This book is dedicated to Richard Cole
who passed on January 1, 1996.
Beloved uncle and role model.

A COMPLETE GUIDE TO THE LOS ANGELES METROLINK COMMUTER TRAIN SYSTEM

Covering Los Angeles, Orange, Riverside, San Bernardino, and Ventura counties

by Edward J. Simburger

Maps and Photography by Edward J. Simburger

ISBN No. 0-9649948-0-1

Maps by Edward J. Simburger
Photography by Edward J. Simburger
Edited by Donald Duke, Golden West Books, San Marino, CA
Cover design and paste-up by Viki Mason, Victoria Graphics, Orange, CA
Printed by Diversified Printing, Brea, CA

Published by: Yerba Seca Publications
                        P. O. Box 975
                        Agoura, CA 91376

Printed in the USA

Contents

Acknowledgements

I have many people who have contributed to this work and who have given their support toward my vision and goal--producing a user friendly guide to public transportation in the Greater Los Angeles Region.

First and foremost I want to acknowledge my wife Theresa Alexandra, who goes by her middle name and likes to be called Alex. She has been with me on most of my adventures in the Greater Los Angeles Region over the past two years and has had to put up with a preoccupied husband who has not had time for anything but "THE BOOK". She has informed me that she has two years of household projects saved up for me--from broken toilets to house painting--to fill all of my "free" time now that the book is finished. I haven't told her about "book signings" and the next edition yet.

Next on my list of major contributors to this project are my mother and father, Laurette and Edward C. Simburger, who celebrate their 51st. year of wedded bliss as this book goes to press. They have come out of retirement to help me sell the advertizing that appears in the station chapters. Without their help I would not have been able to complete my advertizing sales campaign in the time allocated to that phase of the book. They are responsible for all of the ads in the chapters for the Burbank, Glendale and Los Angeles Line, Santa Clarita Line and the Ventura County Line with the exception of Oxnard, Camarillo and Moorpark. Thanks mom and dad!

My aunt Rose Fletcher was also a great help in the advertizing sales arena. She lives in San Clemente and her family operates South Coast Lawnmower (see San Juan Capistrano chapter). She was instrumental in selling the advertizing that appears in the southern Orange County station chapters. Without her help I would not have had the representation that I do have from businesses in that region. Thanks Aunt Rose!

The next person I would like to give credit to is Donald Duke, chief editor and owner of Golden West Books. Donald provided guidance and his expertise in editing initial drafts of my text. He also taught me the tricks of page layout and the rules of writing for publication in book form. Donald has a new book out and for his efforts I have plugged it here with a full-page ad. Thanks Donald!

One evening, in the spring of 1994, after the 17 January Northridge Earthquake, as I was riding one of the overcrowded Santa Clarita Line trains from Los Angeles Union Station to Burbank, I struck up a conversation with Bob Eggert. I told Bob about my project and he told me that he was in the printing business and worked at Anderson Lithograph. Bob offered to help me lay out the book and to make up some dummy books when I finished my manuscript. He gave me his business card and we said our good-byes. Little did he know that I would call him over a year later to take him up on his offer. Bob did the mock-ups and introduced me to Kathleen Shields. Kathleen gave me some estimates for printing the book and ultimately provided me with a quote from KNI, Inc. which was "affordable". Although I would not get rich, at least I could sell the book for more than it cost to produce. Thanks Bob and Kathleen!

Kim Bryant-Dyer, from KNI, referred me to Viki Mason to get my halftones and color separations. When it became clear that KNI could not print my book Kim referred me to Diversified Printing who printed this book. Thanks Kim!

Viki, of Victoria Graphics, has been a sweetheart these last few months by helping me produce the final layout of the pages for each chapter. She has put with late night and early morning calls asking her to pull this map or that page, as I just found another error. Viki also designed the front cover. If you bought this book because the front cover got your attention, I have Viki to thank. Thanks Viki!

The folks at Metrolink have been wonderful! When I was first starting with this project in the spring of 1994, I sent samples of my text to Peter Hidalgo in the publicity department. Peter passed my material on to Gordon Glor. Gordon got the executive director of Metrolink, Mr. Richard Stanger, to review the manuscript. In fact, Mr. Stanger provided some assistance with editing on the "Metrolink" chapter and his words appear as written in that chapter of the book. Thanks Richard!

Gordon Glor continued to be my primary point of contact at Metrolink throughout the period of research and writing. He kept me up-to-date on new line openings. The first time that I thought I was close to finishing the book, Metrolink opened the Orange county line and I added eight new chapters. Then again, new stations came on-line in the cities of Rancho Cucamonga, and San Clemente. Finally, as I was really about to finish, Gordon informed me about the new Inland Empire-Orange County Line. So bach to the Computer. Thanks, Gordon, for all the maps, schedules, fact sheets, and other reference material you provided over the two years it took to complete this book.

Just as I was beginning to sell advertizing to finance the initial printing of this book, Gordon told me to call Joyce Sand, Metrolink's new marketing director. Joyce really put this project in high gear. She opened the doors to Metrolink for me by committing to purchase the inside front cover; sell the books through the Metrolink Store; and also assigned Francisco Oaxaca to provide me with the access to Metrolink's store of artwork. Joyce has since left Metrolink for a better opportunity. Good luck Joyce and thanks!

The Metrolink clip art that appears throughout this book was provided by Francisco, including the Metrolink System Map that appears on the back cover of the book. Thanks, Francisco!

Adrienne Brooks-Taylor has taken over for Joyce and will be heavily involved in marketing the book through Metrolink's publicity department.

I would also like to thank the people at all of the transit agencies and individual cities throughout Southern California who contributed by providing corrections to the text and financial support in the form of advertizing. Without their support some of the information would have been in error or out of date.

Finally, I would like to thank all of the small business owners who had the vision and foresight to believe in this project and purchased advertizing space. As a result of their support this book is now published and I hope that it will help you, the reader, find your way around Southern California "using" the Metrolink and Amtrak trains and connecting bus transportation.

Introduction

I have been a resident of the Los Angeles region all my life. Journeying without my car was not even in my vocabulary. However, something new has been added to the Los Angeles scene. It is called Metrolink. It is true rapid transit and has come into being nearly overnight. The current system connects commuters in six counties: Los Angeles, Orange, Riverside, San Bernardino, San Diego and Ventura, with 44 stations. When complete, the system will include 450 route miles and over 50 stations. In addition, the recent opening of the RED Line at the Civic Center, Blue Line to Long Beach, and the Green Line along the new 105 freeway from Norwalk to LAX, make public transit a real option to visitors and residents alike for getting around the greater Los Angeles region.

Rail rapid transit is a real novelty to a lifelong Los Angeles resident like myself. Since I am unable to use the system myself to get to and from my home, and place of employment, I decided to see what it would be like to go somewhere without my car.

My first adventure was a trip to downtown Los Angeles on the Ventura County Line from Moorpark. After arriving at Union station, I proceeded to the Metrolink Information booth where I was presented with myriad bus schedules and brochures describing various transportation options available to the Metrolink rider wishing to travel from Union Station to his final destination. After pouring over these documents for the better part of an hour, I was able to chart my course for the rest of my adventure in downtown Los Angeles. The experience gave me the idea for this book.

What was needed was a book containing information about station location, facilities, security provisions, parking and transit options for each stop on the system. A book with "How To Get There" instructions using local bus connections for the various points of interest accessible from each Metrolink station. With such a reference book one could actually make maximum use of this new service by knowing in advance "How To Get There."

While writing this book the I have ridden the rails and connecting bus transit to the locations described. In addition, descriptions and critiques of the various points of interest visited are provided to help guide your adventures in exploring the City of Angels.

Author at Metrolink Information Booth - Los Angeles Union Station

Metrolink

Metrolink is the Southern California Regional Rail Authority's (SCRRA) commuter rail system serving six Southern California counties: Los Angeles, Orange, Riverside, San Bernardino, San Diego and Ventura. The Metrolink system presently has 40 stations. The system utilitizes existing railroad tracks and their right-of-way. The system started operation with the opening of the San Bernardino Line, Santa Clarita Line and Ventura County Line on October 26, 1992. Within the first year of operation the system has seen the opening of the Riverside Line, and the extension of the San Bernardino Line from Pomona to San Bernardino. After the January 17 1994, Northridge Earthquake, Metrolink extended the Santa Clarita Line to Lancaster and the Ventura County Line to Oxnard. The Orange County Line opened on March 28, 1994, and the Inland Empire-Orange County Line opened on October 2, 1995. The Inland Empire-Orange County Line was extended from Riverside to San Bernardino on March 4, 1996. The first regularly scheduled weekend service began on the San Bernardino Line at the opening of the Los Angeles County Fair in September 1995.

Virtually overnight Los Angeles has a Rail Rapid Transit System that works. After the January 17, 1994 Northridge Earthquake, stations in Lancaster and Palmdale were opened in seven days.

Metrolink Trains parked at the Moorpark Yard

Metrolink purchased all new equipment for the new intercity commuter rail service. The System is modern, clean and capable of high speed operation.

Metrolink has improved the existing roadbed on which the trains operate. They have installed new all

Regular Adult Fares

Number of Zones	ONE-WAY	ROUND-TRIP	10-TRIP	MONTHLY PASS
1	$3.50	$6.00	$25.00	$80.00
2	$4.50	$8.00	$35.00	$112.00
3	$5.50	$10.00	$45.00	$144.00
4	$6.50	$12.00	$55.00	$176.00
5	$7.50	$14.00	$65.00	$208.00
6	$8.50	$16.00	$75.00	$240.00
7	$9.50	$18.00	$85.00	$272.00

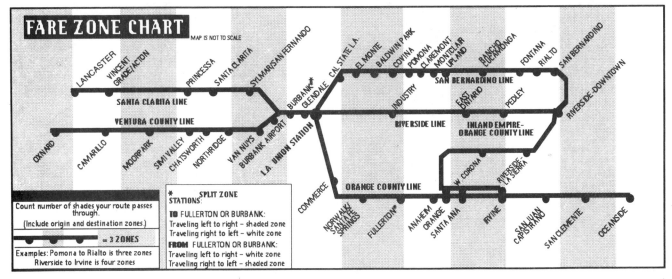

FARE ZONE CHART — MAP IS NOT TO SCALE

Count number of shades your route passes through.
(Include origin and destination zones.)

▬▬▬ = 3 ZONES

Examples: Pomona to Rialto is three zones
Riverside to Irvine is four zones

* SPLIT ZONE STATIONS:
TO FULLERTON OR BURBANK:
Traveling left to right – shaded zone
Traveling right to left – white zone
FROM FULLERTON OR BURBANK:
Traveling left to right – white zone
Traveling right to left – shaded zone

Engineer's Console with Simplified Computerized Control

welded rails so that trains can operate at speeds up to 110 mph. The current operating speed is 79 mph. As Metrolink completes its program of upgrading the roadbed and signaling along the various lines, the resulting improvements in schedules should make Metrolink an even more attractive transportation alternative for Los Angeles commuters.

The SCRRA has contracted with Amtrak for personnel to operate its trains. Each train has an engineer who operates the locomotive and a conductor who is responsible for passenger safety. The stations are unmanned with automated ticket-selling machines located near the boarding platform. The system operates on the honor system. This means passengers may board a train and ride without having to have his ticket checked. The railroad has roving spot checkers who board trains at various points and check tickets. Passengers without a valid ticket are subject to citation (fine). At the discretion of the conductor, or ticket checker, a warning can be issued for not having a valid ticket. If an individual receives three warnings a court case is filed. The offending individual must then appear in court. The fine for not having a valid ticket is $200., plus the penalty, and court costs, which brings the total up to $500. This is a significant deterrent to would-be cheaters.

Metrolink uses a zone system for determining its fares. One-way, round-

trip, 10-trip and monthly passes are available. The fare-zone table on the system map provides the cost for each type of ticket as a function of the number of zones. One-way tickets are valid for three hours for a one-way trip from the station where the ticket was purchased to the selected destination. Round-trip tickets are issued by the machines as two tickets; one valid for three hours from time of purchase and a return ticket valid anytime on the day of

Metrolink Ticket Vending Machine

purchase. A 10-trip ticket is valid for 10 one-way trips within 90 days of purchase. The 10-trip ticket must be validated once per passenger prior to boarding the trains each time you ride. Up to three passengers can use the same 10-trip ticket providing that it is validated once for each passenger for each one-way trip. Ticket validators are located next to the ticket vending machines at each station. Monthly passes are valid for unlimited travel between the station where purchased and the selected destination station during a calendar month. Monthly passes are sold during the last 10 days and first 10 days of any calendar month. Monthly passes must be signed and are valid for travel by the original purchaser only. When using a monthly pass the purchaser may be asked to show a current picture identification, such as a drivers license, passport, etc.

Metrolink offers a 25-percent discount on one-way and round-trip tickets that are purchased and used between 8:30 A.M. and 3:30 P.M. The discount also applies to travel after 6:55 P.M. The discount for youths, 6 to 18 years, during these time periods is 50 percent.

The discount for Seniors (65 and over) and disabled is 50 percent on all trains at all times. Passengers traveling on reduced fare tickets must have valid picture identification showing age or proof of disability such as DMV placard identification card, Social Security Disability Income Certification, L.A. County Transit Operators Association identification card, or other connecting transit operator's reduced fare identification card. Children under 6 years may ride free when accompanied by a fare-paying adult.

The Metrolink ticket vending machines are somewhat intimidating the first time you try to purchase a ticket. The Metrolink Ambassador will help you purchase your ticket if he or she is on duty. The first thing you need to do is select the ticket type, such as one-way, round trip, youth, elderly etc., by pushing the appropriate button on the machine. Next you need to select the destination station by pushing the button listing the name of your destination station. The last step is to pay for your ticket. The machines accept cash in denominations of $1.00, $5.00, $10.00 and $20.00 bills and .05, .10, .25, and Susan B. Anthony $1.00 coins. The machines also accept

Visa and Mastercard.

Each line receives local funding from the cities and/or counties which subsidize the cost of operating the system. Because of this arrangement, multi-zone 10-trip tickets or monthly passes purchased at a station on one line cannot be used on another line. For instance, you purchase a 10-trip 3-zone ticket at the Chatsworth station, on the Ventura County Line, to take you from Chatsworth to L.A. Union Station for your normal daily commuting. Then, on one day you wanted to continue on to Pomona on the San Bernardino Line, you would have to purchase an additional ticket for the Los Angeles to Pomona segment of your ride, or you could purchase a round trip ticket to Pomona at Chatsworth. However, you could not validate your 10-trip ticket at Los Angeles Union Station for the three zone trip from Union Station to Pomona. The only exception to this is on the Riverside and San Bernardino Lines. Monthly passes and 10-trip tickets can be used interchangeably for travel between the same or fewer number of zones. For a visitor to Los Angeles, traveling on one of the Metrolink lines, a 10-trip ticket with the free connecting transit privileges is a real bargain. For information on changes in fares or routes call Metrolink on 808-LINK.

Metrolink passengers may transfer free from the train on all of the local connecting bus lines listed in this book under each station description unless otherwise noted in a particular chapter. In order to transfer you need only to show the bus driver your valid Metrolink ticket. If you need to take a bus to any of the Metrolink stations ask the driver for a transfer. Then when purchasing your one-way or round-trip Metrolink ticket you will receive a $1.00 discount on your Metrolink ticket. However, be prepared to the ticket checker both the valid bus transfer and your Metrolink ticket.

It is this connection with local transit, all along the Metrolink system, that makes the Metrolink a truly usable system for getting around the greater Los Angeles region. This connection is the reason for writing this book. With a system that has as many stations as Metrolink, there are literally hundreds of local transit connections, operated by more than 30 different local entities there is a definite need for a guidebook.

Presently, the Metrolink system is

10-Trip Ticket Validator

designed to operate primarily at peak commute hours. The trains operate only Monday thru Friday except on the San Bernardino Line which has Saturday Service. The trains operate primarily as a one-way system. Trains bring commuters from the many bedroom communities to job sites in the central city. With the combination of Metrolink, Amtrak and supplemental long-haul bus service,most stations have bi-directional service all day long. For visitors to the Los Angeles area who want to use the Metrolink system, this limitation must be taken into account. However, due to the vast size of the greater Los Angeles urban sprawl, one cannot travel from one end of the city to the other by car in less than two to three hours at top freeway speeds. Only on extremely rare occasions can this be accomplished. It is 124 miles from Oxnard, on the western extremity of the Metrolink system, to Riverside on the eastern extremity and, it is 165 miles from Lancaster in the north to Oceanside at the southern extremity. In all this area the only breaks in the urban sprawl are Camp Pendleton located between San Clemente and Oceanside, the mountains between Palmdale and the Santa Clarita Valley, and the farmland between Oxnard and Moorpark in eastern Ventura county. Thus, if you plan to visit the Los Angeles area, and use the Metrolink system, it will be

necessary to book hotels near the various attractions you wish to visit. Plan your Metrolink excursions so that you will be traveling generally toward L.A. Union Station in the early morning or early afternoon hours, and away from L.A. Union Station during late morning to early evening hours for best schedules. Hotel accommodations will be easier to obtain and generally rates are more reasonable in the many outlying communities.

Weekend travel is limited to Saturday Service on the San Bernardino Line Amtrak service available on the San Diegan route which includes most stations on the Ventura County Line and the Orange County Line. This would permit a traveler to get around the area when Metrolink does not operate. One may visit the regions served by Metro Red, Blue and Green lines, which operate seven days a week. The weekends would be a perfect time to settle in at one location with a number of attractions. Some suggestions would be the Anaheim, Antelope Valley (Lancaster), Buena Park, Burbank, downtown Los Angeles, Glendale, Long Beach, Oceanside, Riverside, San Bernardino, San Juan Capistrano or Santa Clarita regions.

Another weekend option for a Los Angeles visitor would be to rent a car (weekend rates are significantly lower than weekday rates) . This would permit a visit to areas of the city that do not presently have convenient Metrolink or other (Red Line, Blue Line or Green Line) rail service. Some of the communities that come to mind are Beverly Hills, West Los Angeles, Santa Monica, Malibu, Venice, as well as others.

Trip Planning

The key element in using Metrolink to travel around Southern California is planning ahead. You will need to know which trains you will ride and what connecting bus transportation you will use from the Metrolink station to your final destination. You need to know the schedule for both the train and bus portions of your trip. The schedules for the trains on each of the seven Metrolink Lines (Ventura County, Santa Clarita, Burbank, Glendale and Los Angeles, San Bernardino, Riverside, Inland Empire-Orange County and Orange County) and the train/bus connection schedules are included in each station chapter of this book.

However, Metrolink, Amtrak and the connecting bus schedules are subject to change at any time without notice. So you should only rely upon the schedules provided in this book for preliminary trip planning.

Once you have completed your preliminary trip planning you should call Metrolink at 808-LINK from any Southern California area code or Amtrak at (800) USA-RAIL for updates to the train departure and arrival times on your itinerary. Next, you should call the appropriate bus operator for the current schedules of the particular bus lines you are planning to use. The phone numbers for all of the bus operators are provided in each station chapter.

On the following page we have provided a Trip Planner to help you plan your trip. Make copies of this trip planner so you can write in the train and bus departure and arrival times for each leg of your trip.

The following is an example of a weekday trip to the Los Angeles Zoo for a traveler staying at the Warner Center Marriott Hotel in Woodland Hills. This traveler wants to arrive at the zoo shortly after the 10:00 opening and depart before the 5:00 P.M. closing.

Since our traveler is staying in the San Fernando Valley he will use the Burbank Metrolink Station for access to the zoo. He will take the MTA 245 bus which will pick him up in front of the Warner Center Marriott at the Topanga Canyon Boulevard and Oxnard Street stop. The bus departs from this stop at

8:40 A.M. and arrives at the Chatsworth Metrolink Station at 9:04 A.M. in time to catch the Metrolink train at 9:49 A.M. The traveler pays the $1.35 bus fare for each person in his party and requests a transfer for use on Metrolink. Arriving at the station our traveler purchases round trip Metrolink tickets at the ticket vending machine. Since he arrived by bus and has a valid bus transfer he selects the *bus-train connection* for a round trip ticket as the ticket type. He selects the *Burbank Station* as his destination station and pays a $5.00 round trip fare for the two-zone trip for each adult in his party. Since he is traveling after 8:30 A.M. he gets a 25% discount off the regular $8.00 round trip fare plus an additional $1.00 discount for the bus transfer.

He boards Metrolink train number 108 and arrives at the Burbank Metrolink Station at 10:18 A.M.. Our traveler then connects with the MTA 96 bus which departs at 10:23 A.M. and arrives at the front gate to the Los Angeles Zoo at 10:41 A.M. Upon boarding the bus our traveler shows the driver his Metrolink ticket for a free transfer from the train to the bus.

After a full day at the zoo our weary traveler catches the 4:21 P.M. MTA 96 bus. He then shows the bus driver his return ticket for a free transfer to the Burbank Metrolink Station. This bus arrives at the Burbank Station at 4:39 P.M. and connects with the Metrolink 105 train which departs the station at 4:43 P.M. The train arrives at the Chatsworth Metrolink Station at 5:09 P.M. and the traveler connects with the MTA 245 bus which departs at 5:25 P.M. At 5:48 P.M. our traveler arrives at the Warner Center Marriott Hotel somewhat rested after the short nap he had on the train ride back from the zoo.

The Trip Planner on the following page shows all of the train and bus times for our traveler's itinerary for an example.

For those of you who live in the Los Angeles region Metrolink can be an ideal vehicle for a weekend getaway to explore another part of our wonderful city. Metrolink trains will whisk you away from your regular jobsite in the central city to a number of exotic sites

which are located all around the Los Angeles region. For example, one could take a train on the Santa Clarita Line on a Friday afternoon for a weekend in the Antelope Valley communities of Lancaster and Palmdale. On the way out to the Lancaster Station in the Antelope Valley one could stop at the Vincent Hill/Acton Station for dinner at the Vincent Hill Restaurant and Saloon and then catch the last train into the Antelope Valley (see Vincent Hill/ Acton Station chapter). Pick the weekend that the California Poppy Festival is being held for a really funfilled time. There are several hotels in the Antelope Valley which have a courtesy van for local transportation and if you stay at any of them they will pick you up at the Lancaster Metrolink Station. Transportation options in the Antelope Valley include Antelope Valley Transit busses, rental cars and your hotel's courtesy van. Another option could be a guided tour with Viola's Tours (see ad in the Lancaster Station Chapter). After your weekend in the Antelope Valley you will catch the Monday Morning Metrolink Train from the Lancaster Metrolink Station back to your work location. Thus you have avoided the normal Friday evening traffic out of town and the Monday morning drive into work and, in the bargain, gained an additional full day for your weekend getaway rather than rushing home on Sunday afternoon so you could be at work on Monday morning.

Suggested destinations somewhat off your standard tourist itineraries that would make excellent destinations for weekend excursions are Oxnard with the Seebee Museum, Channel Islands Harbor and the annual California Strawberry Festival; San Bernardino with the National Orange Show; Riverside with the University of California Campus and many local museums; San Juan Capistrano with the Swallows day Parade, mission, museums and Dana Point Harbor; Oceanside with the beaches, marina, pier, California Surf Museum and Mission San Luis Rey, to name a few. All you need to do is pick a location and go.

4

TRIP PLANNER

EXAMPLE

TRIP	DEPARTURE/DESTINATION	BUS	BUS	BUS	DEPARTURE/DESTINATION	TRAIN	TRAIN	DESTINATION	TRAIN
SEGMENT	LOCATION/ STATION	LINE NUMBER	DEPARTURE TIME	ARRIVAL TIME	LOCATION/ STATION	NUMBER	DEPARTURE TIME	STATION	ARRIVAL TIME
OUTBOUND LEG	WARNER CENTER MARRIOTT	MTA 245	8:40A	9:04A	CHATSWORTH	108	9:49A	BURBANK	10:18A
INTERMEDIATE LEG	BURBANK STATION	MTA 96	10:23A	10:41A	LOS ANGELES ZOO				
INTERMEDIATE LEG									
INTERMEDIATE LEG									
INTERMEDIATE LEG									
RETURN LEG	LOS ANGELES ZOO	MTA 96	4:21P	4:39P	BURBANK STATION	105	4:43P	CHATSWORTH	5:09P
RETURN LEG	BURBANK STATION	MTA 245	5:25P	5:48P	WARNER CENTER MARRIOTT				

TRIP	DEPARTURE/DESTINATION	BUS	BUS	BUS	DEPARTURE/DESTINATION	TRAIN	TRAIN	DESTINATION	TRAIN
SEGMENT	LOCATION/ STATION	LINE NUMBER	DEPARTURE TIME	ARRIVAL TIME	LOCATION/ STATION	NUMBER	DEPARTURE TIME	STATION	ARRIVAL TIME
OUTBOUND LEG									
INTERMEDIATE LEG									
INTERMEDIATE LEG									
INTERMEDIATE LEG									
INTERMEDIATE LEG									
RETURN LEG									
RETURN LEG									

Burbank, Glendale, and Los Angeles Line

The Burbank, Glendale and Los Angeles Line has three stations. They are located at L.A. Union Station, Glendale and Burbank. Metrolink operates 17 trains northbound from L.A. Union Station to Burbank and 18 trains southbound from Burbank to L.A. Union Station Monday thru Friday. Amtrak operates three trains daily in each direction. The schedules below indicate the times and number of trains traveling in each direction on this route at the time of publication. Due to the rapid expansion of Metrolink service please call 808-LINK for current updates to the schedule for Metrolink trains and (800) USA-RAIL for updates on Amtrak trains.

Metrolink Trains Laid-Over at Taylor Yard

BURBANK, GLENDALE, AND LOS ANGELES LINE TRAIN SCHEDULE
SOUTHBOUND FROM BURBANK TO LOS ANGELES

TRAIN NUMBER	METROLINK	METROLINK	METROLINK	METROLINK	METROLINK	METROLINK	METROLINK	METROLINK	METROLINK	METROLINK	AMTRAK
	200	100	102	202	204	104	206	106	208	210	774
DAYS OF OPERATION	M - F	M - F	M - F	M - F	M - F	M - F	M - F	M - F	M - F	M - F	SA.SU.H.
BURBANK	L5:58A	6:03A	6:43A	6:52A	7:22A	7:33A	7:53A	8:12A	8:22A	9:22A	
GLENDALE	L6:04A	6:09A	6:49A	6:58A	7:28A	7:39A	7:59A	8:18A	8:28A	9:28A	9:58A
L.A. UNION STATION	6:18A	6:23A	7:03A	7:12A	7:42A	7:53A	8:13A	8:32A	8:42A	9:42A	10:15A

TRAIN NUMBER	METROLINK	AMTRAK	METROLINK	METROLINK	AMTRAK	AMTRAK	METROLINK	METROLINK	METROLINK	AMTRAK R	METROLINK	AMTRAK
	108	776	110	212	780	782	900	902	214	11	216	786
DAYS OF OPERATION	M - F	DAILY	M - F	M - F	M - F	SA.SU.H.	M - F	M - F	M - F	DAILY	M - F	DAILY
BURBANK	10:18A		3:37P	3:56P			4:53P	5:17P	5:40P		7:54P	
GLENDALE	10:24A	11:55A	3:44P	4:02P	4:35P	4:35P	5:00P	5:24P	5:46P	D6:45P	8:00P	8:26P
L.A. UNION STATION	10:39A	12:10P	4:01P	4:16P	4:55P	4:55P	5:15P	5:39P	6:05P	7:00P	8:15P	8:40P

NORTHBOUND FROM LOS ANGELES TO BURBANK

TRAIN NUMBER	METROLINK	METROLINK	METROLINK	METROLINK	METROLINK	METROLINK	AMTRAK	AMTRAK	AMTRAK R	AMTRAK	METROLINK	METROLINK
	201	901	203	903	905	101	769	771	14	775	103	205
DAYS OF OPERATION	M - F	M - F	M - F	M - F	M - F	M - F	SA.SU.H.	M - F	DAILY	DAILY	M - F	M - F
L.A. UNION STATION	6:32A	6:46A	7:30A	8:02A	8:30A	8:51A	9:15A	9:15A	9:30A	11:35A	1:05P	1:56P
GLENDALE	L6:43A	6:59A	L7:41A	8:14A	8:42A	9:03A	9:28A	9:27A	9:48A	11:48A	1:16P	2:07P
BURBANK	L6:49A	7:10A	L7:47A	8:25A	8:53A	9:09A					1:22P	2:13P

TRAIN NUMBER	AMTRAK	METROLINK	METROLINK	METROLINK	METROLINK	METROLINK	METROLINK	METROLINK	AMTRAK	METROLINK	METROLINK	METROLINK
	779	207	209	105	211	107	213	109	791	215	111	217
DAYS OF OPERATION	DAILY	M - F	M - F	M - F	M - F	M - F	M - F	M - F	SA.SU.H.	M - F	M - F	M - F
L.A. UNION STATION	3:30P	3:45P	4:10P	4:26P	4:57P	5:05P	5:33P	5:41P	5:55P	6:14P	6:24P	8:26P
GLENDALE	3:44P	3:56P	4:21P	4:37P	5:08P	5:16P	5:44P	5:52P	6:09P	6:25P	6:35P	8:37P
BURBANK		4:02P	4:27P	4:43P	5:14P	5:22P	5:50P	5:58P		6:31P	6:41P	8:43P

L: Regular stop to discharge or pick up passengers except train may leave ahead of schedule.

R: Amtrak's Coast Starlight requires advance reservations Call (800) USA-RAIL.

D: Stops to discharge passengers only arrival time approximate.

Metrolink trains with 100 series numbers continue on the Ventura County Line.

Metrolink Trains with 200 series numbers continue on the Santa Clarita Line.

Metrolink trains with 900 series numbers operate only on the Burbank, Glendale and L.A. Union Station Line.

Metrolink Trains dropping off passengers at the Glendale Station

Metrolink Trains at Glendale Station

The Burbank, Glendale and Los Angeles Line is, in reality, a combination of the Metrolink trains serving the Santa Clarita Line, the Ventura County Line and the 900 series trains. Amtrak operates the *San Diegans* to Santa Barbara and the *Coast Starlight* to Seattle on this line. Amtrak and Metrolink tickets are not interchangeable. You must purchase an Amtrak ticket for travel on Amtrak and a Metrolink ticket for travel on Metrolink.

The Burbank, Glendale and Los Angeles Line was originally built by the Southern Pacific Company in the 1880's. Metrolink purchased this route from the Southern Pacific Company along with the Ventura County and Santa Clarita lines. The line is 10.9 miles in length between Burbank and

L.A. Union Station. The alignment roughly follows the Los Angeles River and the Golden State Freeway from downtown L.A. to Burbank. The total running time is approximately 17 minutes. The average speed along the entire route is 38 mph with top speeds of 79 mph. Speed will improve when Metrolink completes its program to improve the roadbed and install new tracks on the approach to L.A. Union Station.

The Glendale Station is located a short distance from Downtown Glendale and the Glendale Beeline shuttle busses provide free connections to downtown for Metrolink Riders.

From the Glendale Station the track passes by numerous industrial plants, warehouses and the Glendale Department of Water & Power Steam Electric Generating Station before passing under the Ventura Freeway S.R. 134. Directly across the L.A. River, along the route from the Glendale Station to the Ventura Freeway, is Griffith Park. About a mile beyond the Ventura Freeway undercrossing the track enters the city of Burbank and quickly passes under the Golden State Freeway I-5 and on to the Burbank Station. Downtown Burbank is located directly across the Golden State Freeway from the station.

Metrolink Trains passing on tracks on each side of the L. A. River

L. A. Union Station

Station Connecting Transit Information

The L.A. Union Station is located at 800. N. Alameda Street. The station can be reached by taking the Alameda Street exit from the Hollywood Freeway (U.S. 101) in downtown Los Angeles. The station is just north of the freeway. Parking is available at the station at a cost of $5.50 per day. Low cost parking is available across the street from the station at the Post Office annex. This station serves downtown Los Angeles and is the "Hub" for the Metrolink System. Connections between all Metrolink lines can be made here. All trains terminate here and all outbound trains originate at the station. All Amtrak trains on the Orange County and Ventura County lines stop at this station. There is a multitude of connecting transit options that can be made from L.A. Union Station starting with the MTA Red Line Subway.

The Red Line Subway has stations at L.A. Union Station right under the Metrolink and Amtrak boarding platforms. The Red Line has four other stations in the downtown Los Angeles district. The Civic Center Station is located at First and Hill streets and serves L.A. City Hall, L.A. County Hall of Administration and Courthouse, and the Los Angeles Music Center. The Pershing Square Station is located

L. A. Union Station

underneath Pershing Square at Fifth and Hill streets. It serves the L.A. Jewelry Center, The California Center atop Bunker Hill, downtown shopping in the Latino dominated shops along Broadway, Grand Central Market and the Central Library. The Seventh Street Metro Center is located at Seventh and Flower streets. It is also the terminus of the Blue Line to downtown Long Beach. Here one finds the Los Angeles

Financial District, Broadway Plaza, Seventh Street Marketplace and the Central Library. All are a short walk from this station. The final station in the downtown L.A. area is the Westlake/MacArthur Park Station located at Wilshire Boulevard and Alvarado streets. MacArthur Park has a nice lake surrounded by manicured grass and treelined walkways. The surrounding slums are a breeding ground for gangs and drugs. The MTA has spent $7.5 million dollars to improve the park and the presence of MTA uniformed police has improved the gang and drug situation. But the neighborhood has a long way to go before I would recommend this neighborhood as a tourist stop at night.

The LADOT Dash Bus provides the most convenient service for getting from place to place in downtown Los Angeles. There are six routes in addition to a Downtown Metrolink Shuttle Bus and a Hollywood Metrolink Shuttle Bus. In addition to the Metrolink Shuttles, routes B and D have stops at L.A. Union Station. Route B has stops at Los Angeles and Alameda Streets in front of L.A. Union Station. Northbound busses serve Chinatown and southbound busses serve the Civic Center, the Financial district and West City. Connections to Route A are located at the First Street

Gateway Transit Plaza Bus Service

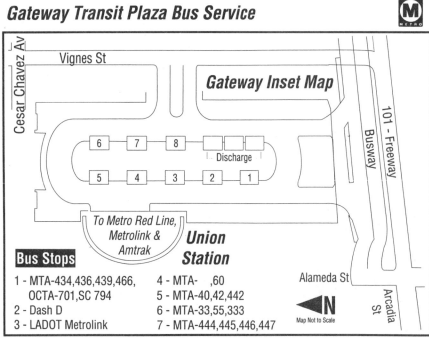

Vignes St

Cesar Chavez Av

Gateway Inset Map

6 7 8
Discharge
5 4 3 2 1

To Metro Red Line, Metrolink & Amtrak

Union Station

101 - Freeway Busway

Alameda St

Arcadia St

N
Map Not to Scale

Bus Stops

1 - MTA-434,436,439,466, OCTA-701,SC 794
2 - Dash D
3 - LADOT Metrolink

4 - MTA- ,60
5 - MTA-40,42,442
6 - MTA-33,55,333
7 - MTA-444,445,446,447

Union Station Gateway Transit Plaza

Watergarden at California Plaza

Points of Interest
California Plaza

The California Plaza is a group of new highrise buildings built on top of Bunker Hill along Grand Avenue Here you can listen to a wide variety of musical groups during the ever popular concerts in the sky held in the California Plaza Amphitheater. The Museum of Contemporary Art is housed in this complex. Across the street from the California Plaza is the Wells Fargo Building which features

and Grand Avenue stop. Connections to Routes C and E busses are at the Fifth Street and Grand Avenue stop. Route D stops at the new Gateway Transit Plaza. Frequency of busses on the six downtown routes vary from 5 to 15 minutes weekdays and 15 to 30 minutes on Saturdays. There is no Saturday service on Route E. There is no Sunday service on any Dash Route. For Information about Dash service call (213) 580-5444.

Los Angeles Union Station

Los Angeles Union Station is the old historic railroad station built in the 1930's. The station houses the Amtrak ticket office and Metrolink information booth. There is a Budget rental car agency, a couple of cafe's and a newsstand in the station. The Dash route "C" bus stops in front of the station.

Gateway Transit Plaza

The new Gateway Transit Plaza is a major element of the Union Station Gateway project which includes the new Los Angeles County Metropolitan Transportation Authority (MTA) Headquarters building. The transit plaza provides connections with MTA 33, 40, 42, 55, 60, 333, 434, 436, 439, 442, 444, 445, 446, 447, 446, Dash Route "D," LADOT Metrolink Shuttle, OCTA 701 and Santa Clarita Transit 701 bus lines. To reach the transit plaza go to your right upon exiting the ramp down from the train boarding platform. Upon exiting the

tunnel to the transit plaza you will find a large salt water aquarium which has native Southern California species which would be found in the environs surrounding Santa Monica Bay.

9

The Los Angeles Skyline from Elysian Park

Rose Garden In Exposition Park

the Wells Fargo Museum. From L.A. Union Station take the southbound LADOT Dash Route B bus to the California Plaza Stop.

California Museum of Science & Industry

The California Museum of Science & Industry is located at 700 State Drive in Exposition Park. The museum features exhibits on our urban environment where you will meet the Globeheads as they learn how to reduce, reuse and recycle. The Aerospace Hall features real aircraft, satellites, and engineering models which trace the history of aircraft and space flight. The amount and importance of the aerospace hardware on display here is second only to the National Air & Space Museum in Washington D.C. In the Technology Hall you can experience interactive hands-on experiments which demonstrate the basic forces of electricity and magnetism, experience a simulated earthquake and witness demonstrations of computer graphics and animation. The Kinsey Hall of Health provides you with the opportunity to test your vital signs and develop a health profile in addition to interactive stage productions for children. The California African American Museum traces African American culture in the United States. The museum is open seven days a week 10:00 A.M. to 5:00 P.M. except for Thanksgiving, Christmas and New Years Day. Admission is free. For

information call (213) 744-2014. See instructions for Exposition Park for connections to Metrolink at L.A. Union Station.

Central Library

The Central Library is located at 630 West 5th Street. It features a modern automated catalogue system, a recent facelift, and expansion. The library building itself is an architectural masterpiece. Murals cover the walls and ceilings. The library is open 10:00 A.M. to 5:30 P.M. Monday, 12:00 P.M. to 8:00 P.M. Tuesday and Wednesday, and 10:00 A.M. to 5:30 P.M. Thursday thru Saturday. Closed Sunday. Take the Metro Red Line to Pershing Square Station or the Dash Route B to the Fifth and Grand stop. For information call (213) 228-7000.

Children's Museum

The Children's Museum is located at 310 N. Main Street in the City Hall

Children's Museum

East shopping mall complex. The museum has touch and feel environmental exhibits, including an art studio, city street and recording studio. The Museum is open on weekends only to the general public from 10:00 A.M. to 5:00 P.M.. Admission is $5.00 for children and adults. Take the southbound DASH Route B bus to the Los Angeles and Alameda Street stop. For information call (213) 687-8825.

Civic Center

Los Angeles Civic Center is the headquarters for Los Angeles City and County Governments. The Civic Center Mall is anchored by Los Angeles City Hall on Spring Street on the east end. As you head, west from City Hall, the next building along the mall is the Criminal Courts building. Next on Temple Street is the County Hall of Records, located between Broadway and Hill. On the south of Temple Street is the Law Library. The County Court House and County Hall of Administration are situated between Hill and Grand. The music center is across Grand. At the top of the hill, on Hope-the west end of the civic center mall, is located headquarters of the Los Angeles Department of Water & Power. In order to reach the Civic Center Mall, from L.A. Union Station, take the Red Line to the Civic Center Station.

China Town

Los Angeles, like most west coast major cities, has a China Town. In China Town there are restaurants and shops featuring Asian delicacies, spices and gifts. The Chinese Historical Society offers guided walking tours of Chinatown the second Saturday of each month. Reservations required, call (213) 621-3171. Catch the northbound DASH Route B bus in front of Union Station on Alameda Street.

Entrance Arch to China Town

Los Angeles City Hall viewed through the Dance Door
located at the Music Center

Convention & Visitors Bureau Information Center

The Los Angeles Convention & Visitors Bureau Information Center is located at 685 S. Figueroa. Call the events hotline, or stop by, and find out all the happenings around Los Angeles.

Open 8:00 A.M. to 5:00 P.M. Monday through Friday, 8:30 A.M. to 5:00 P.M. Saturday. For information by phone call (213) 689-8822. Take the Metro Red Line to Seventh Street/ Metro Center Station.

Dodger Stadium

Dodger Stadium is located on Stadium Way. It is the home of the Los Angeles Dodgers. The stadium was the site for demonstration baseball games during the 1984 Olympics. For information about games and tickets call (213) 224-1400. MTA operates special bus service to games, so call MTA at (213) 626-4455.

Exposition Park

Exposition Park is a 36-square block complex that houses the Los Angeles Memorial Coliseum, Los Angeles Sports Arena, Exposition Park Rose Garden, California Museum of Science & Industry, Natural History Museum of Los Angeles County and the IMAX Theater. Take the LADOT Dash Route B to the Fifth and Grand stop and connect with Dash Route C which connects with Dash Route C-Exposition Park at the Venice/Grand

Parking Garage. MTA Route numbers 444, 446 or 447 located at the Gateway Transit Plaza, will also take you direct to Exposition Park.

Financial District

The Financial District extends north from Seventh Street all the way to the Music Center on First Street along Grand Avenue and Flower Street. In the early part of the 20th century this entire area was once the exclusive Bunker Hill residential district of Los Angeles. In the late 1940's and 1950's this area became an innercity slum. In the 1960's, the Bunker Hill Redevelopment Agency obtained the property and set it aside for high rise development. Since that time it has become the financial center of Greater Los Angeles. The new high rise towers carry the marque of the major financial institutions based in the

Dodger Stadium from Elysian Park

west. There is a network of pedestrian walkways that connect all of the various highrise buildings, sometimes several floors above street level. One can walk from the Arco Plaza at Sixth and Flower, all the way to the Bunker Hill Apartment complex on First Street, without ever having to cross a street at street level. The Financial District also has three shopping centers: Arco Plaza (Sixth and Figueroa); Seventh Street Market-Place (Seventh and Figueroa); and Broadway Plaza (Seventh and Flower).

Take the Metro Red Line to Seventh Street/Metro Center Station from L.A. Union Station or take the southbound LADOT Dash Route B bus.

Flower Market

The Flower Market is on Wall Street at Eighth Street. Here you will find row upon row of fresh-cut and exotic flowers at bargain prices. The only time to arrive is in the predawn hours between 3:00 A.M. and 5:00 A.M. when the selection is best. From L.A. Union Station take the LADOT Dash Route E to the Seventh and Spring streets stop. Then walk one block south to Eighth Street and three blocks east to Wall Street.

Garment District

The Los Angeles Garment District is the second largest in the nation. Centered around Eighth and Los Angeles streets, shops in the district offers shoppers deals on all types of clothing. Here you may buy finished items like shoes and suits or purchase do-it-yourself material from the many fabric shops. The center for the trade is the Cooper Building located at 860 S. Los Angeles Street which is open 9:30 A.M. to 5:30 P.M. Monday thru Saturday, or 11:00 A.M. to 5:00 P.M. on Sunday. Take the LADOT Dash to

Japanese Village in Little Tokyo

Eighth and Spring streets and walk two blocks east to Los Angeles Street.

IMAX Theater in Exposition Park

The IMAX Theater is associated with the California Museum of Science & Industry in Exposition Park. The theater is located at 700 State Drive. IMAX films are the closest thing to being there. With a five-story high and 70-feet wide screen combined with six-channel surround sound, you are in the cockpit of the Space Shuttle when viewing the long running original space movie *The Dream is Alive*. The theater features an ever-changing program of new IMAX movies that put the viewer into the action. For show information call (213) 744-2014. See instructions for Exposition Park for connections to Metrolink at L.A. Union Station.

Japanese American National Museum

The Japanese American National Museum is located at 369 E. First Street in Little Tokyo. This is the first museum dedicated to the experiences of Americans of Japanese descent. The centerpiece of the museum is the magnificently restored sanctuary of the 1925 former Nishi Hongwanji Buddhist temple which now houses the major exhibits. The Japanese American experience is explored in exhibits focusing on the Issei pioneers, American Concentration Camps, and Japanese American soldiers. The museum is open Tuesdays thru Thursday, Saturday and Sunday 10:00 A.M. to 5:00 P.M., Fridays 11:00 A.M. to 8:00 P.M. Closed Mondays, Thanksgiving Day, Christmas and New Years Day. Admission is $4.00 for adults, $3.00 for children ages 6 to 17, students with ID and seniors 62 and over. children under five are free. For information call (213) 625-0414. See Instructions for Little Tokyo for connections with Metrolink at L.A. Union Station.

Jewelry District

In the Los Angeles Jewelry district are found retail and wholesale watch, gem and other jewelry vendors. The Jewelry District is centered around Seventh and Hill streets. As you pass through the various large buildings, including a converted theater at Seventh and Hill, you will pass by individual jewelers selling out of small stalls. Competition is fierce and haggling over price is commonplace. From L.A. Union Station take the Metro Red Line to the Pershing Square Station. Walk two blocks south on Hill to Seventh Street.

Little Tokyo

In Little Tokyo major office and shopping complexes have made this area the largest Japanese community outside Japan. The Japanese American National Museum is located here along with a couple of major Japanese-owned hotels, like the New Otani and Miyako Inn. There are several Japanese restaurants in the district with excellent Japanese cuisine. From L.A. Union Station catch the LADOT DASH Route D to the Los Angeles City Hall Stop. From there you can walk a few blocks east on First Street or transfer to the eastbound LADOT Dash Route A.

Los Angeles Convention Center

The Los Angeles Convention Center was recently expanded and has become the largest convention complex in the West. It is located at Pico and Figueroa streets. The 81,000 square-foot facility is the home to many exhibitions and expos throughout the year. For information on current shows, conventions and expositions call (213) 741-1151. From L.A. Union Station take the southbound LADOT Dash Route B to the Sixth and Grand stop and transfer to the DASH Route E or take the MTA Red Line to the Seventh Street Metro Center station and transfer to the Metro Blue Line. Take the Blue Line to the Pico Station and walk one block west on Pico to the Convention Center.

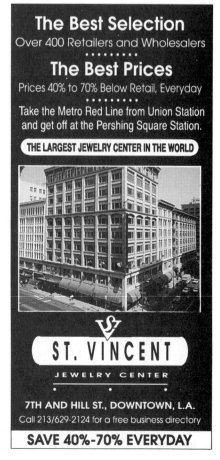

Los Angeles Memorial Coliseum

Dorothy Chandler Pavilion
at the Music Center

Los Angeles
Memorial Coliseum

The Los Angeles Memorial Coliseum is located at 3939 South Figueroa Boulevard in Exposition Park. The Coliseum was originally built for the 1932 Olympic Games in an abandoned gravel pit. Since that time the stadium has been the home field for the USC *Trojans*, Los Angeles *Rams*, Los Angeles *Raiders,* and, at one time, the Los Angeles *Dodgers*. In 1984 the Coliseum was once again the host to the 23rd. Olympic games. Presently the USC *Trojans* call the Coliseum home. For Information on games and events call (213) 748-6131. See instructions to Exposition Park for connections to Metrolink at L.A. Union Station.

Los Angeles Sports Arena

The Los Angeles Sports Arena is located at 3939 South Figueroa Boulevard in Exposition Park. The Sports Arena is home to the Los Angeles Clippers Basketball team and the USC Trojans Basketball team. The Sports Arena was the site of Boxing events during the 1984 Olympics. For ticket information call (213) 748-6131. See instructions for Exposition Park for connections to Metrolink at L.A. Union Station.

Los Angeles Music Center

The Music center is Los Angeles' premier center for the performing arts. The complex includes the Dorothy Chandler Pavilion, Mark Taper Forum

and Ahmanson Theater. Under construction is the Walt Disney Theater, built with funds donated to the Music Center by Walt Disney's widow Lillian Disney. The music center is home to the Los Angeles Philharmonic Orchestra, the Los Angeles Opera and the Ahmanson Theater group. The Music Center is located at First Street and Grand Avenue. Free tours are available 10:00 A.M. to 10:30 A.M. Monday thru Thursday and 10:00 A.M. to noon Saturday. For tour information call (213) 972-7483 and for box office information (213) 972-7211. From L.A. Union Station take the Metro Red Line to the Civic Center Station.

Museum of Contemporary Art

The Museum of Contemporary art is located at 250 South Grand Avenue in the California Plaza Complex. The Museum was founded in 1979 and is the only museum in Los Angeles

Museum of Contemporary Art

devoted to contemporary Art. MOCA collects exhibits and interprets art created since 1940 in all media. The museum facilities were` designed by Japanese architect Arata Isozaki and combine a number of shapes and materials in a whimsical and thoroughly modern way. The museum is open Tuesday through Sunday 11:00 A.M. to 5:00 P.M. and till 8:00 P.M. on Thursday. Closed Mondays, Thanksgiving, Christmas and New Years Day. Admission is $6.00 for adults, $4.00 for seniors 65 and over, and students with student identification, children under 12 are free. For information call (213) 626-6222. From L.A. Union Station take the southbound LADOT Dash Route B Bus to the Third and Grand stop.

Natural History Museum of
Los Angeles County

The Natural History Museum of Los Angeles County is located at 900 Exposition Boulevard in Exposition Park. The museum opened its doors originally in 1913 and has grown to become among one of the nation's major museums in natural and cultural history. Exhibits range from dinosaur fossils to modern mammals in the natural history exhibits. There is an excellent gem and mineral collection. The cultural history exhibits span pre-Columbian cultures of Mexico, Central and South America, Native American cultures of the United States, California History 1540 to 1940 and American History 1492 to 1914. The museum is open 10:00 A.M. to 5:00 P.M. Tuesday thru Sunday. Admission is $6.00 for adults, $3.50 for seniors, $2.00 children age 5 - 12 and children under five are free. For information call (213) 744-3414. See instructions for Exposition Park for connections to

Olvera Street

Metrolink at L.A. Union Station.

Olvera Street

The Pueblo de Los Angeles is the birthplace of L.A. circa 1781. It has dozens of historic buildings, including the Avila Adobe the first house in Los Angeles and the Pico House built by the one-time governor of California under Mexican rule, Pio Pico. Olvera Street is located across the street from the main entrance to Union Station and features authentic Mexican restaurants, boutiques and gift shops. Maps and information are available from the Sepulveda House, 622 N. Main Street which is open 10:00 A.M. to 3:00 P.M. Tours are available; for information call (213) 628-1274.

University of Southern California

The University of Southern California (USC) is located at Exposition Boulevard and Figueroa Street across the street from Exposition Park. USC is well known for its football and basketball teams. The USC Trojans have represented the Pacific Ten in the Rose Bowl game on new years day on a regular bases. The university opened its doors in 1880. At that time the university consisted of a single wood building, 10 facility members and 53 students. Today USC is the second largest private research university in the United States with a student body of 28,000, half of whom are undergraduates. For general campus information call (213) 740-7767.

The university has a number of museums and theaters which offer the students and visitors alike a wide variety of cultural and entertainment opportunities. A listing of these facilities follows:

Museums and Galleries

Arnold Schoenberg Institute

Tours of the archives, library, performance and exhibit halls are available by appointment Monday thru Friday 10:00 A.M. to 4:00 P.M. For Appointment call (213) 740-4090.

Fisher Gallery

Open Thursday thru Friday Noon to 5:00 P.M. and Saturday 11:00 A.M. to 3:00 P.M. For information call (213) 740-4561.

Helen Lindhurst
Architecture Gallery

Open Monday thru Friday 9:00 A.M. to 6:00 P.M. and Saturday Noon to 5:00 P.M. For information call (213) 740-2723.

Helen Lindhurst Fine Arts Gallery

Open Monday thru Friday 9:00 A.M. to 6:00 P.M. and Saturday Noon to 5:00 P.M. For information call (213) 740-2787.

Hancock Memorial Museum

Open Monday thru Friday 10:00 A.M. to 4:00 P.M. For information call (213) 740-0433.

Heritage Hall

Contains all of the athletic trophies and memorabilia relating to USC's athletic history. Four Heisman trophies awarded to USC athletes are on display (Mike Garrett, O.J. Simpson, Charles White, and Marcus Allen).

Theaters

-Bing Theater
-Eileen L. Norris Cinema Theater
-Greenroom Theater
-Arnold Schoenberg Institute
 Performance and Exhibit hall

In addition, the USC Department of Film and Television boasts a Cinema-Television complex which includes two sound stages, a music

University of Southern California

USC Campus

scoring stage, and state-of-the-art studio for video and film editing and animation graphics.

Campus tours are offered with reservations. The tours begin at the Widney Alumni House every hour between 10:00 A.M. and 2:00 P.M. For reservations call (213) 740-2300.

Take the LADOT Dash Route B to the Fifth and Grand stop and Connect with Dash Route C which connects with Dash Route C-Exposition Park at the Venice/Grand Parking Garage. The MTA 444, 446 or 447 lines from the Union Station Gateway Transit Plaza will also take you to the USC campus.

Wells Fargo History Museum

The Wells Fargo History Museum is located at 333 South Grand Avenue. The museum displays tracing the history of California in the Gold Rush days and the part Wells Fargo & Company played in those days. There is a stagecoach in the museum that visitors can sit in and get a feel of how it must have been to ride the stage in those days. Also on display is the Challenge Nugget found by a weekend visitor in 1975 in a tributary to the

Feather River near the town of Challenge. The museum is open 9:00 A.M. to 5:00 P.M. Monday thru Friday. Admission is free. From L.A. Union Station take the southbound LADOT Dash Route B bus to the Third Street and Grand Avenue stop.

Places to Stay

Bonaventure Hotel and Suites

The Bonaventure Hotel and Suites are located at 404 S. Figueroa Street. The hotel phone number is (213) 624-1000. For reservations call (800) 228-3000.

Daimaru Hotel

The Daimaru Hotel is located at 345 E. First Street. The hotel phone number is (213) 621-7704.

Holiday Inn Crowne Plaza

The Holiday Inn Crowne Plaza is located at 3540 S. Figueroa Street. The hotel phone number is (213) 748-4141. For reservations call (800) HOLIDAY.

Hyatt Regency Los Angeles

The Hyatt Regency is located at phone number is (213) 683-1234. For reservations call (800) 233-1234.

Inntowne Hotel Los Angeles

The Inntowne is located at 925 S. Figueroa Street. The hotel phone number is (213) 628-2222.

Little Tokyo Hotel

The Little Tokyo Hotel is located at 327-1/2 E. First Street. The hotel phone number is (213) 617-0128.

Los Angeles Hilton

The Los Angeles Hilton is located at 930 Wilshire Boulevard. The hotel phone number is (213) 629-4321. For reservations call (800) HILTONS.

Metro Plaza Hotel

The Metro Plaza Hotel is located at 711 N. Main Street. The hotel phone number is (213) 680-0200.

Mikado Hotel

The Mikado Hotel is located at 331-1/2 E. First Street. The hotel phone number is (213) 623-9032.

Miyako Inn

The Miyako Inn is located at 328 E. First Street. The hotel phone number is (213) 617-2000.

Orchid Hotel

The Orchid Hotel is located at 819 S. Flower Street. The hotel phone number is (213) 624-5855. For reservations call (800) 874-5855.

Queens Hotel

The Queens Hotel is located at 351 E. First Street. The hotel phone number is (213) 680-3425.

Sheraton Grand Hotel

The Sheraton Grand Hotel is located at 333 S. Figueroa Street. The hotel phone number is (213) 617-1133. For reservations call (800) 325-3535.

The New Otani Hotel & Garden

The New Otani Hotel is located at 120 S. Los Angeles Street. The hotel phone number is (213) 629-1200.

Wyndham Checkers Hotel Los Angeles

The Wyndham Checkers Hotel is located at 535 S. Grand Avenue. The hotel phone number is (213) 624-0000. For reservations call (800) 996-3426.

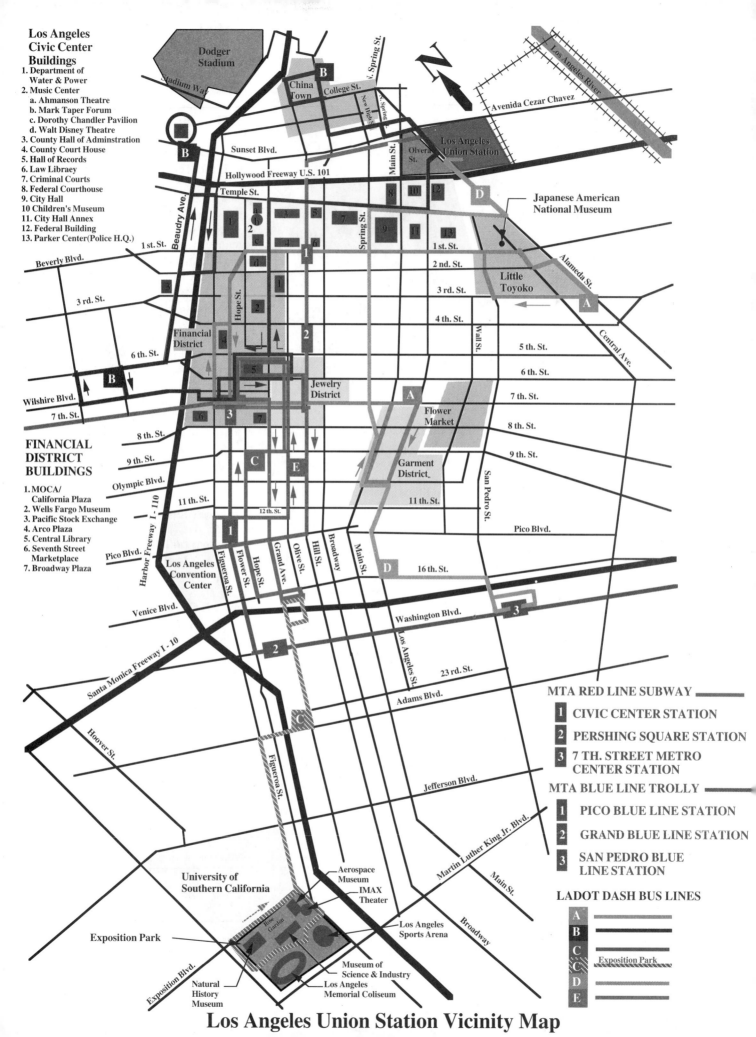

Los Angeles Civic Center Buildings

1. Department of Water & Power
2. Music Center
   a. Ahmanson Theatre
   b. Mark Taper Forum
   c. Dorothy Chandler Pavilion
   d. Walt Disney Theatre
3. County Hall of Adminstration
4. County Court House
5. Hall of Records
6. Law Libraey
7. Criminal Courts
8. Federal Courthouse
9. City Hall
10. Children's Museum
11. City Hall Annex
12. Federal Building
13. Parker Center(Police H.Q.)

FINANCIAL DISTRICT BUILDINGS

1. MOCA/ California Plaza
2. Wells Fargo Museum
3. Pacific Stock Exchange
4. Arco Plaza
5. Central Library
6. Seventh Street Marketplace
7. Broadway Plaza

Dodger Stadium

Stadium Way

China Town

College St.

Sunset Blvd.

Hollywood Freeway U.S. 101

Temple St.

Beaudry Ave.

1 st. St.

Beverly Blvd.

3 rd. St.

Hope St.

Financial District

6 th. St.

Wilshire Blvd.

7 th. St.

8 th. St.

9 th. St.

Olympic Blvd.

11 th. St.

12 th. St.

Pico Blvd.

Harbor Freeway I - 110

Figueroa St.

Flower St.

Hope St.

Grand Ave.

Olive St.

Hill St.

Broadway

Main St.

Los Angeles Convention Center

Venice Blvd.

Santa Monica Freeway I - 10

Hoover St.

University of Southern California

Exposition Park

Exposition Blvd.

Rose Garden

Natural History Museum

Aerospace Museum

IMAX Theater

Los Angeles Sports Arena

Museum of Science & Industry

Los Angeles Memorial Coliseum

New High St.

N. Spring St.

Main St.

N. Spring St.

Olvera St.

Los Angeles Union Statfon

Avenida Cezar Chavez

Los Angeles River

Japanese American National Museum

Spring St.

1 st. St.

2 nd. St.

3 rd. St.

4 th. St.

Wall St.

Little Toyoko

Alameda St.

Central Ave.

5 th. St.

6 th. St.

7 th. St.

Jewelry District

Flower Market

8 th. St.

Garment District

9 th. St.

San Pedro St.

11 th. St.

Pico Blvd.

16 th. St.

Washington Blvd.

Los Angeles St.

23 rd. St.

Adams Blvd.

Jefferson Blvd.

Martin Luther King Jr. Blvd.

Main St.

Broadway

MTA RED LINE SUBWAY
1 CIVIC CENTER STATION
2 PERSHING SQUARE STATION
3 7 TH. STREET METRO CENTER STATION

MTA BLUE LINE TROLLY
1 PICO BLUE LINE STATION
2 GRAND BLUE LINE STATION
3 SAN PEDRO BLUE LINE STATION

LADOT DASH BUS LINES
A
B
C
C   Exposition Park
D
E

Los Angeles Union Station Vicinity Map

Glendale Station

Station Connecting Transit Information

The Glendale Amtrak/Metrolink Station is located at 400 West Cerritos Avenue. Access to the station's 300 car parking lot is via Central Avenue west of San Fernando Road. See map insert for station locale. This Amtrack station of Southwestern architectural style, is manned. The train boarding platform is well lighted, but does not have any shelter. There is a small shelter at the Metrolink ticket vending machine and at the south end of the Amtrak station. The parking lot is also well lighted and maintained. The station has security guards at the platform during the morning and evening rush hours.

The station is served by the Glendale Express Shuttle, Glendale Beeline, and MTA 183 Bus Line. Metrolink passengers may transfer free to connecting MTA Bus Lines 90, 91, 92, 93, 94, 96, 180, 181 from the 183 line.

The Glendale Express Shuttle service meets each Metrolink train between 6:00 A.M. and 9:00 A.M. in the morning and between 3:00 P.M. and 7:00 P.M. in the evening, Monday through Friday. The Glendale Beeline Routes 1 and 2 run every 10 to 12 minutes between 6:00 A.M. and 6:30 P.M. Monday through Friday. Saturday service is every 20 minutes between 9:00 A.M. and 5:00 P.M. For schedule and route updates call the Glendale Beeline at (818) 548-3960.

The MTA 183 line provides extended service from the Glendale Amtrak/Metrolink Station. From the 183 line, connections can be made with the remaining MTA lines serving the

Glendale Station Building

greater Glendale area. For schedule and route updates call MTA at (818) 246-2593.

The station vicinity map provides the routes for bus transit options from the Glendale Metrolink Station. The following tables provide the schedule of bus connections with Metrolink and Amtrak.

Points of Interest
Downtown Glendale

The downtown district of Glendale is located along Central and Brand avenues between Colorado Street and the 134 Freeway. The Downtown district is anchored by the Galleria which occupies the area along Central

GLENDALE STATION WEEKEND BUS CONNECTIONS
SOUTHBOUND TRAINS FROM BURBANK TO LOS ANGELES

TRAIN NUMBER	DAYS OF OPERATION	TRAIN ARRIVAL	MTA 183	GLENDALE BEELINE ROUTE 1 & 2
DAYS OF OPERATION			SA.SU.H.	SATURDAY
BUS FREQUENCY			45 MIN.	20 MIN.
AMTRAK 774	SA.SU.H.	9:58A	9:01/10:13A	9:41/10:00A
AMTRAK 776	DAILY	11:55A	11:01A/12:13P	11:41A/12:00P
AMTRAK 782	SA.SU.H.	4:35P	4:01/5:13P	4:21/4:40P
AMTRAK 11 R	DAILY	D6:45P	7:13P	
AMTRAK 786	DAILY	8:26P		

NORHTBOUND TRAINS FROM LOS ANGELES TO BURBANK

AMTRAK 769	SA.SU.H.	9:28A	9:01/10:13A	9:40A
AMTRAK 14 R	DAILY	9:48A	9:01/10:13A	9:41/10:00A
AMTRAK 775	DAILY	11:48A	11:01A/12:13P	11:41/11:00A
AMTRAK 779	DAILY	3:44P	3:01/4:13P	3:41/4:00P
AMTRAK 791	SA.SU.H.	6:09P	5:58/6:13P	

L: Regular stop to discharge or pick up passengers except train may leave ahead of schedule
R: Amtrak's Coast Starlight requires advance reservations Call (800) USA-RAIL.
D: Stops to discharge passengers only arrival time approximate.

GLENDALE STATION WEEKDAY BUS CONNECTIONS
SOUTHBOUND TRAINS FROM BURBANK TO LOS ANGELES

TRAIN NUMBER	DAYS OF OPERATION	TRAIN ARRIVAL	MTA 183	GLENDALE METROLINK EXPRESS BRAND BLVD. & SAN FERNANDO RD.	GLENDALE BEELINE ROUTE 1 & 2
BUS FREQUENCY			45 MIN.	10 - 20 MIN.	12 MIN.
METROLINK 200	M - F	L6:04A	6:22A	6:10A	6:12A
METROLINK 100	M - F	6:09A	6:05/6:22A	6:10A	6:12A
METROLINK 102	M - F	6:49A	6:43/6:52A	6:51A	6:43/7:00A
METROLINK 202	M - F	6:58A	6:43/7:20A	7:05A	6:55/7:00A
METROLINK 204	M - F	7:28A	7:04/8:22A	7:30A	7:19/7:36A
METROLINK 104	M - F	7:39A	7:04/8:22A	7:42A	7:31/7:48A
METROLINK 206	M - F	7:59A	7:59/8:22A	8:01A	7:43/8:00A
METROLINK 106	M - F	8:18A	7:59/8:22A	8:20A	8:07/8:24A
METROLINK 208	M - F	8:28A	7:59/9:08A	8:30A	8:19/8:36A
METROLINK 210	M - F	9:28A	8:50/10:08A		9:21/9:30A
METROLINK 108	M - F	10:24A	9:54/10:48A		10:19A/10:30A
AMTRAK 776	DAILY	11:55A	11:25A/12:28P		11:45A/12:00P
METROLINK 110	M - F	3:44P	3:40/3:48P	3:40P	3:33/3:48P
METROLINK 212	M - F	4:02P	3:40/4:10P	3:58P	3:57/4:12P
AMTRAK 780	M - F	4:35P	4:25/4:48P	4:34P	4:33/4:36P
METROLINK 900	M - F	5:00P	4:25/5:48P	4:56P	4:57/5:12P
METROLINK 902	M - F	5:24P	5:21/5:48P	5:20P	5:19/5:36P
METROLINK 214	M - F	5:46P	5:21/5:48P	5:40P	5:45/5:48P
AMTRAK 11 R	DAILY	D6:45P	6:48P		
METROLINK 216	M - F	8:00P	6:57P		7:09P
AMTRAK 786	DAILY	8:26P			

NORHTBOUND TRAINS FROM LOS ANGELES TO BURBANK

TRAIN NUMBER	DAYS OF OPERATION	TRAIN ARRIVAL	MTA 183	GLENDALE METROLINK EXPRESS	GLENDALE BEELINE
METROLINK 201	M - F	L6:43A	6:05/6:52A	6:44A	6:48A
METROLINK 901	M - F	6:59A	6:43/7:20A	7:05A	6:57/7:12A
METROLINK 203	M - F	L7:41A	7:04/8:22A	7:42A	7:33/7:48A
METROLINK 903	M - F	8:14A	7:59/8:22A	8:15A	8:09/8:24A
METROLINK 905	M - F	8:42A	7:59/9:08A	8:43A	8:33/8:48A
METROLINK 101	M - F	9:03A	8:50/9:08A		8:57/9:10A
AMTRAK 771	DAILY	9:27A	8:50/10:08A		9:21/9:30A
AMTRAK 14 R	DAILY	9:48A	8:50/10:08A		9:45/9:50A
AMTRAK 775	DAILY	11:48A	11:25A/12:28P		11:45/11:50A
METROLINK 103	M - F	1:16P	1:10/1:20P		1:15/1:20P
METROLINK 205	M - F	2:07P	1:55/2:08P		2:05/2:12P
AMTRAK 779	DAILY	3:44P	3:40/3:48P	3:40P	3:33/3:48P
METROLINK 207	M - F	3:56P	3:40/4:48P	3:52P	3:45/3:48P
METROLINK 209	M - F	4:21P	3:40/4:48P	4:17P	4:09/4:24P
METROLINK 105	M - F	4:37P	4:25/4:48P	4:34P	4:33/4:48P
METROLINK 211	M - F	5:08P	4:25/5:48P	5:04P	4:57/5:12P
METROLINK 107	M - F	5:16P	4:25/5:48P	5:13P	5:09/5:24P
METROLINK 213	M - F	5:44P	5:21/5:48P	5:40P	5:33/5:48P
METROLINK 109	M - F	5:52P	5:21/6:48P	5:49P	5:45/6:00P
METROLINK 215	M - F	6:25P	6:21/6:48P	6:21P	6:21P
METROLINK 111	M - F	6:35P	6:21/6:48P	6:32P	6:33P
METROLINK 217	M - F	8:37P			7:09P

L: Regular stop to discharge or pick up passengers except train may leave ahead of schedule

R: Amtrak's Coast Starlight requires advance reservations Call (800) USA-RAIL.

D: Stops to discharge passengers only arrival time approximate.

Downtown Glendale

between Colorado and Broadway. The Galleria can be reached from the Metrolink station by taking the Glendale Beeline Route 2 bus. Return to Metrolink would be by the Route 1 bus. The city has a new outdoor shopping complex called the Exchange which is located along Brand Boulevard between Maryland and Wilson avenues. The Exchange is centered around the state-of-the-art Mann 8 theaters. The streets have decorative fountains and are lined with upscale boutiques and restaurants.

As you travel north along Brand Boulevard you will encounter the Alex Theater. The theater is accented by a crosswalk across Brand with stanchions on either side of Brand. Further up Brand or Central are located a number of high rise office buildings which serve as the employment center of downtown Glendale. The downtown district is capped on the north by the Red Lion Hotel.

Forest Lawn Memorial Park

Forest Lawn Memorial Park is located at 1712 South Glendale Avenue. Only in Southern California would someone feel that it would be

fitting to develop a cemetery that would at once be a place for a major art museum complex and yet a solemn place for those who are interred here. The park was founded in 1917 by Dr. Hubert Eaton. Since that time it has more than fulfilled the founders vision to develop a great park where the living could enjoy art, architecture and sculpture blended with sweeping lawns and trees alongside the dearly departed.

The major paintings and art works on display at Forest Lawn (Glendale) include *The Last Supper*, stained glass window, the Crucifixion painting, the *Resurrection* painting, a full size recreation of Michelangelo's statue of David, and much more. In addition to the major art works there is the Forest Lawn Museum which houses a fine collection of antiquities of historical and artistic interest.

Visiting hours are 9:00 A.M. to 4:45 P.M. in the Mausoleum-Columbaria where the *Last Supper* is on display, to 4:30 P.M. at the Hall of the *Crucifixion* and *Resurrection* paintings, and to 5:00 P.M. at the Forrest Lawn Museum. Admission is free and children under 16 must be accompanied by an adult. For information call (818) 241-4151. From the Glendale Amtrak/Metrolink Station take the Glendale Beeline Route 2 bus to the Brand Boulevard and Cerritos Avenue stop. Walk one Block east on Cerritos Avenue to Glendale Boulevard and the entrance to Forrest Lawn will be a short distance to the south off of Glendale Boulevard.

The Alex Theater

The Alex Theater is located at 216 N. Brand Boulevard. The theater can be reached from the Metrolink station by taking the Glendale Beeline Route 2

The Alex Theater

bus to the stop between Wilson Avenue and California Avenue. The Theater is located midway between these two streets. The theater presents live stage productions. For current billings and ticket availability call (818) 243-ALEX.

Glendale Community College

Glendale Community College is located at 1500 North Verdugo Road. The college was founded in 1927 to serve the needs of the people of La Crescenta, Glendale and Tujunga. The college moved from the campus of Harvard High School to its present site in 1937. The college occupies a 100-acre campus where it serves its 15,500 students. The college offers an Associates of Arts degree in a variety of majors. The campus has an active theater department which presents a number of student productions during the school year. For general information

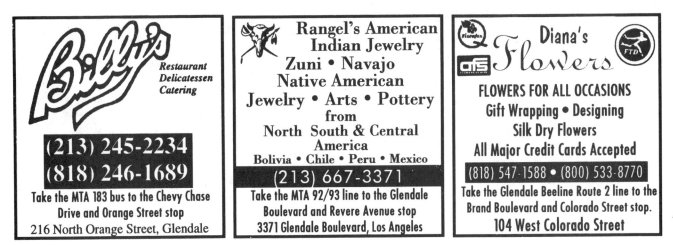

William Mulholland Memorial

Tigers having their Halloween Pumpkin at the L.A. Zoo

call (818) 240-1000. From Metrolink the college can be reached by taking the Glendale Beeline route 1 or 2 bus to the Glendale Galleria stop. There, transfer to the route 4 bus and take it to the Glendale College stop.

Griffith Park

The Los Feliz gateway to Griffith Park is not far from the Metrolink station. However, there is no direct bus service between Metrolink and Griffith Park. To reach the park one must transfer to the westbound MTA 180 or 181 line at Central Avenue and Los Feliz Boulevard from the Glendale Beeline routes 1 & 2 or the MTA 183 line. On the southwest corner of Los Feliz and Riverside Drive is the William Mulholland Memorial erected by the Los Angeles Department of Water & Power. William Mulholland

was the engineer responsible for the original Los Angeles Aqueduct from the Owens Valley. This aqueduct, completed in 1913, brought Owens river water to Los Angeles which hastened the growth of Southern California.

There is a pony ride and train ride just north of the Los Feliz Boulevard and Riverside Drive stop. These attractions have given much joy to the children of Los Angeles and there are long lines on weekends and holidays. Griffith park is the home of the Los Angeles Zoo, the Griffith Observatory, the Greek Theater, Travel Town, and the Autry Museum of Western Heritage. There is also a carousel that has been in operation for as long as I can remember. There are several municipally-operated golf courses within the park. There are

Autry Museum of Western Heritage

several picnic areas, bridal trails and hiking trails within this municipal park. Many of the park attractions are accessible only by car. Those accessible by public bus transportation will be discussed.

Los Angeles Zoo

The northbound MTA 96 line connects with the 180 & 181 lines at Los Feliz and Riverside Drive (see bus instructions for the Griffith Park-Los Feliz Gateway). The 96 line provides service to the Los Angeles Zoo and the Autry Museum of Western Heritage. The Los Angeles Zoo is a major Zoological Park with many endangered animals on display. It is home to a colony of Koala bears displayed in an indoor venue which provides a nighttime environment for these nocturnal animals during the Zoo operating hours. The animal displays are without bars throughout the park.

There is a large flight cage for birds which you can walk through with many rare species. There is a Children Zoo which features an interesting reptile display. Tram service is available for $3.00 for adults, $1.00 for seniors 65+, disabled and children 2 thru 12 . You can get off the tram at any of the six stops and re-board as you desire. The Zoo is open daily 10:00 A.M. to 5:00 P.M. except Christmas. Admission is $8.25 for adults age 13 and over, $3.25 for children 3 thru 12 and $5.25 for seniors 65+. For zoo information call (213) 666-4090.

Autry Museum of Western Heritage

The Autry Museum of Western Heritage is the fulfillment of Gene Autry's dream of a World-Class Museum that would showcase the rich history of the West. Since its opening in November of 1988, the museum has been host to millions of visitors. The museum provides permanent displays in a series of galleries that follow the history of the West from the First Americans to the present day. It has an impressive gallery populated with many prominent nineteenth century western artists.

With Gene Autry being a western movie star in the thirties, it is no surprise that there is a large gallery devoted to the Hollywood western movie stars and their films. The "finale" to your museum experience is a film and special effects extravaganza in

the Heritage Theater adapted for the museum by Walt Disney Imagineering.

The Wells Fargo Theater features films, lectures and live presentations. The George Montgomery Gallery is host to ever-changing traveling exhibitions. Food service is available at the Golden Spur Cafe. The museum is open Tuesdays through Sundays from 10:00 A.M. to 5:00 P.M. and on selected Mondays. The museum is closed Thanksgiving and Christmas. Admission is $7.00 for adults, $5.00 for seniors, $5.00 for students with I.D. and $3.00 for children 2 through 12. For information call (213) 667-2000.

The Griffith Observatory

The Griffith Observatory is located at the north end of Vermont Avenue on the south slope of Mount Hollywood. It can be reached from the Metrolink station by taking the MTA 180 & 181 Bus Line to the Los Feliz and Vermont stop. There you will transfer to the LADOT Dash line 203. The Dash 203 line travels up Vermont Avenue past the Greek Theater to the Observatory. The Observatory building has been featured in many science fiction films over the years and is a well-known Los Angeles landmark.

Griffith Observatory

The Hall of Science features a number of extremely interesting displays. There is a 12-inch telescope which is devoted to public viewing of the heavens. The telescope is open in winter Tuesday thru Sunday from 7:00 P.M. till 9:45 P.M. and in the summer daily from dark till 9:45 P.M. Admission is free. For the Sky Report call (213) 663-8171.

There is a planetarium theater which has a large Zeiss projector for displaying the stars and planets visible from earth. A regular series of different shows are presented over the calendar year. Planetarium admission is $4.00 for adults 13+, $3.00 for seniors 65+ and $2.00 for children 5 thru 12. For information about planetarium shows call (213) 664-1191.

The Observatory presents Laserium light concerts which are presented in the planetarium theater after each evening planetarium show. For information about specific shows, show times, and ticket prices call (818) 997-3624.

The Greek Theater

The Greek Theater is located on Vermont Avenue in Griffith Park. The theater is an outdoor amphitheater which is open during the summer and early fall. The theater presents a number of concerts during its season and features many big name entertainers in the music world. For information about current productions and ticket availability call (213) 665-1927.

Municipal Golf Courses

Along Riverside Drive there is a Municipal Golf Course which is open to the public. The course can be reached by taking the 96 bus from the Los Feliz gateway to the golf course stop.

Places to Stay

Best Western
Golden Key Hotel

The Best Western Golden Key hotel is located at 123 West Colorado Street. The hotel phone number is (818) 247-0111. For reservations call (800) 528-1234.

Econo Lodge

The Econo Lodge is located at 200 West Colorado Street. The hotel phone number is (818) 246-7331. For reservations call (800) 424-4777.

Red Lion Hotel

The Red Lion Hotel is located at 100 West Glenoaks Boulevard between Central Avenue and Brand Boulevard. The hotel phone number is (818) 956-5466. For reservations call (800) 547-8010.

Vagabond Inn

The Vagabond Inn is located at 120 West Colorado Street. The hotel phone number is (818) 240-1700. For reservations call (800) 548-8428.

Greek Theater

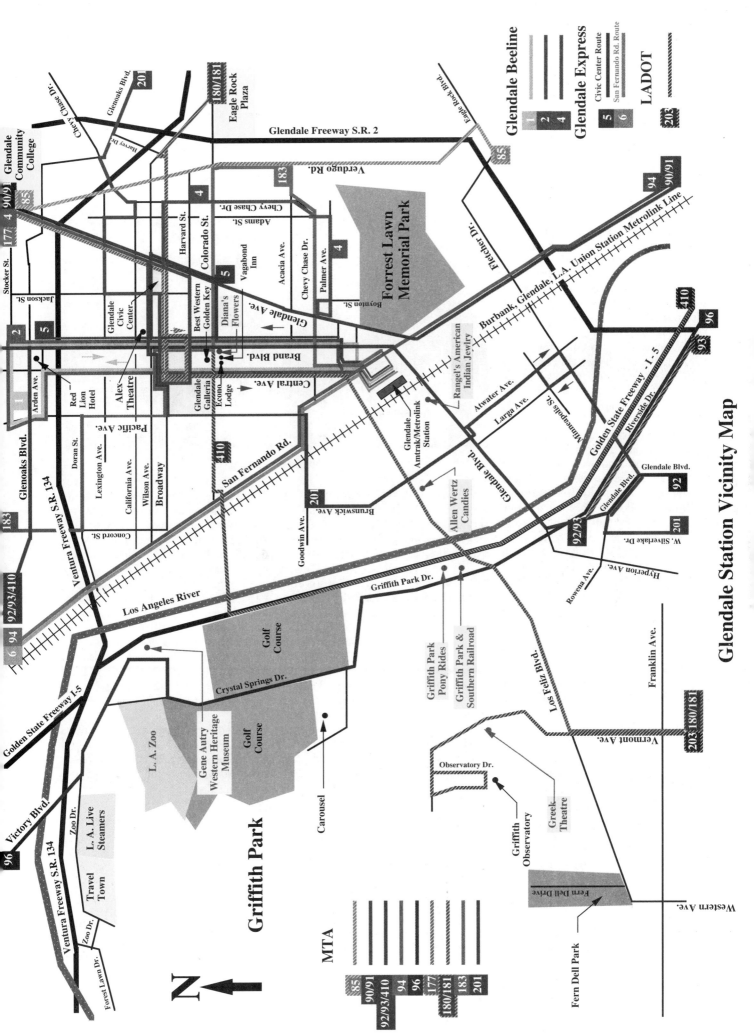

Glendale Station Vicinity Map

Burbank Station

Station Connecting Transit Information

The Burbank Metrolink Station is located at 201 N. Front Street, between the Burbank Electric Power Generating Station and the I-5 Freeway. Access to the station's 300-car parking lot is via Verdugo on the south and Burbank Boulevard on the north. There is also access to/from the station from the southbound Interstate 5 by taking the Verdugo off-ramp which ends on Front Street. Make a right on Front Street and Metrolink is on the left. There is also a pedestrian stairway to Olive for access to "Beautiful Downtown Burbank." See map insert for station locale. The station is manned for the morning and evening rush hours. The station is unmanned for the midday flex trains. The train boarding platform is well lighted but has limited shelter. The parking lot is also well lighted and maintained. Since the January 17, 1994 Northridge Earthquake, the Burbank Metrolink Station has become a major transit hub for the San Fernando Valley.

The station is served by the MTA 96, 152, 154, 164, and 165 lines. In addition the Burbank Local Transit (BLT) Media District Shuttle, Glendale Express Shuttle, Downtown Burbank Shuttle, and Golden State Area/ Burbank Airport Shuttle serve the station.

The eastbound MTA 96 line provides direct service to Griffith Park, L.A. Zoo and Autry Museum of Western Heritage (see Glendale Station). From Griffith Park this line continues through Silverlake to

Burbank Station

Downtown Los Angeles. The westbound MTA 96 line provides service to Studio City and Sherman Oaks. The MTA 152 line provides extended service along Vineland Avenue to Sun Valley, and Roscoe Boulevard to Panorama City, Sepulveda, Northridge and Canoga Park. The MTA 154 line provides extended service along Burbank Boulevard to Van Nuys, and Reseda, and along Tampa Avenue to Northridge. The MTA 164 and 165 lines provide extended service to the same communities along Victory Boulevard and Vanowen Street respectively. The station vicinity map provides the routes for bus transit options from the Burbank Metrolink Station. The table below provides the schedule of bus connections with Metrolink. For schedule and route updates call MTA on (818) 246-2593.

The Burbank Local Transit (BLT) meets every Metrolink train in the morning starting with the 5:59 A.M. arrival of the first train in the morning from Santa Clarita. The last morning shuttle leaves the Metrolink station at 8:53 A.M. There are no shuttle connections with the midday "Flex" trains. The shuttle provides return service arriving at the Metrolink station at 3:30 P.M. The last shuttle arrives at the Metrolink station at 6:42 P.M. The

Golden State Area/Burbank Airport Shuttles are at the Burbank Metrolink Station during the peak hours of 6:30 A.M. to 9:30 A.M. and 3:30 P.M. to 6:30 P.M. For BLT schedule and route updates call (818) 238-5276.

For passengers inbound from Santa Clarita going to the Burbank Airport, the Burbank Airport shuttle will pick you up after you call from the station. There is a special Burbank Airport shuttle phone at the station. Passengers traveling from Los Angeles or from Oxnard can take the Ventura County Line trains to the Burbank Airport Station.

In addition, a number of employers in the Burbank Media District and elsewhere in the San Fernando Valley have shuttle busses for picking up and returning their employees to/from the Burbank Metrolink Station.

Points of Interest

Burbank was born during the Southern California land boom of the 1880's. The city is named for its founder Dr. David Burbank, a New Hampshire born dentist. Dr. Burbank acquired a portion of Rancho San Rafael and Rancho Providencia in 1870. This land became what is now Burbank. Dr. Burbank sold his holdings in 1886 to land speculators who formed the Providencia Land, Water and

BURBANK STATION BUS CONNECTIONS
SOUTHBOUND TRAINS FROM BURBANK TO LOS ANGELES

TRAIN NUMBER	DAYS OF OPERATION	TRAIN ARRIVAL	MTA 96 EASTBOUND 20 - 30 MIN.	MTA 96 WESTBOUND 20 - 30 MIN.	MTA 152 40 - 60 MIN.	MTA 154 45 - 60 MIN.	MTA 164 20 - 30 MIN.	MTA 165 20 - 30 MIN.	BLT GLENDALE EXPRESS SHUTTLE	BLT MEDIA DISTRICT SHUTTLE
METROLINK 200	M - F	L5:58A	5:34/5:59A	5:53/6:19A	5:51/6:25A	6:01A	6:06A	6:05A	6:04A	6:04A
METROLINK 100	M - F	6:03A	5:59/6:18A	5:53/6:19A	5:51/6:25A	6:44A	6:06A	6:05A	6:04A	6:04A
METROLINK 102	M - F	6:43A	6:32/6:45A	6:39/6:59A	5:51/7:22A	6:34/6:44A	6:45A	6:21/6:57A	6:26/6:45A	6:54A
METROLINK 202	M - F	6:52A	6:45/6:58A	6:39/6:59A	5:51/7:22A	6:34/7:34A	6:52/6:57A	6:45/6:57A	6:26/6:55A	6:54A
METROLINK 204	M - F	7:22A	7:12/7:26A	7:20/7:40A	7:07/8:17A	7:19/7:34A	7:18/7:26A	7:09/7:35A	7:17/7:25A	7:34A
METROLINK 104	M - F	7:33A	7:26/7:41A	7:20/7:40A	7:07/8:17A	7:19/7:34A	7:18/7:51A	7:09/7:35A	7:17/7:34A	7:34A
METROLINK 206	M - F	7:53A	7:41/7:56A	7:40/8:01A	7:48/8:17A	7:19/8:14A	7:43/8:21A	7:33/7:55A	7:47/7:56A	7:55A
METROLINK 106	M - F	8:12A	8:11/8:27A	8:01/8:21A	7:48/8:17A	8:04/8:14A	8:08/8:21A	8:00/8:20A	8:11/8:14A	8:13A
METROLINK 208	M - F	8:22A	8:11/8:27A	8:21/8:43A	7:48/9:17A	8:04/8:58A	8:08/8:51A	8:27/8:50A	8:18/8:27A	8:26A
METROLINK 210	M - F	9:22A	8:53/9:23A	9:13/9:34A	9:22/10:17A	8:49/9:43A	9:07/9:50A	9:20/9:50A	8:49A	9:24A*
METROLINK 108	M - F	10:18A	9:53/10:23A	10:04/10:34A	9:54/11:16A	9:34/10:28A	10:07/10:20A	10:10/10:20A		
METROLINK 110	M - F	3:37P	3:25/3:44P	3:29/3:54P	2:54/4:27P	3:11/4:13P	3:28/3:41P	3:34/3:45P		3:30P
METROLINK 212	M - F	3:56P	3:44/4:04P	3:54/4:19P	2:54/4:27P	3:11/4:13P	3:28/4:08P	3:53/4:10P	3:51P	3:48P
METROLINK 900	M - F	4:53P	4:44/5:11P	4:39/4:59P	3:54/5:27P	4:48/5:04P	4:52/5:08P	4:33/5:01P	4:39P	4:37P
METROLINK 902	M - F	5:17P	5:11/5:43P	4:59/5:21P	5:01/5:27P	4:48/5:54P	5:15/5:39P	5:13/5:26P	5:09P	5:16P
METROLINK 214	M - F	5:40P	5:11/5:43P	5:21/5:44P	5:01/6:34P	5:38/5:54P	5:38/6:12P	5:30/5:52P	5:35P	5:33P
METROLINK 216	M - F	7:54P	7:20/8:22P	7:42/8:06P	6:56P	7:23P	7:31/8:00P	7:51P	6:37P	7:48P*

NORTHBOUND TRAINS FROM LOS ANGELES TO BURBANK

TRAIN NUMBER	DAYS OF OPERATION	TRAIN ARRIVAL	MTA 96 EASTBOUND	MTA 96 WESTBOUND	MTA 152	MTA 154	MTA 164	MTA 165	BLT GLENDALE EXPRESS SHUTTLE	BLT MEDIA DISTRICT SHUTTLE
METROLINK 201	M - F	L6:49A	6:45/6:58A	6:39/6:59A	5:51/7:22A	6:34/7:34A	6:57A	6:45/6:57A	6:26/6:55A	6:54A
METROLINK 901	M - F	7:10A	7:12/7:26A	6:59/7:20A	7:07/7:22A	6:34/7:34A	6:52/7:11A	7:09/7:15A	7:07/7:25A	7:15A
METROLINK 203	M - F	L7:47A	7:41/7:56A	7:40/8:01A	7:07/8:17A	7:19/8:14A	7:43/7:51P	7:33/7:55A	7:17/7:49A	7:55A
METROLINK 903	M - F	8:25A	8:11/8:27A	8:21/8:43A	7:48/9:17A	8:04/8:58A	8:08/8:51P	8:27/8:50A	8:18/8:27A	8:26A
METROLINK 905	M - F	8:53A	8:27/9:23A	8:43/9:13A	8:28/9:17A	8:49/8:58A	8:37/9:20A	8:27/9:20A	8:49A	8:54A
METROLINK 101	M - F	9:09A	8:53/9:23A	8:43A/9:13A	8:28/9:17A	8:49/9:43A	9:07/9:20A	8:56/9:20A		9:14A*
METROLINK 103	M - F	1:22P	1:21/1:51P	1:04/1:34P	12:54/2:23P	12:41/1:43P	1:08/1:38P	1:12/1:25P		
METROLINK 205	M - F	2:13P	1:51/2:21P	2:04/2:34P	1:59/2:23P	1:31/2:33P	2:08/2:20P	2:10/2:25P		
METROLINK 207	M - F	4:02P	3:44/4:04P	3:54/4:19P	3:54/4:27P	3:59/4:13P	4:00/4:08P	3:53/4:10P	3:51P	3:48P
METROLINK 209	M - F	4:27P	4:24/4:44P	4:19/4:39P	3:54/4:27P	3:59/5:04P	4:06/4:38P	4:13/4:35P	4:22P	4:19P
METROLINK 105	M - F	4:43P	4:24/4:44P	4:39/4:59P	3:54/5:27P	4:48/5:04P	4:28/5:08P	4:33/5:01P	4:39P	4:37P
METROLINK 211	M - F	5:14P	5:11/5:43P	4:59/5:21P	5:01/5:27P	4:48/5:54P	4:52/5:39P	5:13/5:26P	5:09P	5:06P
METROLINK 107	M - F	5:22P	5:11/5:43P	5:21/5:44P	5:01/5:27P	4:48/5:54P	5:15/5:39P	5:13/5:26P	5:18P	5:16P
METROLINK 213	M - F	5:50P	5:43/6:15P	5:44/6:01P	5:01/6:34P	5:38/5:54P	5:38/6:12P	5:48/5:52P	5:35P	5:33P
METROLINK 109	M - F	5:58P	5:43/6:15P	6:01/6:19P	5:01/6:34P	5:38/6:45P	5:38/6:12P	5:48/6:24P	5:54P	5:52P
METROLINK 215	M - F	6:31P	6:15/7:20P	6:19/6:38P	6:30/6:34P	6:28/6:45P	6:23/6:42P	6:24/6:58P	6:26P	6:23P
METROLINK 111	M - F	6:41P	6:15/7:20P	6:38/6:58P	6:30/7:21P	6:28/6:45P	6:23/7:15P	6:24/6:58P	6:37P	6:35P
METROLINK 217	M - F	8:43P	8:22P	8:06/9:06P	6:56P	8:18P	8:30/8:45P	8:26P		8:36P*

L: Regular stop to discharge or pick up passengers except train may leave ahead of schedule

* Service being provided by Prime Time. Please Call (800) 733-8267 to arrange your pick-up.

Development Company. Burbank later became the San Fernando Valley's first independent city when the voters approved incorporation on July 1, 1911. The movies came to Burbank in a big way in 1926 when First National Pictures started to build a large studio. Today this studio is home of Warner Brothers Studios. Walt Disney built his Studio in Burbank in 1939 and the Studio now houses the headquarters of the giant Walt Disney Corporation. NBC constructed its television studios in Burbank in 1951.

Burbank is also the former home to Lockheed's famous Skunk Works where Kelly Johnson's U-2 and SR-71 Blackbird spy planes were designed and built.

Beautiful Downtown Burbank

The downtown district of Burbank is located directly across Interstate 5 Freeway from the Metrolink station. You can take the any of the MTA lines that stop at the station to San Fernando Road or you can walk via the stairway to Olive Avenue. If you decide to walk take Olive across the Interstate 5 to San Fernando Road.

Along San Fernando Road is the Burbank downtown area called the Burbank Village. There are numerous bookstores dealing in used books and

"Beatiful Downtown Burbank"

many unique old shops such as the Last Grenadier dealing with toy soldiers lining San Fernando Road as you travel north west from Olive. The city has widened the sidewalks in the old downtown shopping district and added head-in parking reminiscent of earlier less hectic times. There are signs of significant improvement in this old shopping district with the addition of several trendy restaurants and boutiques. San Fernando Road terminates at Magnolia Blvd. in Burbank's new Media City Center shopping mall.

Autry Museum of Western Heritage

See Glendale Station for information. Take the southbound MTA 96 line to the museum stop.

Los Angeles Zoo

See Glendale Station for information. Take the southbound MTA 96 line to the zoo stop.

Gordon R. Howard Museum Complex

The Gordon R. Howard Museum Complex is located at 1015 W. Olive Avenue in George Izay Park. Adjacent to the Mentzer House, a victorian home, is a Lockheed F-104 Starfighter named the *Spirit of Burbank*. The museum is named for one of Burbank's prominent citizens. The museum consists of three different museums. The first building that you encounter is the Mentzer House, a late 1880's vintage victorian home which contains period-style furniture. The next museum is the Burbank Memorabilia Museum which has on display photographs detailing the history of the Walt Disney Studio, the NBC Studio, the Lockheed Aircraft Corporation and other prominent business concerns which at one time were important to the economic well being of Burbank. In addition there is an antique doll collection, some native american artifacts, an antique camera collection, turn of the century business machines and many more late 19th and early 20th century artifacts. The museum also has replicas of representative rooms from typical homes, businesses and professional offices such as a turn-of- the-century dentist office.

The final museum in this complex is the Antique Vehicle Museum which has a fire engine, a bus and ten cars. There is a 1937 Rolls Royce Phantom

The Spirit of Burbank

III, a 1939 Daimler, and many more rare cars from the early 1900's. The museum is open 1:00 P.M. to 4:00 P.M. Sundays. For further information call (818) 842-7514. From Metrolink the museum can be reached by taking the MTA 96 bus line to the Olive Avenue at the George Izay Park. The Museum will be one block west on the north side of Olive Avenue.

NBC Television Studio

The NBC Television Studio is located at 3000 W. Alameda Street between Bob Hope Drive and Olive. Contrary to several famous television personalities' statements, the NBC television studios is not located in "Downtown" Burbank, but in the city's Media District. The NBC studio can be reached using the BLT Media District Shuttle to the Alameda and Bob Hope stop. Access to/from Metrolink can also be by taking either the MTA 96 or 152 bus line to the Alameda and Olive stop.

Free tickets for the Tonight Show are distributed daily at 8:00 A.M. at the NBC ticket counter. If you want to get tickets you want to arrive on the first train in the morning to get in line as early as possible. For ticket availability information call (818) 840-3537.

NBC Studio Burbank

There is a 70-minute walking Studio tour at regular intervals between 9:00 A.M. and 3:00 P.M. Monday through Friday. The cost of the tour is $6.00 for adults, $5.50 for seniors 60 and over, $3.75 for children (5-12 years) and children under five are free. The tour is mildly interesting with the highlight being a visit to "Studio One" where the Tonight Show is taped. You may catch a glimpse of one of NBC's Television personalities during your tour, but autograph requests are discouraged by the tour guides. Many of the canned video demonstrations are a bit dated (not in the same league as Universal Hollywood). The low cost of the tour is in line with the overall quality.

Universal Studios Hollywood

Universal Studios Hollywood is located between Hollywood and the San Fernando Valley. The studio can be reached using the MTA 96 or 152 bus lines to the Ventura and Lankershim boulevards stop.

Universal CityWalk

The park is open daily except Thanksgiving and Christmas. The park opens at 9:00 A.M. most of the year and at 7:30 A.M. during the summer. For information on admission prices and exact operating hours call (818) 508-9600.

Universal Studios Hollywood is the original theme park that grew out of the old tram tour of the studio and back-lot. The old tram tour has been expanded by the addition of several new attractions such as *Earthquake*. Today this park also features several rides like *Back to the Future the Ride* and *Backdraft*, stunt shows like the *Miami Vice* and *Wild Wild Wild West*. The theme park is a 10 plus and a major Southern California tourist attraction.

Established adjacent to the theme

Warner Brothers Studio

park is the *Universal CityWalk* with many unique shops, restaurants and Hollywood street performers. If you just want to take in the latest Hollywood blockbuster there is the 18 theater Cineplex Odean. The Universal Amphitheater provides a venue for some of the top concert groups on tour. Call the Amphitheater at (818) 622-4440 for current bookings.

Walt Disney Studio

The Walt Disney Studio is located on Alameda between Buena Vista and Keystone streets. The studio can be reached using the Burbank Media District Shuttle to the Disney studio stop or the MTA 96 or 152 bus line to the Alameda and Buena Vista stop. There is no studio tour and visitors are not allowed on the lot. The new Disney Corporate Headquarters is interesting with the Seven Dwarfs supporting the roof of the building.

Warner Brothers Studio

The Warner Brothers Studio is located at the intersection of Olive Avenue and Hollywood Way. The studio can be reached taking the MTA 96 line to the Olive Avenue and Riverside Drive stop or Burbank Media District Shuttle to Olive Avenue and Hollywood Way stop.

The Studio provides a tour to the general public in small groups. It starts off with an introduction to the studio by the head of the studio tour staff and a short film clip with scenes from many famous Warner Brothers movies. The focus is primarily educational and changes daily depending upon what is being filmed on the lot and the interest of the particular group. The tour that I was on had a total of ten people. We were allowed to roam at will through the "Daily Planet" the set being used at the time of our visit for the television show *The New Adventures of Superman*. The tour group was brought on the set of *A Full House* which was in the process of taping with a live audience for a couple of scenes with Little Richard as guest star. Our guide was extremely knowledgeable about the history of the Warner Brothers Studio and took the time to answer in depth any questions asked. Throughout the lot at the numerous outdoor stages there was evidence of filming in process. The tour was two hours in length and the personal attention was a welcome departure from the canned "behind the scenes" tours offered to the masses at the "Universal Studios Theme Park."

Generally reservations are required but walk-ins sometimes can be accommodated. The tour visits working areas and children under 10 years of age are not allowed. The cost of the tour is $25.00 per person. For tour availability and prices you can call (818) 954-1744.

Woodbury University

Woodbury University is located at 7500 Glenoaks Boulevard on a 22-acre campus. The university can be reached by taking the northbound MTA 92/93/410 line from the First Street and Olive Avenue stop in downtown Burbank to the stop in front of the university main gate. The university was founded in 1884 by F. C. Woodbury as a college of business administration. For its first 103 years the college was located in central Los Angeles. In 1987 the college moved to its present location in the city of Burbank. Today the University has three schools: the School of Architecture and Design, the School of Arts and Science and the School of Business Management. The student body numbers about 1,000 students. For general information call (818) 767-0888.

Places to Stay

Holiday Inn Burbank

The Holiday Inn Burbank is located at 150 E. Angeleno Avenue. The hotel has a shuttle van that will pick you up at the Metrolink station with advance notice. The hotel phone number is (818) 841-4770. For reservations call (800) 465-4329.

Universal Hilton & Towers

The Universal Hilton & Towers is located at 555 Universal Terrace Parkway. Bus transportation to the hotel is the same as Universal Studios. The hotel phone number is (818) 506-2500. For reservations call (800) HILTONS

Sheraton Universal

The Sheraton Universal is located at 333 Universal Terrace Parkway. Bus transportation to the hotel is the same as Universal Studios. The hotel phone number is (818) 980-1212. For reservations call (800) 325-3535.

Ramada Inn Burbank

The Ramada Inn Burbank is located at 2900 N. San Fernando Boulevard. The hotel has a shuttle van that will pick you up at the Metrolink station with advance notice. The hotel phone number is (818) 843-5955. For reservations call (800) 228-2828.

Safari Inn

The Safari Inn is located at 1911 West Olive Avenue. The hotel can be reached by taking the MTA 96 line at to the Olive Avenue and Lamer Street stop. The hotel phone number is (818) 845-8586. For reservations call (800) STAHERE.

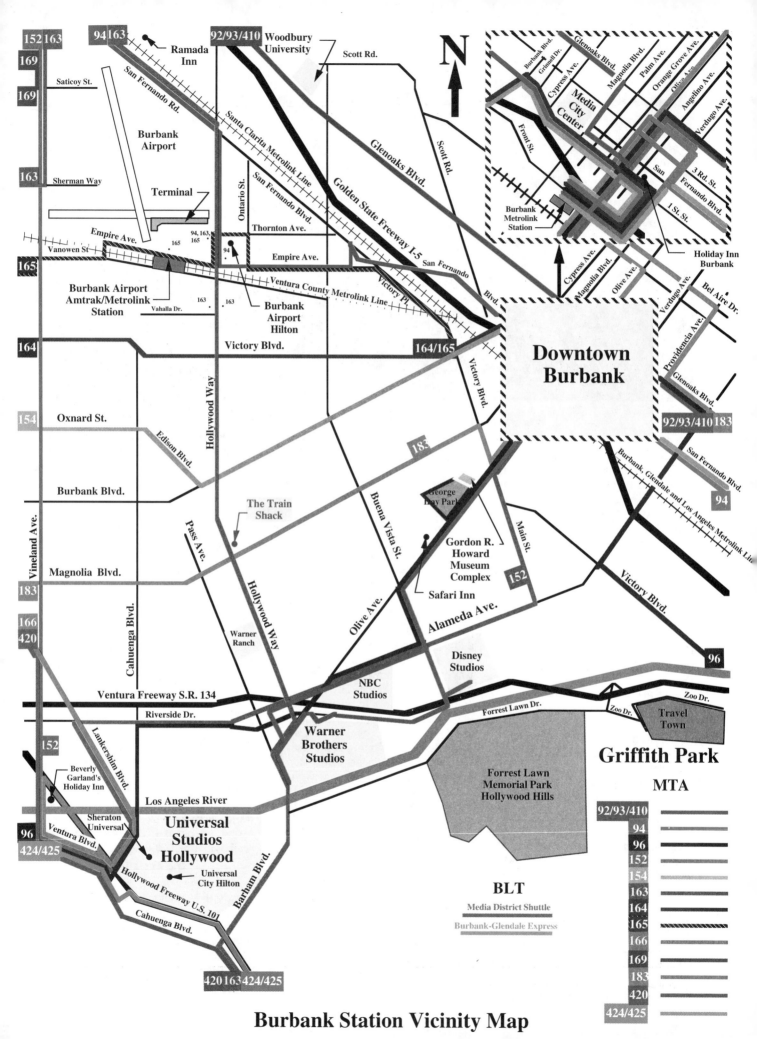

Burbank Station Vicinity Map

Ventura County Line

The Ventura County Line has 11 stations. They are located at L.A. Union Station, Glendale, Burbank, Burbank Airport, Van Nuys, Northridge, Chatsworth, Simi Valley, Moorpark, Camarillo, and Oxnard. For information on the L.A. Union Station, Glendale Station and Burbank Station see the section on the Burbank, Glendale and Los Angeles Line. Amtrak operates four trains daily and Metrolink operates six trains Monday thru Friday in each direction. The schedules below indicate the times and number of trains traveling in each direction on the Ventura County Line at the time of publication. For updates to Metrolink schedules please call 808-LINK in the 213, 310, 714, 805, 818, and 909 area codes. For updates to Amtrak schedules please call (800) USA-RAIL.

Amtrak and Metrolink tickets <u>are not</u> interchangeable. You must purchase an Amtrak ticket for travel on Amtrak and a Metrolink ticket for travel on Metrolink. The only exception to this is for Metrolink Ventura County Line Monthly Pass holders. Monthly Pass holders can purchase "Step-Up Coupon Books" in packs of 10 Coupons for

Metrolink Train In the Santa Susana Pass

$18.00 from Amtrak Ticket agents on the Ventura County Line stations and at L.A. Union Station. The Coupons may be used only on Amtrak trains 771, 772, 775, 776, 779, 780, 781, and 786 Monday thru Friday for trips which originate or terminate at the Ventura County Stations of Simi Valley, Moorpark, Camarillo and Oxnard only. Coupons are not sold on Amtrak trains.

VENTURA COUNTY LINE TRAIN SCHEDULE
SOUTHBOUND FROM OXNARD TO LOS ANGELES

TRAIN NUMBER	METROLINK 100	METROLINK 102	METROLINK 104	AMTRAK 772	METROLINK 106	AMTRAK 774	METROLINK 108	AMTRAK 776	METROLINK 110	AMTRAK 780	AMTRAK 782	11 (R)	AMTRAK 786
DAYS OF OPERATION	M - F	M - F	M - F	M - F	M - F	SA.SU.H	M - F	DAILY	M - F	M - F	SA.SU.H	DAILY	DAILY
OXNARD		5:29A	6:19A	6:50A		8:35A		10:31A		3:17P	3:17P	4:50P	7:05P
CAMARILLO		5:39A	6:29A	7:00A		8:45A							7:15P
MOORPARK	5:12A	5:52A	6:42A	7:13A	7:22A	8:57A			2:39P				7:27P
SIMI VALLEY	5:25A	6:05A	6:55A		7:35A	9:10A		11:14A	2:52P	3:48P	3:48P	5:30P	7:40P
CHATSWORTH	5:38A	6:18A	7:08A		7:47A	9:24A	L9:49A		3:12P		4:02P		7:54P
NORTHRIDGE	5:44A	6:24A	7:14A		7:53A		L9:58A		3:18P				
VAN NUYS	5:51A	6:31A	7:21A	7:49A	8:00A	9:36A	10:06A	11:40A	3:25P	4:15P	4:15P		8:06P
BURBANK AIRPORT	5:59A	6:39A	7:29A	7:56A	8:08A	9:43A	10:14A	11:47A	3:33P	4:23P	4:23P		8:13P
BURBANK	6:03A	6:43A	7:33A		8:12A		10:18A		3:37P				
GLENDALE	6:09A	6:49A	7:39A		8:18A	9:58A	10:24A	11:55A	3:44P	4:35P	4:35P	D6:45P	8:26P
L.A. UNION STATION	6:23A	7:03A	7:53A	8:20A	8:32A	10:15P	10:39A	12:10P	4:01P	4:55P	4:55P	7:00P	8:40P

NORTHBOUND FROM LOS ANGELES TO OXNARD

TRAIN NUMBER	METROLINK 101	AMTRAK 769	AMTRAK 771	14 (R)	AMTRAK 775	METROLINK 103	AMTRAK 779	METROLINK 105	METROLINK 107	METROLINK 109	AMTRAK 781	AMTRAK 791	METROLINK 111
DAYS OF OPERATION	M - F	SA.SU.H	M - F	DAILY	DAILY	M - F	DAILY	M - F	M - F	M - F	DAILY	SA.SU.H	M - F
L.A. UNION STATION	8:51A	9:15A	9:15A	9:30A	11:35A	1:05P	3:30P	4:26P	5:05P	5:41P	5:50P	5:55P	6:24P
GLENDALE	9:03A	9:28A	9:27A	9:48A	11:48A	1:16P	3:44P	4:37P	5:16P	5:52P		6:09P	6:35P
BURBANK	9:09A					1:22P		4:43P	5:22P	5:58P			6:41P
BURBANK AIRPORT	L9:13A	9:39A	9:37A		11:59A	1:26P	3:55P	4:48P	5:26P	6:02P	6:13P	6:21P	6:45P
VAN NUYS	L9:22A	9:48A	9:43A		12:08P	1:35P	4:02P	4:56P	5:35P	6:11P	6:22P	6:32P	6:54P
NORTHRIDGE	L9:29A					1:42P		5:03P	5:42P	6:18P			7:01P
CHATSWORTH	9:37A				12:21P	1:48P		5:09P	5:48P	6:24P		6:45P	7:07P
SIMI VALLEY		10:15A	10:06A	10:19A	12:35P	L2:00P	4:30P	L5:21P	L6:00P	L6:36P		6:57P	L7:19P
MOORPARK		10:30A			12:53P	2:20P		L5:35P	L6:14P	6:55P	7:06P	7:12P	7:38P
CAMARILLO					1:05P			L5:49P	L6:25P		7:16P	7:23P	
OXNARD		10:48A	10:41A	11:01A	1:17P		5:07P	6:02P	6:39P		7:28P	7:35P	

L: Regular stop to discharge or pick up passengers except train may leave ahead of schedule
R: Amtrak's Coast Starlight requires advance reservations Call (800) USA-RAIL
D: Stops to discharge passengers only, arrival time approximate.

Metrolink Train at Moorpark Station

When riding Amtrak you must show the conductor your Monthly Pass and give him one of the Step-Up Coupons. Step-Up Coupons sold for use on the Ventura County Line are not valid for travel on the Orange County Line nor are the "Step-Up Coupons" sold for use on the Orange County Line valid on the Ventura County Line.

The Ventura County Line was originally built by the Southern Pacific Company. The line was built to shorten the original Coast line to San Francisco which was completed in 1894 by way of Santa Paula. Southern Pacific began construction of the Chatsworth tunnels through the Santa Susana Mountains to Simi Valley in 1893. It took 11 years to complete the tunnels. When the Chatsworth cutoff opened in 1904 the tunnels were the longest in the country.

Metrolink purchased several Southern Pacific Lines in the five county region served. Metrolink service to Moorpark from L.A. Union Station began on October 26, 1992.

The original service offered service from Moorpark to Los Angeles with stops at Simi Valley, Chatsworth, Van Nuys, Burbank, and Glendale. The original cost of this line was $94 million for capital improvements, including track, rolling stock and stations. The total length of the original line from Moorpark to L.A. Union

Station is 47 miles.

After the January 17, 1994 Northridge Earthquake, Metrolink opened the Northridge and Camarillo

stations on February 14, 1994. The line was extended 10 miles west from the Moorpark Station to Camarillo. The Northridge Station is located between the Chatsworth and Van Nuys stations in the San Fernando Valley.

On April 4, 1994 Metrolink extended service to Oxnard, bringing the total length of this line to 66 miles with a transit time of 1 hour 34 minutes from Oxnard to L.A. Union Station. All costs for these emergency extensions of the Ventura County Line were funded by the Federal Emergency Management Agency (FEMA).

The Burbank Airport Station was opened for regular passenger service on July 17, 1995. This station is the first multi-modal station to open on the Metrolink system. This station provides direct access to the Burbank Airport allowing local travelers to park their cars at the local Metrolink Station and take the train to the airport, avoiding the drive to the airport and the expense and hassle of parking in one of the airport parking lots. For out-of-town visitors intent on using public transportation, the Burbank Airport should be the number one choice for arrival in the Los Angeles region.

Burbank Airport Station

Station Connecting Transit Information

The Burbank Airport Amtrak/ Metrolink Station is located at 3750 Empire Avenue. This station is a destination station on the Metrolink system. Parking is available at the Burbank Airport, Lot C, two blocks north of the station off Hollywood Way at a rate of $8.00 per day. The Lot C shuttle bus will take you to the train boarding platform. The train boarding platform is well lighted and there is excellent shelter. The station is located directly across the street from the Burbank Airport terminal. Metrolink personnel man the station during the morning and evening rush hours. The station is unmanned midday when the flex trains arrive.

The station is served by the MTA 94, 163 and 165 bus lines. The bus stop for the MTA 165 line is located down the stairs on the north side of the boarding platform on Empire Avenue. The stops for the 94 and 163 lines are located at the intersection of Hollywood Way and Thornton Avenue. The

Burbank Airport Metrolink Station

southbound 94 line has a stop on Empire Avenue on the north side of Hollywood way.

The station vicinity map provides

the routes for bus transit options from the Burbank Airport Amtrak/Metrolink Station. The following tables provide the schedule of bus connections with

BURBANK AIRPORT STATION WEEKDAY BUS CONNECTIONS
SOUTHBOUND TRAINS FROM OXNARD TO LOS ANGELES

TRAIN NUMBER	DAYS OF OPERATION	TRAIN ARRIVAL	MTA 94 SOUTHBOUND 10 - 20 MIN.	MTA 94 NORTHBOUND 10 - 20 MIN.	MTA 163 EASTBOUND 30 - 45 MIN.	MTA 163 WESTBOUND 30 - 45 MIN.	MTA 165 EASTBOUND 20 - 30 MIN.	MTA 165 WESTBOUND 20 - 30 MIN.
BUS FREQUENCY								
METROLINK 100	M - F	5:59A	5:47/6:01A	5:48/6:00A	5:57/6:29A	5:33/6:09A	6:08A	5:39/6:04A
METROLINK 102	M - F	6:39A	6:27/6:51A	6:32/6:42A	6:29/7:00A	6:09/6:55A	6:32/6:56A	6:32/6:44A
METROLINK 104	M - F	7:29A	7:14/7:44A	7:20/7:36A	7:00/7:30A	7:14/7:35A	7:20/7:46A	7:12/7:30A
AMTRAK 772	M - F	7:56A	7:44/8:00A	7:52/7:59A	7:30/8:15A	7:35/8:19A	7:46/8:13A	7:50/8:10A
METROLINK 106	M - F	8:08A	8:00/8:16A	7:59/8:09A	7:30/8:15A	7:35/8:19A	7:46/8:13A	7:50/8:10A
METROLINK 108	M - F	10:14A	10:12/10:29A	10:11/10:26A	9:35/10:15A	9:39/10:19A	9:56/10:26A	10:05/10:35A
AMTRAK 776	DAILY	11:47A	11:37/11:54A	11:34/11:51A	11:36A/12:16P	11:38A/12:18P	11:26/11:56A	11:35A/12:05P
METROLINK 110	M - F	3:33P	3:30/3:39P	3:18/3:46P	2:56/3:36P	3:01/3:41P	3:18/3:38A	3:12/3:37P
AMTRAK 780	M - F	4:23P	4:20/4:33P	4:14/4:26P	4:16/4:53P	4:21/5:08P	4:18/4:38A	4:02/4:27P
AMTRAK 786	DAILY	8:13P	7:36/8:16P	7:57/8:17P	7:53/8:53P	7:40/8:17P	7:39/8:14P	7:43P

NORTHBOUND TRAINS FROM LOS ANGELES TO OXNARD

METROLINK 101	M - F	L9:13A	9:04/9:21A	9:08/9:20A	8:55/9:35A	8:59/9:39A	9:06/9:30A	9:05/9:35A
AMTRAK 771	M - F	9:37A	9:21/9:55A	9:32/9:44A	9:35/10:15A	8:59/9:39A	9:30/9:56A	9:35/10.05A
AMTRAK 775	DAILY	11:59A	11:54A/12:11P	11:51A/12:08P	11:36A/12:16P	11:38A/12:18P	11:56A/12:26P	11:35A/12:05P
METROLINK 103	M - F	1:26P	1:18/1:34P	1:17/1:34P	12:56/1:36P	12:58/1:41P	1:25/1:54P	1:13/1:42P
AMTRAK 779	DAILY	3:55P	3:48/3:57P	3:46/4:00P	3:36/4:16P	4:41/4:21P	3:38/3:58P	3:37/4:02P
METROLINK 105	M - F	4:48P	4:45/4:59P	4:46/4:56P	4:16/4:53P	4:21/5:08P	4:38/4:58P	4:27/4:52P
METROLINK 107	M - F	5:26P	5:24/5:39P	5:16/5:36P	4:53/5:29P	5:08/5:59P	5:15/5:33P	5:18/5:43P
METROLINK 109	M - F	6:02P	5:59/6:19P	5:56/6:06P	5:29/6:07P	5:59/7:05P	5:51/6:10P	5:43/6:08P
AMTRAK 781	M - F	6:13P	5:59/6:19P	6:06/6:15P	6:07/6:57P	5:59/7:05P	6:10/6:34P	6:08/6:39P
METROLINK 111	M - F	6:45P	6:44/7:08P	6:35/6:48P	6:07/6:57P	5:59/7:05P	6:34/7:04P	6:39/7:12P

L: Regular stop to discharge or pick up passengers except train may leave ahead of schedule

Metrolink and Amtrak. For schedule and route updates on MTA lines call (818) 781-5890.

Points of Interest
Burbank Airport

The Burbank Airport is located at 2627 Hollywood Way. The Airport terminal is directly across the street (Empire Avenue) from the Burbank Airport Amtrak/Metrolink Station. This station provides the best and easiest access to the Metrolink system from any of the Los Angeles region's many airports. Travel time from the Burbank Airport Station to Los Angeles Union Station is approximately 25 minutes. With the proper connection a traveler can be in downtown Los Angeles in less than 40 minutes from flight gate arrival time by using this Airport and Metrolink or Amtrak. Travelers using LAX will take from one and one half to two hours to reach downtown Los Angeles. The Airport is served by Alaska Airlines, America West Airlines, American Airlines, Reno Air, SkyWest, Southwest Airlines, and United Airlines.

Burbank Airport Terminal

CBS Studios

The CBS Studios is home to many of the independent Television Production companies which supply television fare to the networks. There is a studio store near the main gate at 4024 Radford Avenue. There are no tours of the studios, however, many of the shows are open to audiences. Tickets for shows can be obtained

BURBANK AIRPORT STATION WEEKEND BUS CONNECTIONS
SOUTHBOUND TRAINS FROM OXNARD TO LOS ANGELES

TRAIN NUMBER	DAYS OF OPERATION	TRAIN ARRIVAL	MTA 94 SOUTHBOUND 10 - 20 MIN.	MTA 94 NORTHBOUND 10 - 20 MIN.	MTA 163 EASTBOUND HOURLY	MTA 163 WESTBOUND HOURLY	MTA 165 EASTBOUND 20 - 30 MIN.	MTA 165 WESTBOUND 20 - 30 MIN.
BUS FREQUENCY								
SATURDAY BUS CONNECTIONS								
AMTRAK 774	SA.SU.H	9:10A	9:05/9:16A	8:58/9:16A	8:27/9:28A	8:47/9:47A	9:06/9:36A	8:44/9:14A
AMTRAK 776	DAILY	11:14A	11:02/11:26A	11:03/11:19A	10:30/11:30A	10:47/11:47A	11:10/11:40A	10:44/11:44A
AMTRAK 782	SA.SU.H	3:48P	3:42/3:57P	3:41/3:53P	3:31/4:31P	2:47/4:47P	3:38/4:08P	3:45/4:15P
AMTRAK 786	DAILY	7:40P	7:34/8:09P	7:36/7:56P	7:38/8:18P	6:59/8:18P	7:31/8:01P	7:04P
SUNDAY & HOLIDAY BUS CONNECTIONS								
AMTRAK 774	SA.SU.H	9:10A	8:55/9:15A	9:05/9:25A	8:26/9:28A	8:49/9:49A	8:36/9:21A	8:52/9:33A
AMTRAK 776	DAILY	11:14A	11:09/11:21A	11:05/11:26A	10:29/11:29A	10:47/11:47A	10:41/11:21A	10:53/11:33A
AMTRAK 782	SA.SU.H	3:48P	3:43/3:58P	3:42/3:57P	3:29/4:29P	2:47/4:47P	3:25/4:06P	3:34/4:14P
AMTRAK 786	DAILY	7:40P	7:09/7:55P	7:27/7:47P	7:37/8:17P	7:38/8:17P	7:10/7:59P	7:03P

NORTHBOUND TRAINS FROM LOS ANGELES TO OXNARD

SATURDAY BUS CONNECTIONS								
AMTRAK 769	SA.SU.H.	9:39A	9:28/9:40A	9:32/9:48A	9:28/10:30A	8:47/9:47A	9:36/10:10A	9:14/9:44A
AMTRAK 775	DAILY	11:59A	11:50A/12:01P	11:50A/12:05P	11:30A/12:30P	11:47A/12:47P	11:40A/12:06P	11:44A/12:14P
AMTRAK 779	DAILY	3:55P	3:42/3:57P	3:53/4:05P	3:31/4:31P	3:47/4:47P	3:38/4:08P	3:45/4:15P
AMTRAK 791	SA.SU.H.	6:21P	6:17/6:37P	6:18/6:31P	5:29/6:28P	5:47/6:59P	6:06/6:34P	5:49/6:24P
SUNDAY & HOLIDAY BUS CONNECTIONS								
AMTRAK 769	SA.SU.H.	9:39A	9:35/9:55A	9:25/9:45A	9:28/10:29A	8:49.9:49A	9:21/10:01A	9:33/10:13A
AMTRAK 775	DAILY	11:59A	11:45A/12:15P	11:46A/12:06P	11:29A/12:29P	11:47A/12:47P	11:21A/12:03P	11:33A/12:13P
AMTRAK 779	DAILY	3:55P	3:43/3:58P	3:42/3:57P	3:29/4:29P	3:37/4:47P	3:25/4:06P	3:34/4:14P
AMTRAK 791	SA.SU.H.	6:21P	6:09/6:34P	6:12/6:27P	5:29/6:27P	5:49/6:59P	6:03/6:40P	6:13/7:03P

CBS Studios

from Audiences Unlimited at their box office located at Fox Television Center located at 5746 Sunset Boulevard in Hollywood.

The ticket window is located near the corner of Sunset Boulevard and Van Ness Avenue. Tickets are offered on a first-come first-served basis between 8:30 A.M. and 6:00 P.M. weekdays. For Tickets by Mail write to Audiences Unlimited, 100 Universal City Plaza, Building 153, Universal City, California 94608. For information by phone call (818) 506-0067.

The studio can be reached from the Burbank Airport Amtrak/Metrolink Station by taking the westbound MTA 165 line to the Vanowen Street and Lankershim Boulevard stop. From there transfer to the southbound MTA 228 line. Take this line to the Ventura Boulevard and Radford Avenue stop. The Studio main entrance is one block north of Ventura Boulevard on Radford Avenue.

Valley Plaza Shopping Center

The Valley Plaza Shopping Center is located along Laurel Canyon Boulevard between Victory Boulevard and Kittridge Street. The shopping center is anchored by a large Sears Store. The shopping center can be reached by MTA 165 line from the Burbank Airport Amtrak/Metrolink Station to the Laurel Canyon Boulevard stop. The shopping center is one block south on Laurel Canyon.

Laurel Plaza Mall

The Laurel Plaza Mall is located at 6100 Laurel Canyon Boulevard in North Hollywood. The Mall is anchored by a Robinsons-May department store. This is a small mall with few retail stores. The mall can be reached by taking the MTA 165 line to the Laurel Canyon Boulevard stop and transfer to the southbound MTA 230 line. Take the 230 line to the Mall stop on Laurel Canyon Boulevard.

Universal Studios Hollywood

See Chapter on Burbank Station for information. From the Burbank Airport Amtrak/Metrolink Station take the southbound MTA 163 line to the Hollywood Way and Riverside Drive stop. Transfer to the westbound MTA 96 line and take it to the Universal city stop. There is a tram that will take you to the studio. The stop for the tram is a short distance up Universal Terrace Parkway from Lankershim Boulevard.

Warner Brothers Studios

See Chapter on Burbank Station for information. From the Burbank Airport Station take the southbound MTA 163 line to the Hollywood Way and Olive Avenue stop. The entrance to the studio tour is at this intersection.

Places to Stay

Best Western Mikado Hotel

The Best Western Mikado Hotel is located at 12600 Riverside Drive, North Hollywood. The hotel phone number is (818) 763-9141. For reservations call (800) 826-2759 nationwide or in California call (800) 433-2239.

Beverly Garland's Holiday Inn

Beverly Garland's Holiday inn is located at 4222 Vineland Avenue, North Hollywood. The hotel has a shuttle bus that provides service to the Burbank Airport and the Burbank Airport Amtrak/Metrolink Station. Call the hotel prior to arrival and they will meet you at the station. The hotel phone number is (818) 980-8000. For reservations call (800) BEVERLY or Holiday Inn reservations on (800) HOLIDAY.

Burbank Airport Hilton

The Burbank Airport Hilton is located at 2500 North Hollywood Way. The hotel has a shuttle van that will pick you up at the Metrolink station. Be sure to specify Burbank Airport Station as they also serve the Burbank station. Call the hotel and let them know when you will be arriving and they will send the van to meet you. The hotel phone number is (818) 843-6000. For reservations call (800) HILTONS.

Sportsmen's Lodge Hotel

The Sportsmen's Lodge Hotel is located at 12825 Ventura Boulevard, Studio City. The hotel has a shuttle bus that provides service to the Burbank Airport and the Burbank Airport Amtrak/Metrolink Station. Call the hotel prior to arrival and they will meet you at the station. The hotel phone number is (818) 769-4700. For reservations call (800) 821-8511 nationwide or (800) 821-1625 in California.

Universal Hilton & Towers

The Universal Hilton & Towers is located at 555 Universal Terrace Parkway. Bus transportation to the hotel from Metrolink is the same as Universal Studios. The hotel phone number is (818) 506-2500. For reservations call (800) HILTONS

Sheraton Universal

The Sheraton Universal is located at 333 Universal Terrace Parkway. Bus transportation to the hotel from Metrolink is the same as Universal Studios. The hotel phone number is (818) 980-1212. For reservations call (800) 325-3535.

Burbank Airport Station Vicinity Map

Van Nuys Station

Station Connecting Transit Information

The Van Nuys Amtrak/Metrolink Station is located at 7720 Van Nuys Boulevard. The station has a 40-car parking lot. The train boarding platform is well lighted. There is good shelter. The parking lot is also well lighted and maintained. The station building is manned by Amtrak personnel during the day.

The station is served by the MTA 169, 233, 420 and 561 bus lines. The bus stop for the MTA lines is located down the stairs from the boarding platform on Van Nuys Boulevard.

LADOT provides shuttle service to/from the Van Nuys Civic Center and Los Angeles Valley College. This service also connects with the Van Nuys/Studio City Dash service. Dash Busses meet the Metrolink trains in the morning and afternoon/evening.

The station vicinity map provides the routes for bus transit options from

Van Nuys Metrolink Station

VAN NUYS STATION WEEKDAY BUS CONNECTIONS
SOUTHBOUND TRAINS FROM OXNARD TO LOS ANGELES

TRAIN NUMBER	DAYS OF OPERATION	TRAIN ARRIVAL	MTA 169 EASTBOUND HOURLY	MTA 169 WESTBOUND HOURLY	MTA 233/561 SOUTHBOUND 10 - 20 MIN.	MTA 233/561 NORTHBOUND 10 - 30 MIN.	MTA 420 SOUTHBOUND 10 - 20 MIN.	MTA 420 NORTHBOUND 10 - 20 MIN.
METROLINK 100	M - F	5:51A	5:15/6:15A	6:15A	5:41/5:53A	5:42/5:56A	5:47/5:55A	5:08/5:58A
METROLINK 102	M - F	6:31A	6:15/7:16A	6:15/7:19A	6:23/6:33A	6:20/6:33A	6:28/6:37A	6:26/6:37A
METROLINK 104	M - F	7:21A	7:16/8:18A	7:19/8:19A	7:13/7:23A	7:08/7:32A	7:20/7:30A	7:15/7:27A
AMTRAK 772	M - F	7:49A	7:16/8:18A	7:19/8:19A	7:43/7:53A	7:44/7:57A	7:40/7:50A	7:45/7:57A
METROLINK 106	M - F	8:00A	7:16/8:18A	7:19/8:19A	7:53/8:03A	7:57/8:07A	7:50/8:10A	7:57/8:03A
METROLINK 108	M - F	10:06A	9:16/10:16A	9:19/10:20A	10:03/10:13A	9:58/10:07A	10:02/10:10A	10:00/10:12A
AMTRAK 776	DAILY	11:40A	11:16A/12:15P	11:20A/12:20P	11:33/11:43A	11:36/11:46A	11:37/11:49A	11:39/11:51A
METROLINK 110	M - F	3:25P	3:15/4:17P	3:19/4:19P	3:23/3:33P	3:20/3:32P	3:20/3:27P	3:23/3:35P
AMTRAK 780	M - F	4:15P	3:15/4:17P	3:19/4:19P	4:13/4:23P	4:09/4:20P	4:14/4:20P	4:13/4:23P
AMTRAK 786	DAILY	8:06P	7:19/8:19P	7:19P	7:41/8:09P	7:54/8:14P	7:57/8:13P	8:00/8:12P

NORTHBOUND TRAINS FROM LOS ANGELES TO OXNARD

METROLINK 101	M - F	L9:22A	9:16/10:16A	9:19/10:20A	9:13/9:23A	9:17/9:28A	9:20/9:30A	9:15/9:29A
AMTRAK 771	M - F	9:43A	9:16/10:16A	9:19/10:20A	9:33/9:53A	9:47/9:58A	9:36/9:46A	9:36/9:51A
AMTRAK 775	DAILY	12:08P	11:16A/12:15P	11:20A/12:20P	12:03/12:13P	12:06/12:16P	11:57A/12:09P	12:00/12:12P
METROLINK 103	M - F	1:35P	1:15/2:15P	1:19/2:19P	1:33/1:43P	1:31/1:40P	1:31/1:41P	1:22/1:36P
AMTRAK 779	DAILY	4:02P	3:15/4:17P	3:19/4:19P	3:53/4:03P	3:50/4:09P	3:58/4:04P	3:51/4:13P
METROLINK 105	M - F	4:56P	4:17/5:19P	4:19/5:19P	4:53/5:03P	4:52/4:58P	4:54/5:01P	4:53/5:03P
METROLINK 107	M - F	5:35P	5:19/6:19P	5:19/6:19P	5:33/5:47P	5:30/5:41P	5:33/5:41P	5:32/5:41P
METROLINK 109	M - F	6:11P	5:19/6:19P	5:19/6:19P	6:10/6:24P	6:05/6:16P	6:07/1:16P	6:08/6:17P
AMTRAK 781	M - F	6:22P	6:19/7:19P	6:19/7:19P	6:10/6:24P	6:16/6:24P	6:16/6:26P	6:17/6:23P
METROLINK 111	M - F	6:54P	6:19/7:19P	6:19/7:19P	6:40/7:00P	6:48/7:03P	6:49/5:59P	6:46/7:02P

L: Regular stop to discharge or pick up passengers except train may leave ahead of schedule

VAN NUYS STATION WEEKEND BUS CONNECTIONS
SOUTHBOUND TRAINS FROM OXNARD TO LOS ANGELES

TRAIN NUMBER	DAYS OF OPERATION	TRAIN ARRIVAL	MTA 233/561	MTA 233/561	MTA 233/561	MTA 233/561	MTA 420	MTA 420	MTA 420	MTA 420
DAYS OF OPERATION			SOUTHBOUND	NORTHBOUND	SOUTHBOUND	NORTHBOUND	SOUTHBOUND	NORTHBOUND	SOUTHBOUND	NORTHBOUND
BUS FREQUENCY			SATURDAY 10 - 20 MIN.	SATURDAY 10 - 20 MIN.	SUNDAY - H. 15 MIN.	SUNDAY - H. 15 MIN.	SATURDAY 10 - 20 MIN.	SATURDAY 10 - 20 MIN.	SUNDAY - H. 10 - 20 MIN.	SUNDAY - H. 10 - 20 MIN.
AMTRAK 774	SA.SU.H	9:36A	9:27/9:42A	9:24/9:37A	9:26/9:41A	9:33/9:49A	9:26/9:47A	9:29/9:40A	FREQUENT	FREQUENT
AMTRAK 776	DAILY	11:40A	11:27/11:42A	11:37/11:54A	11:26/11:41A	11:32/11:49A	FREQUENT	FREQUENT	FREQUENT	FREQUENT
AMTRAK 782	SA.SU.H	4:15P	4:02/4:22P	3:57/4:17P	4:11/4:26P	4:02/4:19P	FREQUENT	FREQUENT	FREQUENT	FREQUENT
AMTRAK 786	DAILY	8:06P	8:02/8:47P	7:57/8:12P	7:40/8:08P	8:02/8:30P	8:03/8:28P	8:03/8:15P	7:55/8:15P	8:00/8:14P

NORTHBOUND TRAINS FROM LOS ANGELES TO OXNARD

AMTRAK 769	SA.SU.H.	9:48A	9:42/9:57A	9:37/9:54P	9:41/9:56A	9:33/9:49A	9:47/9:58A	9:40/9:52A	FREQUENT	FREQUENT
AMTRAK 775	DAILY	12:08P	12:02/12:22P	11:57A/12:17P	11:56A/12:11P	12:02/12:19P	FREQUENT	FREQUENT	FREQUENT	FREQUENT
AMTRAK 779	DAILY	4:02P	3:57/4:22P	3:57/4:17P	3:56/4:11P	3:49/4:19P	FREQUENT	FREQUENT	FREQUENT	FREQUENT
AMTRAK 791	SA.SU.H.	6:32P	6:12/6:37P	6:17/6:37P	6:26/6:41P	6:19/6:49P	FREQUENT	FREQUENT	FREQUENT	FREQUENT

the Van Nuys Metrolink/Amtrak Station. The preceding tables provide the schedule of bus connections with Metrolink and Amtrak. For schedule and route updates on MTA lines call (818) 781-5890 and for updates on LADOT DASH service call (213) 580-5444.

Points of Interest

Van Nuys was the commercial and business center for the San Fernando Valley during the early to mid-20th century. It all began when William Paul Whitsett purchased one-half interest in the one-square-mile town of Van Nuys in 1911. He then proceeded with a grand advertizing campaign which culminated with a barbecue and auction which attracted thousands of Angelinos. Opening day sales totaled $250,000.00. With the bringing of Owens River water to the San Fernando Valley, Van Nuys annexed itself to the City of Los Angeles. In 1933 with the completion of the Van Nuys City Hall the city became the governmental center

View Along Van Nuys Boulevard

for the San Fernando Valley.

Van Nuys was a blue collar community during the 50's 60's and 70's with good jobs provided by the now defunct General Motors plant which was located across the tracks from the Metrolink station. Today along Van Nuys Boulevard pawn shops and bail bond brokers do business from shops that once housed a wide variety of stores that occupied every main street in America in the 40's, 50's and 60's. Expansion into the suburbs and the invention of the shopping mall doomed

Van Nuys City Hall

Valley College Campus

remain independent to this day. Located within the Van Nuys Civic Center is the valley annex for Los Angeles City Hall, the Valley Federal Building, and Los Angeles County Courts. From Metrolink the LADOT Metrolink shuttle can be used in the morning and evening. During the rest of the day the southbound MTA 233, 420 or 561 lines will take you to the Van Nuys Civic Center.

Los Angeles Valley College

Los Angeles Valley College is a two year community college serving the central and eastern San Fernando valley. It is located at 5800 Fulton Avenue. From Metrolink the college can be reached using the LADOT Metrolink Shuttle in the morning and evening. During the rest of the day the Van Nuys/Studio City Dash service provides transportation between the college and the Van Nuys Civic Center where you can connect with the MTA 233, 420 or 561 lines to Metrolink.

Los Angeles Valley College was established in June 1949. It is one of the nine public colleges of the Los Angeles Community College district.

Van Nuys Boulevard to its present condition.

A group headed by actor Tom Selleck purchased the General Motors property recently. Plans of this group are to develop a commercial and retail complex on the property. When this development is completed the area surrounding the Van Nuys Amtrak/Metrolink Station will be vastly improved.

Van Nuys Civic Center

Van Nuys is the governmental administrative center for the San Fernando Valley. Most of the San Fernando Valley is within the Los Angeles city limits. The reason for this is that in 1913 when the City of Los Angeles brought Owens River water into the San Fernando Valley, Los

Angeles made annexation into the city a requirement for access to this new water source. The only holdouts were San Fernando, Burbank and Glendale. They

Donald C. Tillman Water Reclamation Plant Administration Building

The college moved from the campus of Van Nuys High School to its present 105-acre site in 1951. Today the college serves a diverse student body of 16,000 students. The college offers an associate of arts degree in a wide variety of majors. For general campus information call (818) 781-1200.

The college has an historical museum, planetarium and theater on campus. The historical museum contains documents, photographs, and historical artifacts relating to the history of the San Fernando Valley. The museum is located in Bungalow 15 at the south end of campus along Burbank Boulevard. The museum is open 1:00 P.M. to 4:00 P.M. weekdays. For information call (818) 781-1200 ext. 373.

The planetarium has a program of multi-media presentations on a wide variety of astronomical topics which are presented by the astronomy club members. Presentations are held on Friday nights at 8:00 P.M. Admission is $3.50 for adults, $2.50 for senior citizens, club members, and students, and $2.00 for children 8 thru 16. Children under 8 are not admitted. For information on show topics please call (818) 781-1200 ext. 335.

The campus theater offers a number of live stage and film presentations throughout the school year. For information on current presentations please call (818) 781-1200 ext. 353.

The Japanese Garden

The Japanese Garden is located at 6100 Woodley Avenue. The garden is a part of the City of Los Angeles Donald C. Tillman Water Reclamation Plant which is located in the Sepulveda Flood Control Basin Recreation Area. The gardens include three different styles, a Zen garden, a wet strolling garden and a tea garden. Tours are by appointment only. To make a reservation please call (818) 756-8166.

To reach the gardens from the Van Nuys Metrolink Station take LADOT Metrolink Shuttle or MTA 233, 420 or 561 lines to the Van Nuys and Victory Boulevards stop. Transfer to the westbound MTA 164 or 236 line. Take this line to the Woodley Avenue stop. The entrance to the garden is located about one-half mile south of Victory Boulevard. From there you need to walk up to the vehicle entrance to the Donald C. Tillman Water Reclamation Plant and the guard will direct you from there.

Van Nuys Airport

The Van Nuys Airport does not have commercial airline service. It caters primarily to private aircraft and charter air carriers. It is the busiest general aviation airport in the world with 500,000 take-offs and landings per year. The airport began operations in 1927 as a privately-owned and operated airport. It was acquired by the Los Angeles City Department of Airports in 1949.

Places to Stay
Airtel Plaza Hotel

The Airtel Plaza Hotel is located at 7277 Valjean Avenue, adjacent to the Van Nuys Airport. The hotel has a shuttle van that will pick you up at the Van Nuys Metrolink Station. The hotel phone number is (818) 997-7676.

The Japanese Garden

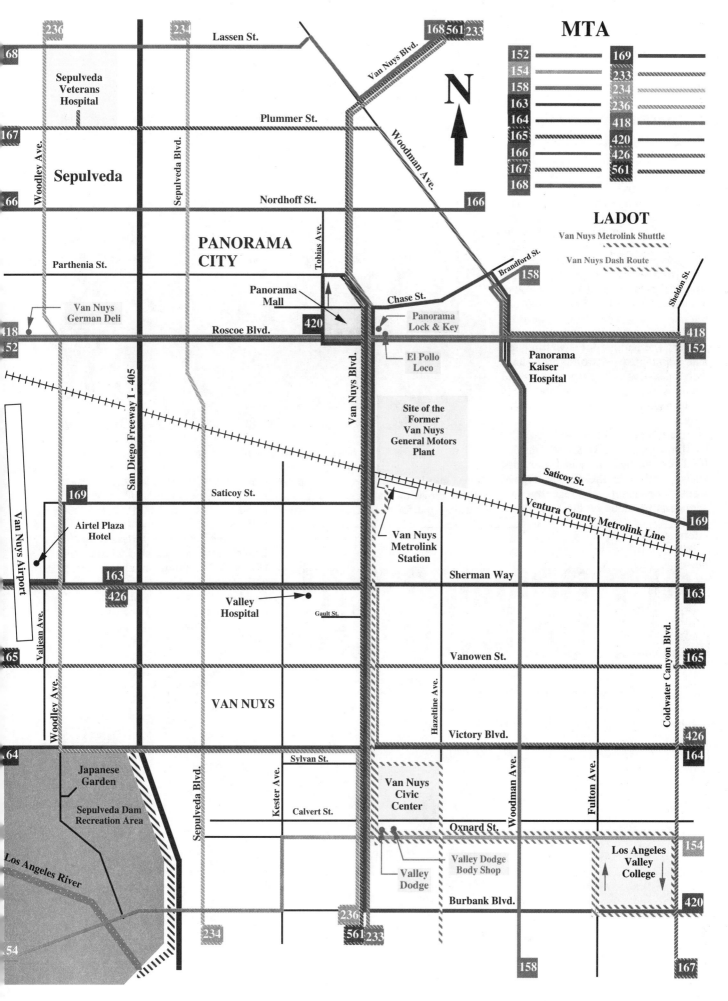

Van Nuys Station Vicinity Map

Northridge Station

Station Connecting Transit Information

The Northridge Metrolink Station is located at 8701 Wilbur Avenue, off Parthenia Street between Reseda Boulevard and Tampa Avenue. The station was one of the new emergency facilities built immediately after the January 17, 1994 Northridge Earthquake. It was completed within 12 days from start of construction by Los Angeles Department of Water & Power crews. The station has a 400-car parking lot. The train boarding platform is well lighted, but there is no shelter. The parking lot is well lighted and maintained. Metrolink personnel man the station during the morning and evening rush hours. The station is unmanned midday when the flex trains arrive.

The station is served by the California State University-Northridge (CSUN) 648 bus line which provides transportation to the CSUN Transit Center on campus. Presently this service is provided by the local Prime

Northridge Metrolink Station

Time Shuttle Van. The bus stop is located across the parking lot from the boarding platform. Service to/from

Metrolink is provided when classes are in session between 7:00 A.M. and Noon and between 3:00 P.M. and 7:00 P.M.

Connecting transportation at the CSUN Transit Center includes the CSUN 647 Campus circulator, CSUN 649 line to UCLA, CSUN 650 Handyman remote lot, and MTA 240 line. Surrounding MTA transit includes the 158, 166, 167, 168, 236, 239, and 240 lines.

NORTHRIDGE STATION TRAIN SCHEDULE
SOUTHBOUND TRAINS FROM
OXNARD TO LOS ANGELES

TRAIN NUMBER	DAYS OF OPERATION	TRAIN ARRIVAL
METROLINK 100	M - F	5:44A
METROLINK 102	M - F	6:24A
METROLINK 104	M - F	7:14A
METROLINK 106	M - F	7:53A
METROLINK 108	M - F	L9:58A
METROLINK 110	M - F	3:18P

NORTHBOUND TRAINS FROM
LOS ANGELES TO OXNARD

TRAIN NUMBER	DAYS OF OPERATION	TRAIN ARRIVAL
METROLINK 101	M - F	L9:29A
METROLINK 103	M - F	1:42P
METROLINK 105	M - F	5:03P
METROLINK 107	M - F	5:42P
METROLINK 109	M - F	6:18P
METROLINK 111	M - F	7:01P

L: Regular stop to discharge or pick up passengers except train may leave ahead of schedule

Campus View CSUN

The station vicinity map provides the routes for bus transit options from the Northridge Metrolink Station and CSUN.

Table below provides the schedule for Metrolink trains that stop at this station. For schedule and route updates call MTA on (818) 781-5890.

Points of Interest

In 1908 the Southern Pacific Company line, which Metrolink presently operates on, was laid through the area. The Biblical name of Zelzah was given to the station stop in the area of present day Northridge. In 1929 the community's name was changed to North Los Angeles, and finally to Northridge in 1938. In the 30's and 40's many celebrities had horse ranches in the Northridge area including Barbara Stanwyck, Harry James, Betty Grable, Monte Montana, etc. In the latter half of the 1960's the last of the great ranchers of the San Fernando Valley, Porter Ranch, was subdivided and 12,000 homes were built on the 4,000 acres.

Today Northridge is the educational center of the San Fernando Valley and is home to California State University-Northridge. The university is the one thing that sets this community apart from the rest of the communities in the Northwestern San Fernando Valley.

CSUN

The university is about one mile from the Metrolink Station. The university provides shuttle service between the station and the university. The university is a part of the 20-campus California State University System and has an enrollment of 25,000 students. It began as the San Fernando Valley Campus of Los Angeles State College of Applied Arts and Sciences. In 1958 the campus was granted independent status and became San Fernando Valley State College with an enrollment of 3,300 students. In June of 1972, the college was granted university status and was renamed California State University-Northridge. It offers Bachelors and Masters degrees in a wide range of majors. The university was severely damaged during the January 17th Northridge Earthquake causing many campus buildings to be closed for repair or rebuilding. The university installed hundreds of portable classrooms and reopened on February 14, 1994. For general information call (818) 885-1200.

There are three art galleries and a theater on campus. The art galleries offer over 40 multicultural events during the school year. For information about current events call (818) 885-2156.

The campus theater offers a number of live stage productions, dance performances, opera performances and concerts during the school year. For information about current productions call the Performing Arts Box Office on (213) 885-3093.

The university is home to the Matadors which field 18 women's and men's Division I NCAA athletic teams competing in a wide variety of sports. For current sporting events call (818) 885-2488.

The Recreational sports office hosts an open gym three nights per week. For information call (818) 885-3225. The 25-yard university swimming pool is open-year round to the public. For information on pool hours call (818) 885-3604.

Northridge Fashion Center

The mall is about one mile from the Metrolink station at Tampa and Nordhoff streets. The mall is the largest such facility in the western San Fernando Valley with 200 stores, including the Broadway, Bullocks, J. C. Penny, Robinson's-May, and Sears.

Places to Stay

Howard Johnson Lodge

The Howard Johnson Lodge is located at 7432 Reseda Boulevard in Reseda. The hotel phone number is (818) 344-0324. For reservations call (800) 523-4825.

METROLINK

41

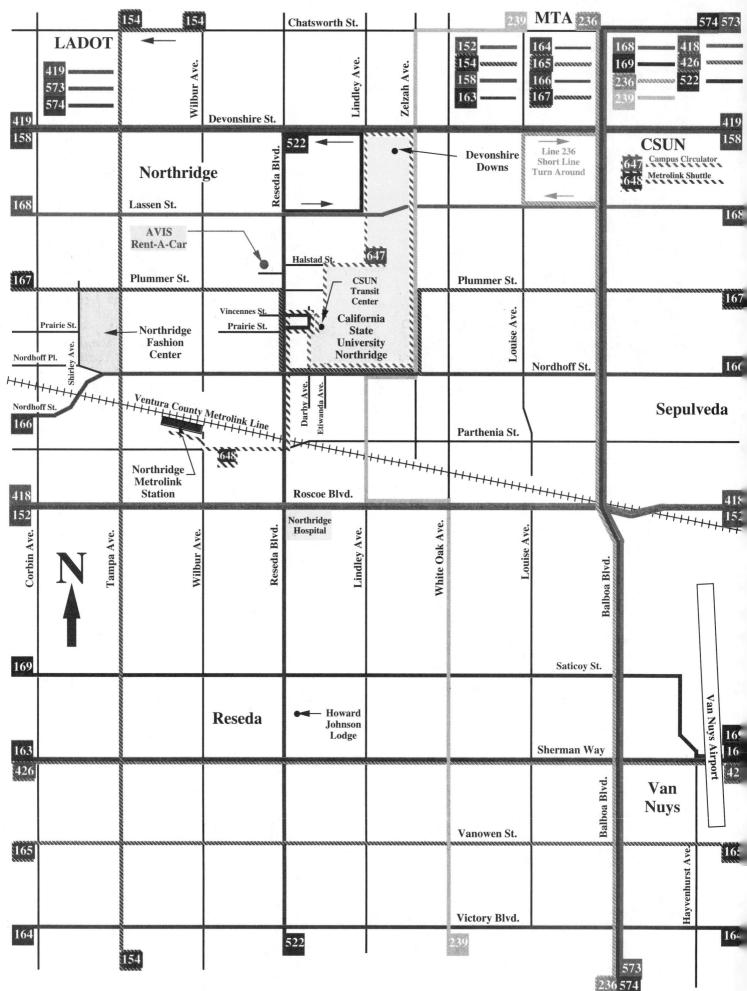

Northridge Station Vicinity Map

Chatsworth Station

Station Connecting Transit Information

The Chatsworth Metrolink Station is located at 21510 Devonshire Street between Owensmouth and Canoga avenues. The station parking lot has entrances on Devonshire Street and Lassen Street. The station can be reached by taking the Topanga Canyon exit from the 118 Freeway. From the 118 go south on Topanga Canyon to Devonshire. Turn left on Devonshire and the station entrance will be on your right just past the railroad tracks. The station has a 483-car parking lot. The train boarding platform is well lighted and has good shelter. The parking lot is also well lighted and maintained. Metrolink personnel man the station during the morning and evening rush hours. The station is unmanned midday when the flex trains arrive. The City of Los Angeles has constructed a new station building which will house a day care center and some retail outlets to serve the growing number of commuters using the Chatsworth Metrolink Station. This facility is scheduled to

Chatsworth Metrolink Station

open in 1996.

The station is served by the MTA 158, 166, 167, 168, 243, 245, Santa Clarita Transit 791 and LADOT 419 bus lines. The bus stop for all of these lines (except the MTA 158 and 168 lines) is located across the parking lot from the boarding platform. The following tables provide the schedule of bus connections with Metrolink and

CHATSWORTH STATION WEEKDAY BUS CONNECTIONS
SOUTHBOUND TRAINS FROM OXNARD TO LOS ANGELES

TRAIN NUMBER	DAYS OF OPERATION	TRAIN ARRIVAL	MTA 158 EASTBOUND 30 - 40 MIN.	MTA 158 WESTBOUND 30 - 40 MIN.	MTA 166 30 MIN.	MTA 167 30 - 60 MIN.	MTA 168 EASTBOUND HOURLY	MTA 168 WESTBOUND HOURLY	MTA 243 15 - 45 MIN.	MTA 245 45 MIN.	SCT 791 COMMUTER EXPRESS	LADOT 419 COMMUTER EXPRESS
METROLINK 100	M - F	5:38A	5:53A			5:45A	5:49A	5:08/6:08A		5:28/5:41A	5:34/5:45A		5:46A
METROLINK 102	M - F	6:18A	5:53/6:23A	6:24A	5:53/6:39A	6:15/6:43A	6:08/7:02A	6:40A	6:01/6:30A	6:18/6:25A	6:35A	6:16/6:31A
METROLINK 104	M - F	7:08A	6:48/7:22A	7:07/7:37A	6:46/7:09A	6:59/7:43A	7:02/8:02A	6:40/7:40A	7:04/7:11A	7:02/7:25A	7:05/7:45A	6:51/7:11A
METROLINK 106	M - F	7:47A	7:22/7:58A	7:37/8:02A	7:42/8:07A	7:40/8:43A	7:02/8:02A	7:40/8:39A	7:40/7:50A	7:43/8:00A	7:45/8:05A	7:31/8:06A
METROLINK 108	M - F	L9:49A	9:38A	9:25A	9:29A	9:20A	9:02A	9:38A	9:10A	9:04A		
METROLINK 110	M - F	3:12P	2:48/3:23P	3:02/3:45P	2:58/3:19P	2:22/3:19P	3:03/4:03P	2:37/3:38P	2:45/3:16P	3:08/3:22P		
AMTRAK 786	DAILY	7:54P	7:34P	7:21P	7:31P	7:17/8:45P	6:03P	7:26P	7:04	7:26/8:25P		

NORTHBOUND TRAINS FROM LOS ANGELES TO OXNARD

METROLINK 101	M - F	9:37A	9:38A	10:03A	10:07A	10:20A	10:02A	9:38A	10:07A	10:10A		
AMTRAK 775	DAILY	12:21P	11:59A/12:49P	11:39A/12:29P	12:24/12:33P	12:20/12:42P	12:02/1:03P	11:37A/12:37P	12:15/12:37P	12:08/12:25P		
METROLINK 103	M - F	1:48P	1:33/2:08P	1:20/2:11P	1:24/1:51P	1:22/2:42P	1:03/2:03P	1:37/2:37P	1:05/2:00P	1:38/2:40P		
METROLINK 105	M - F	5:09P	4:33/5:13P	5:00/5:35P	4:50/5:10P	4:23/5:36P	5:03/6:03P	4:37/5:35P	4:52/5:11P	4:52/5:25P	4:05/5:45P	5:07/5:22P
METROLINK 107	M - F	5:48P	5:13/5:53P	5:35/6:10P	5:45/5:55P	5:23/6:45P	5:03/6:03P	5:35/6:33P	5:33/6:22P	5:32/6:00P	5:45P	5:38/5:58P
METROLINK 109	M - F	6:24P	5:53/6:30P	6:10/6:43P	6:15/6:40P	6:17/6:45P	6:03P	5:35/6:33P	6:16/7:22P	6:08/6:40P		5:58/6:44P
METROLINK 111	M - F	7:07P	6:30/7:34P	6:43/7:21P	6:54/7:45P	6:17/7:45P		6:33/7:26P	7:04/7:22P	6:44/7:33P		6:44/7:09P

L. Regular stop to discharge or pick up passengers except train may leave ahead of schedule

CHATSWORTH STATION WEEKEND BUS CONNECTIONS
SOUTHBOUND TRAINS FROM OXNARD TO LOS ANGELES

TRAIN NUMBER	DAYS OF OPERATION	TRAIN ARRIVAL	MTA 158 EASTBOUND SATURDAY 45 MIN.	MTA 158 EASTBOUND SUNDAY H. 45 - 60 MIN.	MTA 158 WESTBOUND SATURDAY 45 MIN.	MTA 158 WESTBOUND SUNDAY H. 45 - 60 MIN.	MTA 166 SATURDAY HOURLY	MTA 166 SUNDAY H. HOURLY	MTA 167 SA. SU. H. HOURLY	MTA 168 EASTBOUND SATURDAY HOURLY	MTA 168 WESTBOUND SATURDAY HOURLY	MTA 245 SATURDAY HOURLY	MTA 245 SUNDAY H. HOURLY
AMTRAK 774	SA.SU.H	8:35A	8:13/8:58A	8:33/9:33A	7:50/8:44A	8:21/9:21A	8:25/8:40A	8:40A	8:13/8:45A	8:05/9:05A	7:40/8:40A	8:23/8:40A	8:23/8:40A
AMTRAK 782	SA.SU.H	3:17P	2:58/3:48P	3:03/3:48P	2:46/3:31P	2:42/3:27P	2:31/3:40P	2:30/3:40P	2:19/3:43P	3:05/4:05P	2:38/3:38P	2:27/3:40P	2:25/3:40P
AMTRAK 786	DAILY	7:05P	6:33/7:33P	6:33/7:33P	6:40P	6:22/7:19P	6:30/7:45P	6:24P	6:19/7:46P	6:05P	6:35P	6:27P	6:24P

NORTHBOUND TRAINS FROM LOS ANGELES TO OXNARD

AMTRAK 769	SA.SU.H	10:01A	9:43/10:48A	9:33/10:33A	9:29/10:14A	9:21/10:24A	9:31/10:40A	9:25/10:40A	9:16/10:43A	9:05/10:05A	9:39/10:39A	9:25/10:40A	9:23/10:40A
AMTRAK 775	DAILY	12:21P	11:58A/12:43P	12:03/12:48P	11:42A/12:27P	11:24A/12:29P	11:31A/12:40P	11:30A/1240P	12:19/12:43P	12:05/1:05P	11:39A/12:38P	11:25A/12:40P	11:24A/12:40P
AMTRAK 791	SA.SU.H	6:45P	6:33/7:33P	6:33/7:33P	6:40P	6:22/7:19P	6:30/7:45P	6:24P	6:19/7:46P	6:05P	6:35P	6:27P	6:24P

Old Trapper's Lodge

Amtrak. The station vicinity map provides the routes for bus transit options from the Chatsworth Metrolink Station.

The MTA 158 Line has a stop near the station parking lot entrance on Devonshire Street (about 400 yards from the station platform) which provide east-west transportation along Devonshire.

The MTA 168 Line provides east-west transportation along Lassen Street. There is a bus stop for this line near the parking lot entrance on Lassen Street (about 400 yards from the station platform).

For schedule and route updates on MTA lines call MTA on (818) 781-5890 or for LADOT lines call (213) 485-7201.

The Warner Center Transportation Management Organization provides free taxi service to/from the Metrolink station for Warner Center employees only. For information about this service call (818) 710-7767.

Points of Interest

Chatsworth got its start as a relay station on the San Juan and Los Angeles Stagecoach line in 1867. In 1893 the Southern Pacific Railroad came to town with a crew of construction workers to build the tunnels through the Santa Susana Mountains to Simi Valley. The tunnels were finished in 1904 thus completing the Coast Line Route Cutoff to points north.

Today Chatsworth is one of the bedroom communities that is located at the western end of the San Fernando Valley. The Rocketdyne Division of Rockwell International has its headquarters in nearby Canoga Park. A large test facility is located in the Simi Hills to the west of Chatsworth. Neighboring communities of Canoga Park, West Hills and Woodland Hills can be reached on the MTA 245 line. The Warner Center business district along with the Topanga Mall, Promenade Mall and Fallbrook Mall are accessible by the MTA 245 line. The Warner Center has a DASH bus service which provides transportation throughout the business district between 10:55 A.M. and 2:08 P.M. (lunchtime) at 10-minute intervals. The station vicinity map provides the route for this service.

Los Angeles Pierce College

Los Angeles Pierce College is located at 6201 Winnetka Avenue, Woodland Hills. It can be reached on the MTA 243 line from Metrolink. The college is a two-year institution that offers an Associate Arts degree in a wide range of majors.

There is a substantial Agriculture Department at the college and a large part of the campus is a working farm. Tours of the farm are offered to school children

Near the college farm is located the Old Trapper's Lodge. This is one of California's twentieth-century folk art monuments. It represents the life work of John Ehn (1897-1981), a self-taught artist. The "lodge" consists of a grassy park with some picnic tables and benches for visitors. The art of John Ehn consists of "Boot Hill," the lodge and many colorful characters from the old west. Many of these characters are modeled after his family members.

For general campus information call (818) 347-0551.

Orcutt Ranch Horticulture Center

The Orcutt Ranch Horticulture Center is located at 23600 Roscoe Boulevard. The closest bus stop is located at Fallbrook Avenue and Roscoe Boulevard on the MTA 152 line. It is about three-quarters of a mile from the stop to the Ranch. In 1917 William Orcutt used his property in the western San Fernando Valley as a vacation residence. At that time there was a small cabin which Orcutt used during his stays. In 1920 Mr. Orcutt commissioned Mr. C. G. Knipe an architect from Arizona to design a Spanish-style house for the property. This home contained 3060 square feet and had adobe walls which were 16 inches thick. In 1929 Mr. Ernesto Cornejo was hired by the Orcutts as their gardener. He remained at the estate until 1979 when he retired and moved to Montebello, California. He planted the 26 acres surrounding the Orcutt home with many varieties of trees and shrubs which make up the gardens. The rose gardens surrounding the house are spectacular during the spring and summer months.

In 1966, the Los Angeles City Recreation and Parks Department purchased the Orcutt estate and has

Rose Garden at Orcutt Ranch Horticulture Center

operated the property as an Historical Monument and Horticulture facility since that time. The ranch property is used as a wedding site by residents of the San Fernando Valley. On any weekend there will be wedding ceremonies and receptions being held in the gardens.

The Ranch is open 8:00 A.M. to 5:00 P.M. daily. Special docent tours are offered on the last Sunday of each month from 2:00 P.M. to 5:00 P.M. For information call (818) 346-7449.

Topanga Mall

The Topanga Mall is the oldest enclosed mall in the San Fernando Valley. It was one of the original shopping centers that pioneered the concept of grouping a number of smaller retail outlets along with the larger department stores in a single building surrounded by a parking lot. The Topanga Mall included movie theaters and an indoor ice skating rink when it originally opened. Today the Topanga Mall has gone through several renovations and has added Nordstrom's and Montgomery Ward's to the two original anchor department stores (Broadway and May Co.) located at each end of the Mall. A "Fast Food" court has replaced the ice skating rink. The Topanga Mall is located at 6100 Topanga Canyon Boulevard in Canoga Park between Victory Boulevard and Vanowen Street. The mall can be reached by taking the MTA 245 line

from the Chatsworth Metrolink Station.

Promenade Mall

One block south of the Topanga Mall is the Promenade Mall which was built many years after the Topanga Mall. The Promenade Mall has a more upscale atmosphere as compared to the older Topanga Mall with anchors like Bullocks and I. Magnum. The Promenade Mall is located at 6600 Topanga Canyon Boulevard in Warner Center between Erwin and Oxnard streets. The mall can be reached by taking the MTA 245 line from the Chatsworth Metrolink Station.

Fallbrook Mall

The Fallbrook Mall began life as an open air shopping center with a J. C. Penney store and Sears. With the popularity of the covered malls the Fallbrook Mall covered over the

pedestrian walkways and became a covered mall like the Topanga Mall. Today, Mervyns and Target department stores have been added to the mall and the J. C. Penney store has been converted into a J. C. Penney outlet store. The Fallbrook Mall is located at 6633 Fallbrook Avenue in West Hills between Victory Boulevard and Vanowen Street. The mall can be reached by taking the MTA 245 line from the Chatsworth Metrolink Station.

Places to Stay
Summerfield Suites Hotel

The Summerfield Suites Hotel is located at 21902 Lassen Street. The hotel has a shuttle van and will pick you up at the Metrolink Station with advance notice. The hotel phone number is (818) 773-0707. For reservations call (800) 833-4353.

The Chatsworth Hotel

The Chatsworth Hotel is located at 9777 Topanga Canyon Boulevard. The hotel phone number is (818) 709-7054. For reservations call (800) 676-9641.

Ramada Inn

The Ramada Inn is located at 21340 Devonshire Street. The hotel phone number is (818) 98-5289. For reservations call (800) 2RAMADA.

7-Star Suites Hotel

The 7-Star Suites Hotel is located at 21603 Devonshire Street. The hotel phone number is (818) 998-8888. For reservations call (800) 782-7872.

The Warner Center Marriott Hotel

The Warner Center Marriott Hotel is located at 21850 Oxnard Street in Woodland Hills. The hotel phone number is (818) 887-4800. For reservations call (800) 228-9290.

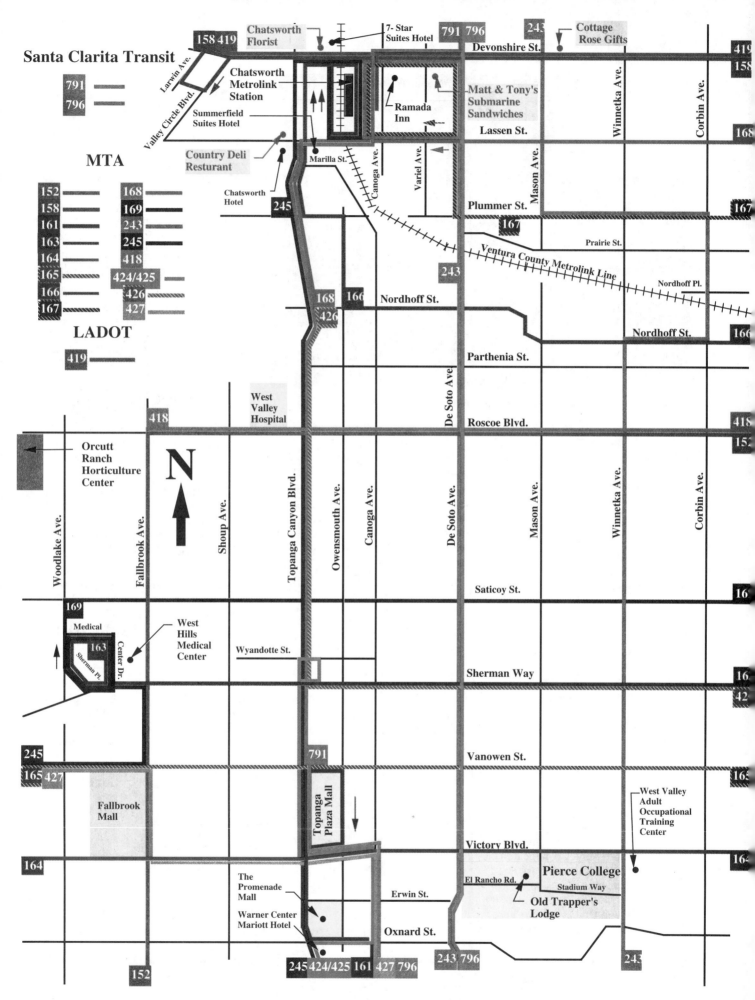

Chatsworth Station Vicinity Map

Simi Valley Station

Station Connecting Transit Information

The Simi Valley Amtrak/Metrolink Station is located at 5050 Los Angeles Avenue. The station can be reached by taking the Stearns Street exit from the 118 Simi Valley Freeway and going south on Stearns Street to Los Angeles Avenue. The station will be about one-quarter mile on your left. See map insert for station locale. The station has a 600-car parking lot. The train boarding platform is well lighted. There is a fair amount of shelter on the boarding platform. The parking lot is also well lighted and maintained.

The Simi Valley Transit bus lines A and B stop at the Metrolink station. Both bus lines follow the same circular route through Simi Valley. The stop for line B is across the street from Metrolink and runs west on Los Angeles Avenue, and the stop for line A is right in front of the station on Los Angeles Avenue and runs east. The station vicinity map provides the routes for bus transit options from the Simi Valley Amtrak/Metrolink Station. The

Simi Valley Metrolink Station

following tables provide the schedule of bus connections with Amtrak and Metrolink. For schedule and route updates call Simi Valley Transit on (805) 584 - 6287. For information on VISTA routes and schedules call (800) 438-1112.

SIMI VALLEY STATION WEEKDAY BUS CONNECTIONS

SOUTHBOUND TRAINS FROM OXNARD TO LOS ANGELES

TRAIN NUMBER	DAYS OF OPERATION	TRAIN ARRIVAL	SIMI VALLEY TRANSIT ROUTE A	SIMI VALLEY TRANSIT ROUTE B
BUS FREQUENCY			30 - 60 MIN.	30 - 60 MIN.
METROLINK 100	M - F	5:25A	5:38A	5:58A
METROLINK 102	M - F	6:05A	5:38/6:11A	5:58/6:19A
METROLINK 104	M - F	6:55A	6:38/7:11A	6:19/6:58A
METROLINK 106	M - F	7:35A	7:11/7:38A	7:19/7:58A
AMTRAK 776	DAILY	11:14A	11:11A/12:11P	10:58/11:58A
METROLINK 110	M - F	2:52P	2:41/3:11P	2:30/2:58P
AMTRAK 780	M - F	3:48P	3:41/4:11P	3:30/3:58P
AMTRAK 11 (R)	DAILY	5:30P	5:11/5:41P	4:58/5:58P
AMTRAK 786	DAILY	7:40P	7:24P	7:26P

NORTHBOUND TRAINS FROM LOS ANGELES TO OXNARD

TRAIN NUMBER	DAYS OF OPERATION	TRAIN ARRIVAL	SIMI VALLEY TRANSIT ROUTE A	SIMI VALLEY TRANSIT ROUTE B
AMTRAK 771	M - F	10:06A	9:11/10:11A	9:58/10:58P
AMTRAK 14 (R)	DAILY	10:19A	10:11/11:11A	9:58/10:58A
AMTRAK 775	DAILY	12:35P	12:11/1:11P	11:58A/12:58P
METROLINK 103	M - F	L2:00P	1:11/2:11P	1:58/2:30P
AMTRAK 779	DAILY	4:30P	4:11/4:41P	3:58/4:58P
METROLINK 105	M - F	L5:21P	5:11/5:41P	4:58/5:30P
METROLINK 107	M - F	L6:00P	5:41/6:11P	5:58/6:30P
METROLINK 109	M - F	L6:36P	6:11/6:41P	6:30/6:58P
MERTOLINK 111	M - F	L7:19P	7:24P	7:26P

L: Regular stop to discharge or pick up passengers except train may leave ahead of schedule

Simi Valley Civic Center

Points of Interest
Simi Valley Civic Center

The Simi Valley Civic Center is home to the City Hall, Library, Senior Citizens Center and the Courthouse where the Rodney King trial of the four Los Angeles Police Officers was held which triggered the 1992 Los Angeles Riots. Both Simi Valley Transit Lines A and B serve the civic center. Take Line A from Metrolink to the courthouse and Line B for return to Metrolink.

Simi Valley is a bedroom community in eastern Ventura County that has grown out of the urban sprawl that overflowed the northwestern San Fernando Valley in the 1960's. The newer housing developments are located at the western end of the valley. The latest addition to Simi Valley is the

SOUTHBOUND TRAINS FROM OXNARD TO LOS ANGELES

TRAIN NUMBER	DAYS OF OPERATION	TRAIN ARRIVAL	SIMI VALLEY TRANSIT ROUTE A	SIMI VALLEY TRANSIT ROUTE B
DAYS OF OPERATION			SATURDAY	SATURDAY
BUS FREQUENCY			HOURLY	HOURLY
AMTRAK 774	SA.SU.H	9:10A	5:38A	5:58A
AMTRAK 776	DAILY	11:14A	11:11A/12:11P	10:58/11:58A
AMTRAK 782	SA.SU.H	3:48P	3:11/4:11P	2:58/3:58P
AMTRAK 11 (R)	DAILY	5:30P	5:11/6:11P	4:58/5:58P
AMTRAK 786	DAILY	7:40P	7:11P	6:58P

NORTHBOUND TRAINS FROM LOS ANGELES TO OXNARD

AMTRAK 769	SA.SU.H.	10:15A	10:11/11:11A	9:58/10:58P
AMTRAK 14 (R)	DAILY	10:19A	10:11/11:11A	9:58/10:58A
AMTRAK 775	DAILY	12:35P	12:11/1:11P	11:58A/12:58P
AMTRAK 779	DAILY	4:30P	4:11/5:11P	3:58/4:58P
AMTRAK 791	SA.SU.H.	6:57P	6:11/7:11P	5:58/6:58P

L: Regular stop to discharge or pick up passengers except train may leave ahead of schedu

Note: Simi Valley Transit Busses do not operate on Sunday

exclusive Wood Ranch community which hosts a PGA golf course.

Ronald Reagan Presidential Library

The Ronald Reagan Presidential Library is located at 40 Presidential Drive. The library can be reached from Metrolink by taking Simi Valley Transit Line A to the Royal Avenue and Madera Road stop. There you must transfer to the Simi Valley Transit Line D. Take this bus to the library.

The library is built around a central courtyard with a reflecting pool reminiscent of early California Mission architecture. The library was dedicated on November 4, 1991, with five living U.S. Presidents in attendance: President Bush, former Presidents Reagan, Carter, Ford and Nixon. The Library is operated by the National Archives & Records Administration. The Library houses an archival collection of documents, photographs, and gifts received by the Reagans during their tenure in the White House. After review by a library archivist, according to provisions of the Presidential Records Act of 1978, documents are made available to the public.

The Library has an extensive museum which houses the memorabilia from the Reagan years in the White House. The museum has a theater in which a film on Reagan's presidency is shown. Throughout the museum are displayed many of the 75,000 gifts given to President and Mrs. Reagan by foreign dignitaries from around the world. The gifts on display include jewelry, paintings, sculpture, furniture and other rare artifacts from the world over. The library regularly rotates the

The Ronald Reagan Presidential Library

Actual Section of the Berlin Wall

gifts on display so each time you visit you can discover the museum all over again.

The museum has a number of permanent gallery displays which chronicle President Reagans life and years in the White House. Along with the history of the Reagan presidency is a strong dose of Reaganism. The museum includes a replica of the Oval office furnished as it was during President Reagan's tenancy. There is a gallery devoted to Mrs. Reagan and her accomplishments as First Lady. Especially notable was memorabilia from her "Just Say No" campaign as a part of the War on Drugs.

In the rear courtyard overlooking the Simi Hills is an actual segment of the Berlin wall which along with the fall of communism was torn down as a direct result of Reagan's defense and

foreign policies. This artifact is the best representation of the legacy of President Reagan's accomplishments in the realm of foreign policy and a reminder to all of us of the evil that dictatorships bring into the world.

The Library is open Monday thru Saturday 10:00 A.M. to 5:00 P.M., Sunday noon to 5:00 P.M. The library is closed Thanksgiving, Christmas and New Year's Day. Admission is $4.00 adults ages 16 to 61, $2.00 seniors age 62+, and free for children under 16 years. For information call (805) 522-8444.

Places to Stay

Clarion Hotel Simi Valley

The Clarion Hotel Simi Valley is located at 1775 Madera Road. The hotel can be reached by taking the Simi Valley Transit Line B bus from the Metrolink station to the first bus stop on Madera Road. The hotel telephone number is (805) 584-6300. For reservations call (800) CLARION.

Motel 6 Simi Valley

The Motel 6 Simi Valley is located at 2566 N. Erringer Road. The hotel can be reached by taking the Simi Valley Transit Line B bus from the Metrolink station to the Cochran Street and Erringer Road stop. The motel telephone number is (805) 526-3533.

Radisson Hotel Simi Valley

The Radisson Hotel Simi Valley is located at 999 Enchanted Way. The hotel has a car which will pick you up at the Metrolink Station with advance notice. The hotel telephone number is (805) 583-2000. For reservations call (800) 333-3333.

Simi Valley Travelodge

The Motel 6 Simi Valley is located at 2550 N. Erringer Road. The hotel can be reached by taking the Simi Valley Transit Line B bus from the Metrolink station to the Cochran Street and Erringer Road stop. The hotel telephone number is (805) 584-6006. For reservations call (800) 578-7878.

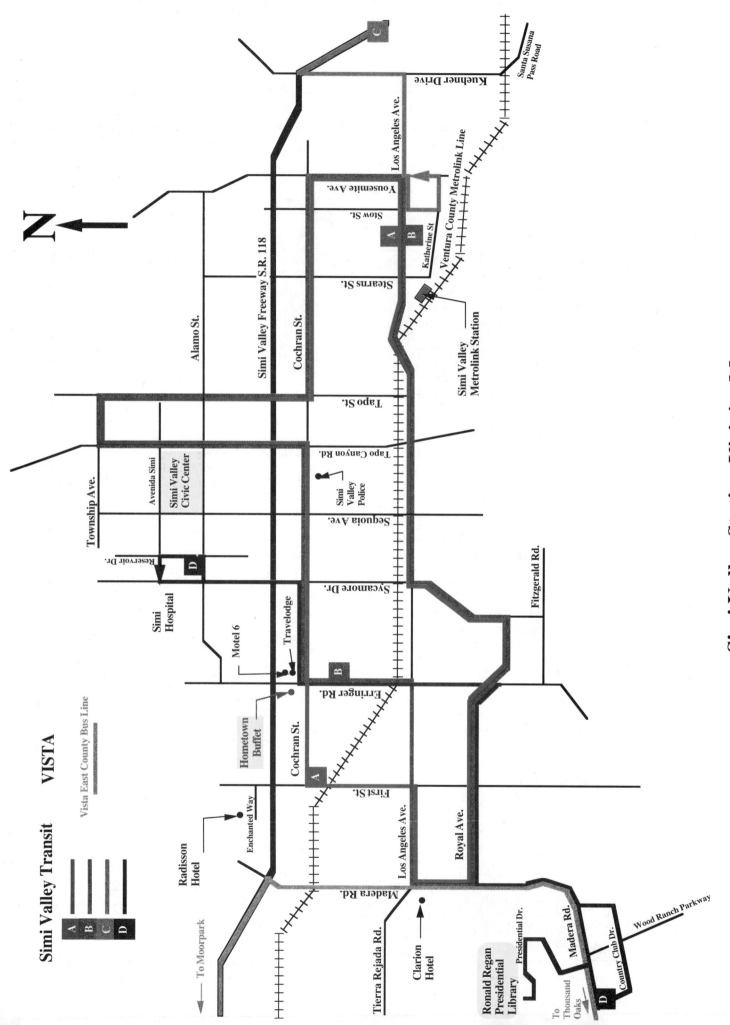

Simi Valley Station Vicinity Map

Moorpark Station

Station Connecting Transit Information

The Moorpark Metrolink Station is located at 300 High Street. Access to the station's 200-car parking lot is via Moorpark Road west of the station. A smaller parking lot with parking for approximately 60 cars is located along High Street. The train boarding platform is well lighted and has limited shelter. The parking lot is also well lighted and maintained.

There is a bus stop on High Street in front of the station for local Moorpark City bus line. Presently the Moorpark City Bus does not provide free transfers to/from Metrolink. The Vista East County Line serves the Moorpark Station. The station vicinity map provides the routes for bus transit options from the Moorpark Metrolink Station. The table below provides the schedule for bus connections with Amtrak and Metrolink. For updates on the Moorpark City bus call (805) 529-6864 and for the Vista bus line call (800) 438-1112.

Moorpark Station

Points of Interest
Downtown Moorpark

Moorpark is a small rural community in eastern Ventura County. It still has the atmosphere of a small farming community. The town is rapidly being engulfed by the urban sprawl of the greater Los Angeles region. Nearby housing tracts have

MOORPARK STATION WEEKEND TRAIN SCHEDULE

SOUTHBOUND TRAINS FROM OXNARD TO LOS ANGELES

TRAIN NUMBER	DAYS OF OPERATION	TRAIN ARRIVAL
AMTRAK 774	SA.SU.H	8:57A
AMTRAK 786	DAILY	7:27P

NORTHBOUND TRAINS FROM LOS ANGELES TO OXNARD

AMTRAK 769	SA.SU.H.	10:30A
AMTRAK 775	DAILY	12:53P
AMTRAK 791	SA.SU.H.	7:12P

MOORPARK STATION WEEKDAY BUS CONNECTIONS

SOUTHBOUND TRAINS FROM OXNARD TO LOS ANGELES

TRAIN NUMBER	DAYS OF OPERATION	TRAIN ARRIVAL	MOORPARK CITY BUS STA STOP	MOORPARK CITY BUS CIVIC CNTR	VISTA EAST
BUS FREQUENCY			HOURLY	HOURLY	HOURLY
METROLINK 100	M - F	5:12A			
METROLINK 102	M - F	5:52A			6:00A
METROLINK 104	M - F	6:42A			7:30A
AMTRAK 772	M - F	7:13A		7:15A	7:30A
METROLINK 106	M - F	7:22A		7:15/8:30A	7:15/7:30A
AMTRAK 774	M - F	8:57A	9:00A	8:30/9:30A	8:25/9:00A
METROLINK 110	M - F	2:39P	2:00/3:00P	2:30/3:30P	2:25/3:00P
AMTRAK 786	DAILY	7:27P			5:57P

NORTHBOUND TRAINS FROM LOS ANGELES TO OXNARD

AMTRAK 775	DAILY	12:53P	11:00A/1:00P	11:30A/1:30P	11:57A/1:40P
METROLINK 103	M - F	2:20P	2:00/3:00P	1:30/2:30P	1:25/2:30P
METROLINK 105	M - F	L5:35P	4:00P	4:30P	5:25/6:20P
METROLINK 107	M - F	L6:14P			5:57/6:20P
METROLINK 109	M - F	6:55P			
AMTRAK 781	M - F	7:06P			
METROLINK 111	M - F	7:38P			

L: Regular stop to discharge or pick up passengers except train may leave ahead of schedule

grown up with large homes in the $300,000 to $400,000 price range where only a few years ago cattle roamed. The downtown district extends from the Metrolink station to the west for about a half-mile where High Street ends at the intersection of Moorpark Road. High Street hosts a number of antique shops, boutiques, restaurants and the Moorpark Melodrama. High Street is lined with a canopy of pepper trees that provide a backdrop which invites one to stroll along this street. The area surrounding Moorpark that has not succumbed to urban sprawl is still ranch land. You know that you have left the big city when you enter the tack and feed store on the corner of High Street and Moorpark Road. Other than the High Street shopping district there is nothing in Moorpark to distinguish this community from any other suburban community which makes up Los Angeles.

Moorpark Melodrama

The Moorpark Melodrama is located at 45 E. High Street. The Moorpark Melodrama & Vaudeville Company is housed in a 1928 vintage theater with a capacity for

View along High Street from Metrolink Station

approximately 306 persons. The theater was originally built in 1928 to replace a wooden structure that housed the silent movie theater known as the *El Rancho*. When it opened it was the only movie theater in eastern Ventura County that exhibited talking motion pictures. From that time till the mid 1950's it was used as a movie theater. The theater was reborn in 1982 as the Magnificent Moorpark Melodrama & Vaudeville Company with a production of *The Drunkard*. The theater has enjoyed tremendous success since then and offers

Reflecting Pool at Moorpark College

downtown Moorpark at 7075 Campus Road. The college can be reached from the Metrolink station using the Moorpark City Bus system or the Ventura County Vista East County Line. The college is a part of the Ventura County Community College District and is a two-year institution offering an Associate of Arts degree in a wide range of majors. The Moorpark College info line is (805) 378-1597. In 1995 the college added a new performing arts theater. For information about current productions call (805) 378-1412.

The college is unique in its Exotic Animal Training and Management program. The college has a mini zoo on campus which has many exotic animals including a lion, tigers, panthers, a water buffalo, a camel and many more. The campus zoo is open to the public on Saturday and Sunday from 11:00 A.M. to 5:00 P.M. The students put on shows on the hour on weekends. Admission is $4.00 for adults, $2.00 for children 2 thru 12, and $3.00 for seniors. The students also put on special shows and events during the school year. For information about special events and shows call (805) 378-1441.

Places to Stay

There are no hotels in Moorpark. See the Simi Valley Station chapter for places to stay.

about six different productions each year in addition to a Christmas production. Show times are 7:00 P.M. Thursdays, 8:00 P.M. on Fridays, 3:00 P.M. and 8:00 P.M. on Saturdays, and 3:00 P.M. on Sundays. On weekends one can take the Amtrak train from Los Angeles that arrives at 12:53 P.M., have lunch and attend the afternoon Matinee at 3:00 P.M. The show usually ends around 6:00 P.M. allowing time for dinner before catching the 7:27 P.M. Amtrak train back to Los Angeles. Tickets are $12.00 for adults and $9.50 for seniors 55 and over and children 11 and under at matinees only. For information about current productions call (805) 529-1212 or (800) 597-1210.

Moorpark College

Moorpark College is located east of

Entrance to Amphitheater at Moorpark College Zoo

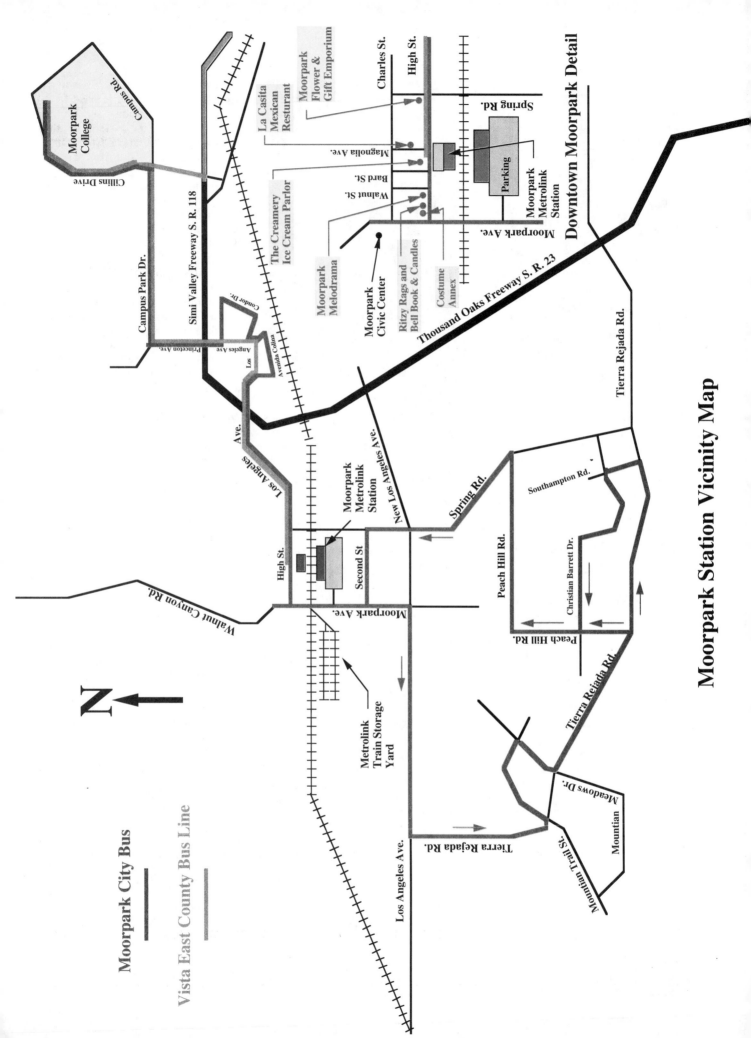

Moorpark Station Vicinity Map

Downtown Moorpark Detail

Moorpark City Bus

Vista East County Bus Line

N

La Casita Mexican Resturant

Moorpark Flower & Gift Emporium

Charles St.

High St.

Spring Rd.

Magnolia Ave.

Bard St.

Walnut St.

Parking

Moorpark Metrolink Station

Moorpark Ave.

The Creamery Ice Cream Parlor

Moorpark Melodrama

Moorpark Civic Center

Ritzy Rags and Bell Book & Candles

Costume Annex

Thousand Oaks Freeway S. R. 23

Moorpark College

Campus Rd.

Cillins Drive

Campus Park Dr.

Simi Valley Freeway S. R. 118

Condor Dr.

Princeton Ave.

Avenida Colina

Los Angeles Ave.

Los Angeles Ave.

Walnut Canyon Rd.

High St.

Second St

Moorpark Metrolink Station

Moorpark Ave.

Metrolink Train Storage Yard

New Los Angeles Ave.

Spring Rd.

Southampton Rd.

Tierra Rejada Rd.

Peach Hill Rd.

Christian Barrett Dr.

Peach Hill Rd.

Tierra Rejada Rd.

Tierra Rejada Rd.

Meadows Dr.

Mountian Trail St.

Mountian

Los Angeles Ave.

Camarillo Station

Station Connecting Transit Information

The Camarillo Metrolink Station is located at 30 Lewis Road. The station can be reached by taking the Lewis Road Exit from the northbound (actually westbound) Ventura Freeway. Turn right on Daily Drive at the end of the offramp. Turn right on Lewis Road and the station will be on your left at the intersection of Ventura Boulevard and Lewis road. From the Southbound (actually eastbound) Ventura Freeway take the Carmen Drive offramp. Turn left at the end of the offramp on Ventura Boulevard. Continue east on Ventura Boulevard till you reach the station at Lewis Road. See map for station locale. The train boarding platform is well lighted but it does not have any shelter. The parking lot is also well lighted and maintained. The station was one of the "three-day miracles" that was constructed by the United States Navy Seabees based in nearby Port Hueneme.

Camarillo has a limited city-operated bus system called Camarillo Area Transit (CAT). There are bus stops on Ventura Boulevard at the intersection of Glenn Avenue for CAT Routes 1 and 2 to Leisure Village and at Ventura Boulevard and Arneill Road for CAT Routes 1 and 2 to Las Posas Plaza. The CAT busses do not connect with any of the Metrolink trains. At this time the CAT does not provide free transfers to/from Metrolink. The Ventura County, Vista Central County and Vista Highway 101 lines serve the Camarillo Metrolink Station. The stops are the same as the CAT bus lines at Ventura Boulevard and Glenn Avenue

Camarillo Station

for southbound busses, and at Ventura Boulevard and Arneill Road for northbound busses. The station vicinity map provides the routes for bus transit options from the Camarillo Metrolink Station. The tables below provide the schedule of bus connections with Metrolink and Amtrak. For updates to the Camarillo City Bus and the Vista Bus call (800) 438-1112.

If you wish to stop in Camarillo, a rental car would be the best way to get around.

Points of Interest
Downtown Camarillo

Camarillo is a small rural community in Ventura County which is becoming an upscale suburb of Greater Los Angeles. The community traces its roots to a Mexican land grant for Rancho Calleguas registered to Jose Pedro Ruiz in 1847. Ruiz later sold the rancho to Adolpho Camarillo. The town adopted Camarillo's name for the community when a post office was established for the community. The city celebrates Adolpho Camarillo's birthday each September with a community celebration and parade.

CAMARILLO STATION WEEKEND TRAIN SCHEDULE

SOUTHBOUND TRAINS FROM OXNARD TO LOS ANGELES

TRAIN NUMBER	DAYS OF OPERATION	TRAIN ARRIVAL
AMTRAK 774	SA.SU.H	8:45A
AMTRAK 786	DAILY	7:15P

NORTHBOUND TRAINS FROM LOS ANGELES TO OXNARD

| AMTRAK 775 | DAILY | 1:05P |
| AMTRAK 791 | SA.SU.H. | 7:23P |

CAMARILLO STATION WEEKDAY BUS CONNECTIONS

SOUTHBOUND TRAINS FROM OXNARD TO LOS ANGELES

TRAIN NUMBER	DAYS OF OPERATION	TRAIN ARRIVAL	CAT ROUTE 1 & 2 TO LAS POSAS	CAT ROUTE 1 & 2 TO LEISURE VIL.	VISTA CENTRAL EASTBOUND	VISTA CENTRAL WESTBOUND	VISTA HIGHWAY 101 SOUTHBOUND	VISTA HIGHWAY 101 NORTHBOUND
BUS FREQUENCY			HOURLY	HOURLY	HOURLY	HOURLY	HOURLY	HOURLY
METROLINK 102	M - F	5:39A				6:02A		
METROLINK 104	M - F	6:29A			6:52A	6:02/7:02A		
AMTRAK 772	M - F	7:00A			6:52/7:52A	6:02/7:02A	8:30A	
AMTRAK 786	DAILY	7:15P	8:37A	8:41A				

NORTHBOUND TRAINS FROM LOS ANGELES TO OXNARD

AMTRAK 775	DAILY	1:05P	12:53/1:40P	12:51/1:44P	12:52/1:52P	12:02/2:02P	12:30/2:30P	11:25A/1:25P
METROLINK 105	M - F	L5:49P	5:46P	5:46P	5:52/5:52P	5:02P		
METROLINK 107	M - F	L6:25P			5:52P			
AMTRAK 781	M - F	7:16P						

L: Regular stop to discharge or pick up passengers except train may leave ahead of schedule

Saint Mary Magdalene Church

Across the street on top of the bluff where downtown Camarillo is located is Saint Mary Magdalene Catholic Church. The church is an excellent example of Spanish Colonial Revival architecture and its distinctive bell tower has become a symbol for the City of Camarillo. The church was built in 1913 as the Camarillo family chapel. The corner stone has an inscription dedicating the church to Juan and Martina Camarillo. The church interior is decorated with beautiful stained glass windows which depict the life of Christ. These windows were selected by Juan Camarillo while on a trip to Europe in 1913. Shortly thereafter, World War I broke out and the windows never left Germany. At the end of World War I a German official noticed several large crates with Juan's name on them and wrote Juan several letters. One got through after the end of World War I and the windows were finally installed in the church in 1919.

Old Downtown Camarillo

Old downtown Camarillo extends along Ventura Boulevard from Metrolink for about a mile. The old downtown district today has several antique shops, restaurants, and gift shops intermingled with real estate and professional offices. There is a new mini-mall complex which is located across the freeway from the old downtown district at Carmen Drive. This is the commercial center of Camarillo.

Camarillo Factory Stores

Camarillo joined many of the outlying communities in 1995 in hosting a new factory outlet shopping center. Camarillo Factory Stores has over 40 factory-direct outlets including: Barneys New York, Esprit, Levis, Bass, Pro Image, Mikasa and more. Camarillo Factory Stores is located off Highway 101 at the Los Posas exit. For info call (805) 445-8520. CAT 1 Line to Las Posas Plaza and CAT Line 2 to Leisure Village serve the outlet center.

Camarillo Airport

The Camarillo Airport is located at Las Posas Road and Pleasant Valley Road. The airport serves the general aviation flying public. It is home to a

museum which features artifacts from the early days in the Camarillo area. Period furniture pieces are on display. The museum is open 1:00 P.M. to 4:00 P.M. Saturday and Sunday. CAT Line 1 to Leisure Village and CAT Line 2 to Las Posas Plaza serve the museum.

Places to Stay

Best Western's Camarillo Inn

The Best Western's Camarillo Inn is located at 295 Daily Drive. The hotel has a shuttle van and will pick you up at the Metrolink Station with advance notice. The hotel phone number is (805) 987-4991. For reservations call (800) 528-1234.

Comfort Inn

The Comfort Inn is located at 984 Ventura Boulevard. The hotel phone number is (805) 987-4188. For reservations call (800) 221-2222.

Country Inn at Camarillo

The Country Inn at Camarillo is located at 1405 Del Norte Road. The hotel phone number is (805) 983-7171. For reservations call (800) 44 RELAX..

Courtyard By Marriott - Camarillo

The Courtyard By Marriott is located at 4994 Verdugo Way. The hotel phone number is (805) 388-1020. For reservations call (800) 321-2211.

Days Inn

The Days Inn is located at 165 Daily Drive. The hotel phone number is (805) 482-0761. For reservations call (800) 329-7466.

Del Norte Inn

The Del Norte Inn is located at 4444 Central Avenue. The hotel phone number is (805) 485-3999. For reservations call (800) 44 RELAX.

Southern California Chapter of the Confederate Air Force. There are several WW II vintage aircraft based at the airport. The airport is the site of the annual Experimental Aircraft Association Fly-in and Air Show. The Fly-in and Air show is held in May of each year. There is no public transportation to the airport at this time.

Pleasant Valley Historical Museum

The Pleasant Valley Historical Museum is located at 720 Las Posas Road. This is a small historical

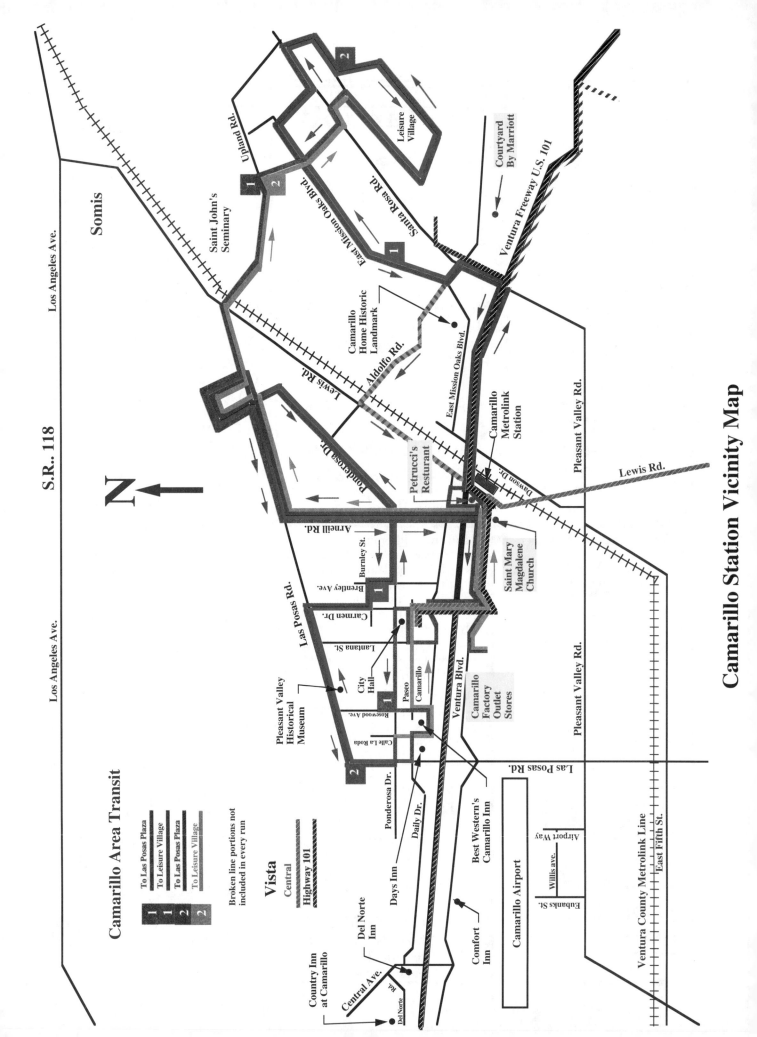

Camarillo Station Vicinity Map

S.R. 118

Somis

Los Angeles Ave.

Los Angeles Ave.

N

Camarillo Area Transit

To Las Posas Plaza
To Leisure Village
To Las Posas Plaza
To Leisure Village

Broken line portions not included in every run

Vista

Central
Highway 101

Country Inn at Camarillo

Central Ave.

Del Norte Rd.

Del Norte

Del Norte Inn

Days Inn

Comfort Inn

Best Western's Camarillo Inn

Camarillo Airport

Eubanks St.

Willis ave.

Airport Way

Ventura County Metrolink Line

East Fifth St.

Las Posas Rd.

Pleasant Valley Rd.

Lewis Rd.

Pleasant Valley Rd.

Ventura Blvd.

Camarillo Factory Outlet Stores

Saint Mary Magdalene Church

Camarillo Metrolink Station

Petrucci's Resturant

East Mission Oaks Blvd.

Aldolfo Rd.

Camarillo Home Historic Landmark

East Mission Oaks Blvd.

Santa Rosa Rd.

Courtyard By Marriott

Ventura Freeway U.S. 101

Upland Rd.

Saint John's Seminary

Leisure Village

Lewis Rd.

Ponderosa Dr.

Arneill Rd.

Burnley St.

Brentley Ave.

Carmen Dr.

Lantana St.

City Hall

Paseo

Camarillo

Rosewood Ave.

Calle La Roda

Ponderosa Dr.

Daily Dr.

Las Posas Rd.

Pleasant Valley Historical Museum

Oxnard Station

Station Connecting Transit Information

The Oxnard Transportation Center is located at 201 E. Fourth Street. The station can be reached by taking the Oxnard Boulevard (Route 1) offramp from the "southbound" (the Freeway actually goes east and west through Oxnard) Ventura 101 Freeway. From the freeway, go south on Oxnard Boulevard to Fourth Street, and turn left. The station is one block away where Fourth Street ends at the intersection with Meta Street. From the "Northbound" Ventura Freeway take the Rose Avenue offramp. Go south on Rose over the freeway to Fifth Street. Turn right on Fifth and continue to Meta Street. Turn right on Meta and the station will be one block north. The train boarding platform is well lighted but there is no shelter. The parking lot is also well lighted and maintained. The station is manned by Amtrak personnel during the day.

Adjacent to the station building South Coast Area Transit (SCAT) has established a Bus Transit Center where the SCAT Routes 1, 2, 3, 4, 5, 6, 7, 8 and 15 stop. In addition, the Ventura County Vista Central Route stops next to the Greyhound stop. The station vicinity map provides the routes for bus transit options from the Oxnard Transportation Center. The following

Oxnard Station

tables provide the schedule of bus connections with Metrolink and Amtrak. For updates to SCAT routes and schedules call (805) 487-4222 or 643-3185.

Outside of the immediate vicinity of the Oxnard Transportation Center the SCAT Route 6 provides service to Ventura via the Ventura Freeway. The Vista Central Route provides service to Camarillo.

Points of Interest

The City of Oxnard is located in the heart of the Santa Clara Valley just south of the City of Ventura in Ventura County. The city is located in one of the richest farming districts in Southern California. The city is the largest in Ventura County with a population of nearly 150,000. While it has experienced steady growth it has not yet

OXNARD STATION WEEKDAY BUS CONNECTIONS
SOUTHBOUND TRAINS FROM OXNARD TO LOS ANGELES

TRAIN NUMBER	DAYS OF OPERATION	TRAIN DEPARTURE	SCAT 1	SCAT 2	SCAT 3	SCAT 4 & 5	SCAT 6	SCAT 7	SCAT 8	SCAT 15	VISTA CENTRAL
BUS FREQUENCY			20 - 30 MIN.	35 MIN.	35 MIN.	30 MIN.	20 MIN.	30 MIN.	30 MIN.	40 - 60 MIN.	HOURLY
METROLINK 102	M - F	5:29A									
METROLINK 104	M - F	6:19A	6:10A	6:18A			6:10A				
AMTRAK 772	M - F	6:50A	6:10A	6:18A			6:10A				
AMTRAK 776	DAILY	10:31A	10:09A	10:30A	10:30A	10:25A	10:30A	10:25A	10:25A	9:55A	9:55A
AMTRAK 780	M - F	3:17P	3:09P	3:10P	3:10P	2:55P	3:10P	2:55P	2:55P	3:15P	2:55P
AMTRAK 11 (R)	DAILY	4:50P	4:49P	4:20P	4:20P	4:25P	4:30P	4:25P	4:25P	3:55P	4:00P
AMTRAK 786	DAILY	7:05P	6:50P	6:40P	6:40P	6:33P	6:39P	6:55P	6:54P	7:00P	5:55P

NORTHBOUND TRAINS FROM LOS ANGELES TO OXNARD

TRAIN NUMBER	DAYS OF OPERATION	TRAIN DEPARTURE	SCAT 1	SCAT 2	SCAT 3	SCAT 4 & 5	SCAT 6	SCAT 7	SCAT 8	SCAT 15	VISTA CENTRAL
AMTRAK 771	M - F	10:41A	10:45A	11:10A	11:10A	11:00A	11:00A	11:00A	11:00A	11:00A	12:05P
AMTRAK 14 (R)	DAILY	11:01A	11:05A	11:10A	11:10A	11:30A	11:20A	11:30A	11:30A	11:40A	12:05P
AMTRAK 775	DAILY	1:17P	1:35P	1:30P	1:30P	1:30P	1:20P	1:30P	1:3OP	2:00P	3:05P
AMTRAK 779	DAILY	5:07P	5:30P	5:35P	5:35P	5:30P	5:20P	5:30P	5:30P	5:40P	
METROLINK 105	M - F	6:02P	6:10P	6:10P	6:10P	6:10P	6:10P	6:10P	6:10P		
METROLINK 107	M - F	6:39P	6:45P	6:45P	6:45P		6:45P	6:45P			
AMTRAK 781	M - F	7:28P									

R: Amtrak's Coast Starlight requires advance reservations Call (800) USA-RAIL

TRAIN NUMBER	DAYS OF OPERATION	TRAIN DEPARTURE	SCAT 1	SCAT 1	SCAT 2 & 3	SCAT 4	SCAT 5	SCAT 6	SCAT 6	SCAT 7	SCAT 8	SCAT 15
DAYS OF OPERATION BUS FREQUENCY			SATURDAY 30 - 40 MIN.	SUNDAY HOURLY	SA. SU. 35 MIN.	SATURDAY HOURLY	SATURDAY HOURLY	SATURDAY 30 MIN.	SUNDAY HOURLY	SATURDAY HOURLY	SATURDAY HOURLY	SA. SU. 40 - 60 MIN.
AMTRAK 774	SA.SU.H	8:35A	8:25A	7:59A	8:10A	7:55A	8:25A	8:20A	8:10A	7:55A	8:25A	7:51A
AMTRAK 776	DAILY	10:31A	10:14A	9:59A	10:30A	9:55A	10:25A	10:20A	10:10A	9:55A	10:25A	10:15A
AMTRAK 782	SA.SU.H	3:17P	3:14P	2:29P	3:10P	2:55P	2:25P	2:50P	2:40P	2:55P	2:25P	3:15P
AMTRAK 11 (R)	DAILY	4:50P	4:24P	4:29P	4:20P	4:00P	4:25P	4:20P	4:40P	3:55P	4:25P	4:11P
AMTRAK 786	DAILY	7:05P	6:44P	7:00P	6:40P	5:55P	6:32P	6:39P	6:10P	7:00P	6:25P	6:58P

NORTHBOUND TRAINS FROM LOS ANGELES TO OXNARD

AMTRAK 769	SA.SU.H.	10:48A	11:00A	11:30A	11:10A	11:30A	11:00A	11:00A	11:20A	11:00A	11:30A	11:20A
AMTRAK 14 (R)	DAILY	11:01A	11:40A	11:30A	11:10A	11:30A	12:00P	11:30A	11:20A	12:00P	11:30A	11:20A
AMTRAK 775	DAILY	1:17P	1:25P	1:30P	1:30P	1:30P	2:00P	1:30P	1:20P	2:00P	1:3OP	1:40P
AMTRAK 779	DAILY	5:07P	5:40P	6:05P	5:35P	5:30P	6:10P	5:30P	5:50P	6:10P	5:30P	6:10P
AMTRAK 791	SA.SU.H.	7:35P										

R: Amtrak's Coast Starlight requires advance reservations Call (800) USA-RAIL

succumbed to the urban sprawl like the rest of Southern California. The primary crop grown on the surrounding farmland is strawberries. Along any of the roads through the area you will find strawberry stands selling the local crop. With over 4,000 acres in strawberry fields, Oxnard has claimed the title of strawberry capital of the United States. The city celebrates the local crop with the annual California Strawberry Festival which is held on the third weekend in May.

The city has seven miles of

beaches, and the Channel Islands Harbor for pleasure craft. Nearby, in Port Hueneme is the Deep Water Port of Port Hueneme and the U.S. Navy Seabee Base.

Within walking distance of the Oxnard Transportation Center is the Carnegie Art Museum, Heritage Square, Old Downtown Oxnard and the Gull Wings Children's Museum. Also within the city limits is Oxnard College.

Oxnard College

Oxnard College is located at 4000 Rice Road. The college is a two-year institution which offers an Associate of Arts Degree in a wide range of majors and an Associate in Science degree for vocational majors. The college can be reached by taking the SCAT Route 7 or 8. For information call (805) 986-5800.

The Carnegie Art Museum

The Carnegie Art Museum is located at 424 South C Street, a short walk from the Oxnard Transportation Center. The Museum is housed in the Carnegie Library, built in 1906, with funds donated by the steel magnate Andrew Carnegie. It is one of 1,678 libraries built by Carnegie during the early part of the 20th century. Today the museum is operated by the City of Oxnard and is not affiliated with the Carnegie Museum of Art in Pennsylvania.

The Museum features traveling exhibits and a permanent collection containing over 200 paintings, photographs and sculptures. The main focus of the museum's collection is on California painters from the 1920's to the present. For information call (805)

Strawberry Stand Oxnard California

60

385-8157. The museum closes between traveling exhibits so calling to verify hours of operations is advised. Normal hours are 10:00 A.M. to 5:00 P.M. Thursday and Saturday, 11:00 to 6:00 P.M. Fridays, and 1:00 P.M. to 5:00 P.M. on Sunday. Admission is $2.00 for adults, $1.50 for seniors and students and $1.00 for children 6 to 16.

Gull Wings Children's Museum

The Gull Wings Children's Museum is located at 418 W. Fourth Street, a short walk from the Oxnard Transportation Center. The museum is geared for pre-school and elementary school children. The museum provides a hands-on learning experience with science exhibits, a model railroad, and hands-on activities with computers and television. The museum is open 1:00 P.M. to 5:00 P.M. Wednesday to Friday and Sunday and 10:00 A.M. to 5:00 P.M. on Saturday. Admission is $3.00 for adults, $2.00 for children 2 to 12 and free for children under 2. For information call (805) 483-3005.

Heritage Square

Heritage Square is located at 715 South A Street and is a short walk from

Heritage Square Downtown Oxnard

the Oxnard Transportation Center. The Square is populated by a number of Victorian homes built in the Oxnard area in the late nineteenth and early twentieth centuries. The houses are occupied by a variety of professional offices, a community theater and a gift shop. You can take a walking tour of the square and get a glimpse of how the people of Oxnard lived 100 years ago. Docents lead tours on Saturdays from 11:00 A.M. to 2:00 P.M.

Petit Playhouse

The Petit Playhouse is located in the lower level of the Victorian Petit Mansion in Heritage Square. This intimate theatre offers a full range of professional productions throughout the year. For information on current productions call (805) 525-6301.

Old Downtown Oxnard

The old downtown shopping district runs for a few blocks along "A" Street on either side of Fifth Street.

Right across the street from the station there are a number of businesses which cater to the local population of hispanic farm workers. This area will transport the adventurous visitor to old Mexico. There are several restaurants and eateries which offer authentic Mexican food the same as you would find in rural parts of Mexico. Additionally, many of the stores offer western wear and many items unique to Mexico.

Channel Islands Harbor

Channel Islands Harbor is located at the west end of Channel Island Boulevard. There is no public transportation at this time to the harbor. A rental car is the best way to get from

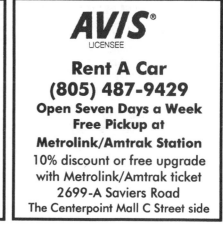

Fisherman's Wharf Channel Islands Harbor

the Oxnard Transportation Center to the harbor. Call Avis Rent-A-Car on (805) 487-9429. The harbor has nine marinas that offer a wide range of amenities. There are traditional small craft slips, commercial fishing docks, luxury slips, and slips for residents of luxury condominium homes.

At the corner of Channel Islands Boulevard and Victoria Avenue is located the Fisherman's Wharf at Channel Islands Harbor. The village has a cape cod architectural style and features several fine restaurants and boutiques.

There are a total of three shopping villages (including Fisherman's Wharf) and over two dozen waterside restaurants. The Harbor Hopper Water Taxi provides transportation to the various venues in the Harbor.

Sportfishing and whale-watching charters are offered at Cisco's Landing located at 4151 S. Victoria Avenue. For information and charter fares call (805) 985-8511. Marine Emporium at Channel Islands Harbor features Gold Coast Sportfishing. For information call (805) 382-0402. In addition, Island Packers offer daily excursions to the nearby Channel Islands. For information call (805) 642-1393.

The Channel Islands Harbor Visitor Center located at Fisherman's Wharf provides information about all of Ventura County. Call (805) 985-4852 or (800) 994-4852 (California only).

Ventura County Maritime Museum

The Ventura County Maritime Museum is located in the Fisherman's

Wharf at Channel Islands Harbor. The museum has exhibits that include maritime art with works dating from 1700 to the present. There is also a large number of model ships tracing the development of ships from 4000 B.C. to the present. There is an exhibit which provide a glimpse into the life of the native Chumash Indians which inhabited the region and the Channel Islands before the coming of the white man. The museum is open 11:00 A.M. to 5:00 P.M. Thursdays through Mondays. Admission is free. For information call (805) 984-6260.

Oxnard Factory Outlet

The Oxnard Factory Outlet is located on Gonzales Road between Rose and Rice avenues. Take the SCAT Route 15 to the Factory Outlet Mall stop. Manufacturers such as The Gap, LA Gear, Bugle Boy, Corning and American Tourister are represented. For information call (805) 485-2244.

Esplanade Mall

The Esplanade Mall is located between Wagon Wheel Road, Vineyard Avenue and the Ventura Freeway. It can be reached by taking the SCAT Route 6. This mall is the major shopping mall in the Ventura-Oxnard area. The anchor department stores are Sears and Robinson-May.

Seabee Museum

The Seabee Museum is located on the Port Hueneme Seabee base. The museum can be reached by taking the SCAT Route 3 to the Ventura Road and Teakwood stop. From there walk one block south along Ventura Road to Sunkist. The main gate to the Seabee base is at the intersection of Sunkist and Ventura Road. The Seabee Museum is about a quarter-mile from

The Seabee Museum

the main gate along the main road into the base. The museum is well worth the half-mile walk from the nearest bus stop. The uniqueness of the museum is the very personal nature of the items on display. All of the items were donated by individual Seabees. The items donated span the time from creation of the Seabees at the outbreak of World War II to the present. The exhibits trace the accomplishments of the Seabees and the work they do all over the world. The mementos were collected by individual servicemen where the Seabees have worked and sometimes fought. Wherever the Seabees go they always leave something behind that, in many parts of the world, is still in use by the people who live there. Admission is free. The museum is open daily 8:00 A.M. to 4:30 P.M.

Places to Stay

Casa Sirena Marina Resort

The Casa Sirena Marina Resort is located at 3605 Peninsula Road, Channel Islands Harbor. The hotel has a shuttle van and will pick you up at the Oxnard Transportation Center with advance notice. The hotel phone number is (805) 985-6311. For reservations call (800) 228-6026.

Oxnard Hilton Inn

The Oxnard Hilton Inn is located at 600 Esplanade Drive. The hotel has a shuttle van and will pick you up at the Oxnard Transportation Center with advance notice. For reservations call (805) 485-9666.

Mandalay Beach Resort

The Mandalay Beach Resort, operated by Embassy Suites, is located at 2101 Mandalay Road on Mandalay Beach. The hotel has a shuttle van and will pick you up at the Oxnard Transportation Center with advance notice. The hotel phone number is (805) 984-2500. For reservations call (800) 433-4600.

Radisson Suite Hotel at River Ridge

The Radisson Suite Hotel is located at 2101 West Vineyard Road next to the River Ridge Golf Course. The hotel has a shuttle van and will pick you up at the Oxnard Transportation Center with advance notice. The hotel phone number is (805) 988-0130. For reservations call (800) 333-3333.

Vagabond Inn

The Vagabond Inn is located at 1245 Oxnard Boulevard. The hotel phone number is (805) 983-0251. For reservations call (800) 522-1555.

Wagon Wheel Motel

The Wagon Wheel Motel is located at 2751 Wagon Wheel Road. The motel phone number is (805) 485-3131.

Channel Islands Motel

The Channel Islands Motel is located at 1001 East Channel Islands Boulevard. The motel phone number is (805) 487-7755.

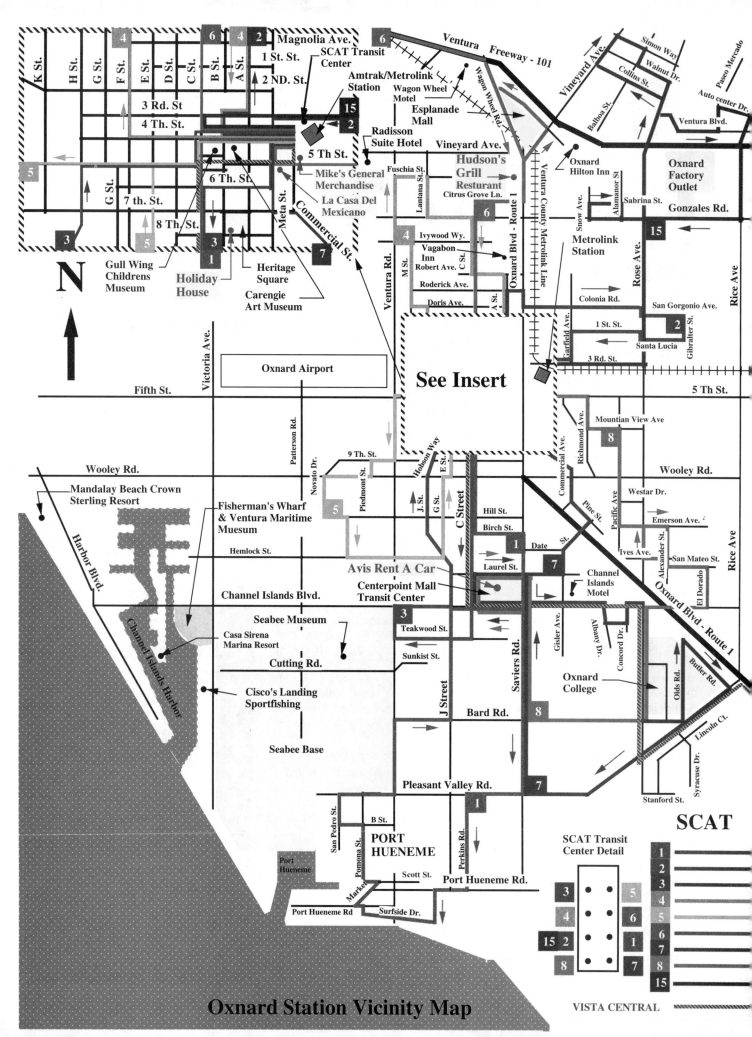

Oxnard Station Vicinity Map

Santa Clarita Line

The Santa Clarita Line has eight stations located at L.A. Union Station, Glendale, Burbank, Sylmar/San Fernando, Santa Clarita, Princessa, Vincent Grade/Acton, and Lancaster. For information on the L.A. Union Station, Glendale Station and Burbank Station see the section on the Burbank, Glendale and Los Angeles Line. Metrolink operates nine trains Monday thru Friday on this line. The schedules below indicate the times and number of trains traveling in each direction on the Santa Clarita Line at the time of publication. Due to the rapid expansion of Metrolink service please call (800) 371-LINK for current updates to the schedule.

The Santa Clarita Line was originally built by the Southern Pacific Company in 1876. This line connected Southern California to the San Joaquin Valley, via the Tehachapi Pass to Bakersfield, and points North. Metrolink purchased the entire Southern Pacific Lines in the five-county region served. Metrolink service to Santa Clarita from L.A. Union Station with intermediate stops at Burbank and Glendale began on October 26, 1992. The original cost of this line was $37.2 million which included the track,

Metrolink Train making connections with Santa Clarita Transit Busses at Santa Clarita Station

Metrolink rolling stock and capital improvements to the line. The original length of this trackage was 34.3 miles, from Santa Clarita to L.A. Union Station. Initial service included stops at Santa Clarita, Burbank, Glendale and L.A. Union Station.

Following the January 17, 1994 Northridge Earthquake, Metrolink extended service 45.6 miles to the Antelope Valley communities of Lancaster and Palmdale. On January 24, 1994 the Palmdale and Lancaster Emergency Stations were opened.

SANTA CLARITA LINE TRAIN SCHEDULE
SOUTHBOUND FROM LANCASTER TO LOS ANGELES

TRAIN NUMBER	METROLINK 200	METROLINK 202	METROLINK 204	METROLINK 206	METROLINK 208	METROLINK 210	SC 795 BUS	METROLINK 212	METROLINK 214	METROLINK 216	SC 795 BUS
DAYS OF OPERATION	M - F	M - F	M - F	M - F	M - F	M - F	M - F	M - F	M - F	M - F	M - F
LANCASTER	4:37A	5:31A	6:01A	6:32A			2:04P				8:04P
VINCENT GRADE/ACTON	4:52A	5:46A	6:16A	6:47A			2:35P				8:35P
PRINCESSA	5:23A	6:17A	6:47A	7:18A	7:48A	8:48A	3:05P	3:19P		7:19P	9:05P
SANTA CLARITA	5:29A	6:23A	6:53A	7:24A	7:53A	8:53A	3:15P	3:26P	5:09P	7:25P	9:15P
SYLMAR/SAN FERNANDO	5:47A	6:41A	7:11A	7:42A	8:11A	9:11A		3:44P	5:29P	7:43P	
BURBANK	L5:58A	6:52A	7:22A	7:53A	8:22A	9:22A		3:56P	5:40P	7:54P	
GLENDALE	L6:04A	6:58A	7:28A	7:59A	8:28A	9:28A		4:02P	5:46P	8:00P	
L.A. UNION STATION	6:18A	7:12A	7:42A	8:13A	8:42A	9:42A		4:16P	6:05P	8:15P	

NORTHBOUND FROM LOS ANGELES TO LANCASTER

TRAIN NUMBER	METROLINK 201	SC 795 BUS	METROLINK 203	SC 795 BUS	METROLINK 205	SC 795 BUS	METROLINK 207	METROLINK 209	SC 795 BUS	METROLINK 211	METROLINK 213	METROLINK 215	SC 795 BUS	METROLINK 217
DAYS OF OPERATION	M - F	M - F	M - F	M - F	M - F	M - F	M - F	M - F	M - F	M - F	M - F	M - F	M - F	M - F
L.A. UNION STATION	6:32A		7:30A		1:56P		3:45P	4:10P		4:57P	5:33P	6:14P		8:27P
GLENDALE	L6:43A		L7:41A		2:07P		3:56P	4:21P		5:08P	5:44P	6:25P		8:37P
BURBANK	L6:49A		L7:47A		2:13P		4:02P	4:27P		5:14P	5:50P	6:31P		8:43P
SYLMAR/SAN FERNANDO	L7:03A		L8:07A		2:24P		L4:13P	4:38P		L5:25P	6:01P	6:42P		8:54P
SANTA CLARITA	L7:27A	7:35A	L8:28A	8:35A	2:44P	2:50P	L4:34P	4:59P	5:30P	L5:46P	L6:22P	L7:02P	7:10P	L9:14P
PRINCESSA	7:39A	7:45A	8:37A	8:45A	2:52P	3:00P	L4:39P		5:40P	L5:51P	L6:27P	7:08P	7:20P	L9:19P
VINCENT GRADE/ACTON		8:15A		9:15A		3:30P	L5:11P		6:10P	L6:23P	L6:59P		7:50P	L9:51P
LANCASTER		8:46A		9:46A		4:01P	5:29P		6:41P	6:41P	7:19P		8:21P	10:10P

L: Regular stop to discharge or pick up passengers except train may leave ahead of schedule

Metrolink Train entering the Tunnel in Soledad Canyon

These stations were built by the U.S. Navy Seabees based at Port Hueneme. Two additional emergency stations were built at Vincent Grade/Acton opening on January 31, 1994, and Princessa in the Santa Clarita Valley opening on February 7, 1994. The Sylmar/San Fernando Station was already under construction. Metrolink accelerated construction with around-the-clock shifts following the earthquake. This allowed initial service from this station to commence on January 26, 1994. All costs for the emergency extension of this line to the Antelope Valley were paid for by FEMA. The original 78-mile commute from Lancaster to L.A. Union Station took 2 hours and 25 minutes. Metrolink, immediately following the earthquake, implemented an extensive rail construction program to straighten much of the line through the mountains between Santa Clarita and the Antelope Valley. By August 1, 1994 the commute time from Lancaster to L.A. Union Station was reduced to 1 hour and 56 minutes, a decrease of 30 minutes running time. The Palmdale Station was forced to close in June 1994 due to safety considerations relating to pedestrian access design issues. The majority of riders from the city of Palmdale used the Vincent Grade/Acton station which has easy access from the Antelope Valley Freeway-Highway 14. Track straightening work was completed by

February 1995, and the route was shortened by one mile. The length of the line is now 77 miles and running time is 1 hour and 43 minutes.

Between the San Fernando Valley and the Antelope Valley the Santa Clarita Line traverses the Newhall Pass and scenic Soledad Canyon. In the Newhall Pass you can catch a glimpse of several Los Angeles Department Of Water and Power facilities. The first you will see is the Sylmar High Voltage Direct Current Converter Station, which transforms high-voltage-direct-current power transmitted from the Bonneville Power Administration dams along the Columbia River in Washington and Oregon. Beyond the Sylmar Converter Station is the Los Angeles Reservoir which is used to store water delivered from the Owens River in the Owens Valley 300 miles north of this point. Directly west of the track is the Metropolitan Water District's Joseph Jensen Water Filtration Plant, which process all water delivered to Southern California on the West Branch of the California Aqueduct. The State water project that brings surplus water from the Feather River in Northern California to parched Southern California. On the hill directly across the freeway is the terminus of the Los Angeles-Owens Valley Aqueduct originally completed in 1913. Occasionally, the aqueduct water can be seen cascading down a rock lined concrete channel when the small hydro-electric generator across San Fernando

Road is down for maintenance. From this point the line parallels the Golden State Freeway I-5 through the Newhall Pass until it enters the Newhall Tunnel.

After leaving the Santa Clarita Valley the line enters Soledad Canyon one of the most scenic parts of Metrolink system. The river in the canyon has running surface water all year round during wet years. As a result of this the canyon floor is lined with cottonwood trees which provide a backdrop for numerous private campgrounds and parks. On weekends, these facilities are always running at capacity with familes getting away from the urban sprawl located just over the mountains separating Soledad Canyon from the San Fernando and Santa Clarita Valleys. The track is never far from the canyon floor and the canyon is quite narrow in places resulting in some spectacular views from the train as it traverses the canyon on to the top of Vincent Grade. About midway through Soledad Canyon some of the exotic landscape of Vasquez Rocks State Park can be seen to the north of the train. This area was a favorite location site for many Hollywood studios making western epics. About three quarters of the way through the canyon the train passes the Shambala Wild Animal Preserve. The preserve is directly across the river from the Metrolink route. If you look carefully you may catch a glimpse of elephants, lions, leopards, giraffes and other wild animals. The preserve is not open to the public and is operated by Melanie Griffith's mother.

After leaving Soledad Canyon the line traverses the Vincent Grade Pass into the Antelope Valley. The terrain dramatically changes from that of the costal mountains to that of the high desert as you arrive at the Vincent Grade/Acton Station.

From the Vincent Grade/Acton Station the line follows Sierra Highway on into the City of Palmdale. The line passes the Palmdale City Hall as it intersects Palmdale Road the main street of Palmdale. From downtown Palmdale the line continues to follow Sierra Highway past the location of the abandoned Palmdale Station on the way to Lancaster. The line terminates at the downtown Lancaster Station where you can connect with the Antelope Valley Transit Authority's bus system for access to the cities of Lancaster and Palmdale.

San Fernando / Sylmar Station

Station Connecting Transit Information

The San Fernando/Sylmar Metrolink Station is located at 12219 First Street in the city of San Fernando. The station can be reached by taking the Hubbard Street exit from the I-210. Go west on Hubbard Street to the station which will be on your right. From the 118 Freeway take the San Fernando Road exit and go north to Hubbard. Turn right on Hubbard and the station will be on your left just across the railroad tracks. The station has a 400-car parking lot. The train boarding platform is well lighted and has good shelter. The parking lot is well lighted and maintained. Metrolink personnel man the station during the morning and evening rush hours. Security guards patrol the station and parking lot all day.

The station is served by the MTA 92-93-410, 94, 230, 239, 561 and LADOT 574 Express. The station vicinity map provide the routes for bus transit options from the San Fernando/Sylmar Metrolink Station.

San Fernando / Sylmar Metrolink Station

The following table provides the schedule of bus connections with Metrolink.

Outside of the immediate vicinity of the San Fernando / Sylmar Metrolink station the MTA 92 / 93 and 410 lines provides service along Glenoaks Boulevard to Pacoima, Sun Valley, and

SAN FERNANDO/SYLMAR STATION BUS CONNECTIONS
SOUTHBOUND TRAINS FROM LANCASTER TO LOS ANGELES

TRAIN NUMBER	DAYS OF OPERATION	TRAIN ARRIVAL	MTA 92-93-410	MTA 94 NORTHBOUND	MTA 94 SOUTHBOUND	MTA 230	MTA 239	MTA 561	LADOT 574
BUS FREQUENCY			20 - 40 MIN.	10 -15 MIN.	10 - 15 MIN.	30 MINUTES	40 - 60 MIN.	30 MIN.	COMMUTER
METROLINK 200	M - F	5:47A	5:26/5:49A	5:39/5:55A	5:46/5:58A	6:04A	6:02A	5:49A	5:49A
METROLINK 202	M - F	6:41A	6:24/6:55A	6:29/6:42A	6:32/6:44A	6:35/6:43A	6:26/7:18A	6:32/6:45A	7:09A
METROLINK 204	M - F	7:11A	7:08/7:25A	6:52/7:12A	6:58/7:14A	7:00/7:24A	7:04/7:18A	6:56/7:35A	
METROLINK 206	M - F	7:42A	7:08/8:04A	7:22/7:50A	7:30/7:46A	7:15/7:44A	7:04/8:06A	7:20/8:06A	
METROLINK 208	M - F	8:11A	7:53/8:26A	8:06/8:14A	8:02/8:19A	8:06/8:25A	7:44/8:47A	7:44/8:37A	
METROLINK 210	M - F	9:11A	9:02/9:27A	9:03/9:15P	9:09/9:26A	9:06/9:24A	9:04/9:36A	8:50/9:37A	
METROLINK 212	M - F	3:44P	3:16/3:55P	3:37/3:51P	3:37/3:49P	3:37/4:03P	3:39/4:17P	3:27/4:04P	
METROLINK 214	M - F	5:29P	5:09/6:18P	5:19/5:39P	5:10/5:30P	5:17/5:43P	5:03/5:37P	5:17/5:26P	
METROLINK 216	M - F	7:43P	7:05P	7:42/7:55P	7:08/7:49P	7:28/8:09P	7:09P	7:27P	5:39P

NORTHBOUND TRAINS FROM LOS ANGELES TO LANCASTER

TRAIN NUMBER	DAYS OF OPERATION	TRAIN ARRIVAL	MTA 92-93-410	MTA 94 NORTHBOUND	MTA 94 SOUTHBOUND	MTA 230	MTA 239	MTA 561	LADOT 574
METROLINK 201	M - F	L7:03A	6:45/7:25A	6:52/7:12A	6:58/7:14A	7:00/7:04A	6:26/7:18A	6:56/7:05A	7:09A
METROLINK 203	M - F	L8:07A	7:53/8:26A	8:06/8:14A	8:02/8:19A	8:06/8:25A	7:44/8:47A	7:44/8:37A	
METROLINK 205	M - F	2:24P	1:55/2:29P	2:21/2:37P	2:23/2:32P	2:10/2:39P	1:49/2:40P	1:55/2:25P	
METROLINK 207	M - F	L4:13P	3:56/4:24P	4:05/4:19P	4:02/4:15P	3:57/4:23P	3:39/4:17P	3:57/4:26P	
METROLINK 209	M - F	4:38P	4:32/4:56P	4:33/4:47P	4:30/4:44P	4:37/4:43P	4:23/4:57P	4:27/4:46P	
METROLINK 211	M - F	L5:25P	5:09/6:18P	5:19/5:29P	5:10/5:30P	5:17/5:43P	5:03/5:37P	5:17/5:26P	5:11P
METROLINK 213	M - F	6:01P	5:39/6:18P	5:57/6:07P	5:50/6:15P	5:57/6:05P	5:43/6:14P	5:49P	5:39P
METROLINK 215	M - F	6:42P	6:28/6:45P	6:41/6:51P	6:39/7:08P	6:36/7:09P	6:26/7:01P	6:40P	6:13P
METROLINK 217	M - F	8:54P	8:43P	8:42/9:02P	8:31/9:31P	8:45/9:09P	8:01P	7:27P	

L: Regular stop to discharge or pick up passengers except train may leave ahead of schedule

The Convento at the San Fernando Mission

Burbank, continuing on to Glendale along Brand Boulevard. The MTA 94 line provides service along San Fernando Road to Pacoima, Sun Valley, Burbank Airport, Burbank and Glendale. The stop for the 94 line is at the corner of Truman and Hubbard streets. The 230 line operates along Laurel Canyon Boulevard to Ventura Boulevard serving Pacoima, Sun Valley, North Hollywood and Studio City. The 239 line operates over Rinaldi in the east-west direction and then traverses the valley in the north-south direction along Zelzah and White Oak avenues. The 239 line serves Granada Hills, Northridge, Reseda and Encino. The 561 line provides service along Van Nuys Boulevard to Van Nuys. It continues via the 405 Freeway to West Los Angeles serving UCLA. Leaving West Los Angeles it continues on the 405 Freeway to the Fox hills Mall in Culver City and the Los Angeles International Airport.

From the San Fernando/Sylmar station one can take the LADOT 574 Express Bus line serving communities in West Los Angeles and the South Bay not served by Metrolink.

For updated schedules and complete route maps for MTA call (818) 781-5890 and for LADOT call (213) 485-7201.

Points of Interest

San Fernando, the "First City of the Valley" grew from its proximity to

Mission San Fernando Rey. It was named after the Spanish Saint / King in 1791. By the early 1800's the community of San Fernando had become the center for trade and commerce. Here, farm crops, wine and

livestock produced by local Indians were bought and sold. Contrary to popular belief, the earliest documented gold discovery in California was at nearby Placerita Canyon on March 9, 1842 by Don Francisco Lopez, the mayordomo of the mission. A small gold rush ensued, but died out after the discovery of gold at Sutter's Mill.

The City of San Fernando was incorporated in 1874. It is the only community in the San Fernando Valley, other than Burbank and Glendale, that did not annex itself to Los Angeles for access to Owens River water. Today the city occupies 2.42 square miles in the northeastern corner of the San Fernando Valley and is completely surrounded by the city of Los Angeles. The commercial center of the city is along San Fernando Road and Brand Boulevard. The San Fernando Mall has transformed the city's old downtown shopping district along San Fernando Road into a lively commercial area with an hispanic flavor reflecting the ethnic background of the majority of the residents of this city.

San Fernando Mission

The San Fernando Mission is

The Gardens in Brand Park

Los Angeles reclaimed the Mission and completed restoration in 1941.

Today the mission is operated as a museum depicting life in the San Fernando Valley in the early 1800's. Mass is still celebrated daily in the mission church. The mission is open daily 9:00 A.M. to 4:15 P.M. Admission is $4.00 for adults $3.00 for children 7 to 15 years and seniors. Children under 7 are free. For information call the mission at (818) 361-0186.

To reach the mission from the San Fernando/Sylmar Metrolink Station take the MTA 94 bus line to the Truman Street and Maclay Avenue stop where you will transfer to the MTA 234 line. Take the westbound 234 line to the Brand Boulevard and Columbus Avenue stop. Walk one block north on Columbus Avenue to San Fernando Mission Boulevard, the mission will be on your right on San Fernando Mission Boulevard. Take time to stroll through the gardens of Brand Park which occupies the land between the bus stop on Brand and San Fernando Mission Boulevards.

located 15151 San Fernando Mission Boulevard in Mission Hills. The mission was the 17th of California's missions founded by the Franciscan Order in 1797. The first church at San Fernando was completed the same year and was blessed on November 28. Work on the permanent church was started in 1804 and was completed on December 6, 1806. This church was restored in 1941 only to be destroyed on February 9, 1971 by the Sylmar Earthquake. A replica of the church was dedicated on November 4, 1974. The mission buildings were once again severely damaged by the January 17, 1994 Northridge Earthquake. Above the altar stands a life-sized wooden statue of the mission's namesake San Fernando, Rey de Espana (1198-1252). This statue was sent to California by the King of Spain at the time of the founding of the mission and has occupied its place above the altar ever since, except for the time it resided in Saint Ferdinand's church in the nearby town of San Fernando when the mission was abandoned by the church.

The Convento Building was begun in 1810 and completed in 1812. This structure was unique in architectural style with its wide portico formed by a colonnade of 21 arches. The church abandoned the mission in the mid-1800's. The Convento was used by the Butterfield Stage Line from 1857 to 1861 on the Los Angeles to San Francisco route. In the 1880's it was used by the Porter Land & Water Company to accommodate ranch hands and for store-rooms. The Archdiocese of

Andres Pico Adobe

La Casa de Geronimo Lopez

Los Angeles Mission College

Los Angeles Mission College is located at 13356 Eldridge Avenue in Sylmar. The college is a two-year institution and a part of the Los Angeles Community College District. The college offers an Associate of Arts Degree in a wide range of majors. For information about the college call (818) 364-7600.

The college can be reached from the San Fernando/Sylmar Metrolink Station by taking the MTA 94 bus line to the Truman Street and Maclay Avenue stop where you will transfer to the MTA 234 line. Take the eastbound 234 line to the Hubbard Street and Eldridge Avenue stop. The college is located at the southeast corner of Hubbard Street and Eldridge Avenue.

Andres Pico Adobe

The Andres Pico Adobe is located at 10940 Sepulveda Boulevard in Mission Hills. The adobe was built in 1834 by Andres Pico, the brother of Pio Pico who was the Governor of California. It was severely damaged during the January 17, 1994 Northridge Earthquake. The Adobe is the headquarters of the San Fernando Valley Historical Society and is open Wednesday thru Sunday 1:00 P.M. to 4:00 P.M. For information call (818) 365-7810.

The Adobe is just a few blocks southwest of the San Fernando Mission and the same bus lines serve the Adobe. The Brand Boulevard and Sepulveda Boulevard stop is the closest one to the Adobe.

La Casa de Geronimo Lopez

La Casa de Geronimo Lopez is located at 1100 Pico Ave. The house was constructed by Valentin Lopez in 1882. The seven room house has 19th century furniture on display. The library has a collection of rare local history books. There is a small park and garden surrounding the house with picnic tables. The house is open 11:00 A.M to 3:00 P.M. Wednesday and Saturday, and 1:00 P.M. to 4:00 P.M. on Sunday. Admission is free but donations are gladly accepted.

Places to Stay

Best Western Mission Hills Inn

The Best Western Mission Hills Inn is located at 10621 Sepulveda Boulevard in Mission Hills. To reach the hotel you can use the MTA 94 line and transfer to the MTA 234 line. The hotel phone number is (818) 891 - 1771. For reservations call (800) 528-1234.

Roxford Inn

The Roxford Inn is located at 14955 Roxford Street in Sylmar. To reach the hotel you can take the northbound MTA 94 bus line to the Foothill Boulevard and Roxford Street stop. The hotel phone number is (818) 367-0141. For reservations call (800) 894-3003.

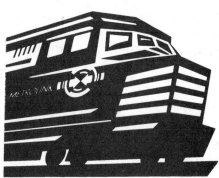

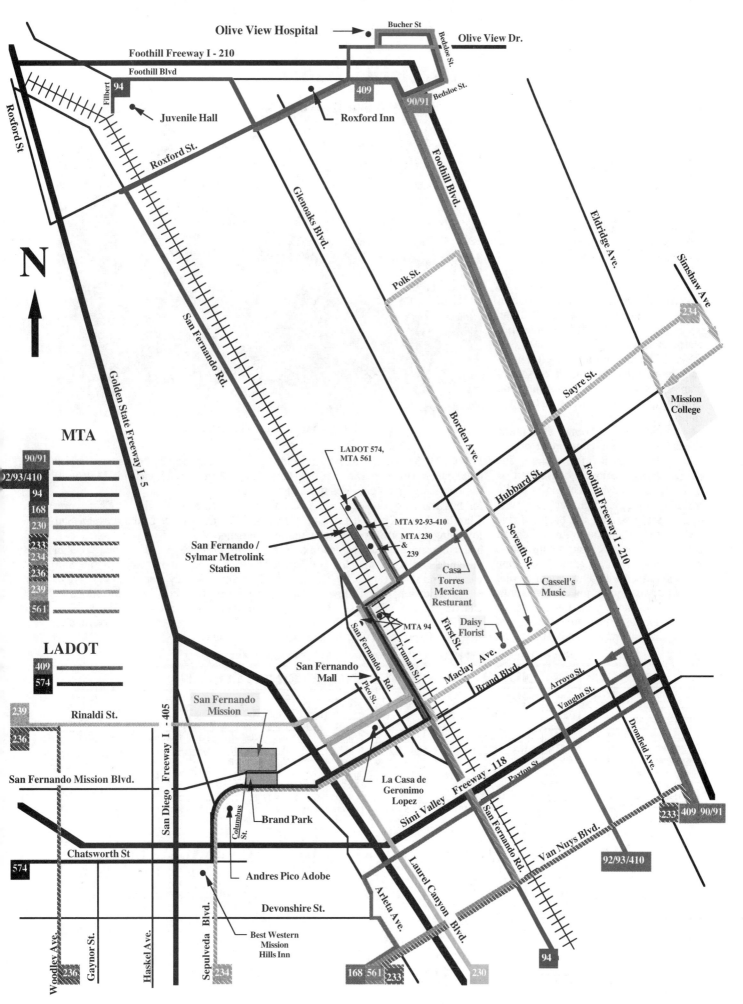

San Fernando / Sylmar Station Vicinity Map

Santa Clarita Station

Station Connecting Transit Information

The Santa Clarita Metrolink Station is located at 22122 Soledad Canyon Road. The station can be reached by taking the Magic Mountain Parkway exit from the I - 5 Freeway. Go east to Valencia Boulevard and turn left. Valencia Boulevard becomes Soledad Canyon Road at the intersection of Bouquet Canyon Road. The station will be about one-mile on your right. See map insert for station locale. The station has a 500-car parking lot. The train boarding platform is well lighted and has good shelter. The parking lot is well lighted and maintained. Metrolink personnel man the station in the morning and evening. Security guards patrol the station and parking lot 24 hours a day.

Santa Clarita Transit has made Metrolink a major component of the local public transit infrastructure. The Santa Clarita Station is configured so that all busses have direct access to the train boarding platform. Each bus route is scheduled so that the busses arrive before each Metrolink train and depart after train departure. This set up allows for two-way transfers between the train and the busses with a minimum of wait time for passengers. However, you must be quick to make your transfer as the bus or train does not wait for stragglers. Santa Clarita Transit Lines 10, 15, 20,

Santa Clarita Metrolink Station

25, 30, 31, 35, 40, 50 and 55 provide local bus service to the station. The station vicinity map provides the routes for bus transit options from the Santa Clarita Metrolink Station. The following table provides the schedule of bus connections with Metrolink. For schedule and route updates call Santa Clarita Transit on (805) 294-1287.

In addition, the following Santa Clarita Transit Express Bus Lines provide service from the station:
• 795: Express service to Lancaster

with stops at the Via Princessa, Vincent Grade/Acton and Lancaster Metrolink stations.
• 796: Express service to Chatsworth and Warner Center in the western San Fernando Valley.
• 793/798: Express service to Van Nuys and Sherman Oaks in the San Fernando Valley and the Van Nuys FlyAway Terminal for connections to Los Angeles International Airport
• 799: Express service to Los Angeles Civic Center.

SANTA CLARITA STATION BUS CONNECTIONS
SOUTHBOUND TRAINS FROM LANCASTER TO LOS ANGELES

TRAIN NUMBER	DAYS OF OPERATION	TRAIN ARRIVAL	SCT 10 CASTAIC 20 VAL VERDE	SCT 10 & 20 SHADOW PINES	SCT 15 & 25 NEWHALL	SCT 30 & 31 MAGIC MTN.	SCT 30 & 31 SECO CANYON	SCT 35 LYONS AVE.	SCT 40 BOUQUET CYN.	SCT 50 LYONS AVE.	SCT 795
BUS FREQUENCY			30 MINUTES	30 MINUTES	30 MINUTES	30 MINUTES	30 MINUTES	30 MINUTES	30 MINUTES	30 MINUTES	
METROLINK 200	M - F	5:29A	5:20/6:18A	5:20/6:18A	5:20/6:18A	5:20A	5:51A	5:20/6:18A	5:20/6:18A	5:20/6:18A	5:15A
METROLINK 202	M - F	6:23A	6:13/6:48A	6:13/6:48P	6:13/6:48A	6:13A	5:49/6:48A	6:13/6:48A	6:13/6:48A	6:13/6:48A	
METROLINK 204	M - F	6:53A	6:43/7:18A	6:43/7:18A	6:43/7:15A	6:43A	7:18A	6:43/7:18A	6:43/7:18A	6:43/7:18A	6:43A
METROLINK 206	M - F	7:24A	7:13/7:33A	7:13/7:48A	7:10/7:45A	7:13/7:48A	7:48A	7:13/7:48A	7:13/7:48A	7:13/8:13A	
METROLINK 208	M - F	7:53A	7:43/8:20A	7:43/8:22A	7:43/8:20A	7:43/8:20A	8:20A	7:43/8:20A	7:43/8:20A	7:43/8:13A	
METROLINK 210	M - F	8:53A	8:43/9:20A	8:45/9:22P	8:45/9:20A	8:45/9:20A	8:45/9:20A	8:43/9:20A	8:43/9:20A	8:43/9:20A	
METROLINK 212	M - F	3:26P	3:15/4:00P	3:15/4:00P	3:15/4:00P	3:15/4:00P	3:15/4:00P	3:18/4:00P	3:20/4:00P	3:15/4:39P	3:15P
METROLINK 214	M - F	5:09P	4:56/5:30P	4:56/5:30P	4:56/5:30P	5:02/5:27P	4:56/5:28P	4:56/5:30P	4:56/5:30P	4:15/5:30P	
METROLINK 216	M - F	7:25P	7:22/7:30P	7:22/7:30P	7:22/7:30P	6:51P	7:00/7:30P	7:22/7:30P	7:22/7:30P	7:22/7:30P	

NORTHBOUND TRAINS FROM LOS ANGELES TO LANCASTER

TRAIN NUMBER	DAYS OF OPERATION	TRAIN ARRIVAL	SCT 10 CASTAIC 20 VAL VERDE	SCT 10 & 20 SHADOW PINES	SCT 15 & 25 NEWHALL	SCT 30 & 31 MAGIC MTN.	SCT 30 & 31 SECO CANYON	SCT 35 LYONS AVE.	SCT 40 BOUQUET CYN.	SCT 50 LYONS AVE.	SCT 795
METROLINK 201	M - F	L7:27A	7:13/7:33A	7:13/7:48A	7:10/7:45A	7:13/7:48A	7:48A	7:13/7:48A	7:13/7:48A	7:13/8:13A	7:35A
METROLINK 203	M - F	L8:28A	8:13/8:35A	8:13/8:52A	8:15/8:50A	8:15/8:50A	8:13/8:50A	8:13/8:50A	8:13/8:50A	8:15/9:20A	8:35A
METROLINK 205	M - F	2:44P	2:15/2:50P	2:15/2:52P	2:15/2:50P	2:15/2:50P	2:15/2:50P	2:15/2:50P	2:15/2:50P	2:15/3:25P	2:50P
METROLINK 207	M - F	L4:34P	4:31/4:39P	4:31/4:39P	4:31/4:39P	4:23/5:04P	4:31/4:39P	4:31/4:39P	4:31/4:39P	4:15/4:39P	
METROLINK 209	M - F	4:59P	4:56/5:04P	4:56/5:04P	4:56/5:04P	4:23/5:04P	4:56/5:04P	4:56/5:04P	4:56/5:04P	4:15/5:04P	5:30P
METROLINK 211	M - F	L5:46P	5:25/5:51P	5:43/5:51P	5:23/5:51P	5:27/5:51P	5:28/5:52P	5:43/5:51P	5:40/5:51P	5:36/5:51P	
METROLINK 213	M - F	L6:22P	6:19/6:27P	6:19/6:27P	6:19/6:27P	6:16/6:27P	6:19/6:27P	6:19/6:27P	6:19/6:27P	6:19/6:27P	
METROLINK 215	M - F	L7:02P	7:00/7:08P	7:00/7:08P	7:00/7:08P	6:51P	7:00/7:08P	7:00/7:08P	7:00/7:08P	6:57/7:08P	7:10P
METROLINK 217	M - F	L9:14P	9:10P	9:21P				9:10/9:21P			

L: Regular stop to discharge or pick up passengers except train may leave ahead of schedule

Points of Interest

Santa Clarita is one of the new communities that has experienced explosive growth over the last 10 to 15 years. This is due mainly to the lack of affordable housing in the nearby San Fernando Valley. The area includes Newhall and Saugus, two long standing towns, that have been a part of the landscape since the late 1800's. The first township in the Santa Clarita Valley was Newhall. It was named after Henry Mayo Newhall, the man who sold the railroad right-of-way to the Southern Pacific Company for one dollar in 1875. The town site was also sold for another dollar. The state's first producing oil well began operation the same year in Pico Canyon. This was followed by the first oil refinery in Railroad Canyon. In the early 1900's the Hollywood movie community started to use the Santa Clarita Valley as a location backdrop for western epics. Film making in the area continues to this day. Much of the local landscape such as Vasquez Rocks is familiar to people the world over due to the motion pictures filmed here over the years.

The area is home to the William S. Hart Park and Museum, College of the Canyons, California Institute of the Arts, Saugus Swapmeet, Mountasia, Six Flags Hurricane Harbor and Six Flags Magic Mountain theme park. Nearby are the Placerita Nature Center, Castaic Lake, a man-made reservoir on the West Branch of the California Aqueduct, which brings Northern California water into parched Southern California and the Angeles National Forrest.

William S. Hart Park and Museum

The William S. Hart Park and Museum is the bequest of Hart to the people of Los Angeles following his death in 1946, at the age of 81. Hart acquired a ranch in Newhall in 1925 after completing his last film *Tumbleweeds*. He commissioned Los Angeles architect Arthur Kelly to design a Spanish Colonial Revival-style home on his property. When completed in 1927, Hart christened the home La Loma de los Vientos (Hill of the Winds). During his years at the ranch, Hart amassed a substantial collection of western art and native American artifacts. Today the house is a

La Loma de Los Vientos

museum which stands not only as a tribute to Hart and his accomplishments, but as a window to view life in the American west as perceived in the early part of the 20th century. Hart, a western figure on the screen, became friends with other western figures such as Will Rogers, Wyatt Earp, and many important western artists. As a result of these relationships, today Hart's home has original works on display from artists such as Charles M. Russell, C. C. Cristadoro, James Montgomery Flagg and Frederick Remington.

The museum offers free guided tours from mid-September to mid-June on Wednesday through Friday 10:00 A.M. to 1:00 P.M. (last tour starts at 12:30 P.M.), Saturday and Sunday 11:00 A.M. to 4:00 P.M. (last tour starts at 3:30 P.M.). In the summer, tours are offered Wednesday thru Sunday 11:00 A.M. to 4:00 P.M. (last tour starts at 3:30 P.M.). On weekends a shuttle operates between the parking area and the Hart Museum which is located at the top of a hill overlooking the park. For information call the museum on (805) 254-4584.

Historic Saugus Railroad Station

The park includes hiking and nature trails, large picnic areas, historic ranch buildings, a wedding site, campground, a barnyard zoo (which includes a herd of bison) and pony rides on weekends. Also on the park grounds is the nineteenth century Saugus Railroad Station which was moved from its original site in Saugus, five miles away, by the Santa Clarita Historical Society. The station is open to the public 1:00 P.M. to 4:00 P.M. Saturdays and Sundays. For park information call (805) 259-0855 and for information on the railroad station call (805) 254-1275.

The park is located at 24151 San Fernando Road, Newhall, California. To reach the park and museum from Metrolink take the Santa Clarita Transit 15 bus line to the park stop.

Saugus Swapmeet

The Saugus Swapmeet is held every Sunday of the year. The swapmeet opens at 7:00 A.M. and closes at 3:00 P.M. with gates locked by 5:00 P.M. This is one of the largest swapmeets in Los Angeles County, attracting sellers from all over the Southern California region. For $20.00 a seller can obtain a space at the swap meet to sell anything from last year's unwanted Christmas gifts to rare antiques that lay hidden in one's attic or garage. Many vendors are professional swapmeet sellers that offer new merchandise to potential buyers. The swapmeet has a number of food and beverage vendors that sell hamburgers, hot dogs, tacos, and other assorted refreshments. Admission for buyers is $1.00 for adults 12 and over. Children under 12 are free. For information call

(805) 259-3886.

College of the Canyons

The College of the Canyons opened in September 1969, with 800 students attending classes in temporary quarters at Hart High School in Newhall. A 153.4-acre site was purchased in the newly created planned community of Valencia. Construction of the facilities, now serving a student body of 8,000, was completed in 1982. The college is a two-year institution and offers an Associate of Arts degree in a wide range of majors. The Administration Building Gallery foyer houses rotating displays of student art and the Cougar Cafe is home to many musical events throughout the year. For admission forms and general information call (805) 259-7800. To reach the college from the Santa Clarita Metrolink Station take the Santa Clarita Transit 15 or 25 bus.

California Institute of the Arts

The California Institute of the Arts (CalArts) was the first institution of higher learning in the United States created specifically to grant degrees to students of the visual and performing arts. With the guidance of founders Walt and Roy Disney and Lulu May Von Hagen, Cal Arts was created with the merger of two Los Angeles professional schools, The Los Angeles Conservatory of music, founded in 1883, and the Chouinard Art Institute, founded in 1921. The school officially opened its doors in 1970 at temporary quarters in Burbank, California. In November 1971, the school moved to its present location in Valencia. Today the institute is comprised of five independent schools: Art, Dance, Film/Video, Music, Theater, and a

Mountasia

Division of Critical Studies. The Institute offers Bachelor of Fine Arts and Master of Fine Arts degrees. The faculty staff, alumni and students have a long list of credentials that include award winning filmmakers, Broadway performers and world class artists with works on display in several art museums.

Tours of the Institute are conducted Monday through Friday at 1:30 P.M., during the academic year. During the summer classes are not in session and tour hours vary. Special events and student performances from the schools of Music, Dance and Theater are offered throughout the year. For information about campus activities and tour reservations call (805) 253-7875. The Institute can be reached from the Santa Clarita Metrolink Station by taking the Santa Clarita Transit 15 or 25 bus.

Mountasia

Mountasia family fun center is a mini amusement park and miniature golf complex. The park offers 36 holes of exciting miniature golf complete with putt through caves and waterfalls, a state-of-the-art roller skating rink, splashing bumper boats, fast race karts, batting cages and a giant game room with all the latest arcade, video and redemption games. There is a Mcdonalds Express inside for fast food.

There is no admission to Mountasia. You pay only for the attractions you wish to use.

Mountasia is located at 21516 Golden Triangle Road. For information call (805) 253-4FUN. From Metrolink take the Santa Clarita Transit 10, 20 or 50 line to the Soledad Canyon Road and Golden Triangle Road stop. Bring your Metrolink Ticket or Santa Clarita Transit transfer for a special discount.

Six Flags Hurricane Harbor

Six Flags Hurricane Harbor is located right next door to Magic Mountain. It is Southern California's only theme water park.

Shipwreck shores is the place where Red Eye the Pirate left an abandoned ship. From here you can see the 45-foot volcano with waterfalls.

In Castaway Cove children under 54 inches tall have a world of their own with pint-sized water slides and a fortress with pirate's hidden treasure to be found by the adventurous.

The River Cruise is just the place to relax and recharge on the hot Santa Clarita summer afternoons. The river winds around the entire park, with the various adventures beckoning around each bend in the river. In the Forgotten Sea you can ride a raft in the surf.

For the adventurous, you can ride down one of the 400 foot slides, plummet over Tiki Falls or dare to climb Taboo Tower and take one of the three escape routes - the 45 degree drop over Daredevil Plunge, the "bumpy" Escape Chute or the spiraling Secret Passage.

Magic Mountain

The park is open daily in summer and on weekends from early September through October 1. For information on operating hours and admission prices call (805) 255-4100.

To reach the park from the Santa Clarita Metrolink Station take the Santa Clarita Transit 30 bus weekdays and the 10, 20, or 30 bus on weekends.

Six Flags Magic Mountain

Six Flags Magic Mountain is a major theme park in the Southern California region. The park specializes in roller coaster thrill rides. *Colossus,* one of the largest wood frame coasters in the country; *Revolution*, the worlds first looping coaster; and *Viper,* which twists you upside down seven times, populate this park. The newest addition to the park is *Batman the Ride* a suspended roller coaster which rockets you through dual outside vertical loops

with nothing but air beneath your feet. This park is not for the faint hearted. People with physical limitations, such as heart conditions or back problems, are restricted. The intense nature of most of the major rides in this park make it a popular venue for the local junior and senior high school set. None of the major attractions can accommodate small children. There are a limited number of rides provided for small children throughout the park, such as those located in *Bugs Bunny World*. During the period of March through October there is a Dolphin and Sea Lion show. New this year is the *Batman Stunt Show*. Live rock and roll entertainment is presented on weekend evenings. Nights are topped off by the *Batman Nights* Fireworks and Laser Extravaganza.

The park is open weekends all year, daily during spring break, early May till

early September, and Christmas vacation. For information as to operating hours and admission prices call (805) 255-4100. To reach Magic Mountain from the Santa Clarita Metrolink Station take the Santa Clarita Transit 30 bus weekdays and the 10, 20, or 30 bus on weekends.

Valencia Town Center Mall

The Valencia Town Center Mall is located a few miles west of the Metrolink Station near the intersection of Magic Mountain Parkway and McBean Parkway. The mall features a carousel and family entertainment center. The mall can be reached by taking Santa Clarita Transit 15, 25, 30, 31, or 35 bus lines from the Santa Clarita Metrolink Station.

Places to Stay
Valencia Hilton Garden Inn

The Valencia Hilton Garden Inn is located at 27710 The Old Road in Valencia. The hotel telephone number is (805) 254-8800. For reservations call (800) HILTONS.

Best Western Ranch House Inn

The Best Western Ranch House Inn is located at 27413 Tourney Road in Valencia. The hotel telephone number is (805) 255-0555. For reservations call (800) 528-1234.

Hampton Inn Valencia

The Hampton Inn Valencia is located at 25259 The Old Road in Newhall. The hotel telephone number is (805) 253-2400. For reservations call (800) HAMPTON.

Santa Clarita Motel

The Santa Clarita Motel is located at 24971 San Fernando Road in Newhall. The motel telephone number is (805) 259-2800. For reservations call (800) 34-MOTEL

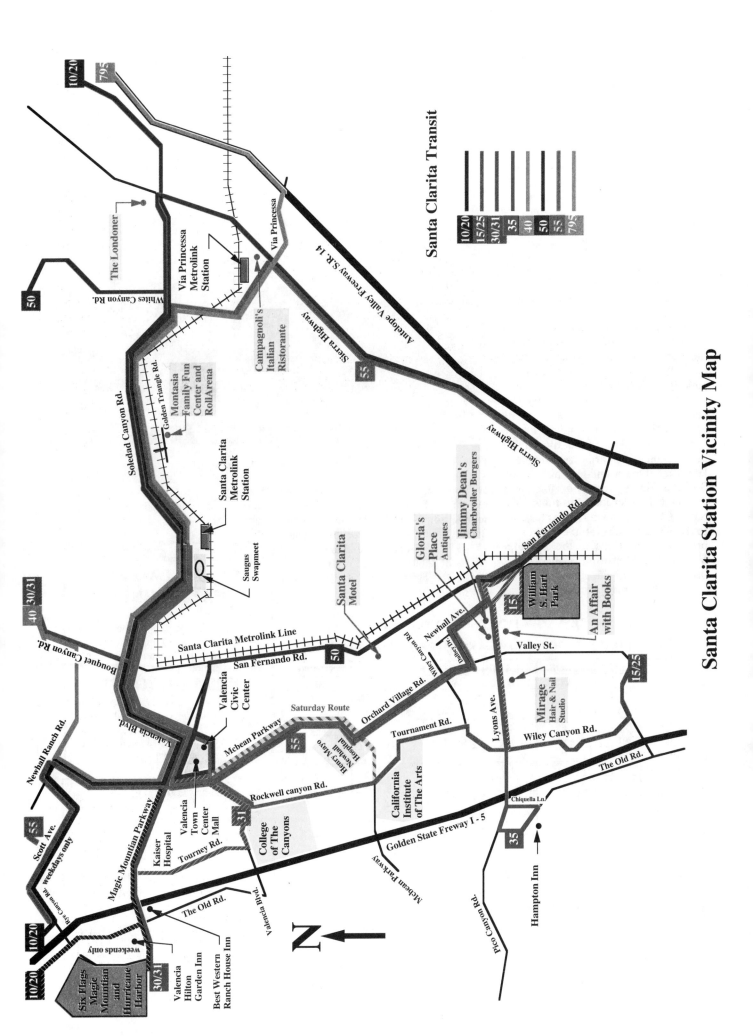

Santa Clarita Transit

	10/20
	15/25
	30/31
	35
	40
	50
	55
	795

Santa Clarita Station Vicinity Map

The Londoner

White's Canyon Rd.

Via Princessa Metrolink Station

Via Princessa

Campagnoli's Italian Ristorante

Soledad Canyon Rd.

Golden Triangle Rd.

Montasia Family Fun Center and RollArena

Santa Clarita Metrolink Station

Saugus Swapmeet

Antelope Valley Freeway S.R. 14

Sierra Highway

Sierra Highway

Santa Clarita Metrolink Line

San Fernando Rd.

Bouquet Canyon Rd.

Santa Clarita Motel

Gloria's Place Antiques

Jimmy Dean's Charbroiler Burgers

San Fernando Rd.

William S. Hart Park

An Affair with Books

Newhall Ave.

Dalbey Dr.

Valley St.

Mirage Hair & Nail Studio

Lyons Ave.

Wiley Canyon Rd.

Wiley Canyon Rd.

Orchard Village Rd.

Valencia Civic Center

Saturday Route

Mcbean Parkway

Henry Mayo Newhall Hospital

Rockwell canyon Rd.

Tournament Rd.

California Institute of The Arts

The Old Rd.

Chiquella Ln.

Golden State Freeway I - 5

Mcbean Parkway

Hampton Inn

Pico Canyon Rd.

Newhall Ranch Rd.

Scott Ave.

Rye Canyon Rd. weekdays only

Magic Mountain Parkway

Kaiser Hospital

Valencia Town Center Mall

Tourney Rd.

College of The Canyons

Valencia Blvd.

The Old Rd.

Valencia Hilton Garden Inn

Best Western Ranch House Inn

Six Flags Magic Mountain and Hurricane Harbor

weekends only

N

Princessa Station

Station Connecting Transit Information

The Princessa Metrolink Station is located at 19201 Via Princessa. The station can be reached by taking the Via Princessa offramp from the Antelope Valley Freeway - Highway 14. Go northwest on Via Princessa and the station will be on your right about one-half mile past Sierra Highway. The station has a 420-car parking lot. The train boarding platform is well lighted, but does not have any shelter. The parking lot is also well lighted and maintained. Metrolink personnel man the station in the morning and evening. Security guards patrol the station and parking lot all day.

Presently there is no local bus connections at the Princessa Metrolink Station. The nearest bus stop is for the Santa Clarita Transit 50 line at the intersection of Via Princessa and Sierra Highway about a one-half mile away. See the vicinity map for the Santa Clarita Station for local bus routes. The Santa Clarita Transit 795 express bus to Lancaster stops at the station to provide connections to the Antelope Valley for Metrolink trains which originate or terminate here.

The Princessa station was added as

Princessa Metrolink Station

an emergency station to serve the residents of Canyon Country, and to relieve some of the pressure on the Santa Clarita Station after the January 17, 1994, Northridge Earthquake. Points of Interest and places to stay in the Santa Clarita Valley can be reached

from the Santa Clarita Station where there is a wide range of public transportation options.

PRINCESSA STATION BUS CONNECTIONS

SOUTHBOUND TRAINS FROM LANCASTER TO LOS ANGELES

TRAIN NUMBER	DAYS OF OPERATION	TRAIN ARRIVAL	SCT 50 VALENCIA	SCT 50 METROLINK	SCT 795 BUS
BUS FREQUENCY			30-60 MIN	30-60 MIN	
METROLINK 200	M - F	5:23A	5:50A		5:05A
METROLINK 202	M - F	6:17A	5:50/6:43A	6:43A	
METROLINK 204	M - F	6:47A	6:43/7:13A	6:43/7:33A	6:33A
METROLINK 206	M - F	7:18A	7:13/7:43A	6:43/7:33A	
METROLINK 208	M - F	7:48A	7:43/8:38A	7:33/8:43A	
METROLINK 210	M - F	8:48A	8:45/9:45A	8:43/9:43A	
METROLINK 212	M - F	3:19P	2:50/3:50P	2:40/3:43P	3:05P
METROLINK 216	M - F	7:19P		6:50P	

NORTHBOUND TRAINS FROM LOS ANGELES TO LANCASTER

METROLINK 201	M - F	7:39A	7:13/7:43A	7:33A	7:45A
METROLINK 203	M - F	8:37A	7:43/8:47A	7:33/8:43A	8:45A
METROLINK 205	M - F	2:52P	2:50/3:50P	2:40/3:43P	3:00P
METROLINK 207	M - F	L4:39P	3:50/5:04P	3:43/4:50P	
METROLINK 211	M - F	L5:51P	5:29/5:55P	4:50/6:03P	
METROLINK 213	M - F	L6:27P	5:55/6:36P	6:03/6:50P	
METROLINK 215	M - F	7:08P	6:36P	6:50P	7:20P
METROLINK 217	M - F	L9:19P			

L: Regular stop to discharge or pick up passengers except train may leave ahead of schedule

Vincent Grade/Acton Station

Station Connecting Transit Information

The Vincent Grade/Acton Metrolink Station is located at 550 W. Sierra Highway in Acton. The station can be reached by exiting the Sierra Highway offramp from the Antelope Valley Freeway (Highway 14) at the top of the Vincent Grade. Go west on Sierra Highway and the station will be on your left. The station features a 250-car parking lot, which is both well-lighted and patrolled. The train boarding platform is also well lighted, and some passenger shelter is available. A Metrolink Ambassador is present during the morning and evening commute times.

The Vincent Grade/Acton Station was built immediately following the Northridge Earthquake of January 17, 1994. If you get off the train here your only transportation out of the area is the next train or Santa Clarita Transit Line 795 express bus to Santa Clarita or Lancaster! Be careful, if you want to stop here and enjoy the solitude, that you are not getting off the last evening train. There are no hotels or accommodations within walking distance of the station!

Santa Clarita Transit Line 795 provides six round trips each weekday linking the Santa Clarita and Antelope valleys. This line provides connections with Metrolink trains at the Santa Clarita and Via Princessa stations. Every Line 795 trip stops at the Vincent Grade/Acton station. The one-

Vincent Grade/Acton Metrolink Station

way adult fare between the station and either the Antelope or the Santa Clarita valleys is three dollars. Riders may also use a valid AVTA transfer or Metrolink monthly pass as a partial credit toward the Line 795 fare. Call Santa Clarita Transit at (805) 294-1287 for further information.

Points of Interest

The Acton area is home to a wide variety of quality restaurants. Among these is the highly regarded Vincent Hill Resturant and Saloon, located directly across Sierra Highway from the station. This establishment is open for dinner at 3:30 P.M daily. One could catch the first train to Lancaster from Los Angeles in the afternoon arriving Vincent Hill/Acton at 5:11 P.M. and have dinner at this restaurant. However, be sure to be finished before the last train leaves at 9:51 P.M., otherwise it will be a long night out in the desert before the first train back to L.A. arrives at 4:52 A.M. the next morning, or Monday morning if you try this on a Friday night. Remember Metrolink

does not run on weekends.

Directly across the station parking lot is Vincent Hill Arena, home to a growing number of equestrian and rodeo events.

For additional infromation within the Acton area call the chamber of commerce at (805) 269-5785.

VINCENT GRADE/ACTON STATION BUS CONNECTIONS
SOUTHBOUND FROM LANCASTER TO LOS ANGELES

TRAIN NUMBER	DAYS OF OPERATION	TRAIN ARRIVAL	SCT 795
BUS FREQUENCY			
SCT 795	M - F		4:35A
METROLINK 200	M - F	4:52A	
METROLINK 202	M - F	5:46A	
SCT 795	M - F		5:53A
METROLINK 204	M - F	6:16A	
METROLINK 206	M - F	6:47A	
SCT 795	M - F		9:35A
SCT 795	M - F		10:35A
SCT 795	M - F		12:35P
SCT 795	M - F		2:35P
NORTHBOUND FROM LOS ANGELES TO LANCASTER			
SCT 795	M - F		8:15A
SCT 795	M - F		9:15A
SCT 795	M - F		10:30A
SCT 795	M - F		12:30P
SCT 795	M - F		3:30P
METROLINK 207	M - F	L5:11P	
SCT 795	M - F		6:10P
METROLINK 211	M - F	L6:23P	
METROLINK 213	M - F	L6:59P	
SCT 795	M - F		7:50P
METROLINK 217	M - F	L9:51P	

L: Regular stop to discharge or pick up passengers except train may leave ahead of schedule

Vincent Hill Restaurant & Saloon

Palmdale

Blackbird Airpark

The Palmdale Metrolink Station was one of the "3-day Miracles" that Metrolink constructed after the January 17, 1994 Northridge Earthquake. This station was located directly adjacent to the Palmdale International Airport on land provided by the Lockheed Advanced Development Company. This temporary facility was forced to close in June 1994 due to safety considerations relating to pedestrian access design issues. To compensate for this closure, the City of Palmdale contributed significantly to passenger amenity upgrades at the nearby Acton/Vincent Grade Metrolink Station.

Some of the points of interest within the Palmdale area may not be accessible by local fixed-route public transit. However, the Antelope Valley Transit Authority (AVTA) offers a fully-accessible dial-a-ride service which covers much of the Palmdale area.

For access to the AVTA bus system it is suggested that you use the Lancaster Metrolink Station. The Palmdale vicinity map provides the routes for the AVTA lines in Palmdale. For schedule and route updates for AVTA call (805) 945-9445.

A rental car is another option for getting around the Antelope Valley.

Points of Interest

The city of Palmdale was established in 1886, when nearly 60 families of Swiss and German descent arrived in the Antelope Valley. Journeying westward from Nebraska, these immigrants initially mistook the Joshua trees for a palm. Hence, the city's first name, Palmenthal.

The original settlement of Palmenthal was located three miles southeast from the current civic center. The new settlers faced many challenges in their attempts to farm in this arid climate. Questions of land title led to further complications, resulting in departure of most of the original families by 1899. Today nothing but the cemetery on 20th Street East is left as evidence of Palmenthal. The new town of Palmdale, created by the Southern Pacific Company, came into existence in 1899.

Today Palmdale is home to more than 110,000 residents. One of the city's best known points of interest is the USAF Plant 42 where the B-1 and B-2 bombers and the space shuttle are built. The Lockheed Advanced Development Company also maintains a large facility here.

Nearly 80 percent of Palmdale's workforce commutes out of the valley for employment reasons. In addition to morning and evening Metrolink trains, AVTA provides a growing number of peak-hour commuter-express trips linking the Antelope Valley with points in the Los Angeles basin.

Blackbird Airpark

The Blackbird Airpark is located at the intersection of Avenue P and 25th Street East. There is no public transit access to the park. On display are examples of Lockheed's A-12 and SR-71A aircraft. The A-12 was the first Blackbird built and the first to fly completing its maiden flight on April 26, 1962. It was used as a flight test vehicle throughout its career and never flew an operational mission. The SR-71A was delivered to the Strategic Air Command in 1968 and performed operational missions with the 9th Strategic Reconnaissance Wing at Beale AFB, California, until 1987, when it was retired due to structural over-stress.

There is a small gift shop and information center housed in a trailer in the park. A staff of volunteers from the Air Force Flight Test Center Museum man the visitor information center. The park is open 10:00 A.M. to 5:00 P.M. Friday thru Sundays. Admission is free.

Antelope Valley Indian Museum

Antelope Valley Mall

The Antelope Valley Mall, the area's premier retail center is located at 1233 West Avenue P near the intersection of Avenue P and 10th Street West. The mall can be reached by the AVTA Red, Green and Orange lines. The adult one-way fare is seventy-five cents, and convenient transfers may be made at this location.

Antelope Valley Indian Museum

The Antelope Valley Indian Museum (Avenue M, between 150th and 170th streets) is located in the northeast corner of Los Angeles County, approximately 17 miles east of the Antelope Valley Freeway. There is no fixed-route public transit service to the museum. However, the AVTA offers a fully-accessible dial-a-ride service which will take you to the museum. Call AVTA at (805) 945-9445 for further information.

Noted local artist Howard Arden Edwards developed his homesteaded 160 acres of Antelope Valley land in 1928. Edwards and his family built their dream home on the site. A Swiss chalet is nestled between large granite boulders which form an integral part of the structure. You actually climb upon these rocks as you travel from the Kachina Hall to the California Hall which Edwards designed to house his vast collection of prehistoric and historic Native American artifacts.

Following Edward's departure from the Antelope Valley in the late 1930's, the home was sold to Grace Oliver. Oliver added her own collection of Native American artifacts and operated the facility as the Antelope Valley Indian Museum from the early 1940's thru the 1970's. In 1979 the State of California purchased the museum and in the 1980's the State Parks designated it as one of its regional museums.

Today, the museum's collection emphasize the Southwestern, California and Great Basin Native Americans.

The museum is open every weekend 11:00 A.M. to 3:00 P.M. October thru June. Admission is $2.00 for adults, $1.00 children 6 - 12 years of age. Guided tours are available Tuesdays and Thursdays only, by appointment. For information call (805) 942-0662.

Places to Stay

Ramada Inn

The Ramada Inn is located at 300 West Palmdale Blvd. The AVTA Orange line serves the hotel. The hotel phone number is (805) 273-1200. For reservations call (800) 228-2828.

Holiday Inn

The Holiday Inn is located at 38630 Fifth St. West. The AVTA Orange line serves the hotel. The hotel phone number is (805) 947-8055. For reservations call (800) HOLIDAY.

Super 8 Motel

The Super 8 Motel is located at 200 West Palmdale Blvd. The AVTA Orange line serves the hotel. The hotel phone number is (805) 273-8000. For reservations call (800) 800-8000.

E - Z 8 Motel

The E-Z 8 Motel is located at 430 West Palmdale Blvd. The AVTA Orange Line serves the hotel. The hotel phone number is (805) 273-6400. For reservations call (800) 32-MOTEL.

Kachina Hall at the Antelope Valley Indian Museum

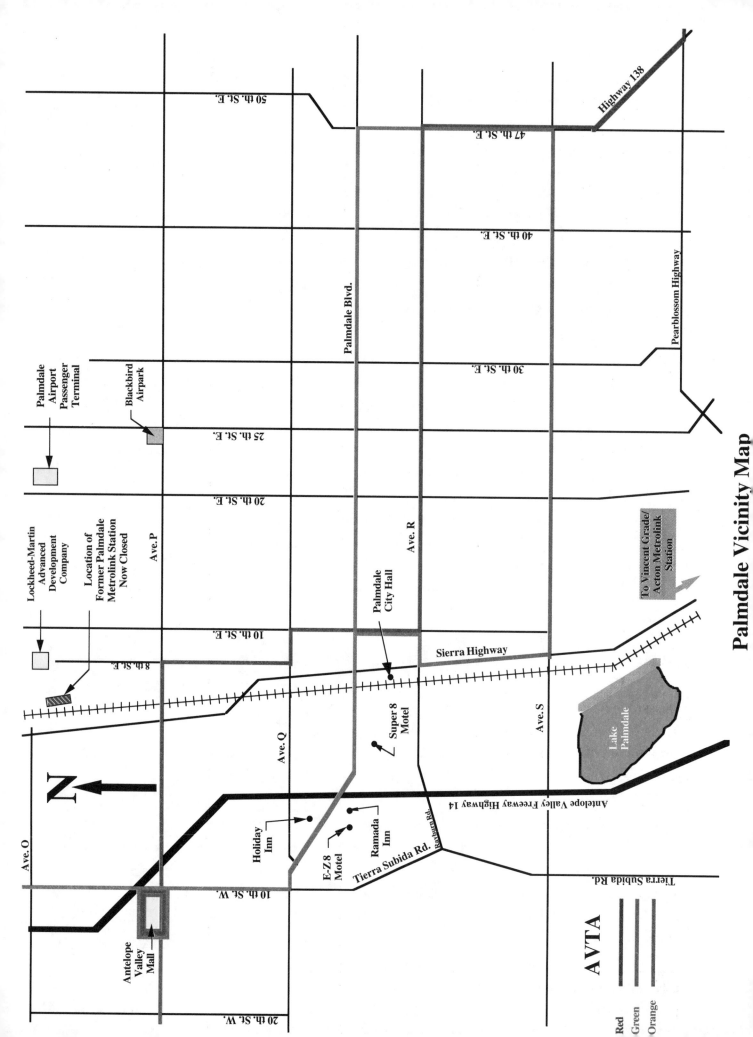

Palmdale Vicinity Map

Lancaster Station

Station Connecting Transit Information

The Lancaster Metrolink Station is located at 44812 North Sierra Highway. The station can be reached by taking the Avenue I exit from the Antelope Valley Freeway (Highway 14). Head east on Avenue I to Sierra Highway. Turn right on Sierra Highway. Just past Lancaster Boulevard the station will be on your left. The station has a 500-car parking lot which is well lighted. There is a new station building which has indoor restrooms for Metrolink riders. The train boarding platform is well lighted and has excellent shelter. A Metrolink ambassador is on duty during the morning and evening rush hours.

The Lancaster Metrolink Station is served by the Antelope Valley Transit Authority (AVTA) Blue Line. The nearest stop for this line is located on Lancaster Boulevard between the tracks and Sierra Highway. The AVTA Green Line also stops nearby, at the intersection of Lancaster Boulevard and Division Street. This stop is a short two-block walk from the Lancaster Metrolink Station. The station vicinity map provides the routes for bus transit options from the Lancaster Metrolink

Lancaster Metrolink Station

Station. The following table provides the schedule of bus connections with Metrolink. For schedule and route updates call AVTA at (805) 945-9445.

AVTA operates eight local routes throughout the Antelope Valley. Its service area stretches from Lancaster to Acton, and from Lake Hughes to eastern

Palmdale.

Metrolink train service to the Antelope Valley is supplemented each weekday by Santa Clarita Transit's Line 795. This line provides six round trips from the Lancaster Metrolink Station to the Santa Clarita Metrolink Station, where convenient connections

LANCASTER STATION BUS CONNECTIONS
SOUTHBOUND TRAINS FROM LANCASTER TO LOS ANGELES

TRAIN NUMBER	DAYS OF OPERATION	TRAIN ARRIVAL	AVTA BLUE WESTBOUND	AVTA BLUE EASTBOUND	AVTA GREEN SOUTHBOUND	AVTA GREEN NORTHBOUND
BUS FREQUENCY			HOURLY	HOURLY	HOURLY	HOURLY
METROLINK 200	M - F	4:37A				
METROLINK 202	M - F	5:31A				
METROLINK 204	M - F	6:01A			5:58A	
METROLINK 206	M - F	6:32A	6:17A	5:56A	6:08A	
SCT 795 BUS	M - F	2:04P	1:56P	1:17P		1:40P
SCT 795 BUS	M - F	8:04P	7:56P	7:17P		7:51P

NORTHBOUND TRAINS FROM LOS ANGELES TO LANCASTER

SCT 795 BUS	M - F	8:46A	9:24A	8:56A	8:58A	
SCT 795 BUS	M - F	9:46A	10:24A	9:56A	10:08A	
METROLINK 207	M - F	5:29P	6:24P	5:56P		5:40P
SCT 795 BUS	M - F	6:41P	7:24P	6:56P		6:51P
METROLINK 211	M - F	6:41P	7:24P	6:56P		6:51P
METROLINK 213	M - F	7:19P	7:24P	7:56P		7:40P
SCT 795 BUS	M - F	8:21P				
METROLINK 217	M - F	10:10P				

Antelope Valley Fairgrounds

to/from Los Angeles may be made. The one-way adult fare is $3.00. For information on schedules call Santa Clarita Transit at (805) 294-1287.

Visitors to the Antelope Valley may wish to secure a rental car, as many of the local points of interest (e.g., Edwards Air Force Base, the California Poppy Preserve, Blackbird Airpark and the Antelope Valley Indian Museum) are not accessible by public transportation.

Another option would be to arrange a guided tour with one of the local tour operators such as Viola Tours. Voila Tours can be reached at (805) 943-2301.

Points of Interest

The city of Lancaster is located at the northern most terminus of the Santa Clarita Line in the Antelope Valley. The city, along with its neighbor to the south, Palmdale, shares the Antelope Valley with Edwards Air Force Base. The base is famous for being the home of the Air Force's Flight Test Center, NASA Dryden Flight Research Center, and the Space Shuttle Orbiter landing site.

Within the city limits, points of interest include the Lancaster Museum and Art Gallery, Western Hotel Museum, Aerospace Walk of Fame, Antelope Valley Fairgrounds, the Lancaster Performing Arts Center and Antelope Valley College. Downtown Lancaster is located along Lancaster Boulevard west of the Metrolink station.

The Lancaster Museum and Art Gallery, Western Hotel Museum, Performing Arts Center and City Hall are all located within a few blocks of the Metrolink station.

Approximately 15 miles west of the city is the California Poppy Reserve which includes more than two square

miles of land set aside for the preservation of the California Poppy-the state flower. The city celebrates the blooming of this colorful flower with the California Poppy Festival held in mid-April each year.

Western Hotel Museum

The Western Hotel Museum is located at 557 W. Lancaster Boulevard about two blocks west of the Metrolink station. The hotel was built in 1888, and was initially known as the Antelope Valley Hotel with Louis Von Rockabrand as proprietor. The hotel changed hands and named the Gillwyn Hotel in 1891. Around 1900 the name was changed to the Western Hotel. In 1908 George Webber purchased the property from the Los Angeles Brewing Company. Around 1912/13 George transferred title to the property to his wife Myrtie who lived on the property until old age forced her to a convalescent hospital in 1971. Myrtie died in 1978 at the age of 110. In 1989 the city of Lancaster took possession of the property after years of effort by local school students and the Western Hotel Historical Society to save the hotel from destruction. The hotel has on display

Western Hotel Museum

numerous artifacts tracing the history of the Antelope Valley. The hotel museum has several small rooms outfitted with displays tracing the life of the native Americans who lived in the Antelope Valley and artifacts from the early pioneers who settled in the Antelope valley in the late 1800's. The museum is open Friday thru Sunday 12:00 Noon to 4:00 PM daily. Admission is free.

Antelope Valley Fair

The Antelope Valley Fairgrounds are located at 155 East Avenue I. The Antelope Valley Fair is held during late

Fields at the Poppy Preserve

August thru early September each year. During the rest of the year special events and exhibits are held at the fairgrounds.

The fairgrounds can be reached by taking the AVTA Blue line to Division Street from Metrolink and transferring to the northbound AVTA Green Line. One can also walk from Metrolink east on Lancaster Boulevard to Division Street. From there take the Green Line. Admission to the Antelope Valley Fair is $5.00 for adults, $3.00 for juniors 6 thru 12 and senior citizens. For information call (805) 948-6060 .

California Poppy Reserve

The California Poppy Reserve is located 15 miles west of Lancaster and is normally accessible only by private car. To reach the reserve, take Avenue I west until it becomes Lancaster Road. Follow the signs directing you to the reserve. The reserve has a visitors center which serves as the wildflower interpretative center and hosts a museum dedicated to the memory of the late preservationist and artist Jane Pinheiro. The Poppy Reserve is open 9:00 A.M. to 4:00 P.M. during "Poppy Season." Admission is $5.00 per vehicle. For information on the Reserve call (805) 942-0662.

Lancaster Museum and Art Gallery

The Lancaster Museum and Art Gallery is located on Sierra Highway directly across from the Metrolink station. The museum features

constantly changing traveling exhibits. The museum closes between exhibits so you need to call them at (805) 723-6250

to verify hours and obtain information about current exhibits. The museum is open Tuesday thru Saturday 11:00 A.M. to 4:00 P.M., and 1:00 P.M. to 4:00 P.M. Sunday.

The Lancaster Performing Arts Center

The Lancaster Performing Arts Center is located at 750 West Lancaster Boulevard between Fig and Fern avenues about five blocks west of the Metrolink station. The center features a wide variety of live productions which include both stage plays and music concerts of all types. For information on current productions call (805) 723-5950.

Antelope Valley College

The Antelope Valley College is located at 3041 W. Avenue K. From the Metrolink station take the AVTA Blue Line to the Avenue K and 30th Street stop. The college is a two year community college offering Associate of Arts Degrees in a wide range of majors. The college features an art gallery with

Lancaster's Poppy Festival

new shows monthly including nationally recognized artists as well as student artists. For information call (805) 942-3241.

California Poppy Festival

The California Poppy Festival is held in mid-April of each year in the Lancaster City Park. The festival is a combination crafts fair and music festival. For the most adventurous, hot air balloon and helicopter rides beckon. Free bus rides leave about every 10 minutes to take you on a one and one-half hour tour of the California Poppy Reserve.

There are numerous stages placed at various locations around the festival grounds that feature Mexican, Country Western and Rock and Roll Music. A wide variety of food is served in each of two food courts which also have music stages. The festival offers two days of family fun without the alcohol. For information call (805) 723-6077.

Lancaster Factory Stores

The Lancaster Factory stores are located just off the Antelope Valley Freeway (Highway 14) on Lancaster Boulevard. Among the stores located there are factory outlets representing Levi's, Bugle Boy, Carole Little, Bass, Van Heusen and L.A. Gear, just to name a few. The outlet center can be reached from the Metrolink station by taking the AVTA Green Line to the Lancaster Boulevard and Valley Central Way stop.

Places to Stay
Antelope Valley Inn
Best Western

The Antelope Valley Inn is located at 44055 N. Sierra Highway. The hotel provides free shuttle service to/from the Lancaster Metrolink Station. Call the hotel on (805) 948-4651 and give your arrival time and they will send the van to meet you at Metrolink. For reservations call (800) 528-1234.

Desert Inn

The Desert Inn is located at 44219 N. Sierra Highway. The hotel provides free shuttle service to/from the Lancaster Metrolink Station. Call the hotel on (805) 948-8401 and give your arrival time and they will send the van to meet you at Metrolink.

E-Z 8 Motel

The E-Z 8 Motel is located at 43530 N. 17th Street W. The motel phone number is (805) 945-9477. For reservations call (800) 326-6835.

Motel 6

The Motel 6 is located at 43540 N. 17th Street W. The motel phone number is (805) 948-0435.

Rio Mirada Inn

The Rio Mirada Inn is located at 1651 W. Avenue K. The hotel phone number is (805) 949-3423. For reservations call (800) 522-3050.

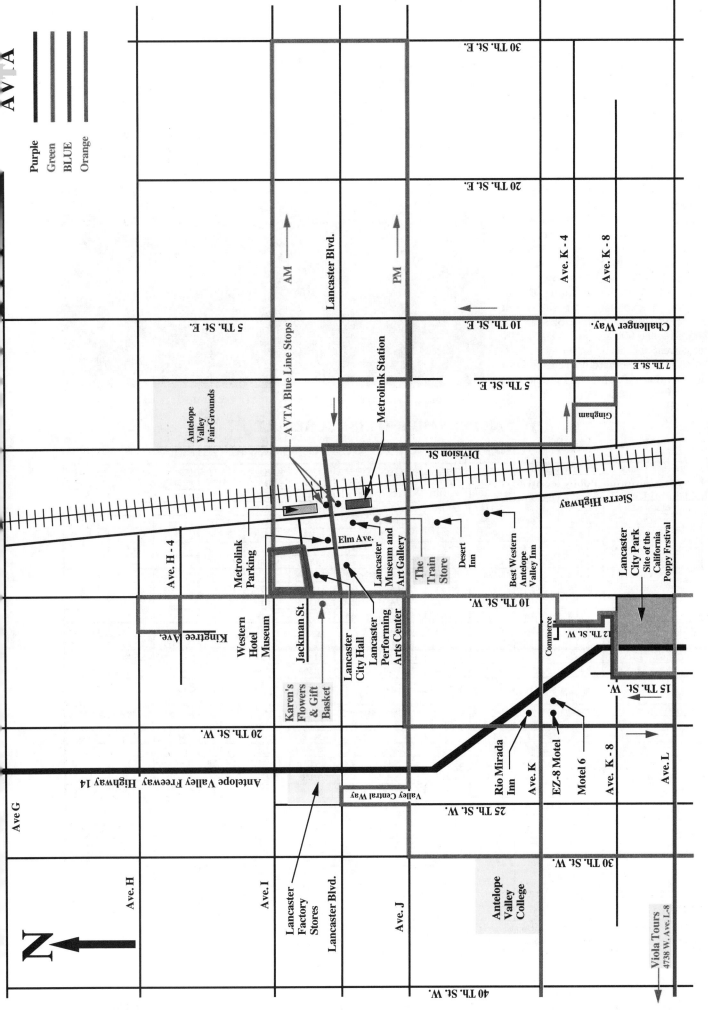

Lancaster Station Vicinity Map

San Bernardino Line

The San Bernardino Line has 13 stations located at L.A. Union Station, California State University Los Angeles (Cal State L.A.), El Monte, Baldwin Park, Covina, Pomona, Claremont, Montclair, Upland, Rancho Cucamonga, Fontana, Rialto and San Bernardino. Metrolink operates 12 trains in each direction Monday thru Friday. The schedules below indicate the times and number of trains traveling in each direction on the San Bernardino Line at the time of publication. Due to the rapid expansion of Metrolink service, please call from 213, 310, 714, 805, 818, and 909 area codes 808-LINK for current updates to the schedule.

The San Bernardino Line follows the Southern Pacific alignment east from Union Station out to the county

Metrolink Train traveling in the center of the San Bernardino Freeway

SAN BERNARDINO LINE SCHEDULE

WESTBOUND FROM SAN BERNARDINO TO LOS ANGELES

TRAIN NUMBER	METROLINK 301	METROLINK 303	METROLINK 305	METROLINK 307	METROLINK 309	METROLINK 311	METROLINK 313	METROLINK 315	METROLINK 317	METROLINK 319	METROLINK 321	METROLINK 323
DAYS OF OPERATION	M - F	M - F	M - F	M - F	M - F	M - F	M - F	M - F	M - F	M - F	M - F	M - F
SAN BERNARDINO	4:22A	5:11A	5:47A	6:17A	6:55A		10:30A	1:21P	2:35P			L6:28P
RIALTO	4:30A	5:19A	5:55A	6:25A	7:03A		10:38A	1:29P	2:43P			L6:35P
FONTANA	4:35A	5:24A	6:00A	6:30A	7:08A		10:43A	1:34P	2:48P			L7:11P
RANCHO CUCAMONGA	*4:42A	*5:32A	*6:08A	*6:38A	*7:16A	7:48A	10:51A	1:42P	L2:56P		L5:31P	
UPLAND	4:49A	5:39A	6:15A	6:45A	7:23A		10:57A	1:48P	L3:02P			L7:32P
MONTCLAIR	4:54A	5:44A	6:20A	6:50A	7:30A	7:59A	11:02A		L3:07P	L4:18P		
CLAREMONT	4:57A	5:47A	6:24A	6:53A	7:34A	8:02A	11:06A	1:57P	L3:10P		L5:44P	L7:40P
POMONA	5:01A	5:51A	6:28A	6:57A	7:37A	8:05A	11:10A	2:01P	L3:14P			
COVINA	5:11A	6:01A	6:38A	7:08A	7:47A	8:16A	11:21A	2:11P				
BALDWIN PARK	5:16A	6:06A	6:49A	7:13A	7:52A		11:26A	2:16P			L6:01P	L8:03P
EL MONTE	5:24A	6:14A	6:53A	7:21A	8:00A	L8:28A	L11:34A	2:24P	L3:39P	L4:48P	L6:09P	L8:11P
CAL STATE L.A.	L5:34A	L6:24A	L7:03A	L7:31A	L8:10A	L8:38A	L11:44A	L2:34P	L3:51P	L4:58P	L6:20P	L8:21P
L.A. UNION STATION	5:46A	6:36A	7:14A	7:45A	8:21A	8:49A	11:56A	2:49P	4:05P	5:15P	6:32P	8:33P

EASTBOUND FROM LOS ANGELES TO SAN BERNARDINO

TRAIN NUMBER	METROLINK 300	METROLINK 302	METROLINK 304	METROLINK 306	METROLINK 308	METROLINK 310	METROLINK 312	METROLINK 314	METROLINK 316	METROLINK 318	METROLINK 320	METROLINK 322
DAYS OF OPERATION	M - F	M - F	M - F	M - F	M - F	M - F	M - F	M - F	M - F	M - F	M - F	M - F
L.A. UNION STATION	6:18A	8:54A	11:13A	1:02P	3:20P	4:20P	4:51P	5:23P	5:51P	6:42P	7:23P	8:45P
CAL STATE L.A.	L6:33A	L9:04A	L11:23A	L1:12P	L3:29P	L4:30P	L5:01P	L5:32P	L6:00P	L6:52P	L7:33P	L8:55P
EL MONTE	L6:51A	L9:14A	11:34A	1:21P	L3:38P	L4:40P	5:11P	5:42P	6:10P	7:02P	7:43P	9:05P
BALDWIN PARK	L6:59A	9:24A	11:44A	1:30P	3:48P	L4:50P	5:21P	5:52P	6:21P	7:11P	7:52P	9:14P
COVINA		9:29A	11:49A	1:35P	3:53P	L4:56P	L5:27P	5:58P	6:27P	7:16P	7:57P	9:19P
POMONA	L7:21A	9:40A	12:00P	1:45P	L4:03P	L5:06P	L5:38P	6:10P	6:38P	7:26P	8:08P	9:29P
CLAREMONT	L7:25A	9:44A	12:04P	1:49P	L4:06P	L5:10P	L5:42P	6:14P	6:42P	7:30P	8:12P	9:33P
MONTCLAIR		9:47A	12:07P	1:53P	4:10P	L5:14P	L5:47P	6:19P	6:47P	7:33P	8:15P	9:37P
UPLAND	L7:33A	9:52A	12:12P	1:58P		L5:19P	L5:52P	L6:24P	L6:52P	L7:40P	L8:20P	9:42P
RANCHO CUCAMONGA	7:39A	9:58A	12:18P	L2:05P		5:25P	L5:58P	L6:30P	L6:58P	L7:46P	L8:26P	L9:48P
FONTANA		L10:07A	L12:27P	2:12P			L6:07P	L6:39P	L7:07P	L7:56P	L8:36P	L9:57P
RIALTO		L10:12A	L12:32P	2:17P			L6:12P	L6:44P	L7:12P	L8:01P	L8:41P	L10:02P
SAN BERNARDINO		10:21A	12:41P	2:26P			6:22P	6:54P	7:22P	8:12P	8:53P	10:12P

L: Regular stop to discharge or pick up passengers except train may leave ahead of schedule

* Passengers at the Rancho Cucamonga Station will board these trains from the south platform (nearest the parking lot)

Metrolink Trains laid over the weekend at the San Bernardino Station

Metrolink Trains Laid Over the Weekend at the San Bernardino Metrolink Station

The San Bernardino Line was the first Metrolink line to initiate weekend service on Saturdays with the opening of the Los Angeles County Fair on September 9, 1995.

line between Pomona and Claremont. From there the line uses the alignment that was originally built by the Atchison, Topeka & Santa Fe Railroad in 1885. This rail line continues east through Cajon Pass to the desert towns of Victorville and Barstow, before running across the desert toward Arizona. Metrolink purchased the entire right-of way on the San Bernardino alignment with the exception of an approximate one-mile segment between Rancho Road and the San Bernardino depot. Metrolink has constructed on this track a passenger train flyover to avoid crossing yard tracks. The original cost of this line was $120 million which included the track, Metrolink rolling stock and capital improvements to the line. The original length of this route was 31.1 miles, running from Pomona to L.A. Union Station when the route opened on October 26, 1992. Initial service included stations at L.A. Union Station, El Monte, Covina and Pomona.

Additional stations were added at Claremont on December 7, 1992, and Montclair on February 22, 1993. The line was extended to its full 57-mile length with the opening of stations at Upland, Rialto and San Bernardino on May 17, 1993. The Baldwin Park Station opened on May 24, 1993, and the Fontana Station opened on November 20, 1993. The final two stations, Cal State LA and Rancho Cucamonga, opened on November 1, 1994.

SAN BERNARDINO LINE SATURDAY SCHEDULE

WESTBOUND FROM SAN BERNARDINO TO LOS ANGELES

TRAIN NUMBER	METROLINK 391	METROLINK 393	METROLINK 395	METROLINK 397
DAYS OF OPERATION	SATURDAY	SATURDAY	SATURDAY	SATURDAY
SAN BERNARDINO	7:23A	10:50A	2:45P	6:05P
RIALTO	7:30A	10:57A	2:52P	6:12P
FONTANA	7:35A	11:02A	2:57P	6:17P
RANCHO CUCAMONGA	7:42A	11:09A	3:04P	6:24P
UPLAND	7:49A	11:16A	3:11P	6:31P
MONTCLAIR	7:54A	11:21A	3:16P	6:36P
CLAREMONT	7:58A	11:25A	3:20P	6:40P
POMONA	8:02A	11:29A	3:24P	6:44P
COVINA	8:12A	11:39A	3:34P	6:54P
BALDWIN PARK	8:17A	11:44A	3:39P	6:59P
EL MONTE	8:25A	11:52A	3:47P	7:07P
CAL STATE L.A.	L8:35A	L12:02P	L3:57P	L7:17P
L.A. UNION STATION	8:48A	12:15P	4:10P	7:30P

EASTBOUND FROM LOS ANGELES TO SAN BERNARDINO

TRAIN NUMBER	METROLINK 390	METROLINK 392	METROLINK 394	METROLINK 396
DAYS OF OPERATION	SATURDAY	SATURDAY	SATURDAY	SATURDAY
L.A. UNION STATION	9:10A	12:28P	4:25P	7:45P
CAL STATE L.A.	9:20A	12:38P	4:35P	7:55P
EL MONTE	9:30A	12:48P	4:45P	8:05P
BALDWIN PARK	9:39A	12:57P	4:54P	8:14P
COVINA	9:45A	1:03P	5:00P	8:20P
POMONA	9:56A	1:13P	5:11P	8:31P
CLAREMONT	10:00A	1:17P	5:15P	8:35P
MONTCLAIR	10:04A	1:22P	5:19P	8:39P
UPLAND	L10:09A	L1:27P	L5:24P	L8:44P
RANCHO CUCAMONGA	L10:15A	L1:33P	L5:30P	L8:50P
FONTANA	L10:24A	L1:42P	L5:39P	L8:59P
RIALTO	L10:29A	L1:47P	L5:44P	L9:04P
SAN BERNARDINO	10:38A	1:56P	5:53P	9:13P

L: Regular stop to discharge or pick up passengers except train may leave ahead of schedule

California State University Los Angeles Station

Station Connecting Transit Information

The California State University Los Angeles (Cal State L.A.) Metrolink Station is located at 5150 State University Drive. The station entrance is located on the campus of Cal State L.A. Metrolink has designated this station a destination station and has not provided any parking.

The station can be reached by taking the Eastern Avenue exit from the San Bernardino Freeway I-10. From the I-10 go north on Eastern to Campus Road and turn right. Continue on Campus Road to Circle Drive and turn Left. The station will be on your right adjacent to the bus turn-out. There is limited street parking on the north side of Circle Drive just past the station.

The station is below the Cal State L.A. Bus Station for the El Monte Busway. There is an elevator from the campus level to the busway station level. A second elevator will take you from the busway station level to the

California State University Los Angeles Metrolink Station

CAL STATE L.A. STATION BUS CONNECTIONS
WESTBOUND TRAINS FROM SAN BERNARDINO TO LOS ANGELES

TRAIN NUMBER	DAYS OF OPERATION	TRAIN ARRIVAL	MTA 65	MTA 170	MTA 256 NORTHBOUND	MTA 256 SOUTHBOUND	MTA 487 WESTBOUND	MTA 487 EASTBOUND	SPIRIT ROUTE 5	ACT ROUTE 1
BUS FREQUENCY			20 - 40 MIN.	HOURLY	30 - 60 MIN.	30 - 60 MIN.	20 - 60 MIN.	20 - 60 MIN.	30 MIN.	15 MIN.
METROLINK 301	M - F	L5:34A	5:40A	6:00A	6:02A	5:49A	6:05A	6:13A		5:50A
METROLINK 303	M - F	L6:24A	6:17/6:35A	7:00A	6:02/6:37A	6:19/6:45A	6:05/6:25A	6:13/6:44A	*6:30A	6:35A
METROLINK 305	M - F	L7:03A	6:47/7:15A	6:45/8:00A	6:37/7:07A	6:45/7:19A	6:55/7:12A	6:44/7:17A	6:45/*7:10A	6:45/7:05A
METROLINK 307	M - F	L7:31A	7:21/7:35A	6:45/8:00A	7:07/7:33A	7:19/7:49A	7:19/7:33A	7:17/7:53A	7:15/*7:40A	7:30/7:35A
METROLINK 309	M - F	L8:10A	7:55/8:25A	7:50/9:00A	8:05/8:38A	7:49/8:23A	7:50/8:35A	7:53/8:23A	7:45/8:15A	8:00A
METROLINK 311	M - F	L8:38A	8:35/9:10A	7:50/9:00A	8:38/9:23A	8:23/8:58A	8:35/9:05A	8:23/8:53A	8:15/8:45A	8:30A
METROLINK 313	M - F	L11:44A	11:12A/12:10P	10:46/11:59A	11:03/11:53A	11:08/11:58A	11:24A/12:24P	11:26A/12:26P	11:15/11:45A	
METROLINK 315	M - F	L2:34P	2:32/2:40P	1:49/3:00P	2:23/3:13P	2:26/3:16P	2:24/2:57P	2:30/2:57P	2:15/2:45P	3:30P
METROLINK 317	M - F	L3:51P	3:32/4:10P	3:49/4:00P	3:13/4:03P	3:16/4:01P	3:29/4:00P	3:27/3:52P	3:45/4:15P	3:40/4:00P
METROLINK 319	M - F	L4:58P	4:47/5:15P	4:50/5:00P	4:33/5:03P	4:49/5:37P	4:28/5:00P	4:57/5:15P	*4:45/*5:15P	4:55/5:00P
METROLINK 321	M - F	L6:20P	6:16/6:35P	5:50/7:00P	5:38/6:23P	5:37/6:24P	6:05/6:45P	6:13/6:33P	*6:15P	6:10P
METROLINK 323	M - F	L8:21P	8:16/8:30P	7:38P	7:52/8:47P	8:01/9:01P	8:10/9:10P	7:54/8:54P		

EASTBOUND TRAINS FROM LOS ANGELES TO SAN BERNARDINO

METROLINK 300	M - F	L6:33A	6:17/6:35A	7:00A	6:02/6:37A	6:19/6:45A	6:25/6:55A	6:13/6:44A	6:45A	6:35P
METROLINK 302	M - F	L9:04A	9:00/9:10A	8:50/10:00A	8:38/9:23A	8:58/9:30A	8:35/9:05A	8:53/9:26A	8:45/9:15A	9:00A
METROLINK 304	M - F	L11:23A	11:12/11:25A	10:46/11:59A	11:03/11:53A	11:08/11:58A	10:26/11:24A	10:26/11:26A	11:15/11:45P	
METROLINK 306	M - F	L1:12P	12:42/1:35P	12:46/2:00P	12:43/1:33P	12:48/1:38P	12:24/1:24P	12:26/1:25P	12:45/1:15P	
METROLINK 308	M - F	L3:29P	3:02/3:40P	2:49/4:00P	3:13/4:03P	3:16/4:01	2:57/4:00P	3:27/3:52P	3:15/3:45P	3:25/3:30P
METROLINK 310	M - F	L4:30P	4:22/4:40P	3:49/5:00P	4:03/4:33P	4:01/4:49P	4:28/5:00P	4:17/4:38P	4:15/*4:45P	4:25/4:45P
METROLINK 312	M - F	L5:01P	4:47/5:15P	4:50/6:00P	4:33/5:03P	4:49/5:37P	5:00/5:30P	4:57/5:15P	*4:45/*5:15P	4:55/5:15P
METROLINK 314	M - F	L5:32P	5:18/5:55P	4:50/6:00P	5:03/5:38P	4:49/5:37P	5:30/6:05P	5:15/5:33P	*5:15/*5:45P	5:25/5:45P
METROLINK 316	M - F	L6:00P	5:48/6:35P	5:50/7:00P	5:38/6:23P	5:37/6:24P	5:30/6:45P	5:53/6:13P	*5:45/*6:15P	5:55P
METROLINK 318	M - F	L6:52P	6:49/7:35P	6:46/7:00P	6:23/7:07P	6:24/7:01P	6:45/7:20P	6:33/7:08P		6:40P
METROLINK 320	M - F	L7:33P	7:26/7:35P	6:46P	7:07/7:52P	7:01/8:01P	7:20/8:10P	7:08/7:54P		6:55P
METROLINK 322	M - F	L8:55P	8:16/9:30P	7:38P	8:47/9:47P	8:01/9:01P	8:10/9:10P	8:54P		

L: Regular stop to discharge or pick up passengers except train may leave ahead of schedule

* Indicates peak hour route for Spirit Route 5.

CAL STATE L.A. STATION SATURDAY BUS CONNECTIONS
WESTBOUND TRAINS FROM SAN BERNARDINO TO LOS ANGELES

TRAIN NUMBER	DAYS OF OPERATION	TRAIN ARRIVAL	MTA 65	MTA 256 NORTHBOUND	MTA 256 SOUTHBOUND	MTA 487 WESTBOUND	MTA 487 EASTBOUND
BUS FREQUENCY			HOURLY	HOURLY	HOURLY	HOURLY	HOURLY
METROLINK 301	SATURDAY	L8:35A	7:39/9:00A	7:56/8:56A	8:09/9:09A	7:50/8:50A	8:03/9:03A
METROLINK 303	SATURDAY	L12:02P	11:45A/1:00P	11:54A/12:54P	11:12A/12:12P	11:54A/12:51P	11:59A/12:59P
METROLINK 305	SATURDAY	L3:57P	3:45/4:00P	2:57/3:57P	3:12/4:12P	3:51/4:50P	3:55/4:57P
METROLINK 307	SATURDAY	L7:17P	6:38P	6:56/7:56P	7:10/8:10P	6:47/7:47P	6:55/7:54P

EASTBOUND TRAINS FROM LOS ANGELES TO SAN BERNARDINO

METROLINK 300	SATURDAY	9:20A	8:39/10:00A	8:56/9:54A	9:09/10:12A	8:50/9:50A	9:03/10:03A
METROLINK 302	SATURDAY	12:38P	11:45A/1:00P	11:54A/12:54P	12:12/1:12P	11:54A/12:51P	11:59A/12:59P
METROLINK 304	SATURDAY	4:35P	3:45/5:00P	3:57/4:56P	4:12/5:12P	3:51/4:50P	3:55/4:57P
METROLINK 306	SATURDAY	7:55P	7:38P	6:56/7:56P	7:10/8:10P	7:47/8:47P	7:54/8:54P

L: Regular stop to discharge or pick up passengers except train may leave ahead of schedule

City of Monterey Park

Photo Courtesy of the City of Monterey Park

In addition, the MTA 483/485, 484, 487/489, 490, 491, 497, Foothill Transit 480/481, 482, 486, 488, 492, 494, 495, and 498 lines stop at the Cal State L.A. bus station. For schedule updates on MTA lines call (818) 443-1307 and for Foothill Transit lines call (800) RIDE INFO.

The communities of Alhambra, City Terrace, Monterey Park and San Gabriel are easily assessable from the Cal State L.A. Metrolink station. The station vicinity map provides the routes for the bus lines serving these communities.

The City of Monterey Park operates its own bus line called SPIRIT. SPIRIT lines provide convenient schedules within Monterey Park. The one way fare is 50 cents. MTA and Metrolink passes and transfers are accepted for fare payment. For route and schedule updates call (818) 307-1388.

The City of Alhambra operates the Alhambra Community Transit (ACT)

Metrolink platform. The train boarding platform is well lighted and has excellent shelter because it is located below the El Monte Busway.

The station is served by the MTA 65, 170, and 256, the Alhambra Community Transit (ACT) Route 1, the Monterey Park SPIRIT Route 5 and the Children's Court Shuttle. The bus stops for these lines are located at the campus level along the bus turnout on Circle Drive. The preceding tables provide the schedule for connections between these bus lines including the MTA 487 line and Metrolink.

which provides fixed route local bus service from the Cal State L.A. Metrolink Station and within the city. One way fares are 25 cents. For route and schedule updates call (818) 289-1220.

The Children's Court Shuttle provides transportation Monday thru Friday between the Metrolink station, Los Angeles County Children's Court, Los Angeles County Sheriff's Headquarters and other related county offices in the local area. Shuttle Loop 1 operates on 7-minute intervals 6:30 A.M. to 9:28 A.M. and 3:53 P.M. to 5:56 P.M. Shuttle Loop 3 operates on 30 minute intervals (:39, :09) 9:33 A.M. to 6:18 P.M.

Points of Interest

All of the communities surrounding the Cal State L.A. Station were a part of the Mission San Gabriel de Archangel after the founding of the mission in 1771 by Fathers Pedro Cambon and Angel Somera. Prior to that the area was inhabited by Shoshone Indians who were renamed Gabrielinos after the mission.

Monterey Park got its beginnings when Richard Garvey, a mail rider for

Sreet Scene at Alhambra Chinese New Year Festival

the U.S. Army, settled down in the area. Garvey began developing land by bringing in spring water from near the Hondo River. He constructed a 54-foot high dam to form Garvey lake which is still Monterey Park's primary source of water today. In the 1920's, a real estate developer named Peter Snyder developed Midwick View Estates, a residential subdivision near the Midwick Country Club. Hoping to rival posh developments such as Beverly Hills and Bel-Air, Snyder built a lavish 240-foot waterfall which he

called *The Cascades* at the entrance to the tract on El Portal Place, just off Atlantic Boulevard. The city renamed this landmark *Heritage Falls* in 1991.

Today the majority population of the cities of Alhambra and Monterey Park are of Asian decent. The signs along the thoroughfares in these communities sport both English and Chinese writing. Some of the best Chinese and Asian restaurants in Southern California are located here. Many Chinese restaurants feature authentic Hong Kong style fare and many famous Hong Kong restaurants have established outlets in the community.

The communities of Alhambra, Monterey Park and San Gabriel each hold an annual Chinese New Year celebration and parade. Monterey Park's festivities feature the Flower Market Festival and Food Fair which is held on Garvey Avenue between Ramona Street and Garfield Avenue. The festivities are capped by a Chinese New Year Parade on Garvey Avenue between Atlantic Boulevard and the Ramona Street entrance to the Flower Market Festival. Monterey Park's celebration was held on the last weekend in January in 1995. For information call the Chamber of Commerce on (818) 280-3864.

Alhambra and San Gabriel combine their festivities and hold a Street Festival along Valley Boulevard between Atlantic Boulevard and Garfield Avenue. The Chinese New Year Parade route extends along Valley Boulevard from Del Mar Avenue in San Gabriel to the Garfield Avenue entrance to the Street Festival. The Alhambra and San Gabriel celebration was held on the first weekend in February 1995. For information call the Alhambra Chamber

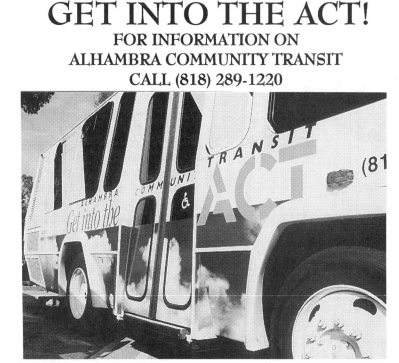

METROLINK

Statue of Confucius on the Cal State L.A. Campus

of Commerce on (818) 282-8481.

The downtown district in the city of San Gabriel is still dominated by the San Gabriel Mission. The architecture of the buildings surrounding the mission in the downtown district are of a California-mission style. There are several restaurants, a Fine Art Gallery, many boutiques, antique stores and the San Gabriel Civic Auditorium. Downtown San Gabriel can be reached by taking eastbound MTA 487 bus line at the Cal State L.A. Busway Station on the El Monte Busway. The Ramona Street and Mission Drive Stop is adjacent to the San Gabriel Mission. The downtown district of San Gabriel extends north along Ramona Street from Mission Drive.

California State University Los Angeles

The university was founded in 1947 by action of the California State Legislature. From 1947 to 1958 Cal State L.A. was situated on the Los Angeles City College campus. In 1958 ten new buildings on the present campus site were occupied by the student and faculty. Today the university has a student body of 18,000. For general campus information call (213) 343-3000.

The Fine Arts Gallery on campus generally organizes three professionally curated exhibitions each year. In addition, there is an annual student show, biannual faculty exhibits and graduate thesis exhibitions. Exhibition hours are Noon to 5:00 P.M. Monday thru Thursday during school quarters (Fall, Winter and Spring). For further information call (213) 343-4010.

The Music Department produces 130 concerts and recitals per year. Fifteen of these are Faculty Artist Recitals and the remainder are student performances. For information call (213) 343-4060.The Theatre Arts and Dance Department presents an average of 12 student productions per year. For information about current productions call (213) 343-4118.

The Harriet & Charles Luckman Fine Arts Complex features a performing arts theater and fine arts gallery. Numerous professional stage and music productions are held each year. For information call (213) 466-1767.

East Los Angeles College

East Los Angeles College is located at 1301 Avenida Cesar Chavez in Monterey Park. To reach the college from the Cal State L.A. Metrolink Station take the Spirit Route 5 to the stops along Floral Drive between Hillside Street and Atlantic Boulevard. The college is a two-year junior college founded in 1945 by the Los Angeles City Board of Education. The college opened for classes on the campus of Garfield High School with an enrollment of 380 students. The college moved to its present 82-acre site in 1948. Today the college enrolls approximately 14,000 students from the surrounding communities. The college offers an Associates of Arts Degree in a variety of disciplines. For general information call (213) 265-8650.

The Harriet & Charles Luckman Fine Arts Complex

San Gabriel Civic Auditorium

Monterey Park Historical Museum

The Monterey Park Historical Museum is located in Garvey Ranch Park at 781 South Orange Avenue in Monterey Park. To reach the museum from Metrolink take the Monterey Park Spirit Route 5 bus to the Atlantic Boulevard and Riggin Avenue stop. Transfer to the SPIRIT Route 1 bus which will take you to the Monterey Park City Hall. Spirit Route 1 will become Spirit Route 3 at city hall and you can take it without transferring to the Garvey Park stop at Orange and Graves avenues. The museum is housed in the Garvey Ranch House and has artifacts on display from the early 1900's. The museum is open each Saturday and Sunday from 2:00 P.M. to 4:00 P.M. For Information call (818) 281-9994.

San Gabriel Civic Auditorium

The San Gabriel Civic Auditorium is located at 320 South Mission Drive. From Metrolink take the MTA 487 line. The auditorium features productions by The Music Theatre of Southern California and the Pasadena Dance theatre. For information on productions call (800) 474-2484.

San Gabriel Fine Arts Gallery

The San Gabriel Fine Arts Gallery is located at 343 South Mission Drive. From Metrolink take the MTA 487 line. Gallery exhibits change monthly. The Gallery is open Noon to 4:00 P.M. Tuesday thru Saturday. For information call (818) 282-1448.

San Gabriel Mission

San Gabriel Mission

The San Gabriel Mission is located at 537 West Mission Drive. From Metrolink take the MTA 487 line. The mission complex today includes the mission church built between 1791 and 1805. It is the oldest structure of its kind south of Monterey. Architecturally, it is unique among the California Missions with a Moorish influence expressed by the fortress-like appearance and vaulted roof. The gardens and cemetery which were first consecrated in 1778 is the oldest cemetery in Los Angeles County. There are over 6,000 Gabrielino Indians buried in the mission cemetery. The museum building, completed in 1812, originally served as the sleeping quarters of the mission fathers and a series of work rooms and storage areas.

The mission grounds are open 9:30 A.M. to 4:14 P.M. daily. The mission is closed Easter, Thanksgiving and Christmas. Admission is $3.00 for adults and $1.00 for children. Call (818) 282-5191 Ext. 52 for information.

Places to Stay

Best Western Alhambra Inn

The Best Western Alhambra Inn is located at 2451 W. Main Street. The hotel has van which will pick you up at the Metrolink station. The hotel phone number is (818) 284-5522. For reservations call (800) 528-1234.

Lincoln Plaza Hotel Monterey Park

The Lincoln Plaza Hotel is located at 123 S. Lincoln Avenue. The hotel phone number is (818) 579-2707.For reservations call (800) 423-2668.

Quality Inn Alhambra

The Quality Inn Alhambra is located at 2221 W. Commonwealth Avenue. The hotel phone number is (818) 300-0003. For reservations call (800) 221-2222.

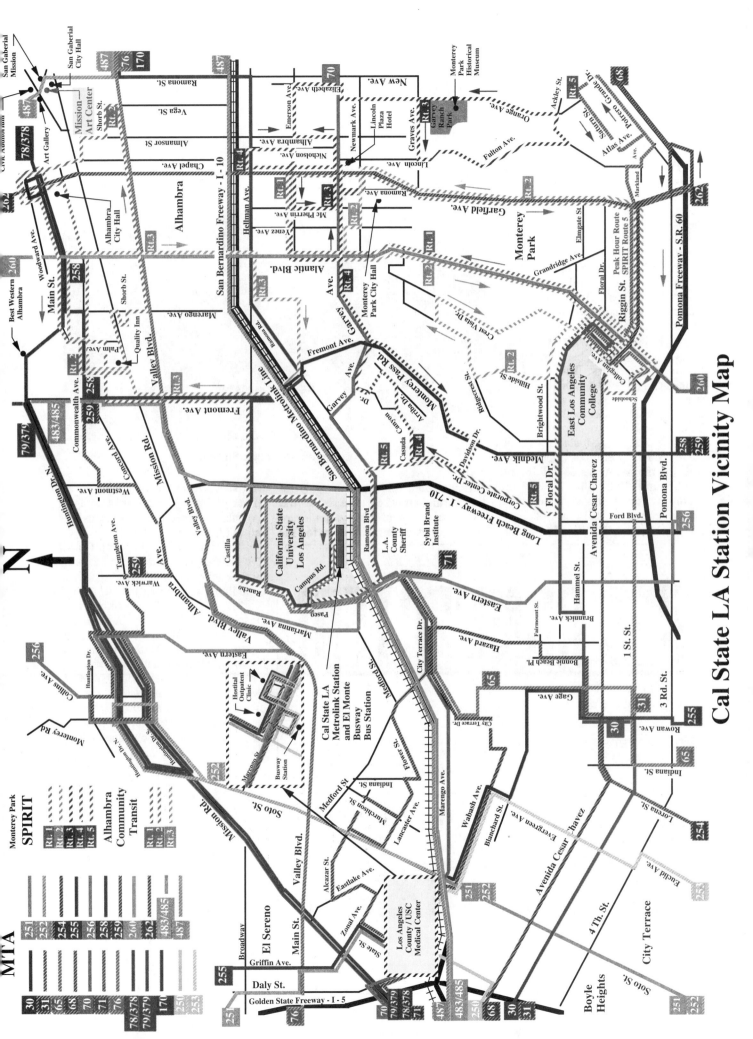

Cal State LA Station Vicinity Map

El Monte Station

Station Connecting Transit Information

The El Monte Metrolink Station is located at 10925 Railroad Street. The station can be reached by taking the Valley Boulevard exit from the I-10 Freeway. Go west on Valley to Tyler Avenue and turn right. Go one block to Railroad Avenue. The station will be on your left. The station has a 316-car parking lot that is well lighted and maintained. The train boarding platform is well lighted with limited shelter. Metrolink Security and El Monte Police Department personnel man the station during the morning and evening rush hours. The station is unmanned midday when the flex trains arrive.

The station is served by the MTA 76 and 268 bus lines, Foothill Transit 721 Fastrax line, El Monte Trolley and the El Monte Metrolink Shuttle. The stop for the MTA eastbound 76 and southbound 268 lines is at the southwest corner of Valley Boulevard and Tyler Avenue on Tyler. Both lines go directly to the El Monte Bus

El Monte Metrolink Station

Terminal from this stop. The stop for the northbound 268 line is at the northeast corner of Valley Boulevard and Tyler Avenue. The stop for the

westbound 76 line is on the northwest corner of Valley Boulevard and Tyler Avenue. For schedule and route updates call MTA on (818) 443-1307.

The stop for the Foothill Transit 721 Fastrax is in the station parking lot. For schedule and route updates call Foothill Transit on (800) RIDE INFO.

The El Monte Bus Terminal is at the eastern terminus of the busway from downtown Los Angeles, built along the center divider of the San Bernardino Freeway. This bus station is served by both Foothill Transit and the MTA. Every bus line that operates in the City of El Monte has a stop at this bus station except the El Monte Trolley. In addition, Greyhound operates a long-haul bus terminal at this location.

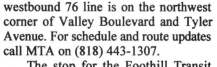

The El Monte Trolley is a local bus system that uses street trolleys. The Trolley Station is on Center Avenue and Valley Boulevard directly across the street from the Metrolink Station. Presently, the trolley does not provide free transfers from Metrolink. The fare is 25 cents per boarding. There are five different routes. The trolleys operate Monday thru Friday between 5:54 A.M. and 7:30 P.M. and on Saturday between 9:40 A.M. and 6:20 P.M. Departures from the El Monte Trolley Station are on 40-minute centers. For further information call the El Monte Trolley at (818) 443-7384.

El Monte also operates the El Monte Metrolink Shuttle. Route 1 provides transportation from the Metrolink station to El Monte Civic Center. Route 2 provides transportation to Flair Business park.

The station vicinity map provides the routes for bus transit options from the El Monte Metrolink Station. The following tables provide the schedule for bus connections with Metrolink.

Points of Interest

El Monte has a long Hispanic

EL MONTE STATION WEEKDAY BUS CONNECTIONS
WESTBOUND TRAINS FROM SAN BERNARDINO TO LOS ANGELES

TRAIN NUMBER	DAYS OF OPERATION	TRAIN ARRIVAL	MTA 76 WESTBOUND 15 MINUTES	MTA 76 EASTBOUND 15 MINUTES	MTA 268 NORTHBOUND 40 MINUTES	MTA 268 SOUTHBOUND 40 MINUTES	FOOTHILL 721 COMMUTER	EL MONTE TROLLY ALL LINES HOURLY	EL MONTE METROLINK SHUTTLE ALL LINES
METROLINK 301	M - F	5:24A	5:17/5:37A		5:34A	5:58A		5:54A	5:25A
METROLINK 303	M - F	6:14A	6:06/6:20A	6:05/6:35A	5:34/6:19A	5:58/6:35A	6:19A	6:39A	6:15A
METROLINK 305	M - F	6:53A	6:51/7:03A	6:35/7:01A	6:19/6:54A	6:35/7:15A		6:30/7:19A	6:53A
METROLINK 307	M - F	7:21A	7:15/7:27A	7:01/7:27A	6:54/7:34A	7:15/8:01A	7:26A	7:15/7:55A	7:23A
METROLINK 309	M - F	8:00A	7:54/8:07A	7:49/8:03A	7:34/8:20A	7:15/8:01A		7:55/9:00A	8:00A
METROLINK 311	M - F	L8:28A	8:20/8:33A	8:18/8:32A	8:20/9:00A	8:01/8:29A	8:33A	7:55/9:00A	
METROLINK 313	M - F	L11:34A	11:30/11:45A	11:23/11:38A	11:00/11:40A	11:16/11:59A		10:56/11:40A	
METROLINK 315	M - F	2:24P	2:28/2:42P	2:22/2:37P	2:16/2:59P	1:59/2:39P		2:16/2:58P	
METROLINK 317	M - F	L3:39P	3:40/3:53P	3:31/3:46P	2:59/3:45P	3:19/4:19P		3:34/4:10P	
METROLINK 319	M - F	L4:48P	4:36/5:00P	4:43/5:00P	4:37/5:24P	4:19/4:58P		4:08/4:54P	
METROLINK 321	M - F	L6:09P	5:56/6:26P	6:02/6:19P	6:09/6:59P	5:36/6:21P		6:08/6:10P	
METROLINK 323	M - F	L8:11P	7:47/8:27P	7:51/8:14P	6:59P	7:34P		7:26P	

EASTBOUND TRAINS FROM LOS ANGELES TO SAN BERNARDINO

METROLINK 300	M - F	L6:51A	6:39/7:03A	6:35/7:01A	6:19/6:54A	6:35/7:15A		6:30/7:19A	
METROLINK 302	M - F	L9:14A	9:00/9:15A	9:12/9:27A	9:00/9:40A	8:48/9:22A		8:31/9:40A	
METROLINK 304	M - F	11:34A	11:30/11:45A	11:23A/11:38A	11:00/11:40A	11:16/11:59A		10:56/11:40A	
METROLINK 306	M - F	1:21P	1:15/1:30P	1:08/1:23P	1:00/1:40P	1:19/1:59P		12:56/1:40P	
METROLINK 308	M - F	L3:38P	3:26/3:53P	3:31/3:46P	2:59/3:45P	3:19/4:19P	3:33P	3:32/4:10P	3:36P
METROLINK 310	M - F	L4:40P	4:36/5:00P	4:29/4:43P	4:37/5:24P	4:19/4:58P	4:35P	4:08/4:54P	4:37P
METROLINK 312	M - F	5:11P	5:00/5:26P	5:00/5:12P	4:37/5:24P	4:58/5:36P		4:46/5:32P	5:09P
METROLINK 314	M - F	5:42P	5:26/5:56P	5:26/5:48P	5:24/6:09P	5:36/6:21P	5:38P	5:30/6:10P	5:39P
METROLINK 316	M - F	6:10P	5:56/6:26P	6:09/6:19P	6:09/6:59P	5:36/6:21P		6:08/6:10P	6:09P
METROLINK 318	M - F	7:02P	6:26/7:03P	7:00/7:16P	6:59P	7:00/7:34P	6:57P	6:46P	7:00P
METROLINK 320	M - F	7:43P	7:03/7:47P	7:36/7:51P		7:34P		7:26P	
METROLINK 322	M - F	9:05P	8:27/9:15P	8:44/9:17P					

L: Regular stop to discharge or pick up passengers except train may leave ahead of schedule

EL MONTE STATION SATURDAY BUS CONNECTIONS
WESTBOUND TRAINS FROM SAN BERNARDINO TO LOS ANGELES

TRAIN NUMBER	DAYS OF OPERATION	TRAIN ARRIVAL	MTA 76 WESTBOUND 20 - 30 MIN.	MTA 76 EASTBOUND 20 - 30 MIN.	MTA 268 NORTHBOUND HOURLY	MTA 268 SOUTHBOUND HOURLY	EL MONTE TROLLY ALL LINES HOURLY
METROLINK 301	SATURDAY	8:25A	8:19/8:34A	8:14/8:36A	8:19/9:19A	7:33/8:33A	9:40A
METROLINK 303	SATURDAY	11:52A	11:48A/12:03P	11:40/11:55A	11:19A/12:19P	11:35A/12:35P	11:34A/12:20P
METROLINK 305	SATURDAY	3:47P	3:40/4:00P	3:45/4:00P	3:19/4:19P	3:35/4:35P	3:34/4:20P
METROLINK 307	SATURDAY	7:07P	6:49/7:19P	6:52/7:10P	6:19/7:19P	6:30/7:34P	6:54P

EASTBOUND TRAINS FROM LOS ANGELES TO SAN BERNARDINO

METROLINK 300	SATURDAY	9:30A	9:19/9:34A	9:20/9:40A	9:19/10:19A	8:33/9:33A	9:40A
METROLINK 302	SATURDAY	12:48P	12:48/1:03P	12:43/12:58P	12:19/1:19P	12:35/1:35P	12:14/1:00P
METROLINK 304	SATURDAY	4:45P	4:42/5:04P	4:30/4:58P	4:19/5:16P	4:35/5:35P	4:14/5:00P
METROLINK 306	SATURDAY	8:05P	7:49/8:25P	7:50/8:14P	7:19P	7:34P	6:54P

L: Regular stop to discharge or pick up passengers except train may leave ahead of schedule

Queen Anne Cottage

of Rancho Santa Anita which included the original Hugo Reid homestead in 1875. Baldwin lived on the ranch until his death in 1909. On the banks of Lake Baldwin, near the Hugo Reid Adobe, is the Queen Anne Cottage which Baldwin built for his fourth wife, 16-year old Lillie Bennett, as a honeymoon gift in early 1885. The house was never lived in by the owners as Lillie and Baldwin separated in late 1885. Baldwin converted the cottage to a memorial to his third wife, Jennie Dexter, who had died in 1881. The cottage was used as a guest house and for entertaining guests to the rancho. It is familiar to many people around the world as it has been used for many motion pictures and for the opening scenes of the long running television show *Fantasy Island*.

Behind the Hugo Reid Adobe is the old Santa Anita Railroad Station that was built about 1890 on the Santa Fe main line through the city. The station is open Tuesdays and Wednesdays from 10:00 A.M. to 4:00 P.M., and on the first Sunday of each month from 1:00 P.M. to 4:00 P.M.

The arboretum is open 9:00 A.M. to 5:00 P.M. daily except, Christmas. Ticket sales are from 9:00 A.M. to 4:30

influence which is preserved in the atmosphere of the main shopping district. The El Monte Valley Mall is the old downtown shopping district. From Metrolink you need only walk down Center Avenue past Valley Boulevard to Valley Mall Boulevard. The street is one lane in each direction with head in parking. The sidewalks have been widened for pedestrian traffic and the street is lined with large olive trees. The overall effect is of a small town with an Hispanic flavor. The mall's success is evidenced by the volume of foot traffic and absence of empty storefronts along Valley Mall Boulevard.

The Arboretum of Los Angeles County

The Arboretum of Los Angeles County is located at 301 N. Baldwin Avenue, Arcadia. It can be reached from Metrolink by taking the northbound MTA 268 line to the arboretum stop.

The arboretum is located on a 127-acre portion of the 13,319 acre Rancho Santa Anita, granted to "Don Perfecto" Hugo Reid by Mexico in 1839. The Hugo Reid Adobe is the original house constructed by Hugo Reid in 1840 with the help of Native American laborers known as the Gabrielino Indians. They were so named because they were converted to christianity at the nearby Mission San Gabriel. These people settled in the vicinity of Lake Baldwin,

fed by freshwater springs, which provided a year round supply of water. The Indians were hunters who gathered and lived directly off the land before the arrival of the Spanish.

Elias Jackson ("Lucky") Baldwin obtained ownership of a 40-acre section

Santa Anita Park

P.M. Admission is $5.00 for adults, $3.00 for seniors over 62 and students with ID, and $1.00 for children 5 thru 12. Children 4 and under are free. For information call (818) 821-3222.

Santa Anita Park

Santa Anita Park is located at 285 West Huntington Drive in Arcadia. The track can be reached by taking the northbound MTA 268 line to the Santa Anita Fashion Park Shopping Mall stop. From there you need to walk toward Baldwin Avenue and Gate 8 which provides pedestrian access to the track. It is about 200 to 300 yards from the bus stop to the Gate 8 entrance; then about the same distance back to the entrance to the track. The entrance to the track is about 100 yards from the bus stop but there is a fence which separates the mall parking from the racetrack parking. The long walk is to discourage racetrack patrons who want to avoid the $3.00 parking fee by parking in the mall parking lot. If you want to avoid the long walk you can exit the 268 bus at the Baldwin Avenue and Huntington Drive stop and transfer to the eastbound MTA 79/379 bus which runs along Huntington Drive. The MTA 79/379 bus will take you to the MTA lot at the east end of the Santa Anita Park parking lot.

Thoroughbred horse racing began in the area when Lucky Baldwin opened the first Santa Anita race course on Thanksgiving day in 1907. Baldwin's original track operated for two years. This track closed on March 1, 1909 after Baldwin's death. The original track is the site of the Arcadia County Park.

Under the leadership of Dr. Charles H. Strub the Los Angeles Turf Club purchased part of the Baldwin land on which Santa Anita Racetrack was built. The present day track opened on December 25, 1934.

Thoroughbred racing is featured at two meetings during the year. The Oak Tree Meet is held each year October through mid-November. The regular Santa Anita meet is December 26 through late April. Racing is normally Wednesday through Sunday. There are special racing days on some Mondays and on an occasional Tuesday. For information call (818) 574-RACE.

Santa Anita Fashion Park

Santa Anita Fashion Park is located at 400 South Baldwin Avenue in Arcadia. The mall can be reached by taking the MTA 268 bus from the El Monte Metrolink Station..

Places to Stay

There are no hotels with easy access to the El Monte Metrolink Station. You can stay near Santa Anita Park where there are several good hotels along Huntington Drive. Take the MTA 268 line to Santa Anita Fashion Park stop and transfer to the MTA 79 line. Take the 79 line to the stop between First and Second avenues on Huntington Drive. There you will transfer to the Foothill Transit 187 line which will take you to the hotel district along Huntington Drive.

Some of the hotels have a courtesy van which will service customers within a five-mile radius. The El Monte Metrolink station is just under five miles from the hotel district. You may need to mention this when calling for pick-up.

Embassy Suites Hotel

The Embassy Suites Hotel is located at 211 E. Huntington Drive, Arcadia. The hotel has a van which will pick you up at the station with advance notice. The hotel phone number is (818) 445-8525. For reservations call (800) EMBASSY.

Hampton Inn Hotel

The Hampton Inn Hotel is located at 311 E. Huntington Drive, Arcadia. The hotel phone number is (818) 574-5600. For reservations call (800) HAMPTON.

Holiday Inn Monrovia

The Holiday Inn is located at 924 W. Huntington Drive, Monrovia. The hotel phone number is (818) 357-1900. For Reservations call (800) HOLIDAY.

Residence Inn by Marriott

The Residence Inn is located at 321 E. Huntington Drive, Arcadia. The hotel has a van which will pick you up at the station with advance notice. The hotel phone number is (818) 446-6500. For reservations call (800) 331-3131.

Wyndham Garden Hotel

The Wyndham Garden Hotel is located at 700 W. Huntington Drive, Monrovia. The hotel has a van which will pick you up at the station with advance notice. The hotel phone number is (818) 357-5211. For reservations call (800) 822-4200.

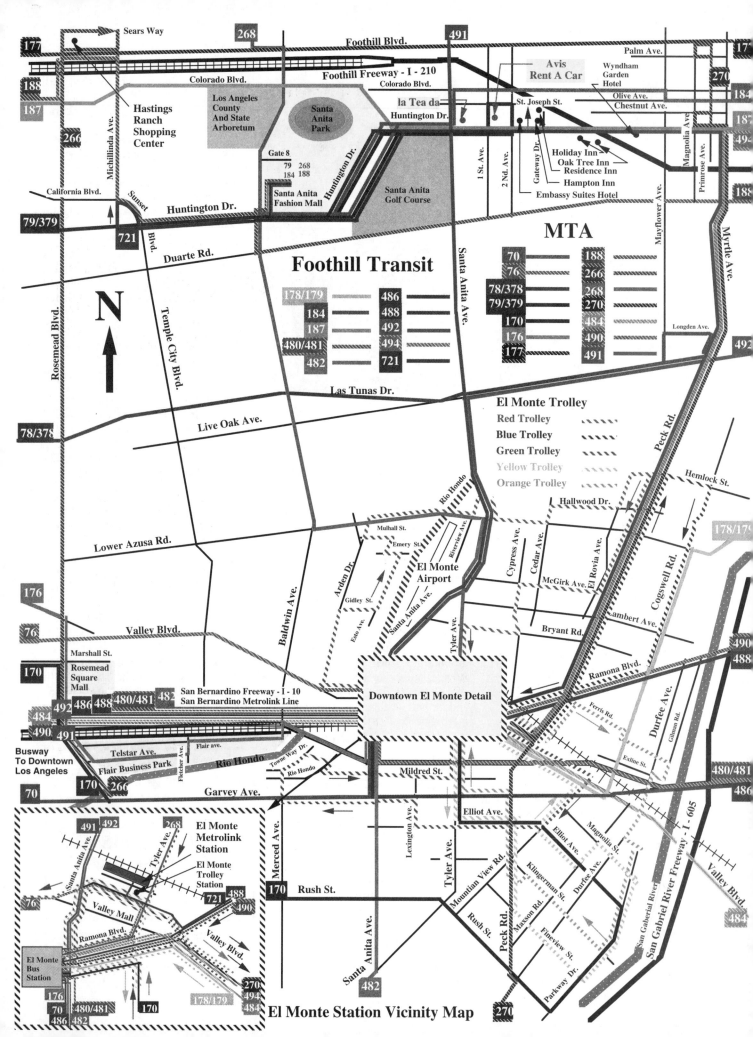

Baldwin Park Station

Station Connecting Transit Information

The Baldwin Park Metrolink Station is located at 3825 Downing Avenue. The station can be reached by taking the Puente Avenue exit from the eastbound I-10. Take Puente Avenue northeast to Pacific Avenue. Turn Left on Pacific and go to Downing. Turn right on Downing and the station parking lot will be on your left. From the Westbound I-10 take the west Covina Parkway exit. Go northwest and the West Covina Parkway becomes Pacific. Continue on Pacific to Downing as above. The station has a 300-car parking lot. The train boarding platform is well lighted and has a fair amount of shelter. The parking lot is well lighted and maintained. Metrolink personnel man the station during the morning and evening rush hours. The station is unmanned midday when the flex trains arrive.

The station is served by the Foothill Transit 178, 179, 272, and 274 bus lines. The bus stop for these lines is located on Downing Avenue directly in front of the station.

The MTA 490 line serves the station with stops on Ramona Boulevard at Bogart Avenue. The

Baldwin Park Metrolink Station

MTA 490 line provides East/West travel along Ramona Boulevard and San Bernardino Road in the vicinity of the Baldwin Park Metrolink Station.

The West Covina Shuttle provides shuttle service from the West Covina Civic Center parking structure. Rides to/from Metrolink are free to Metrolink riders. Fare for rides on the Red and Blue routes is 25 cents. For information on the West Covina Shuttle call (818) 915-4934.

The station vicinity map provides the routes for bus transit options from the Baldwin Park Metrolink Station. The following tables provide the

BALDWIN PARK STATION WEEKDAY BUS CONNECTIONS

WESTBOUND TRAINS FROM SAN BERNARDINO TO LOS ANGELES

TRAIN NUMBER	DAYS OF OPERATION	TRAIN ARRIVAL	FOOTHILL 178/179 WESTBOUND 30-40 MIN.	FOOTHILL 178/179 EASTBOUND 30-40 MIN.	FOOTHILL 272 NORTHBOUND 15-30 MIN	FOOTHILL 272 SOUTHBOUND 15-30 MIN	FOOTHILL 274 NORTHBOUND HOURLY	FOOTHILL 274 SOUHTBOUND HOURLY	MTA 490 WESTBOUND 30 MINUTES	MTA 490 EASTBOUND 30 MINUTES	WEST COVINA METROLINK SHUTTLE 30 MINUTES
BUS FREQUENCY											
METROLINK 301	M - F	5:16A			5:24A	5:23A			5:39A	4:59/5:29A	5:17A
METROLINK 303	M - F	6:06A	6:35A	6:13A	5:54/6:09A	5:53/6:08A	6:06/6:43A	5:39/6:39A	5:59/6:19A	5:17/6:12A	5:59/6:09A
METROLINK 305	M - F	6:49A	6:35/7:02A	6:13/6:51A	6:39/6:54A	6:38/6:53A	6:43/7:09A	6:39/7:49A	6:37/6:51A	6:43/7:11A	6:39A
METROLINK 307	M - F	7:13A	7:02/7:45A	7:13A	7:09/7:24A	7:08/7:23A	7:09/8:09A	6:39/7:49A	7:05/7:20A	7:11/7:46A	7:09/7:17A
METROLINK 309	M - F	7:52A	7:45/8:05A	7:51/8:13A	7:39/7:54A	7:38/7:53A	7:09/8:09A	7:49A	7:35/7:58A	7:46/8:17A	7:49/7:53A
METROLINK 313	M - F	11:26A			11:09/11:39A	11:23/11:53A			10:53/11:26A	11:17/11:47A	
METROLINK 315	M - F	2:16P			2:09/2:39P	1:53/1:23P			1:56/2:26P	2:07/2:37P	
METROLINK 321	M - F	L6:01P	5:45/6:15P	5:51/6:13P	5:54/6:09P	5:53/6:08P	5:06/6:06P	5:59/7:04P	5:56/6:27P	6:01/6:21P	5:50/6:21P
METROLINK 323	M - F	L8:03P	7:05P	6:51P	7:39/8:09P	7:53/8:23P	7:11P	7:04/8:10P	8:03/9:06P	7:55/8:55P	

EASTBOUND TRAINS FROM LOS ANGELES TO SAN BERNARDINO

METROLINK 300	M - F	L6:59A	6:35/7:02A	6:51/7:13A	6:54/7:09A	6:53/7:08A	6:43/7:09A	6:39/7:49A	6:51/7:05A	6:43/7:11A	6:39/7:17P
METROLINK 302	M - F	9:24A	8:05A	8:13A	9:09/9:39A	9:23/9:38A	8:09A		9:20/9:50A	9:17/9:47A	
METROLINK 304	M - F	11:44A			11:39A/12:09P	11:23/11:53A			11:26/11:46A	11:17/11:47A	
METROLINK 306	M - F	1:30P			1:09/1:39P	1:23/1:53P			1:26/1:56P	1:07/1:37P	
METROLINK 308	M - F	3:48P	4:05P	3:51P	3:39/3:54P	3:23/3:53P	4:04P	3:59P	3:26/3:50P	3:47/4:07P	3:46/3:48P
METROLINK 310	M - F	L4:50P	4:45/5:05P	4:13/4:51P	4:39/4:54P	4:53/5:08P	4:04/5:06P	3:59/4:59P	4:46/5:21P	4:47/5:07P	4:40/4:51P
METROLINK 312	M - F	5:21P	5:05/5:45P	5:13/5:51P	5:09/5:24P	5:08/5:23P	5:06/6:06P	4:59/5:59P	5:21/5:56P	5:07/5:27P	5:10/5:22P
METROLINK 314	M - F	5:52P	5:45/6:15P	5:51/6:13P	5:39/5:54P	5:38/5:53P	5:06/6:06P	4:59/5:59P	5:21/5:56P	5:44/6:01P	5:50/5:53P
METROLINK 316	M - F	6:21P	6:15/6:35P	6:13/6:51P	6:09/6:24P	6:08/6:23P	6:06/7:11P	5:59/7:04P	5:56/6:27P	6:01/6:21P	6:14/6:21P
METROLINK 318	M - F	7:11P	7:05P	6:51P	7:09/7:39P	7:08/7:23P	6:06/7:11P	7:04/8:10P	6:59/7:24P	6:51/7:23P	
METROLINK 320	M - F	7:52P			7:39/8:09P	7:23/7:53P	7:11P	7:04/8:10P	7:24/8:03P	7:23/7:55P	
METROLINK 322	M - F	9:14P			9:09/9:39P	8:53/9:23P		8:10P	9:06/10:06P	8:55/9:55P	

L: Regular stop to discharge or pick up passengers except train may leave ahead of schedule

View along Maine Street

TRAIN NUMBER	DAYS OF OPERATION	TRAIN ARRIVAL	FOOTHILL 272 NORTHBOUND	FOOTHILL 272 SOUTHBOUND	MTA 490 WESTBOUND	MTA 490 EASTBOUND
BUS FREQUENCY			HOURLY	HOURLY	HOURLY	HOURLY
METROLINK 301	M - F	8:17A	7:43/8:43A	7:21/8:21	7:43/8:43A	7:54/8:34A
METROLINK 303	M - F	11:44A	11:43A/12:43P	11:21A/12:21P	11:43A/12:43P	11:40A/12:40P
METROLINK 305	M - F	3:39P	2:43/3:43P	3:21/4:21P	2:43/3:43P	2:40/3:40P
METROLINK 307	M - F	6:59P	6:43P	6:21P	6:36/7:16P	6:35/7:45P

BALDWIN PARK STATION SATURDAY BUS CONNECTIONS

WESTBOUND TRAINS FROM SAN BERNARDINO TO LOS ANGELES

EASTBOUND TRAINS FROM LOS ANGELES TO SAN BERNARDINO

METROLINK 300	M - F	9:39A	8:43/9:43A	9:21/10:21A	8:43/9:43A	9:34/10:35A
METROLINK 302	M - F	12:57P	12:43/1:43P	12:21/1:21P	12:43/1:43P	12:40/1:40P
METROLINK 304	M - F	4:54P	4:43/5:43P	4:21/5:21P	4:43/5:43P	4:40/5:35P
METROLINK 306	M - F	8:14P			8:03/9:06P	7:45/8:55P

L: Regular stop to discharge or pick up passengers except train may leave ahead of schedule

schedule of bus connections with Metrolink. For schedule and route updates call Foothill Transit at (800) RIDE-INFO or (818) 967-3147 and MTA at (818) 443-1307.

Points of Interest

Pio Pico, California's last Mexican Governor, acquired a land grant that took in most of the San Gabriel Valley after secularization of the San Gabriel Mission in 1834. In 1845 Pico sold the Rancho La Puente to William Workman and John Rowland. After a series of financial misfortunes Workman mortgaged the rancho to "Lucky" Baldwin for $220,000. Shortly thereafter Workman committed suicide.

Baldwin took position of the property and eventually founded the community of Baldwin Park. After Baldwin's death a portion of the property was sold to a man named Unruh. This property later became the city of West Covina.

Downtown Baldwin Park

The Baldwin Park City Hall is directly across the tracks from Metrolink on Pacific Avenue. Pacific turns into Maine Avenue at the intersection with Ramona Boulevard. The downtown shopping district for Baldwin Park runs along Ramona Boulevard and north along Maine Avenue.

The Plaza at West Covina

The Plaza at West Covina is a major shopping mall serving the communities of Baldwin Park and West Covina. The mall can be reached by taking the West Covina Shuttle or the Foothill Transit 274 line.

Places to Stay

San Gabriel Valley Marriott

The San Gabriel Valley Marriott is located at 14635 Baldwin Park Towne Center. The hotel provides free shuttle service to/from the Baldwin Park Metrolink Station. Call the hotel on (818) 962-6000 and give your arrival time and they will send the van to meet you at Metrolink. For reservations call (800) 228-9290.

Howard Johnson Hotel

The Howard Johnson Hotel is located at 14624 Dalewood Street. The hotel telephone number is (818) 962-8761. For reservations call (800) 770-HOJO.

Travelodge

The Travelodge is located at 13921 Francisquito Avenue. The hotel telephone number is (818) 814-0808. For reservations call (800) 578-7878.

WEST COVINA'S FREE METROLINK SHUTTLE SERVICE

Free Metrolink Shuttle Service to and from the Baldwin Park Metrolink Station. The SHUTTLE now provides connections to the Baldwin Park Metrolink train station, located on Downing Street at Pacific Avenue next to the Baldwin Park Civic Center. Just park your car on the top deck of the West Covina Civic Center parking structure, catch the SHUTTLE in front of the parking structure at Sunset Avenue and Sunset Place, and ride directly to Metrolink.

AM	SCHEDULE				
Depart West Covina Civic Center	Arrive Metrolink Station	Metrolink Due	Depart Metrolink Station	Arrive West Covina Civic Center	
5:50	5:59	6:07	6:09	6:19	
6:29	6:39	6:45	6:46	6:57	
6:59	7:09	7:16	7:17	7:29	
7:40	7:49	7:51	7:53	8:03	
PM	**SCHEDULE**				
Depart West Covina Civic Center	Arrive Metrolink Station	Metrolink Due	Depart Metrolink Station	Arrive West Covina Civic Center	
3:38	3:46	3:47	3:48	3:58	
4:30	4:40	4:50	4:51	5:01	
5:00	5:10	5:21	5:22	5:30	
5:30	5:50	5:52	5:53	6:01	
6:02	6:14	6:20	6:21	6:31	

FOR WEST COVINA RESIDENTS, THERE IS A $20/MONTH SUBSIDY FOR METROLINK MONTHLY PASSES. THE METROLINK PASSES MUST BE PURCHASED FROM THE FOOTHILL TRANSIT STORE. LOCATED AT 100 N. BARRANCA AVE, WEST COVINA 1-800-743-3463. FOR A SCHEDULE UPDATE CALL THE CITY OF WEST COVINA AT 818-814-8430. TO CALL THE SHUTTLE OPERATOR 818-915-4934.

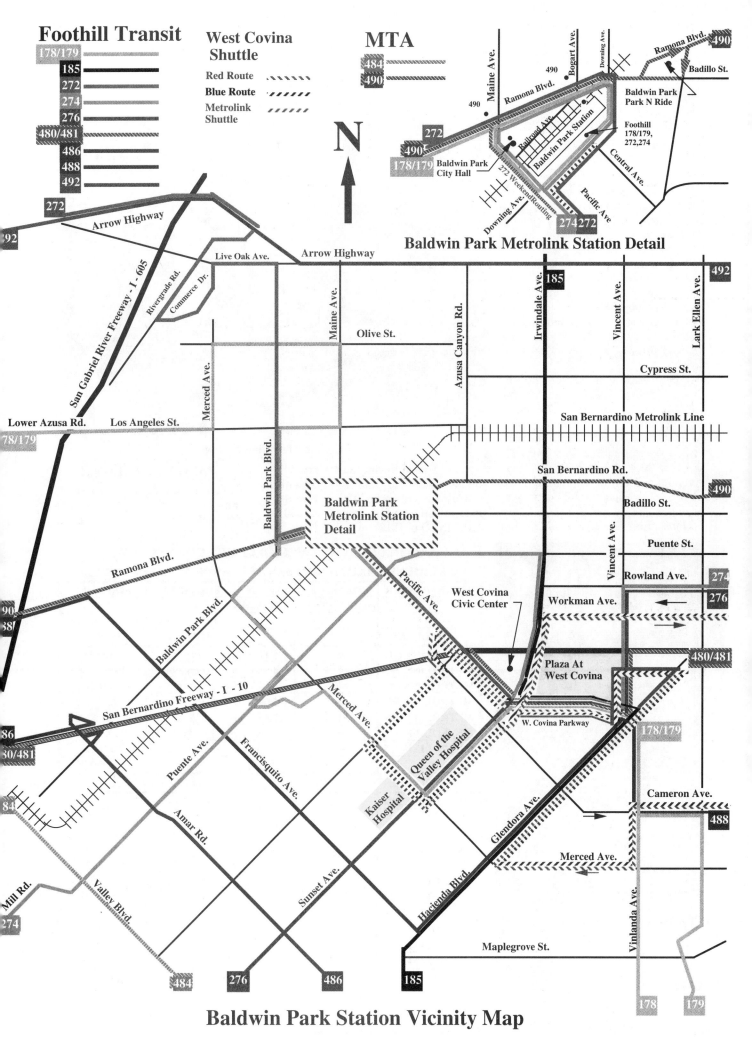

Foothill Transit

178/179
185
272
274
276
480/481
486
488
492

272
92

West Covina Shuttle

Red Route
Blue Route
Metrolink Shuttle

MTA

484
490

N

Baldwin Park Metrolink Station Detail

Maine Ave.
Bogart Ave.
Downing Ave.
Ramona Blvd.
490
Badillo St.
490
Ramona Blvd.
490
Baldwin Park Park N Ride
272
490
Railroad Ave.
Baldwin Park Station
Foothill 178/179, 272,274
178/179
Baldwin Park City Hall
272 WeekendRouting
Central Ave.
Downing Ave.
Pacific Ave.
274 272

Baldwin Park Metrolink Station Detail

Arrow Highway
Live Oak Ave.
Arrow Highway
Commerce Dr.
Rivergrade Rd.
San Gabriel River Freeway - I - 605
Maine Ave.
Olive St.
Azusa Canyon Rd.
Irwindale Ave.
185
Vincent Ave.
Lark Ellen Ave.
492
Cypress St.
Lower Azusa Rd.
Los Angeles St.
Merced Ave.
Baldwin Park Blvd.
San Bernardino Metrolink Line
78/179
San Bernardino Rd.
490
Badillo St.
Baldwin Park Metrolink Station Detail
Ramona Blvd.
Puente St.
Vincent Ave.
Rowland Ave.
274
West Covina Civic Center
Workman Ave.
276
Pacific Ave.
90
88
Baldwin Park Blvd.
Plaza At West Covina
480/481
San Bernardino Freeway - I - 10
Merced Ave.
W. Covina Parkway
178/179
86
Puente Ave.
Francisquito Ave.
Queen of the Valley Hospital
Kaiser Hospital
30/481
Cameron Ave.
84
Amar Rd.
Glendora Ave.
488
Sunset Ave.
Hacienda Blvd.
Merced Ave.
Mill Rd.
Vinlanda Ave.
Valley Blvd.
274
Maplegrove St.
185
484
276
486
178
179

Baldwin Park Station Vicinity Map

Covina Station

Station Connecting Transit Information

The Covina Metrolink Station is located at 600 N. Citrus Avenue. The station can be reached by taking the Citrus Avenue exit from the I-10 and I-210 Freeways. From the I-10 go north on Citrus to the station. From the 210 go south on Citrus. The station has a 250-car parking lot. The train boarding platform is well lighted but has limited shelter. The parking lot is well lighted and maintained. Metrolink personnel man the station during the morning and evening rush hours. The station is not manned midday when the flex trains arrive.

The station is served by the Foothill Transit 274 bus line. The bus stop for the northbound 274 line is located on the northeast corner of Citrus Avenue and Front Street on Front Street. The stop for the southbound 274 line is at the southeast corner of Citrus Avenue and Front Street on Front Street. The station vicinity map provides the routes for bus transit options from the Covina Metrolink

Covina Metrolink Station

Station. The following tables provide the schedule for connections with Metrolink. For schedule and route updates call Foothill Transit at (800) RIDE-INFO or (818) 967-3147.

Points of Interest

Covina is one of the many small communities contained in the San Gabriel Valley in Eastern Los Angeles

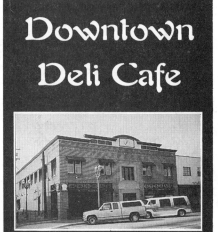
COVINA STATION WEEKDAY BUS CONNECTIONS

WESTBOUND TRAINS FROM SAN BERNARDINO TO LOS ANGELES

TRAIN NUMBER	DAYS OF OPERATION	TRAIN ARRIVAL	FOOTHILL 274 NORTHBOUND	FOOTHILL 274 SOUTHBOUND
BUS FREQUENCY			HOURLY	HOURLY
METROLINK 301	M - F	5:11A	5:19A	5:12A
METROLINK 303	M - F	6:01A	5:19/6:39A	5:12/6:12A
METROLINK 305	M - F	6:38A	5:19/6:39A	6:12/7:22A
METROLINK 307	M - F	7:08A	6:39/7:16A	6:12/7:22A
METROLINK 309	M - F	7:47A	7:43/8:43A	7:22/8:29A
METROLINK 311	M - F	8:16A	7:43/8:43A	7:22/8:29A
METROLINK 313	M - F	11:21A	10:36/11:36A	10:26/11:26A
METROLINK 315	M - F	2:11P	1:36/2:36P	1:26/2:26P

EASTBOUND TRAINS FROM LOS ANGELES TO SAN BERNARDINO

METROLINK 302	M - F	9:29A	8:43/9:36	8:29/9:31A
METROLINK 304	M - F	11:49A	11:36A/12:36P	11:26A/12:26P
METROLINK 306	M - F	1:35P	12:36/1:36P	1:26/2:26P
METROLINK 308	M - F	3:53P	3:36/4:39P	3:26/4:26P
METROLINK 310	M - F	L4:56P	4:39/5:43P	4:26/5:26P
METROLINK 312	M - F	L5:27P	4:39/5:43P	5:26/6:31P
METROLINK 314	M - F	5:58P	5:43/6:43P	5:26/6:31P
METROLINK 316	M - F	6:27P	5:43/6:43P	5:26/6:31P
METROLINK 318	M - F	7:16P	6:43/7:48P	6:31/7:37P
METROLINK 320	M - F	7:57P	7:48P	7:37P
METROLINK 322	M - F	9:19P		

L: Regular stop to discharge or pick up passengers except train may leave ahead of schedule

COVINA STATION SATURDAY BUS CONNECTIONS

WESTBOUND TRAINS FROM SAN BERNARDINO TO LOS ANGELES

TRAIN NUMBER	DAYS OF OPERATION	TRAIN ARRIVAL	FOOTHILL 274 NORTHBOUND	FOOTHILL 274 SOUTHBOUND
BUS FREQUENCY			HOURLY	HOURLY
METROLINK 391	SATURDAY	8:12A	7:30/8:37A	7:29/8:29A
METROLINK 393	SATURDAY	11:39A	10:44/11:44A	11:30A/12:30P
METROLINK 395	SATURDAY	3:34P	2:44/3:44P	3:30/4:30P
METROLINK 397	SATURDAY	6:54P	6:41/7:41P	6:30P

EASTBOUND TRAINS FROM LOS ANGELES TO SAN BERNARDINO

METROLINK 390	SATURDAY	9:45A	9:44/10:44A	9:30/10:30P
METROLINK 392	SATURDAY	1:03P	12:44/1:44P	12:30/1:30P
METROLINK 394	SATURDAY	5:00P	4:44/5:41P	4:30/5:30P
METROLINK 396	SATURDAY	8:20P	7:41P	

County. The city was established on a 2,000 acre tract that was purchased from the Hollenbeck holdings in 1882 by J. S. Phillips. Phillips hired Frederick Eaton, a young engineer at the time, to survey the area. Eaton observed that the San Gabriel mountains formed a natural cove around the vineyards on this tract of land. He coined the word Covina to describe the area which became the name of the new township.

The community is bordered by Azusa on the north and West Covina on the south. To the north, in Azusa, the Azusa Pacific University, and in Glendora, the Citrus Community College, are easily reached on the Foothill Transit 274 line. To the south, in West Covina, the Eastland Mall and West Covina Hotel District are easily reached on the same line.

Downtown Covina

The downtown district of Covina is within walking distance from the Covina Metrolink Station. The downtown area extends from San Bernardino Road on the north to Badillo Avenue on the south along Citrus Avenue. San Bernardino Road is just two short blocks south of the Covina Station.

In the past few years the downtown district has experiences a major facelift and today is home to a thriving antique district. In addition, there are two bookstores, several trendy restaurants, boutiques, and coffee bars. Near the intersection of Citrus Avenue and Badillo Avenue is the Covina Valley Playhouse.

Covina Valley Playhouse

The Covina Valley Playhouse is located at 104 North Citrus Avenue. The Playhouse features a number of professional stage and musical productions during the year. For information about current productions call (818) 339-5135.

Firehouse & Jail Museum

The Covina Valley Historical Society operates the Firehouse and Jail Museum located to the rear of the Covina City Hall. The museum has on display turn-of-the-century fire equipment that was used by the Covina Fire Department. In addition there is a display of the jail facility used in the early days of Covina's existence. The Museum is open Sundays 1:00 P.M. to 3:00 P.M. For information call (818) 332-9523.

Azusa Pacific University

Azusa Pacific University is located at 901 E. Alosta Avenue in Azusa. The university can be reached by taking the northbound Foothill Transit 274 line from the Covina Metrolink Station. Azusa Pacific University is an independent church-related university. Five religious organizations are affiliated with the university. They are the Brethren in Christ, the Church of God,

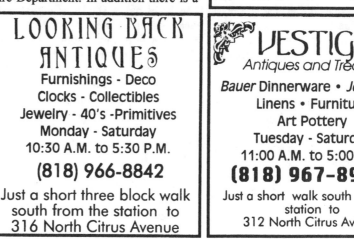

Historic Downtown Covina

the Free Methodist Church, the Missionary Church and the Salvation Army. For general information call (800) TALK-APU.

Citrus Community College

The Citrus Community College is located at 1000 West Foothill Boulevard, Glendora. The college was founded in 1915 under the leadership of Dr. Floyd S. Hayden, who helped to bring the community college movement to California. Today the college serves more than 10,000 students who attend classes at the 104 acre campus. It is a two-year institution that offers an Associate Arts degree.

The college has a strong performing arts department and is home to the Haugh Performing Arts Center. The center has a full schedule of live productions featuring many well known performers. The 1994-95 season featured stars such as Waylon Jennings, The Moscow Classical Ballet, Della Reese, Ed Asner and many others. For information on current productions and ticket prices call the center box office at (818) 963-9411.

Eastland Mall

The Eastland Mall is located just north of the San Bernardino Freeway between Barranca Street and Citrus Avenue. This mall is the smaller of the two malls located in the city of West Covina. The mall serves as a major bus transfer point for the Foothill Transit lines serving the communities in the vicinity of the Covina Metrolink Station. Additionally, the city of West Covina operates a shuttle service which provides transportation between the Eastland Mall and The Plaza at West Covina (see chapter on Baldwin Park Station for information). From Metrolink take the southbound Foothill Transit 274 bus.

Places to Stay

The West Covina Hotel District can be reached by taking the Foothill Transit 274 line to the Eastland Mall stop. From the Eastland mall take the eastbound West Covina Shuttle to Restaurant Row.

Best Western West Covina Hotel

The Best Western is located at 3275 E. Garvey Avenue, West Covina. The hotel phone number is (818) 915-1611. For reservations call (800) 528-1234.

Embassy Suites Resort Covina

The Embassy Suites Resort is located at 1211 East Garvey Avenue. The hotel has a shuttle van that will pick you up at the Covina Metrolink Station with advance notice. The hotel phone number is (818) 915-3441. For reservations call (800) EMBASSY.

Hampton Inn

The Hampton Inn is located at 3145 E. Garvey Avenue, West Covina. The hotel phone number is (818) 967-5800. For reservations call (800) HAMPTON.

Holiday Inn

The Holiday Inn is located at 3223 E. Garvey Avenue, West Covina. The hotel phone number is (818) 966-8311. For reservations call (800) HOLIDAY.

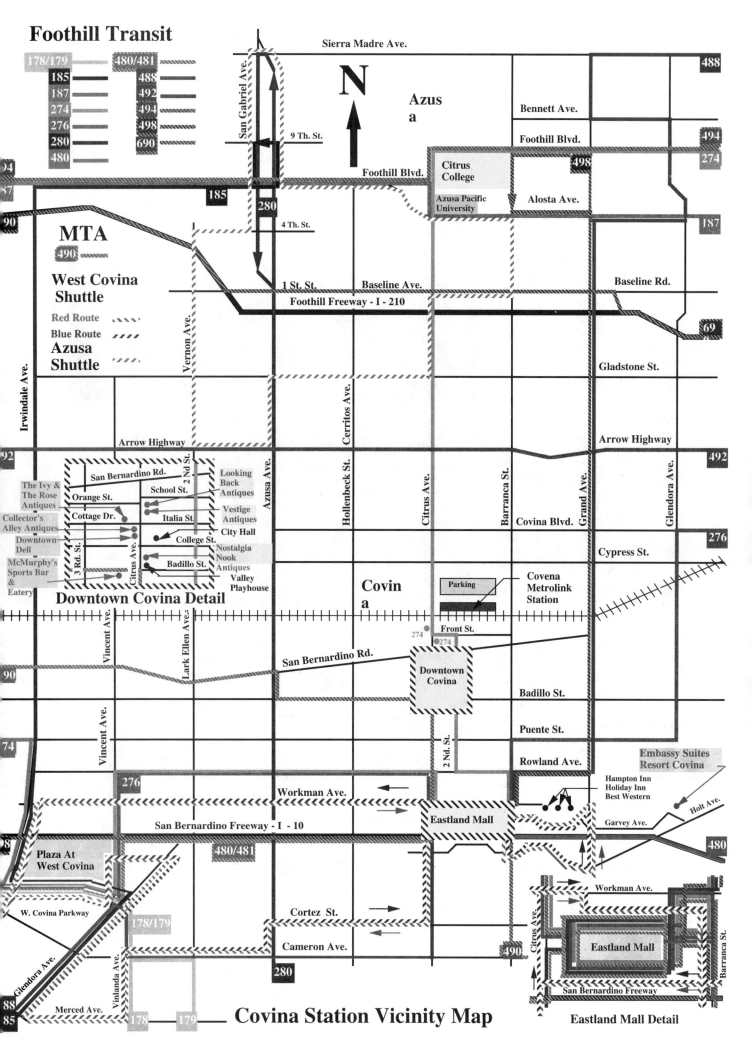

Foothill Transit

178/179
480/481
185
488
187
492
274
494
276
498
280
690
480

MTA
490

West Covina Shuttle

Red Route
Blue Route

Azusa Shuttle

Sierra Madre Ave.

N

Azusa

Bennett Ave.
488

Foothill Blvd.
494

San Gabriel Ave.

9 Th. St.

Foothill Blvd.

Citrus College

Azusa Pacific University

Alosta Ave.
498
274

185

280

4 Th. St.

94
87
90

1 St. St.
Baseline Ave.
Baseline Rd.

Foothill Freeway - I - 210

187

Vernon Ave.

69

Gladstone St.

Irwindale Ave.

Arrow Highway
Cerritos Ave.
Arrow Highway

92

Downtown Covina Detail

San Bernardino Rd.
2 Nd St.

Looking Back Antiques

The Ivy & The Rose Antiques

Orange St.

School St.

Vestige Antiques

Collector's Alley Antiques

Cottage Dr.

Italia St.

City Hall

Downtown Deli

College St.

Nostalgia Nook Antiques

McMurphy's Sports Bar & Eatery

3 Rd. St.

Citrus Ave.

Badillo St.

Valley Playhouse

Azusa Ave.
Hollenbeck St.
Citrus Ave.
Barranca St.
Grand Ave.
Glendora Ave.

492

Covina Blvd.

276

Cypress St.

Covina

Parking

Covena Metrolink Station

274
274

Front St.

San Bernardino Rd.

Downtown Covina

Badillo St.

90

Vincent Ave.
Lark Ellen Ave.

Puente St.

2 Nd. St.

74

Rowland Ave.

Embassy Suites Resort Covina

276

Workman Ave.

Hampton Inn
Holiday Inn
Best Western

Holt Ave.

San Bernardino Freeway - I - 10

Eastland Mall

Garvey Ave.

480

Plaza At West Covina

480/481

Cortez St.

Workman Ave.

W. Covina Parkway

178/179

Citrus Ave.

Eastland Mall

Barranca St.

Glendora Ave.

Vinlanda Ave.

Cameron Ave.

490

88
85

Merced Ave.

178
179

280

San Bernardino Freeway

Covina Station Vicinity Map

Eastland Mall Detail

Pomona Station

Station Connecting Transit Information

The Pomona Metrolink Station is located at 205 Santa Fe Street. The station has a 205-car parking lot. The train boarding platform is well lighted but with limited shelter. The parking lot is well lighted and maintained. Metrolink personnel man the station during the morning and evening rush hours. The station is unmanned midday when the flex trains arrive.

The station is served by the Foothill Transit 291 and 492 bus lines. The bus stop for these lines is located on Santa Fe Street next to the driveway into the station parking lot.

The Valley Connection serves the Pomona Metrolink Station. This dial-a-ride service will take you anywhere in the Pomona and Claremont area free, as long as your departure point or destination is the Metrolink station. Reservations are required so call (909) 620-9820 before leaving.

The station vicinity map provides the routes for bus transit options from the Pomona Metrolink Station. The following tables provide the schedule for bus connections with Metrolink. For schedule updates call Foothill Transit at (800) RIDE-INFO or (818) 967-3147.

Points of Interest

The portion of the Pomona Valley where the City of Pomona is now

Pomona Metrolink Station

situated was a part of the San Jose land grant given by the Mexican governor of California to two solders, Ignacio Palomares and Ricardo Vejar in 1837. In 1863 Vejar's portion of the rancho passed to two Los Angeles merchants and then to Louis Phillips in 1866. In 1875 Phillips sold the property to some land developers and the city of Pomona was founded. Today the city is the site of the Los Angeles County Fair and is the commercial center of the Pomona

Valley.

Los Angeles County Fair

The Pomona Fairplex is the site of the Los Angeles County Fair. The Fair is the largest county fair in the country. It is larger than most state fairs. The fair runs from early September to early October. The fair features a wide variety of exhibits including arts, crafts, agriculture, livestock, and commercial themes. There is a racetrack with thoroughbred racing and parimutuel

POMONA STATION SATURDAY BUS CONNECTIONS
WESTBOUND TRAINS FROM SAN BERNARDINO TO LOS ANGELES

TRAIN NUMBER	DAYS OF OPERATION	TRAIN ARRIVAL	FOOTHILL 291 NORTHBOUND 30 MIN.	FOOTHILL 291 SOUTHBOUND 30 MIN.	FOOTHILL 492 WESTBOUND 30 MINUTES	FOOTHILL 492 EASTBOUND 30 MINUTES
BUS FREQUENCY						
METROLINK 391	SATURDAY	8:02A	7:24*/8:24A*	7:29*/8:29A*	7:18*/8:18P*	7:19*/8:24A*
METROLINK 393	SATURDAY	11:29A	10:54*/11:54A*	10:59*/11:59A*	11:20*/12:20P*	10:28A*/12:28P*
METROLINK 395	SATURDAY	3:24P	2:54*/3:54P*	2:59*/3:29P*	2:20*/4:20P*	2:28*/4:28P*
METROLINK 397	SATURDAY	6:44P	6:24*/6:54P*	6:29*/6:59P*	6:18P*	6:24/7:24P*

EASTBOUND TRAINS FROM LOS ANGELES TO SAN BERNARDINO

METROLINK 390	SATURDAY	9:56A	9:24*/10:24A*	9:29*/10:29A*	9:20*/10:20A*	9:24*/10:28P*
METROLINK 392	SATURDAY	1:13P	12:54*/1:24P*	12:59*/1:29P*	12:20*/2:20P*	12:28*/1:28P*
METROLINK 394	SATURDAY	5:11P	4:54*/5:24P*	4:59*/5:29P*	4:20*/6:18P*	4:28*/5:28P*
METROLINK 396	SATURDAY	8:31P				7:24P*

L: Regular stop to discharge or pick up passengers except train may leave ahead of schedule

* Bus Stops at corner of Garey Avenue and Arrow Highway and NOT at Pomona Metrolink Station

POMONA STATION WEEKDAY BUS CONNECTIONS
WESTBOUND TRAINS FROM SAN BERNARDINO TO LOS ANGELES

TRAIN NUMBER	DAYS OF OPERATION	TRAIN ARRIVAL	FOOTHILL 291 NORTHBOUND	FOOTHILL 291 SOUTHBOUND	FOOTHILL 492 WESTBOUND	FOOTHILL 492 EASTBOUND
BUS FREQUENCY			15 - 30 MIN.	15 - 30 MIN.	30 MINUTES	30 MINUTES
METROLINK 301	M - F	5:01A	5:27A	5:05A	5:24A	
METROLINK 303	M - F	5:51A	5:27/5:51A	5:35/6:05A	5:24/5:54A	6:06A
METROLINK 305	M - F	6:28A	6:27/6:42A	6:20/6:35A	6:26/6:56A	6:06/6:36A
METROLINK 307	M - F	6:57A	6:42/6:57A	6:50/7:05A	6:56/7:26A	6:36/7:12A
METROLINK 309	M - F	7:37A	7:27/7:42A	7:35/7:50A	7:26/7:56A	7:12/7:42A
METROLINK 311	M - F	8:05A	7:57/8:12A	7:50/8:05A	7:56/8:27A*	7:42/8:07A
METROLINK 313	M - F	11:10A	10:53*/11:23A*	11:05*/11:35A*	10:57*/11:27A*	11:04*/11:34A*
METROLINK 315	M - F	2:01P	1:53*/2:23P*	12:35*/1:05P*	1:57*/2:32P*	1:34*/2:34P*
METROLINK 317	M - F	L3:14P	2:53*/3:24P*	3:04*/3:19P*	3:02*/3:32P*	3:04*/3:34P*

EASTBOUND TRAINS FROM LOS ANGELES TO SAN BERNARDINO

METROLINK 300	M - F	L7:21A	7:12/7:27A	7:20/7:35A	6:56/7:26A	7:12/7:42A
METROLINK 302	M - F	9:40A	9:23*/9:53A*	9:35*/10:05A*	9:27*/9:57A*	9:32*/10:02A*
METROLINK 304	M - F	12:00P	11:53A*/12:23P*	11:35A*/12:05P*	11:27A*/12:27P*	11:34A*/12:34P*
METROLINK 306	M - F	1:45P	1:23*1:53P*	1:05*/1:35P*	1:27*/1:57P*	1:34*/2:04P*
METROLINK 308	M - F	L4:03P	3:54*/4:09P*	3:49*/4:05P	3:32*/4:32P	3:34*/4:35P*
METROLINK 310	M - F	L5:06P	4:57/5:12P	5:05/5:20P	5:02/5:32P	4:35*/5:35P
METROLINK 312	M - F	L5:38P	5:27/5:42P	5:35/5:50P	5:32/6:02P	5:35/6:04P
METROLINK 314	M - F	6:10P	5:57/6:12P	6:05/6:20P	6:02/6:32P	6:04/6:34P
METROLINK 316	M - F	6:38P	6:27/6:42P	6:35/6:50P	6:32/7:02P	6:34/7:36P*
METROLINK 318	M - F	7:26P	6:54*/7:53P*	7:05*/735P*	7:02/7:32P	6:34/7:36P*
METROLINK 320	M - F	8:08P	7:53*/8:53P*	7:35*/8:35P*	7:32/8:30P*	7:36/8:38P
METROLINK 322	M - F	9:29P	8:53*/9:53P*	8:35*/9:35P*	8:30P*	8:38/9:38P

L: Regular stop to discharge or pick up passengers except train may leave ahead of schedule

* Bus Stops at corner of Garey Avenue and Arrow Highway and NOT at Pomona Metrolink Station

wagering. There is also a large fun zone with a wide variety of carnival rides. The fair is a must if you are visiting Los Angeles during its run. For the rest of the year the Fairplex complex is used for a variety of festivals and trade shows. During my visit while researching this book there was an art and craft show called Springfest and a computer show at the Fairplex complex. For information about activities at Fairplex call (909) 623-3111.

Metrolink has a station platform located at the corner of the Fairplex parking lot. Metrolink stops at this station when the Los Angeles County Fair is open. The fair runs a parking lot tram to/from the Fairplex Metrolink Station to the general admission gate. The Fairplex station is not used the rest of the year.

From the Pomona Metrolink Station, the Fairplex complex can be

Fairplex Grounds

reached by taking the Foothill Transit 291 line to the Garey Avenue and McKinley Avenue stop. From there you walk about one-third mile east along McKinley Avenue to the Fairplex complex at McKinley Avenue and White Avenue.

La Casa Primera de Rancho San Jose

The adobe La Casa Primera is located at 1569 North Park Avenue. It was the first house built in the Pomona Valley in the year 1837 by Don Ignacio Palomares. The Palomares lived in the house for 17 years, then they moved about a mile north to the Palomares Adobe. The house is presently owned by the city of Pomona and the Pomona Valley Historical Society conducts tours on Sundays between 2:00 P.M. and 5:00 P.M. Admission is $2.00. The adobe is located about one-block north of the Garey and McKinley avenues stop on the Foothill Transit 291 line.

Palomares Adobe

The Palomares Adobe is located at 491 East Arrow Highway. The Adobe was the second home built by Don Ignacio Palomares on the northern portion of Rancho San Jose in 1854. The one story, 13-room house, is built in what has come to be called California Ranch style. In the 1930's the city of Pomona took over the ruins of the original Palomares Adobe and began the task of restoration and preservation. Restoration was completed in 1940 and today the house is furnished in period pieces with many items from the original Adobe. The Adobe is open to the public from 2:00 P.M. to 5:00 P.M. on Sundays. Admission is free but donations are welcome. From Metrolink, the Adobe can be reached on foot by walking down to Arrow Highway and going east on Arrow Highway past Garey to Palomares Park where the Adobe is located. For information call (909) 620-2300.

University of La Verne

The University of La Verne is a private nonsectarian institution. The university is located at 1950 Third Street. in the city of La Verne. It offers both undergraduate and graduate degrees in a wide range of majors. The University was founded in 1891 as Lordsburg College by members of the Church of the Brethren. Both the

La Casa Primera

college and the surrounding town were renamed La Verne in 1917. Today the University has campuses in a number of sites in California, Alaska, Greece and Italy. The main campus of the university is located in the city of La Verne where the majority of its 6,000 students attend classes. The university can be reached from the Pomona Metrolink Station by taking westbound Foothill Transit 492 bus line to the Bonita Avenue and D Street stop. For general information call (909) 593-3511.

Pomona Antique District

The Pomona Antique district is located along Second Street (Pomona Mall East) in downtown Pomona. In addition there are several boutiques and restaurants throughout the surrounding

downtown district of Pomona. Downtown Pomona and the Antique District can be reached by taking the Foothill Transit 291 line from the Metrolink Station.

Places to Stay
Sheraton Suites Fairplex

The Sheraton Suites Fairplex is located at 601 West McKinley Avenue. The hotel provides free shuttle service to/from the Pomona or Fairplex (when in operation) Metrolink station. Call the hotel at (909) 622-2220 and give your arrival time and they will send the van to meet you at Metrolink. For reservations call (800) 325-3535.

Lemon Tree Motel

The Lemon Tree Motel is located at 1700 Gillette Road. The hotel phone number is (909) 623-6404.

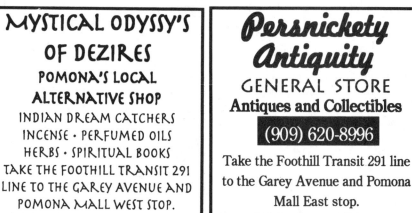

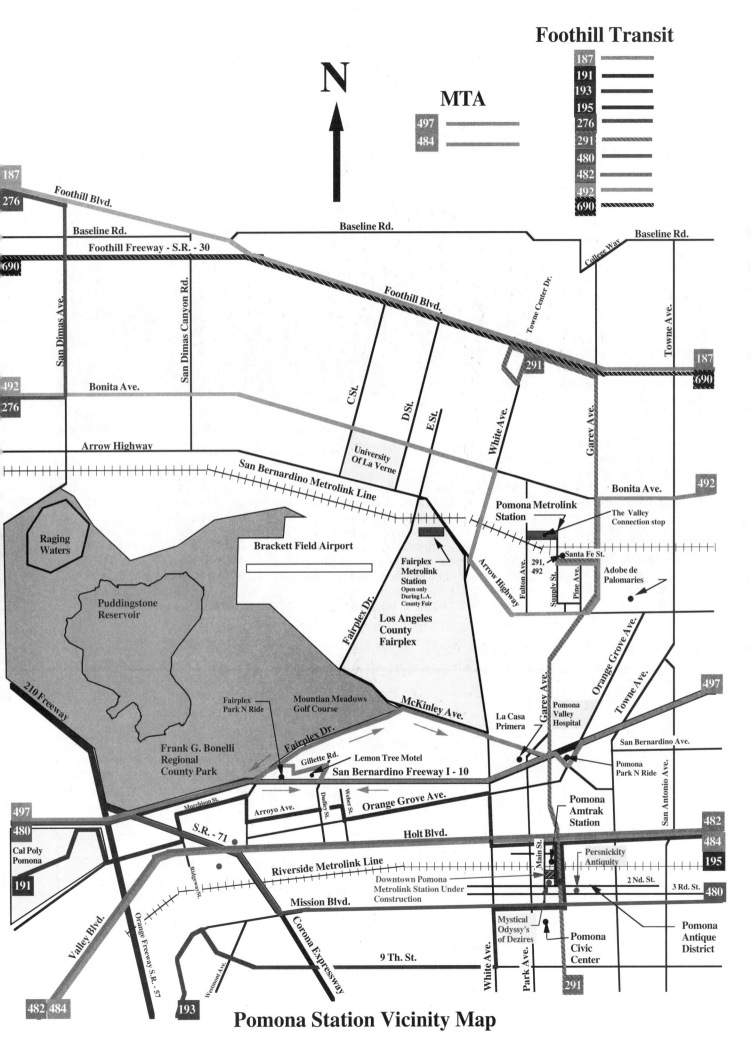

Pomona Station Vicinity Map

Claremont Station

Station Connecting Transit Information

The Claremont Metrolink Station is located at 200 W. First Street. The station can be reached by taking the Indian Hill Boulevard exit from the I-10 Freeway. From the I-10 go north on Indian Hill Boulevard to First Street. Turn right on First and the station will be on your right between Yale and Harvard Avenues. The parking lot for Metrolink commuters is located further up First Street just pass College Avenue.

The bus stops at the Claremont Transit Center are located in front of the commuter Park 'n Ride lot along First Street. The transit center has a 380-car parking lot. The train boarding platform is well lighted but has limited shelter. The parking lot is also well lighted and maintained. Claremont Transit Store personnel man the station building during the day.

The Claremont Transit Center building was completed in 1927 in the California Spanish Colonial Revival Architectural style. It replaced the original wood frame and clapboard station built by the Santa Fe in 1887. The original station was in the Gothic

Claremont Metrolink Station

Victorian style similar to many of the old homes that still populate the village. Today the station building is occupied by the Claremont Transit store operated by the City of Claremont. There you can get updates on routes and schedules for Foothill

Transit bus routes, Metrolink trains, MTA bus lines, LADOT Dash buses, Omni Transit bus lines and much more. The transit store also sells a map of Claremont for $1.00.

The station is served by the Foothill Transit 187, 292, 480, 492,

CLAREMONT STATION WEEKDAY BUS CONNECTIONS

WESTBOUND TRAINS FROM SAN BERNARDINO TO LOS ANGELES

TRAIN NUMBER	DAYS OF OPERATION	TRAIN ARRIVAL	FOOTHILL 187	FOOTHILL 292 NORTHBOUND HOURLY	FOOTHILL 292 SOUTHBOUND HOURLY	FOOTHILL 480 WESTBOUND 15-30 MIN.	FOOTHILL 480 EASTBOUND 15-30 MIN.	FOOTHILL 492 WESTBOUND 30 MINUTES	FOOTHILL 492 EASTBOUND 30 MINUTES	FOOTHILL 690 EASTBOUND COMMUTER	FOOTHILL 690 WESTBOUND COMMUTER
BUS FREQUENCY			30-60 MIN.								
METROLINK 301	M - F	4:57A	5:03A			4:45/5:00A	4:28/5:29A	5:15A			4:38/5:10A
METROLINK 303	M - F	5:47A	5:59A		5:59A	5:44/6:12A	5:29/5:50A	5:45/6:16A			5:40/6:15A
METROLINK 305	M - F	6:24A	5:59/6:29A	6:33A	5:59/6:59A	6:12/6:25A	5:50/7:13A	6:16/6:46A	6:18/6:48A		6:15/6:45A
METROLINK 307	M - F	6:53A	5:59/7:00A	6:33/7:33A	5:59/6:59A	6:40/6:58A	5:50/7:13A	6:47/7:16A	6:48/7:24A		6:45/7:25A
METROLINK 309	M - F	7:34A	7:03/8:00A	7:33/8:33A	6:59/7:59A	7:23/7:42A	7:13/7:43A	7:16/7:46A	7:24/7:54A	7:25A	
METROLINK 311	M - F	8:02A	7:48/9:00A	7:33/8:33A	7:59/8:59A	7:53/8:11A	7:43/8:10A	7:46/8:17A	7:54/8:42A		
METROLINK 313	M - F	11:06A	10:35/11:59A	10:33/11:31A	11:01A/12:01P	10:37/11:11A	11:01/11:16A	10:47/11:17A	10:44/11:14A		
METROLINK 315	M - F	1:57P	1:35/1:59P	1:31/2:31P	1:01/2:01P	1:37/2:11P	1:48/2:03P	1:47/2:22A	1:44/2:14P		
METROLINK 317	M - F	L3:10P	2:35/3:14P	2:31/3:31P	3:01/4:01P	2:41/3:11P	3:03/3:18P	2:52/3:22P	2:43/3:14P		
METROLINK 321	M - F	L5:44P	5:23/5:56P	5:31/6:31P	5:01/5:59P	5:39/6:19P	5:23/5:51P	5:22/5:52P	5:20/5:48P	5:40/6:15P	
METROLINK 323	M - F	L7:40P	7:23/8:08P	7:33/8:33P	6:59/7:59P	7:39/8:18P	7:21/7:51P	7:22/7:50P	7:06/7:47P	7:25P	

EASTBOUND TRAINS FROM LOS ANGELES TO SAN BERNARDINO

METROLINK 300	M - F	L7:25A	7:03/7:30A	6:33/7:33A	6:59/7:59A	7:23/7:42A	7:13/7:43A	7:16/7:46A	7:24/7:54A		7:15/7:45A
METROLINK 302	M - F	9:44A	9:18/10:00A	9:33/10:33A	8:59/10:01A	9:37/10:11A	9:30/9:57A	9:16/9:46A	9:42/10:12A		
METROLINK 304	M - F	12:04P	11:35A/12:59P	11:31A/12:31P	12:01/1:01P	11:37A/12:11A	12:03/12:18P	11:47A/12:17P	11:44A/12:14P		
METROLINK 306	M - F	1:49P	1:35/1:59P	1:31/2:31P	1:01/2:01P	1:37/2:11P	1:48/2:03P	1:47/2:22P	1:44/2:14P		
METROLINK 308	M - F	L4:06P	3:35/4:11P	3:31/4:31P	4:01/5:01P	4:01/4:16P	4:02/4:22P	3:52/4:22P	3:44/4:14P	4:38P	
METROLINK 310	M - F	L5:10P	4:53/5:11P	4:31/5:31P	5:01/5:59P	4:54/5:11P	5:03/5:23P	4:52/5:22P	4:50/5:20P	4:38/5:40P	
METROLINK 312	M - F	L5:42P	5:23/5:56P	5:31/6:31P	5:01/5:59P	5:39/6:19P	5:32/5:46P	5:22/5:52P	5:20/5:48P	5:40/6:15P	
METROLINK 314	M - F	6:14P	5:53/7:07P	5:31/6:31P	5:59/6:59P	5:39/6:19P	6:09/6:24P	5:52/6:22P	6:17/6:47P	5:40/6:15P	
METROLINK 316	M - F	6:42P	6:23/7:00P	6:31/7:33P	5:59/6:59P	6:19/6:56P	6:32/6:44P	6:22/6:52P	6:17/6:47P	6:15/6:45P	
METROLINK 318	M - F	7:30P	7:23/8:02P	7:23/8:02P	6:59/7:59P	7:09/7:39P	7:21/7:51P	7:22/7:50P	7:06/7:47P	7:25P	
METROLINK 320	M - F	8:12P	8:08/9:02P	7:33/8:33P	7:59P	7:39/8:18P	8:05/8:16P	7:50/8:20P	7:47/8:49P		
METROLINK 322	M - F	9:33P	8:56/10:02P	8:33P		9:09/10:09P	9:10/9:38P	9:20P	8:49/9:49P		

L: Regular stop to discharge or pick up passengers except train may leave ahead of schedule

WESTBOUND TRAINS FROM SAN BERNARDINO TO LOS ANGELES

TRAIN NUMBER	DAYS OF OPERATION	TRAIN ARRIVAL	FOOTHILL 187 WESTBOUND HOURLY	FOOTHILL 292 NORTHBOUND HOURLY	FOOTHILL 292 SOUTHBOUND HOURLY	FOOTHILL 480 WESTBOUND 15-30 MIN.	FOOTHILL 480 EASTBOUND 15-30 MIN.	FOOTHILL 492 WESTBOUND HOURLY	FOOTHILL 492 EASTBOUND HOURLY
BUS FREQUENCY									
METROLINK 301	SATURDAY	7:58A	6:56/8:30A	7:34/8:34A	7:01/8:01A	7:56/8:11A	7:30/8:30A	7:09/8:09A	7:28/8:34A
METROLINK 303	SATURDAY	11:25A	11:03/11:30A	10:34/11:34A	11:01A/12:01P	11:12/11:26A	11:00/11:30A	11:10A/12:10P	10:38/11:38A
METROLINK 305	SATURDAY	3:20P	2:33/3:30P	2:34/3:34P	3:01/4:01P	3:12/3:42P	3:00/3:21P	3:10/4:10P	2:38/3:38P
METROLINK 307	SATURDAY	6:40P	6:33/7:03P	6:34/7:34P	6:01/7:01P	5:57/6:42P	6:36/6:56P	6:09P	6:34/7:34P

EASTBOUND TRAINS FROM LOS ANGELES TO SAN BERNARDINO

TRAIN NUMBER	DAYS OF OPERATION	TRAIN ARRIVAL	FOOTHILL 187	FOOTHILL 292	FOOTHILL 292	FOOTHILL 480	FOOTHILL 480	FOOTHILL 492	FOOTHILL 492
METROLINK 300	SATURDAY	10:00A	9:03/10:30A	9:34/10:34A	9:01/10:01A	9:56/10:12A	9:45/10:00A	9:10/10:10A	9:34/10:38A
METROLINK 302	SATURDAY	1:17P	1:03/1:30P	12:34/1:34P	1:01/2:01P	1:12/1:26P	1:15/1:30P	1:10/2:10P	12:38/1:38P
METROLINK 304	SATURDAY	5:15P	4:33/6:03P	4:34/5:34P	5:01/6:01P	4:57/5:57P	5:06/5:21P	5:09/6:09P	4:38/5:38P
METROLINK 306	SATURDAY	8:35P	7:57P	8:34P	8:01P	8:27/9:27P	8:26/9:21P		7:34P

L: Regular stop to discharge or pick up passengers except train may leave ahead of schedule

and 690, bus lines. The bus stops for these lines are located directly in front of the station on First Street. The station vicinity map provides the routes for bus transit options from the Claremont Metrolink Station. The following tables provide the schedule for bus connections with Metrolink.

Outside of the immediate vicinity of the Claremont Metrolink Station the 187 line provides service to La Verne, Glendora, Azusa, Duarte, Arcadia and Pasadena. The 292 line provides service to Pomona and Montclair. The 480 line provides service to Los Angeles with stops in Pomona, Covina, West Covina, El Monte, Cal State L.A., and L.A. County USC Medical Center. The 492 line provides service from Montclair to Pomona, La Verne, Glendora, Covina, Azusa, El Monte and finally Los Angeles via the El Monte-Los Angeles Busway on the I-10 Freeway. The 690 line provides express service to La Verne, Glendora, Azusa,

Monrovia and Pasadena via the I-210 Freeway.

For updated schedules, and complete route maps for Foothill Transit lines call (800) RIDE-INFO or (818) 967-3147; for Omnitrans lines call (800) 966-6428; and for MTA lines call (818) 443-1307.

The same bus lines also stop at the Claremont Transit Center which is located about one and a half blocks west of the station stop. If you miss the bus at the station you may be able to catch it at the transit center as they layover there.

Points of Interest

Claremont is a college town which grew up with the Claremont Colleges since its founding in 1887. Claremont was created by the Santa Fe Railway inorder to sell railroad land to easterners in the late 1880's. The real estate boom never materialized and Claremont would have disappeared if not for the fact that one of the board members of

the land company was a member of the local Congregational Church. The church was attempting to establish a college in the area. The land company was persuaded to donate land and a building in the new Claremont township which became Pomona College. The town today is reminiscent of a New England college town with many businesses and homes with a

Claremont Village

Claremont College Campus

mixture of New England and Victorian architecture.

The Village

The Village is the original township laid out by the Santa Fe Railway in 1887. Today the village is home to numerous upscale boutiques, antique shops, art galleries, and fine restaurants. All of the streets are lined with mature shade trees, wide sidewalks and numerous benches for the weary shopper to stop and rest. There are sidewalk cafes for refreshments and watching the passersby.

Claremont Colleges

The Claremont Colleges are located north of First Street and east of College Avenue. The campus extends about one mile to the north and is bounded by Foothill Boulevard. The colleges are a group of institutions modeled after the Oxford model. Each college was founded as a separate educational corporation, with its own degree, faculty, support, etc. Today the Claremont Colleges are home to Pomona College, Scripps College, Claremont-McKenna College, Harvey Mudd College, Pitzer College, Claremont Graduate School, and the School of Theology at Claremont.

The Colleges are host to a number of museums, galleries, and performing arts venues such as: The Clark Humanities Museum, the Bridges Auditorium Museum, the Montgomery Gallery, the Lang Gallery, the Salathe Gallery, Founders Room at the Honnold Library, Bridges Auditorium, Seaver Theater, Mudd Theater and many more. The Claremont Colleges prepare a calendar for special events at the various venues on campus. Copies of the calendar can be obtained by calling (909) 621-8028.

Rancho Santa Ana Botanic Garden

The Rancho Santa Ana Botanic Garden is located at 1500 North College Avenue off Foothill Boulevard. From Metrolink take the westbound Foothill Transit 187 line to the Foothill Boulevard and north College Avenue Stop. The garden's entrance is at the north end of College Avenue behind the School of Theology. The garden was founded by Susanna Bixby Bryant in memory of her father John W. Bixby. The garden was originally located on historic Rancho Santa Ana in Orange County. It was relocated to Claremont in 1951.

The garden is primarily a botanical research and educational institution which offers graduate degrees in botany and is associated with the Claremont Colleges. The 40 acres of the garden are devoted to displays of native California plants. Displays include a Home Demonstration Garden populated with drought-tolerant plants, a Desert Garden, a Costal Garden and many more. The plant science center houses

The San Gabriel Mountains from the Rancho Santa Ana Garden

the administrative offices, research offices and laboratories, library, auditorium and a small gift shop. Admission is free, but donations are accepted. The garden is open daily 8:00 A.M. till 5:00 P.M., it is closed New Year's Day, Fourth of July, Thanksgiving Day and Christmas Day.

Places to Stay

The Claremont Inn

The Claremont Inn is located at 555 West Foothill Boulevard. The hotel has a van which will pick you up at the Claremont Metrolink Station. Call the hotel before your arrival and

tell them when your train will arrive and they will pick you up. The hotel phone number is (909) 626-2411. For reservations call (800) 821-0341 within

California or outside California call (800) 854-5733.

Howard Johnson

Howard Johnson is located at 721 Indian Hill Boulevard. The hotel has a van which will pick you up at the Claremont Metrolink station. Call the hotel before your arrival and tell them when your train will arrive and they will pick you up. The hotel phone number is (909) 626-2431. For reservations call (800) 654-2000.

Ramada Inn

Ramada Inn is located at 840 Indian Hill Boulevard The hotel can be reached by taking the Foothill Transit 480 bus line to the stop just south of I-10. The hotel phone number is (909) 621-4831. For Reservations call (800) 322-6559.

Claremont Travelodge

The Claremont Travelodge is located at 736 Indian Hill Boulevard. The hotel can be reached by taking the Foothill Transit 480 bus line to the stop just north of I-10. The hotel phone number is (909) 626-5654. For reservations call (800) 255-3050.

Victorian Home In Claremont Village

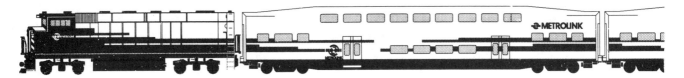

115

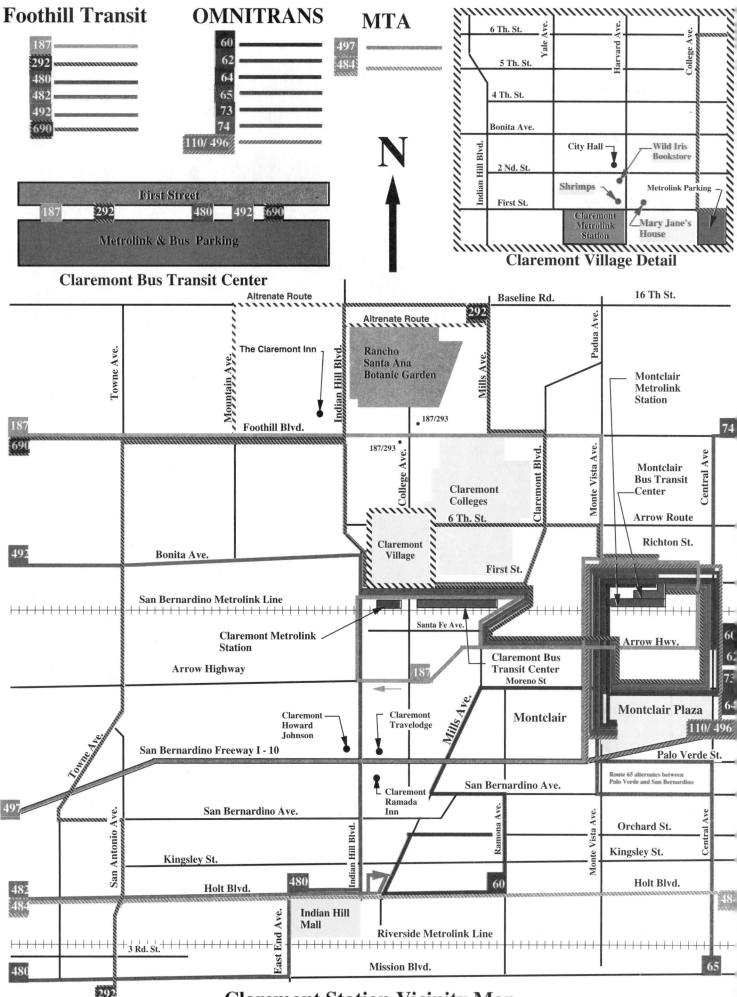

Foothill Transit

187
292
480
482
492
690

OMNITRANS

60
62
64
65
73
74
110/ 496

MTA

497
484

Claremont Bus Transit Center

First Street

187   292   480   492   690

Metrolink & Bus Parking

N

Claremont Village Detail

6 Th. St.
5 Th. St.
4 Th. St.
Bonita Ave.
2 Nd. St.
First St.

Yale Ave.
Harvard Ave.
College Ave.
Indian Hill Blvd.

City Hall
Wild Iris Bookstore
Shrimps
Metrolink Parking
Claremont Metrolink Station
Mary Jane's House

Claremont Station Vicinity Map

Altrenate Route
Baseline Rd.
16 Th. St.
Altrenate Route
292
Rancho Santa Ana Botanic Garden
Padua Ave.

Towne Ave.
Mountain Ave.
Indian Hill Blvd.
The Claremont Inn
Mills Ave.

187/293

187
690
Foothill Blvd.
187/293
College Ave.
Claremont Blvd.
Monte Vista Ave.
Central Ave
74

Montclair Metrolink Station

Claremont Colleges
6 Th. St.
Montclair Bus Transit Center
Arrow Route
Richton St.

492
Bonita Ave.
Claremont Village
First St.

San Bernardino Metrolink Line
Santa Fe Ave.
Arrow Hwy.
60

Claremont Metrolink Station
187
Claremont Bus Transit Center
Moreno St
62
73

Arrow Highway
Claremont Howard Johnson
Claremont Travelodge
Montclair
Montclair Plaza
64
110/ 496

San Bernardino Freeway I - 10
Claremont Ramada Inn
Palo Verde St.

497
San Bernardino Ave.
San Bernardino Ave.
Route 65 alternates between Palo Verde and San Bernardino

Towne Ave.
San Antonio Ave.
Ramona Ave.
Monte Vista Ave.
Central Ave
Orchard St.
Kingsley St.
Kingsley St.
Holt Blvd.

482
484
Holt Blvd.
480
Indian Hill Blvd.
East End Ave.
Indian Hill Mall
60
48

480
3 Rd. St.
Riverside Metrolink Line
292
Mission Blvd.
65

Montclair Station

Station Connecting Transit Information

The Montclair Metrolink Station is located at 5091 Richton Street. The station can be reached by taking the Central Avenue exit from the I-10. Go north on Central to Richton Street. Turn left on Richton. The station will be on your left at the new Montclair Bus Transit Center. The station/transit center has a 750-car parking lot. The train boarding platform is well lighted with good shelter. The parking lot is well lighted and maintained. There is a day care center located on the Montclair Transit Center property. Metrolink personnel man the station during the morning and evening rush hours. The station is not manned midday when the flex trains arrive.

The station is served by the Foothill Transit 187, 292, 480, 492 and 690 bus lines, the MTA 497 Express bus to Los Angeles, and Omnitrans 60, 62, 64, 65, 73, and 74 bus lines. Omnitrans and Riverside Transit Agency operate the Inland

Montclair Metrolink Station

Empire Connection 110, and 496 lines which stop at the Montclair Transit Center. The station vicinity map provides the routes for bus transit options from the Montclair Metrolink Station. The following tables provide the schedule for bus connections to Metrolink.

Outside of the immediate vicinity of the Montclair Metrolink Station the Foothill Transit 492 line provides service to Claremont, Pomona, La Verne, Glendora, Covina, Azusa, El Monte and finally Los Angeles via the El Monte - Los Angeles Busway on the I-10 Freeway. The Foothill Transit 187 provides service to Azusa, Arcadia and Pasadena and the 292 line to Pomona. The Omnitrans 60 line provides service to Upland, and Rancho Cucamonga, the 62 and 64 lines to Upland and Chino, the 65 line to Ontario and Chino Hills, the 73 and 74 lines to Upland, Rancho Cucamonga and Fontana.

The Montclair Bus Transit Center provides a number of express bus lines which compete with Metrolink service. The MTA 497 line provides commuter service between the Montclair Bus Transit Center and Los Angeles via the I-10 Freeway with stops at Pomona Park 'n Ride, El Monte Bus Station, California State University Los Angeles and L.A. County USC Medical Center before arriving in Los Angeles.

The Foothill Transit 480 line provides express service via the San

MONTCLAIR STATION WEEKDAY BUS CONNECTIONS
WESTBOUND TRAINS FROM SAN BERNARDINO TO LOS ANGELES

TRAIN NUMBER	DAYS OF OPERATION	TRAIN ARRIVAL	OMNITRANS 60 SOUTHBOUND 30 MINUTES	OMNITRANS 60 NORTHBOUND 30 MINUTES	OMNITRANS 62 DIRECTION A HOURLY	OMNITRANS 62 DIRECTION B HOURLY	OMNITRANS 64 30 MINUTES	OMNITRANS 65 30 MINUTES	OMNITRANS 73 EASTBOUND HOURLY	OMNITRANS 73 WESTBOUND HOURLY	OMNITRANS 74 EASTBOUND HOURLY	OMNITRANS 74 WESTBOUND HOURLY
METROLINK 301	M-F	4:54A	5:40A				4:50/4:56A		4:49/5:04A	4:32/5:32A	5:40A	4:57A
METROLINK 303	M-F	5:44A	5:40/6:16A	6:08A		4:50/6:27A	5:40/5:50A	4:49/5:44A	5:32/6:18A	5:40/6:44A	5:42/6:41A	
METROLINK 305	M-F	6:20A	6:16/6:47A	6:08/6:38A	6:16/6:35A	6:17/6:27A	5:40/7:00A	5:55/6:31A	6:18/7:18A	5:40/6:44A	5:42/6:41A	6:17/7:21A
METROLINK 307	M-F	6:50A	6:47/7:20A	6:38/7:08A	6:16/7:39A	6:48/7:27A	6:47/7:00A	5:55/7:04A	6:18/7:18A	6:44/7:54A	6:41/7:41A	6:17/7:21A
METROLINK 309	M-F	7:30A	7:20/7:50A	7:08/7:38A	6:16/7:39A	6:48/8:27A	7:23/7:30A	7:00/7:31A	7:18/8:18A	6:44/7:54A	6:41/7:41A	7:21/8:21A
METROLINK 311	M-F	7:59A	7:50/8:20A	7:38/8:08A	7:34/8:39A	6:48/8:27A	7:51/8:00A	7:49/8:04A	7:18/8:18A	7:54/8:56A	7:41/8:41A	7:21/8:21A
METROLINK 313	M-F	11:02A	10:50/11:20A	10:38/11:08A	10:34/11:39A	10:20/11:27A	10:53/11:30A	10:59/11:04A	10:18/11:18A	10:56/11:56A	10:41/11:41A	10:21/11:21A
METROLINK 317	M-F	L3:07P	2:50/3:20P	2:38/3:08P	2:34/3:39P	2:20/3:27P	2:53/3:30P	2:59/3:31P	2:18/3:18P	2:56/3:56P	2:41/3:41P	2:21/3:21P
METROLINK 319	M-F	L4:18P	3:50/4:20P	4:08/4:38P	3:34/4:39P	3:20/4:27P	3:53/4:30P	3:59/4:31P	3:18/4:18P	3:56/4:56P	3:41/4:41P	3:21/4:21P

TRAIN NUMBER	DAYS OF OPERATION	TRAIN ARRIVAL	OMNITRANS 110 HOURLY	OMNITRANS 496 HOURLY	FOOTHILL 187 EASTBOUND 30-60 MIN.	FOOTHILL 187 WESTBOUND 30-60 MIN.	FOOTHILL 292 HOURLY	FOOTHILL 480 15-30 MIN.	FOOTHILL 492 30 MINUTES	FOOTHILL 690 COMMUTER	MTA 497 COMMUTER
METROLINK 301	M-F	4:54A	5:32A	6:05A		4:09/5:09A		5:17A	5:05A	5:03A	4:58A
METROLINK 303	M-F	5:44A	5:27/6:40A	6:05A	5:50A	5:53/6:07A	5:50A	5:37/6:00A	6:05A	6:01A	5:45A
METROLINK 305	M-F	6:20A	5:27/6:40A	5:53/7:15A	5:50/6:53A	6:07/6:37A	6:50A	6:00/6:28A	6:35A	6:28A	6:21A
METROLINK 307	M-F	6:50A	6:24/7:40A	5:53/7:15A	5:50/6:53A	6:37/7:06A	6:42/6:50A	6:00/7:00A	6:29/7:05A	7:08A	6:55A
METROLINK 309	M-F	7:30A	7:27/7:40A	6:53/8:05A	6:53/7:38A	7:06/7:36A	6:42/7:50A	7:23/7:41A	6:59/7:35A	7:38A	7:55A
METROLINK 311	M-F	7:59A	7:27/9:01A	7:53/8:05A	7:38/8:08A	7:36/8:06A	7:42/8:50A	7:53/8:00A	7:36/8:05A		8:20A
METROLINK 313	M-F	11:02A	10:59A/12:01P	10:43A/12:55P	10:27/11:27A	10:06/11:06A	10:42/11:52A	10:28/11:26A	10:56/11:05A		
METROLINK 317	M-F	L3:07P	2:55/3:56P	2:10/3:35P	2:27/3:27P	2:51/3:21P	2:40/3:52P	2:39/3:11P	2:56/3:10P		
METROLINK 319	M-F	L4:18P	3:55/4:56P	3:28/4:35P	3:58/4:43P	3:51/4:19P	3:40/4:52P	4:14/4:20P	3:56/4:40P		

EASTBOUND TRAINS FROM LOS ANGELES TO SAN BERNARDINO

TRAIN NUMBER	DAYS OF OPERATION	TRAIN ARRIVAL	OMNITRANS 60 SOUTHBOUND 30 MINUTES	OMNITRANS 60 NORTHBOUND 30 MINUTES	OMNITRANS 62 DIRECTION A HOURLY	OMNITRANS 62 DIRECTION B HOURLY	OMNITRANS 64 30 MINUTES	OMNITRANS 65 30 MINUTES	OMNITRANS 73 EASTBOUND HOURLY	OMNITRANS 73 WESTBOUND HOURLY	OMNITRANS 74 EASTBOUND HOURLY	OMNITRANS 74 WESTBOUND HOURLY
METROLINK 302	M-F	9:47A	9:20/9:50A	9:38/10:08A	9:34/10:39A	9:20/10:27A	9:23/10:00A	9:26/10:04A	9:18/10:18A	8:56/9:56A	9:41/10:41A	9:21/10:21A
METROLINK 304	M-F	12:07P	11:50A/12:20P	11:38A/12:08P	11:34A/12:39P	11:20A/12:27P	11:53A/12:30P	11:59A/12:31P	11:18A/12:18P	11:56A/12:56P	11:41A/12:41P	11:21A/12:21P
METROLINK 306	M-F	1:53P	1:50/2:20P	1:38/2:08P	1:34/2:39P	1:20/2:27P	1:53/2:00P	1:26/2:04P	1:18/2:18P	12:56/1:56P	1:41/2:41P	1:21/2:21P
METROLINK 308	M-F	4:10P	3:50/4:20P	4:08/4:38P	3:34/4:39P	3:20/4:27P	3:53/4:30P	3:59/4:31P	3:18/4:18P	3:56/4:56P	3:41/4:41P	3:21/4:21P
METROLINK 310	M-F	L5:14P	4:50/5:20P	5:08/5:38P	4:34/5:39P	4:20/5:27P	4:53/5:30P	4:59/5:31P	4:18/5:18P	4:56/5:56P	4:41/5:41P	4:21/5:21P
METROLINK 312	M-F	L5:47P	5:20/5:50P	5:38/6:08P	5:34/6:39P	5:20/6:27P	5:23/6:00P	5:26/6:04P	5:18/6:18P	4:56/5:56P	5:41/6:41P	5:21/6:21P
METROLINK 314	M-F	6:19P	5:50/6:20P	6:08/6:41P	5:34/6:39P	5:20/6:27P	5:53/6:30P	5:59/6:50P	6:18/7:18P	5:56/6:56P	5:41/6:41P	5:21/6:21P
METROLINK 316	M-F	6:47P	6:20/6:50P	6:41/7:15P	6:34P	6:23	6:23/7:00P	6:45/6:50P	6:18/7:18P	5:56/6:56P	6:41/7:41P	6:21/7:21P
METROLINK 318	M-F	7:33P	7:20/7:50P	7:15/8:20P		7:23P	7:23/7:56P	7:26/8:00P	7:18/8:18P	6:56/7:56P	6:41/7:41P	7:21/8:21P
METROLINK 320	M-F	8:15P	7:50/8:20P	7:15/8:20P			7:51/9:03P	7:55/9:08P	7:18/8:18P	7:56/8:56P	7:41/8:35P	7:21/8:21P
METROLINK 322	M-F	9:37P	8:50/9:42P	8:20/9:42P			8:58P	9:03P	9:16P	8:56/9:46P	8:35P	9:13/9:56P

TRAIN NUMBER	DAYS OF OPERATION	TRAIN ARRIVAL	OMNITRANS 110 HOURLY	OMNITRANS 496 HOURLY	FOOTHILL 187 EASTBOUND 30-60 MIN.	FOOTHILL 187 WESTBOUND 30-60 MIN.	FOOTHILL 292 HOURLY	FOOTHILL 480 15-30 MIN.	FOOTHILL 492 30 MINUTES	FOOTHILL 690 COMMUTER	MTA 497 COMMUTER
METROLINK 302	M-F	9:47A	8:59/10:01A	9:28/10:48A	9:08/9:57A	9:06/10:06A	9:42/9:52A	9:40/10:00A	9:24/10:05A		
METROLINK 304	M-F	12:07P	11:59A/1:01P	10:43A/12:55P	11:27A/12:27P	12:06/1:06P	11:40A/12:52P	11:45A/12:26P	11:56A/12:35P		
METROLINK 306	M-F	1:53P	12:59/2:01P	12:45/2:20P	1:27/2:27P	1:06/2:06P	1:40/2:52P	1:45/2:00P	1:26/2:10P		
METROLINK 308	M-F	4:10P	3:55/4:56P	3:28/4:35P	3:58/4:43P	3:51/4:19P	3:40/4:52P	4:04/4:20P	3:56/4:10P		3:49P
METROLINK 310	M-F	L5:14P	4:55/6:19P	4:28/5:43P	5:13/5:43P	4:49/5:19P	4:40/5:50P	4:34/5:28P	5:04/5:40P	4:47P	4:59P
METROLINK 312	M-F	L5:47P	4:55/6:19P	5:23/6:35P	5:43/6:13P	5:19/6:04P	5:40/5:50P	5:35/6:10P	5:34/6:10P	5:19P	5:36P
METROLINK 314	M-F	6:19P	6:07/6:19P	5:23/6:35P	6:13/6:43P	6:04/7:07P	5:40/6:50P	6:03/6:45P	6:02/6:40P	5:49P	6:11P
METROLINK 316	M-F	6:47P	6:07/7:16P	6:23/7:35P	6:43/7:13P	6:04/7:07P	6:40/6:50P	6:44/6:58P	6:34/7:10P	6:24P	6:44P
METROLINK 318	M-F	7:33P	7:07/8:04P	7:23/7:35P	7:13/7:58P	7:07/8:08P	6:40/7:50P	7:29/8:07P	7:18/7:40P	6:54P	7:27P
METROLINK 320	M-F	8:15P	7:59P	7:23P	7:58/8:48P	8:08/9:08P	7:42P	7:56/8:37P	7:59/9:10P	7:34P	7:47P
METROLINK 322	M-F	9:37P			8:48/9:48P	9:08/10:08P	8:42P	9:18/10:00P	9:01P		9:01P

L: Regular stop to discharge or pick up passengers except train may leave ahead of schedule

Bernardino Freeway I-10 to downtown Los Angeles. The 690 line provides express service to Azusa and Pasadena via the Foothill Freeway I-210.

The MTA 497 and Foothill Transit 480 lines operate in parallel with Metrolink and compete with the train for passengers who work in the Central City.

The Inland Empire Connection 110 line provides express service between San Bernardino and Montclair via the I-10 Freeway with intermediate stops at Bloomington Park 'n Ride and Ontario Airport. The Inland Empire Connection 496 line provides express service from Riverside to Montclair.

For updated schedules and complete route maps call: MTA at (818) 443-1307 or (909) 620-1871; Foothill Transit at (800) RIDE-INFO; Omnitrans at (909) 983-2671 from Montclair; Riverside Transit Agency at (800) 800-7821.

Points of Interest

Montclair, a city of 28,000 residents, is located in the eastern San Gabriel Valley. The community was known as Monte Vista until 1958 when the residents voted to change the name to Montclair, two years after incorporation. The community is bordered by Upland on the east,

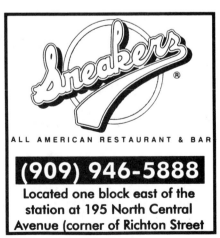

MONTCLAIR STATION SATURDAY BUS CONNECTIONS
WESTBOUND TRAINS FROM SAN BERNARDINO TO LOS ANGELES

TRAIN NUMBER	DAYS OF OPERATION	TRAIN ARRIVAL	OMNITRANS 60 SOUTHBOUND	OMNITRANS 60 NORTHBOUND	OMNITRANS 62 DIRECTION A	OMNITRANS 62 DIRECTION B	OMNITRANS 64	OMNITRANS 65	OMNITRANS 73	OMNITRANS 74 EASTBOUND
BUS FREQUENCY			HOURLY	HOURLY	HOURLY	HOURLY	30 MINUTES	30 MINUTES	HOURLY	HOURLY
METROLINK 301	SATURDAY	7:54A	8:50A	7:08/8:08A	8:39A	8:30A	7:50/8:00A	7:30/8:05A	8:00A	7:41/8:41A
METROLINK 303	SATURDAY	11:21A	10:50/11:50A	11:08A/12:08P	10:34/11:39A	11:20/11:30P	10:53/11:30A	11:00/11:35A	10:55A/12:00P	10:41/11:41A
METROLINK 305	SATURDAY	3:16P	2:50/3:50P	3:08/4:08P	2:34/3:39P	2:20/3:30P	2:53/3:30P	3:00/3:35P	2:55/3:00P	2:41/3:41P
METROLINK 307	SATURDAY	6:36P	5:50/6:38P	6:08/6:51P	5:34/6:39P	5:30P	6:19P	6:00P	5:55/7:00P	5:41P

TRAIN NUMBER	DAYS OF OPERATION	TRAIN ARRIVAL	OMNITRANS 74 WESTBOUND	OMNITRANS 110	OMNITRANS 496	FOOTHILL 187 EASTBOUND	FOOTHILL 187 WESTBOUND	FOOTHILL 292	FOOTHILL 480	FOOTHILL 492 EASTBOUND
BUS FREQUENCY			HOURLY	HOURLY	HOURLY	HOURLY	HOURLY	HOURLY	15 - 60 MIN.	HOURLY
METROLINK 301	SATURDAY	7:54A	8:16A	6:42/8:05A	7:28/8:35A	7:53/8:53A	7:38/8:38A	7:43/8:52A	7:41/8:00A	7:38/8:00A
METROLINK 303	SATURDAY	11:21A	11:16A/12:16P	10:59A/12:05P	10:53A/12:40P	10:53/11:53A	10:38/11:38A	10:43/11:52A	11:11/11:30A	10:49A/12:00P
METROLINK 305	SATURDAY	3:16P	3:16/4:16P	2:59/4:05P	1:58/4:10P	2:23/3:23P	2:38/3:38P	2:43/2:52P	3:11/3:30P	2:49/4:00P
METROLINK 307	SATURDAY	6:36P	6:16/7:05P	5:59P	5:58/7:10P	5:23/6:23P	6:09/7:09P	5:43/6:52P	6:33/7:30P	5:49P

EASTBOUND TRAINS FROM LOS ANGELES TO SAN BERNARDINO

TRAIN NUMBER	DAYS OF OPERATION	TRAIN ARRIVAL	OMNITRANS 60 SOUTHBOUND	OMNITRANS 60 NORTHBOUND	OMNITRANS 62 DIRECTION A	OMNITRANS 62 DIRECTION B	OMNITRANS 64	OMNITRANS 65	OMNITRANS 73	OMNITRANS 74 EASTBOUND
BUS FREQUENCY			HOURLY	HOURLY	HOURLY	HOURLY	30 MINUTES	30 MINUTES	HOURLY	HOURLY
METROLINK 302	SATURDAY	10:04A	9:50/10:50A	9:08/10:08A	9:34/10:39A	9:20/10:30A	9:53/10:30P	10:00/10:35A	9:55/11:00A	9:41/10:41A
METROLINK 304	SATURDAY	1:22P	12:50/1:50P	1:08/2:08P	12:34/1:39P	1:20/1:30P	12:23/1:30P	1:00/1:35P	12:55/2:00P	12:41/1:41P
METROLINK 304	SATURDAY	5:19P	4:50/5:50P	5:08/6:08P	4:34/5:39P	4:20/5:30P	4:53/5:30P	5:00/5:35P	4:55/6:00P	4:41/5:41P
METROLINK 306	SATURDAY	8:39P	7:36P	6:51P					7:49P	7:49P

TRAIN NUMBER	DAYS OF OPERATION	TRAIN ARRIVAL	OMNITRANS 74 WESTBOUND	OMNITRANS 110	OMNITRANS 496	FOOTHILL 187 EASTBOUND	FOOTHILL 187 WESTBOUND	FOOTHILL 292	FOOTHILL 480	FOOTHILL 492 EASTBOUND
BUS FREQUENCY			HOURLY	HOURLY	HOURLY	HOURLY	HOURLY	HOURLY	15 - 60 MIN.	HOURLY
METROLINK 302	SATURDAY	10:04A	9:16/10:16A	9:59/11:05A	9:28/11:05A	9:53/10:53A	9:38/10:38A	9:43/10:52A	9:56/10:15A	9:45/11:00A
METROLINK 304	SATURDAY	1:22P	1:16/2:16P	12:59/2:05P	12:23/2:15P	12:53/2:23P	12:38/1:38P	12:43/1:52P	1:11/1:30P	12:49/2:00P
METROLINK 306	SATURDAY	5:19P	5:16/6:16P	4:59/6:15P	5:03/6:10P	4:23/5:23P	4:38/6:09P	4:43/5:52P	5:18/5:45P	4:49/6:00P
METROLINK 308	SATURDAY	8:39P	7:05P	6:59P	6:58P	7:49P	8:09P	7:43P	8:38/9:15P	

L: Regular stop to discharge or pick up passengers except train may leave ahead of schedule

Claremont and Pomona on the west, and Ontario on the south. The main attraction in the city is the Montclair Plaza Shopping Mall which is located less than a mile from the Montclair Metrolink Station.

Montclair Plaza

Montclair Plaza is the largest mall complex in the Inland Empire. The mall features a food court, over 175 specialtiy stores and hosts Nordstrom, Robinson's-May, The Broadway, JC Penney and Sears department stores.

Surrounding the mall is the Montclair entertainment center which offers many distinctive restaurants, comedy theaters, night spots and movie theaters.

The mall complex and entertainment centercan be reached by taking the Omnitrans 60, 62, 64, 65, 73, and 74 lines.

Places to Stay

There are no hotels in Montclair. The nearest hotels would be in Claremont. See Claremont station for hotel information.

Montclair Bus Transit Center

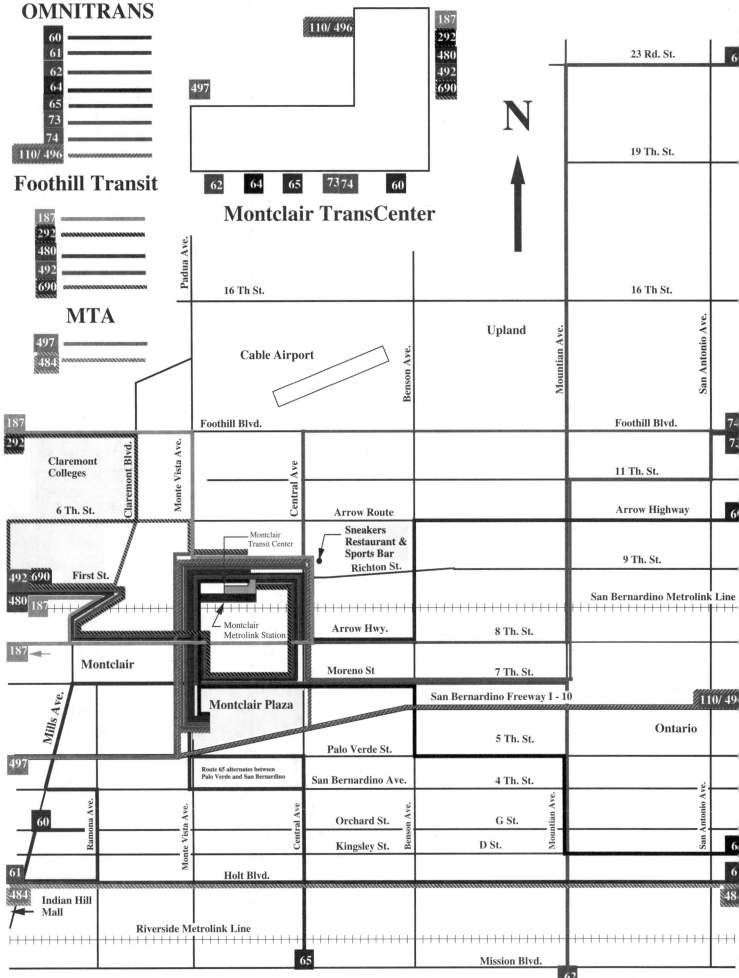

OMNITRANS

60
61
62
64
65
73
74
110/ 496

Foothill Transit

187
292
480
492
690

MTA

497
484

110/ 496   187
292
480
492
690

497

62 64 65 73 74 60

Montclair TransCenter

N

23 Rd. St.   6

19 Th. St.

16 Th. St.   16 Th. St.

Padua Ave.

Upland

Benson Ave.

Mountian Ave.

San Antonio Ave.

Cable Airport

Foothill Blvd.   Foothill Blvd.   74

187   75
292

Claremont Colleges

Claremont Blvd.

Monte Vista Ave.

Central Ave

6 Th. St.   11 Th. St.

Arrow Route   Arrow Highway   6

Montclair Transit Center   Sneakers Restaurant & Sports Bar
Richton St.   9 Th. St.

492 690   First St.

480 187   San Bernardino Metrolink Line

Montclair Metrolink Station   Arrow Hwy.   8 Th. St.

187 ←   Montclair   Moreno St   7 Th. St.

Mills Ave.   San Bernardino Freeway I - 10   110/ 49

Montclair Plaza   Ontario

497   Palo Verde St.   5 Th. St.

Route 65 alternates between Palo Verde and San Bernardino   San Bernardino Ave.   4 Th. St.

San Antonio Ave.

60   Ramona Ave.   Monte Vista Ave.   Central Ave   Orchard St.   Benson Ave.   G St.   Mountian Ave.   6

Kingsley St.   D St.

61   Holt Blvd.   6

484   Indian Hill Mall   48
←

Riverside Metrolink Line

65   Mission Blvd.   62

Montclair Station Vicinity Map

Upland Station

Station Connecting Transit Information

The Upland Metrolink Station is located at 300 East A Street. The station can be reached by taking the Euclid Avenue exit from the I-10 Freeway. From the I-10 go north on Euclid Avenue to A Street and turn right. The station is a block up A Street just past Second Avenue. There are two parking lots serving the station. One is just west of Second Avenue and the other is just east of Fourth Avenue along A Street. The combined capacity is 250 cars. The train boarding platform is well lighted and has a fair amount of shelter. The parking lot is well lighted and maintained. Metrolink personnel man the station during the morning and evening rush hours. The station is unmanned midday when the flex trains arrive.

The station is served by the Omnitrans 62 bus line. There is a bus stop located across "A" Street from the parking lot west of the station. The bus stops at this stop only in the morning and evening rush hours. During the rest

Upland Metrolink Station

of the day you can catch the bus at the stops at the corner of Ninth Street and Euclid Avenue which is about two blocks from the station.

The Omnitrans bus transfer center in downtown Ontario can be reached by taking the southbound Omnitrans 62 bus. From there you can reach the

Ontario International Airport via the Omnitrans 71 line. In addition the Graber Olive House and the Ontario Museum of History & Art are easily accessible using this line from the Upland Metrolink Station. For more info about these venues see the chapter for the East Ontario Metrolink Station.

The station vicinity map provides the routes for bus transit options from the Upland Metrolink Station. The following tables provide the schedule for bus connections with Metrolink. For schedule and route updates call Omnitrans on (800) 966-6428.

Points of Interest

Upland was once an important commercial hub in the eastern San Gabriel Valley as evidenced by the citrus fruit packing plant adjacent to the Metrolink station. Today Upland retains a part of its heritage as a small farming community in its Old Town Upland shopping district. The shopping district extends about one to two blocks in all directions from the intersection of Second Avenue and Ninth Street where there is a large gazebo in the center of the intersection. The gazebo has become the town's

UPLAND STATION WEEKDAY BUS CONNECTIONS
WESTBOUND TRAINS FROM SAN BERNARDINO TO LOS ANGELES

TRAIN NUMBER	DAYS OF OPERATION	TRAIN ARRIVAL	OMNI TRANS 62 DIRECTION A HOURLY	OMNI TRANS 62 DIRECTION B HOURLY
BUS FREQUENCY				
METROLINK 301	M - F	4:49A		
METROLINK 303	M - F	5:39A		
METROLINK 305	M - F	6:15A	6:14A	6:06A
METROLINK 307	M - F	6:45A	6:14/7:14A	6:06/7:40A*
METROLINK 309	M - F	7:23A	7:14/8:18A*	6:06/7:40A*
METROLINK 313	M - F	10:57A	10:18*/11:18A*	10:40*/11:40A*
METROLINK 315	M - F	1:48P	1:18*/2:18P*	1:40*/2:40P*
METROLINK 317	M - F	L3:02P	2:18*/3:18P*	2:40*/3:40P*
METROLINK 323	M - F	L7:32P	7:15P*	6:46P

EASTBOUND TRAINS FROM LOS ANGELES TO SAN BERNARDINO

METROLINK 300	M - F	L7:33A	7:14/8:18A*	6:06/7:40A*
METROLINK 302	M - F	9:52A	9:18*/10:18P*	9:40*/10:40A*
METROLINK 304	M - F	12:12P	11:18*A/12:18P*	11:40A*/12:40P*
METROLINK 306	M - F	1:58P	1:18*/2:18*P	1:40*/2:40P*
METROLINK 310	M - F	L5:19P	5:18*/6:14P	4:40*/5:41P
METROLINK 312	M - F	L5:52P	5:18*/6:14P	5:41/6:46P
METROLINK 314	M - F	L6:24P	6:14/7:15P*	5:41/6:46P
METROLINK 316	M - F	L6:52P	6:14/7:15P*	6:46P
METROLINK 318	M - F	L7:40P	7:15P*	
METROLINK 320	M - F	L8:20P		
METROLINK 322	M - F	9:42P		

UPLAND STATION SATURDAY BUS CONNECTIONS
WESTBOUND TRAINS FROM SAN BERNARDINO TO LOS ANGELES

METROLINK 301	SATURDAY	7:49A	8:18A*	7:40*/8:40A*
METROLINK 303	SATURDAY	11:16A	10:18*/11:18A*	10:40*/11:40A*
METROLINK 305	SATURDAY	3:11P	2:18*/3:18P*	2:40*/3:40P*
METROLINK 307	SATURDAY	6:31P	6:18P*	5:30*/6:37P*

EASTBOUND TRAINS FROM LOS ANGELES TO SAN BERNARDINO

METROLINK 300	SATURDAY	L10:09A	9:18*10:18A*	9:40*/10:40A*
METROLINK 302	SATURDAY	L1:27P	1:18*/2:18P*	12:40*/1:40P*
METROLINK 304	SATURDAY	L5:24P	5:18*/6:18P*	4:30*/5:30P*
METROLINK 306	SATURDAY	L8:44P		

L: Regular stop to discharge or pick up passengers except train may leave ahead of schedule
* Bus stops at Ninth Street and Euclid Avenue.

The Art Room

Antiques & Fine Art
Furniture • Collectibles
Crystal • Porcelain
Conveniently located one and
one half blocks north of the station
at 210 North Second Avenue
(909) 946-8160

The Gazebo In Downtown Upland

trademark and is used in many of the events held in the downtown district throughout the year. Second Avenue and Ninth Street has a variety of upscale boutiques, antique shops and restaurants. The number and quality of the antique shops in the Upland Antique District rival any similar district found in Southern California. At the east end of Ninth Street is the Grove Theater.

The Grove Theater

The Grove Theater is located at the corner of Third Avenue and Ninth Street, about two blocks from Metrolink. The theater features live stage performances presented by the Grove Productions with an occasional performance by a big name entertainer. Performances are normally held at 7:29 P.M. on Fridays and Saturdays and at 3:00 P.M. on Sundays. For current billings call "The Grove" on (909) 920-4343.

Old Rancher's Cannery Cellar

The Cannery Cellar is a unique gift and gourmet shop located in the basement of the Old Rancher's Cannery. The shop specializes in tree-ripened California almonds and olives. The shop is located at 167 S. Sultana Avenue. It is a short two-block walk from the Upland Metrolink Station. The shop is open 9:30 A.M. to 5:00 P.M. Monday through Sunday. For information call (909) 985-0618.

Places to Stay

See the chapter on the East Ontario Station. The city of Upland proper does not have any hotels.

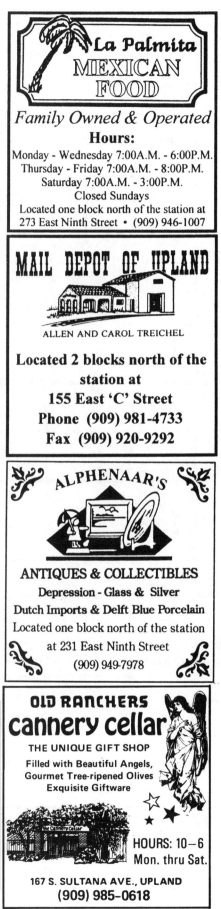
123

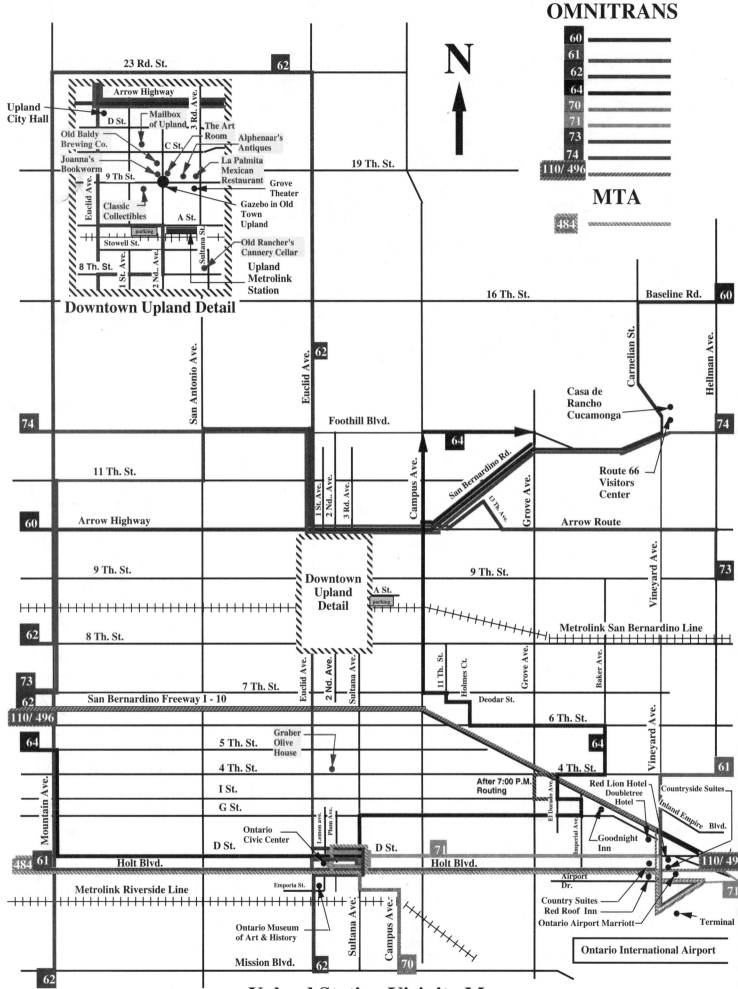

OMNITRANS

60
61
62
64
70
71
73
74
110/ 496

MTA

484

N

Downtown Upland Detail

23 Rd. St.

62

Arrow Highway

Upland City Hall

D St.

Mailbox of Upland

3 Rd. St.

The Art Room

Old Baldy Brewing Co.

C St.

Alphenaar's Antiques

Joanna's Bookworm

La Palmita Mexican Restaurant

9 Th. St.

Euclid Ave.

Grove Theater

Gazebo in Old Town Upland

Classic Collectibles

A St.

parking

Stowell St.

Sultana St.

Old Rancher's Cannery Cellar

Upland Metrolink Station

8 Th. St.

1 St. Ave.

2 Nd. Ave.

19 Th. St.

Baseline Rd.

60

16 Th. St.

San Antonio Ave.

Euclid Ave.

62

Foothill Blvd.

Carnelian St.

Hellman Ave.

Casa de Rancho Cucamonga

74

64

74

San Bernardino Rd.

Grove Ave.

Route 66 Visitors Center

11 Th. St.

1 St. Ave.

2 Nd. Ave.

3 Rd. Ave.

Campus Ave.

13 Th. Ave.

60

Arrow Highway

Arrow Route

Vineyard Ave.

9 Th. St.

9 Th. St.

73

Downtown Upland Detail

A St.

parking

Metrolink San Bernardino Line

62

8 Th. St.

Euclid Ave.

2 Nd. Ave.

Sultana Ave.

11 Th. St.

Holmes Ct.

Grove Ave.

Baker Ave.

73

7 Th. St.

Deodar St.

62

San Bernardino Freeway I - 10

6 Th. St.

110/ 496

64

5 Th. St.

Graber Olive House

4 Th. St.

64

Vineyard Ave.

61

4 Th. St.

I St.

After 7:00 P.M. Routing

Red Lion Hotel

Countryside Suites

Mountain Ave.

G St.

El Dorado Ave.

Doubletree Hotel

Inland Empire Blvd.

Ontario Civic Center

Lemon ave.

Plum Ave.

Goodnight Inn

Imperial Ave

D St.

D St.

71

Holt Blvd.

484

61

Holt Blvd.

110/ 49

Metrolink Riverside Line

Emporia St.

Airport Dr.

71

Country Suites
Red Roof Inn

Ontario Museum of Art & History

Sultana Ave.

Campus Ave.

70

Ontario Airport Marriott

Terminal

Mission Blvd.

62

Ontario International Airport

Upland Station Vicinity Map

Rancho Cucamonga Station

Station Connecting Transit Information

The Rancho Cucamonga Metrolink Station is located at 11208 Azusa Court. The station can be reached by taking the Milliken Avenue exit from the San Bernardino Freeway I-10. From the I-10 go north on Milliken to Seventh Street and turn left. Go one block and turn right on Anaheim Place at the end of Seventh Street. Go one block north on Anaheim Place and turn left on Azusa Ct. which terminates in the station parking lot. From the southbound Ontario Freeway I-15 take the Foothill Boulevard offramp and turn right. Go east on Foothill to Milliken Ave and turn left. The station will be on your right just past the undercrossing for the tracks. From the northbound Ontario Freeway I-15 take the Fourth Street offramp and go east on Fourth Street to Milliken Avenue. Turn right on Milliken and go north to Seventh Street. The station has a 300-car parking lot. The train boarding platform is well lighted and has excellent shelter. The parking lot is well lighted and maintained. Metrolink personnel man the station during the morning and evening rush hours. The station is not manned midday when the flex trains arrive.

The station is served by the Omnitrans 61 bus line. The bus stops are located in the Omnitrans bus transit center which is a part of the Rancho Cucamonga Metrolink Station. There is limited bus service to the station and if you arrive on a midday train or miss the Omnitrans 61 bus you will have a one-half mile walk to the nearest bus stop for the Omnitrans 73 bus which is located at Arrow Route and Milliken Avenue.

The station vicinity map provides the routes for bus transit options from the Rancho Cucamonga Metrolink Station. The following tables provide the schedule for bus connections with Metrolink. For schedule and route updates call Omnitrans on (800) 966-6428.

The area surrounding the Ontario International Airport is easily accessible from the Rancho Cucamonga Metrolink Station. Omnitrans 61 line serving the station provides access to the airport. For information about points of interest

Rancho Cucamonga Metrolink Station

RANCHO CUCAMONGA STATION WEEKDAY BUS CONNECTIONS
WESTBOUND TRAINS FROM SAN BERNARDINO TO LOS ANGELES

TRAIN NUMBER	DAYS OF OPERATION	TRAIN ARRIVAL	OMNI TRANS 61 SOUTHBOUND	OMNI TRANS 61 NORTHBOUND
BUS FREQUENCY		ARRIVAL	HOURLY	HOURLY
METROLINK 301	M - F	*4:42A	5:18A	
METROLINK 303	M - F	*5:32A	5:18/6:04A	
METROLINK 305	M - F	*6:08A	6:04/7:11A	
METROLINK 307	M - F	*6:38A	6:04/7:11A	
METROLINK 309	M - F	*7:16A	7:11A	
METROLINK 311	M - F	7:48A		
METROLINK 313	M - F	10:51A		
METROLINK 315	M - F	1:42P		
METROLINK 317	M - F	L2:56P		
METROLINK 321	M - F	L5:31P		5:29/6:34P

EASTBOUND TRAINS FROM LOS ANGELES TO SAN BERNARDINO

METROLINK 300	M - F	7:39A	7:11A	
METROLINK 302	M - F	9:58A		
METROLINK 304	M - F	12:18P		
METROLINK 306	M - F	L2:05P		
METROLINK 310	M - F	5:25P		5:29P
METROLINK 312	M - F	L5:58P		5:29/6:34P
METROLINK 314	M - F	L6:30P		5:29/6:34P
METROLINK 316	M - F	L6:58P		6:34P
METROLINK 318	M - F	L7:46P		
METROLINK 320	M - F	L8:26P		8:33P
METROLINK 322	M - F	L9:48P		

L: Regular stop to discharge or pick up passengers train may leave ahead of schedule

* Passengers will board these trains from the south platform which is nearest the parking lot.

Train 323 waits for approximately 30 minutes near Rialto for eastbound train 314 to pass.

"Imagine...

*If Rancho Cucamonga were a fragrance
it would be eucalyptus, citrus blossoms,
and the bouquet of wine.*

*If Rancho Cucamonga were a feeling
it would be creative, distinctive,
and proud.*

*If Rancho Cucamonga were an image
it would be snow capped mountains,
inviting neighborhoods,
and contemporary development...*

...Imagine Rancho Cucamonga."

CIVIC CENTER

For more information and a video introduction:
Rancho Cucamonga Redevelopment Agency
P.O. Box 807, Rancho Cucamonga, CA 91729 • (714) 989-1851

Casa de Rancho Cucamonga

RANCHO CUCAMONGA STATION SATURDAY TRAIN SCHEDULE		
WESTBOUND TRAINS FROM SAN BERNARDINO TO LOS ANGELES		
TRAIN NUMBER	DAYS OF OPERATION	TRAIN ARRIVAL
METROLINK 391	SATURDAY	7:42A
METROLINK 393	SATURDAY	11:09A
METROLINK 395	SATURDAY	3:04P
METROLINK 397	SATURDAY	6:24P
EASTBOUND TRAINS FROM LOS ANGELES TO SAN BERNARDINO		
METROLINK 390	SATURDAY	L10:15A
METROLINK 392	SATURDAY	L1:33P
METROLINK 394	SATURDAY	L5:30P
METROLINK 396	SATURDAY	L8:50P

L: Regular stop to discharge or pick up passengers train may leave ahead of schedule

Chaffey College Campus

and hotels surrounding the airport see the chapter for the East Ontario Station on the Riverside Line.

There is **no Saturday** bus service to the Rancho Cucamonga Metrolink Station at this time. Connections with the Omnitrans 73 and 74 bus lines can be made at the Fontana Metrolink Station on Saturday.

Points of Interest

The first residents of the Rancho Cucamonga area were the Serrano-Shoshone Indians who migrated into the area in the 12th century. They were later called Gabrielinos after the San Gabriel Mission. At the end of the mission era in 1839, the Mexican government granted Tiburaco Tapia 13,000 acres of land which he called the Cucamonga Rancho. During the mission era the land was used for sheep and cattle grazing, but Tapia decided that the sandy soil and plentiful water sources would be ideal for growing grapes. As a result of this, Tapia established the first commercial winery in California which today is known as the Thomas Vineyards.

A local legend asserts that shortly before his death, Tapia went out one night and buried his fortune to keep it safe. He died without revealing the location of his hidden treasure. It has not been found to this day.

John Rains and his wife Dona

Merced bought the Rancho from Tapia's heirs for $8,500 in 1858. Rains greatly expanded the original Tapia Vineyards. In 1860, Rains built the first burnt-brick house in California, Casa de Rancho Cucamonga, or the Rains House. Rains was murdered by unknown assailants on November 11, 1862. Dona, his widow, remarried Jose Clement Carrillo and went on to raise her five children by Rains and had another four children with Carrillo. She died in 1907.

Canadians George and William Chaffey settled in Ontario in 1882, purchased land in Rancho Cucamonga, and subdivided it. Chaffey College of Agriculture of the University of Southern California was founded by George and William in 1883.

In the latter part of the 19th century and the first half of the 20th century the Rancho Cucamonga area was initially an agricultural area with the primary crop being grapes for the 20 local wineries. These included Secundo Guasti's Italian Vineyard Company, and the Virginia Dare Winery.

In the 1950's the population of the area began to grow and vineyards began to give way to housing tracks and industrial parks. The city was incorporated on November 8, 1977. Today the vineyards are almost all gone as well as the wineries. In their place is a city of 115,000 residents. The city has its own minor league baseball team, the Rancho Cucamonga *Quakes*, and a new modern baseball stadium.

Casa de Rancho Cucamonga

Casa de Rancho Cucamonga was the home of John Raines and Dona Merced, his wife. Dona was a rich heiress and John wasted no time in investing her money in three rancho's and the Bella Union Hotel in Los Angeles. In the spring of 1861 the Raines moved into their new brick house with their three children. The house was built by Ohio brickmasons who moved to Cucamonga from Los Angeles. Bricks were made on the site by Joseph Mullaly. The original cost was about $18,000, quite a sum for the time. The house today is a National Historic Landmark and is operated by the San Bernardino County Museum. Docents who are members of the Casa de Rancho Cucamonga Historical Society welcome guests from 10:00 A.M. to 4:30 P.M. Wednesday thru Sundays. Admission is free, but donations are welcome. To reach the house from the Rancho Cucamonga station take the Omnitrans 61 line to the Foothill Boulevard and Haven Avenue stop. Transfer to the westbound Omnitrans 74 line and go to the Foothill Boulevard and Vineyard Avenue stop. The house is one block north of Foothill Boulevard just off Vineyard.

Chaffey College

Chaffey College is a two-year to its present site in 1960. The college traces its roots to the Chaffey College of Agriculture founded by George and

Rancho Cucamonga Baseball Stadium

William Chaffey on March 17, 1883. The college was originally located at Fourth Street and Euclid in Ontario. The college closed in the early 1900's due to insufficient financial resources. In 1906 the college's endowment from the Chaffeys was legally separated from the University of Southern California and the Chaffey Union High School District became beneficiary of the College trust. In 1916 the Chaffey Junior College of Agriculture added a postgraduate department to the high school. A separate junior college district was formed in 1922. In 1957 voters approved bonds to develop a campus for the college separate from the high school facility.

Today the college serves the local community on a 200-acre campus which includes a Planetarium, the Wignall Art Museum/Gallery and a 350-person capacity theater. The planetarium has a full schedule of lectures and shows during the school year. Admission is $4.00. For information about current shows call (909) 941-2758. The Wignall Art Museum/Gallery is open Monday thru Friday 12:00 Noon to 4:00 P.M. and Sunday 2:00 P.M. to 4:00 P.M. For information call (909) 987-1737 Ext. 475 or 477. For information about student productions in the campus theater call (909) 941-2425. For general campus information call (909) 987-1737.

The college can be reached by taking the Omnitrans 61 line to the college stop at the end of the line.

Rancho Cucamonga Baseball Stadium

The Rancho Cucamonga Baseball Stadium is located at Arrow Route and Rochester Avenue. The stadium is the home of the Rancho Cucamonga *Quakes*, a minor league baseball team. For game dates and times call (909) 481-5252. Ticket prices vary from $3.00 to $5.00 for box seats during the 1995 season. The stadium can be reached by taking the Omnitrans 61 line to the Haven Avenue and Arrow Route stop. There you would transfer to the eastbound Omnitrans 73 line and take it to the Arrow Route and Rochester

Avenue stop.

Route 66 Visitor's Center

The historic Route 66 passes through the city of Rancho Cucamonga along Foothill Boulevard. Most of the immigrants traveling to Southern California from the eastern states used this route in the 1940's, 1950's and 1960's; time long before the Interstates replaced the old route. The visitor's center and museum have photo's of the old route and memorabilia from the era when Route 66 crossed most of this nation east to west. The center is located at 7965 Vineyard Avenue just off Foothill Boulevard behind the Thomas Winery building which today is a restaurant. To reach the center from the Rancho Cucamonga Station take the Omnitrans 61 line to the Foothill Boulevard and Haven Avenue stop. Transfer to the westbound Omnitrans 74 line and go to the Foothill Boulevard and Vineyard Avenue stop.

Terra Vista Town Center Mall

Terra Vista Town Center is Rancho Cucamonga's new outdoor mall. The shopping center features a Montgomery Ward, Mervyn's and Target department stores, Edwards Cinemas, an outdoor food court and a total of over 70 specialty shops. The center is located at Haven and Foothill boulevards. The center can be reached by taking the Omnitrans 61 line to the Foothill Boulevard and Haven Avenue stop.

Places to Stay

Best Western Heritage Inn

The Best Western Heritage Inn is located at 8179 Spruce Avenue. The hotel phone number is (909) 466-1111. For reservations call (800) 528-1234.

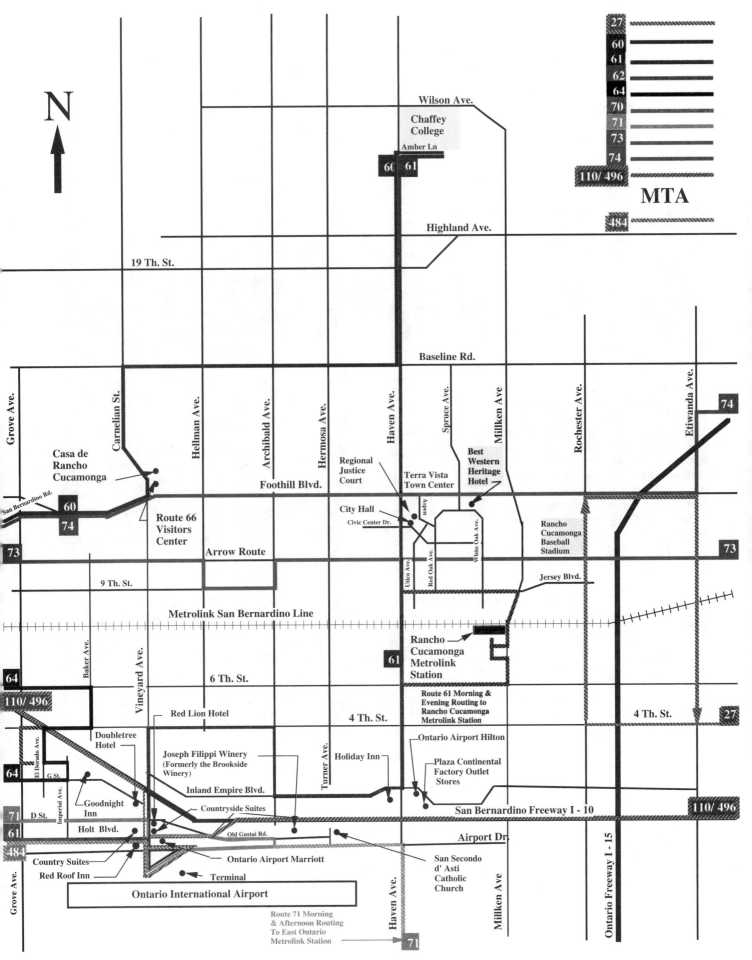

Rancho Cucamonga Station Vicinity Map

Fontana Station

Station Connecting Transit Information

The Fontana Metrolink Station is located at 16777 Orange Way. The station can be reached by taking the Sierra Avenue exit from the San Bernardino Freeway I-10. From the I-10 go north on Sierra Avenue to Orange Way, and turn left. The station will be on your left just off Sierra Avenue. The station has a 348-car parking lot. The train boarding platform is well lighted and has excellent shelter. The parking lot is also well lighted and maintained. Metrolink personnel man the station during the morning and evening rush hours. The station is not manned midday when the flex trains arrive.

The station is served by the Omnitrans 14, 20, 21, 23, 73 and 74 bus lines. The bus stops are located in the Omnitrans Bus Transit Center which is a part of the Fontana Metrolink Station. The station vicinity map provides the routes for bus transit options from the Fontana Metrolink Station. The following tables provide the schedule for bus connections with Metrolink. For schedule and route updates call Omnitrans on (088) 966-6428.

Fontana Metrolink Station

Points of Interest

Active development of the area known today as Fontana did not begin until the early 1900's. The Fontana Development Company acquired the land that is today Fontana. It began as a community called Rosena. A. B. Miller changed the name to Fontana in 1913, and built a community based upon diversified agriculture. This included citrus, grain, grapes, poultry and swine. In 1942 Kaiser Steel built a steel mill in Fontana. Fontana soon became

FONTANA STATION WEEKDAY BUS CONNECTIONS

WESTBOUND TRAINS FROM SAN BERNARDINO TO LOS ANGELES

TRAIN NUMBER	DAYS OF OPERATION	TRAIN ARRIVAL	OMNITRANS 14	OMNITRANS 20	OMNITRANS 20	OMNITRANS 21	OMNITRANS 23	OMNITRANS 23	OMNITRANS 73	OMNITRANS 74
				DIRECTION A	DIRECTION B		DIRECTION A	DIRECTION B		
BUS FREQUENCY			15 MINUTES	45 MINUTES	45 MINUTES	HOURLY	HOURLY	HOURLY	HOURLY	HOURLY
METROLINK 301	M - F	4:35A	4:30/4:50A	5:20A					4:38A	5:15A
METROLINK 303	M - F	5:24A	5:15/5:50A	6:05A	5:48A				5:35A	6:04A
METROLINK 305	M - F	6:00A	5:55/6:20A	5:52/6:05A	6:26A	5:55/6:02A	5:54/6:11A		5:31/6:39A	5:55/6:04A
METROLINK 307	M - F	6:30A	5:55/6:35A	5:52/6:50A	6:23/7:10A	5:55/6:48A	5:54/7:13A	6:47A	5:31/6:39A	5:55/7:03A
METROLINK 309	M - F	7:08A	7:00/7:20A	6:45/7:35A	7:01/7:10A	6:40/7:48A	7:02/7:13A	7:47A	6:34/7:38A	6:46/8:07A
METROLINK 313	M - F	10:43A	10:30/10:50A	10:30/10:50A	10:15/11:05A	9:40/10:48A	10:15/11:20A	9:42/10:47A	10:33/11:38A	9:51/11:07A
METROLINK 315	M - F	1:34P	1:30/1:35P	1:30/1:35P	1:15/2:13P	12:40/1:48P	1:15/2:20P	12:42/1:47P	1:33/1:41P	12:51/2:07P
METROLINK 317	M - F	2:48P	2:45/2:50P	2:15/3:05P	2:00/2:55P	2:40/3:05P	2:15/3:20P	2:42/3:47P	2:35/3:38P	1:51/3:07P
METROLINK 323	M - F	L7:11P	7:00/7:12P	6:53P	6:30/7:25P	6:40/8:00P	7:08P	6:42/7:37P	6:33/7:38P	6:51/8:16P

EASTBOUND TRAINS FROM LOS ANGELES TO SAN BERNARDINO

METROLINK 302	M - F	L10:07A	10:00/10:20A	9:45/10:35A	9:30/10:20A	9:40/10:48A	9:15/10:20A	9:42/10:47A	9:33/10:38A	9:51/10:07A
METROLINK 304	M - F	L12:27P	12:15/12:35P	12:00/12:50P	11:45A/12:35P	11:40A/12:48P	12:15/1:20P	11:42A/12:47P	11:33A/12:38P	11:51A/1:07P
METROLINK 306	M - F	L2:12P	2:00/2:20P	1:30/2:20P	2:00/2:13P	1:40/3:05P	1:15/2:20P	1:42/2:47P	1:33/2:40P	1:51/3:02P
METROLINK 312	M - F	L6:07P	6:00/6:11P	6:00/6:13P	5:45/6:43P	5:40/6:48P	5:15/6:20P	5:42/6:42P	5:33/6:40P	5:51/6:16P
METROLINK 314	M - F	L6:39P	6:30/6:43P	6:00/6:58P	6:30/6:43P	5:40/6:48P	6:15P	5:42/6:42P	6:33/6:40P	5:51/7:07P
METROLINK 316	M - F	L7:07P	7:00/7:12P	6:53P	6:30/7:25P	6:40/8:00P	6:15P	6:42/7:37P	6:33/7:38P	6:51/7:07P
METROLINK 318	M - F	L7:56P	7:45/8:02P	7:38P	7:20P	7:40/8:00P	7:08P	7:33P	7:33/8:45P	7:50/8:16P
METROLINK 320	M - F	L8:36P	7:45/8:55P		8:04P	7:40/8:48P			8:33/8:45P	7:50/9:05P
METROLINK 322	M - F	L9:57P	9:17/10:29P			9:25/10:24P			9:30P	9:31P

L: Regular stop to discharge or pick up passengers except train may leave ahead of schedule

FONTANA STATION SATURDAY BUS CONNECTIONS

WESTBOUND TRAINS FROM SAN BERNARDINO TO LOS ANGELES

TRAIN NUMBER	DAYS OF OPERATION	TRAIN ARRIVAL	OMNITRANS 14	OMNITRANS 20	OMNITRANS 20	OMNITRANS 21	OMNITRANS 23	OMNITRANS 23	OMNITRANS 73	OMNITRANS 74
				DIRECTION A	DIRECTION B		DIRECTION A	DIRECTION B		
BUS FREQUENCY			30 MINUTES	45 MINUTES	45 MINUTES	HOURLY	HOURLY	HOURLY	HOURLY	HOURLY
METROLINK 391	SATURDAY	7:35A	7:15/7:50A	8:00A	7:30/8:20A	8:20A	8:15A	7:50A	7:45A	7:35/8:05A
METROLINK 393	SATURDAY	11:02A	10:45/11:20A	11:00/11:05A	10:30/11:20A	10:15/11:20A	10:10/11:15A	10:45/11:50A	11:00/11:45A	10:40/11:05A
METROLINK 395	STAURDAY	2:57P	2:45/3:20P	2:45/3:35P	2:15/3:05P	2:15/3:20P	2:10/3:15P	2:45/3:50P	2:00/3:45P	2:40/3:05P
METROLINK 397	SATURDAY	6:17P	6:15/6:20P	5:45P	6:00P	5:50P	6:10P	5:45P	6:00/6:45P	5:40P

EASTBOUND TRAINS FROM LOS ANGELES TO SAN BERNARDINO

METROLINK 390	SATURDAY	L10:24A	10:15/10:50A	10:15/11:05A	9:45/10:35A	10:15/11:20P	10:10/11:15A	9:45/10:50A	10:00/10:45A	9:40/11:05A
METROLINK 392	SATURDAY	L1:42P	1:15/1:50P	1:15/2:05P	1:30/2:20P	1:15/2:20P	1:10/2:15P	12:45/1:50P	1:00/1:45P	1:40/2:05P
METROLINK 394	SATURDAY	L5:39P	5:15/5:50P	5:00/5:50P	5:15/6:05P	5:15P	5:10P	4:45/5:50P	5:00/5:45P	4:40/6:05P
METROLINK 396	SATURDAY	L8:59P	7:45P						7:57P	

L: Regular stop to discharge or pick up passengers except train may leave ahead of schedule

Southern California's leading steel producer. In the late 1970's Kaiser Steel cut down production and in 1984 closed the mill. The plate steel and rolling mill was acquired by California Steel Company and continues to produce steel products today.

Today Fontana is a city of 97,000 residents where housing tracts have replaced the orange groves and vineyards of yesterday. The old downtown district lies north of the Metrolink tracks along Sierra Avenue. The business district is comprised of a number of buildings that date back to the 1920's.

Mary Vagle Science and Nature Center

The Mary Vagle Science and Nature Center is located at 11501 Cypress Avenue. There is no public transit access to the center. The center is located in the Jurupa Hills Regional Park. It has displays of reptiles and exhibits of stuffed animals which were donated by local taxidermists Joe and Mary Vagle. The primary use of the center today is the headquarters of the Fontana Native American Indian Center. It is also a focal point for local group activities in the surrounding Jurupa Hills Regional Park. The surrounding park has three miles of hiking trails, a one-acre pond and the ninth most significant petroglyph site in the State of California. The center is open Monday, Wednesday and Thursday 10:00 A.M. to 2:00 P.M., Tuesday 6:00 P.M. to 9:00 P.M. and Saturday 9:00 A.M. to 12:00 noon. The center is closed Friday and Sunday. For Information call (909) 350-7635.

Mary Vagle Science & Nature Center:

Places to Stay

Fontana Comfort Inn

The Fontana Comfort Inn is located at 16780 Valley Boulevard. The hotel phone number is (909) 822-3350. For Reservations call (800) 221-2222.

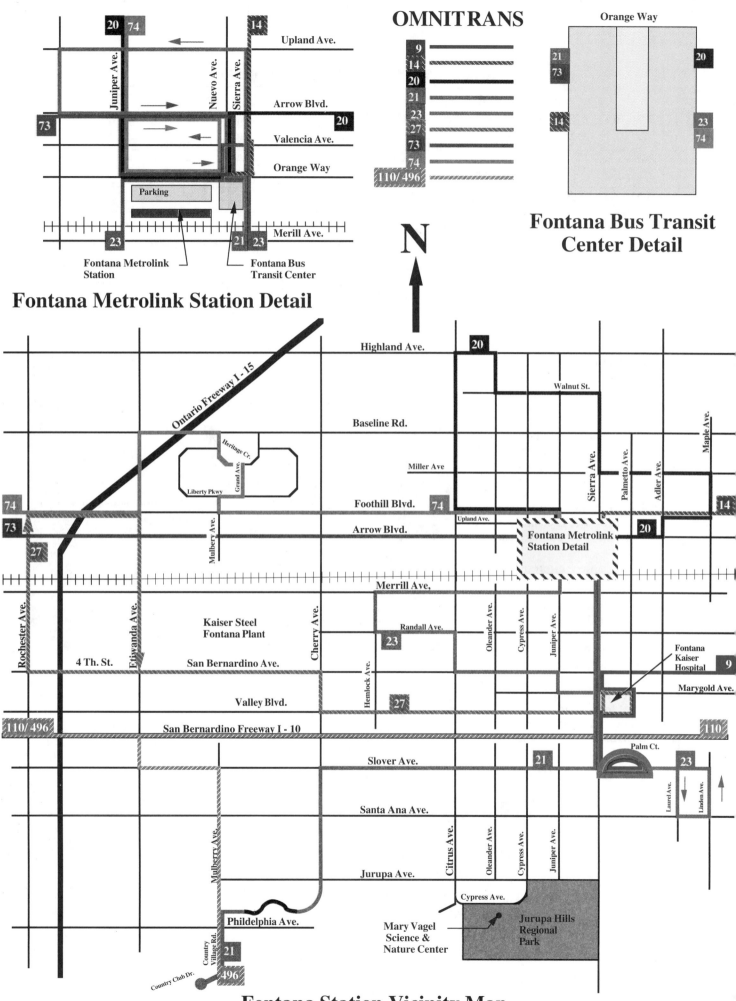

OMNITRANS

Fontana Metrolink Station Detail

20 74   14   Upland Ave.

Juniper Ave.   Nuevo Ave.   Sierra Ave.

Arrow Blvd.   20

73   Valencia Ave.

Orange Way

Parking

23   21 23   Merill Ave.

Fontana Metrolink Station   Fontana Bus Transit Center

9
14
20
21
23
27
73
74
110/ 496

Fontana Bus Transit Center Detail

Orange Way

21 73   20

14   23 74

N

Fontana Station Vicinity Map

Highland Ave.   20

Walnut St.

Ontario Freeway I - 15

Baseline Rd.

Heritage Cr.   Miller Ave

Grand Ave.   Sierra Ave.   Palmetto Ave.   Adler Ave.   Maple Ave.

Liberty Pkwy

74   Foothill Blvd.   74   14

Mulbery Ave.   Arrow Blvd.   Upland Ave.   20

73

Fontana Metrolink Station Detail

27

Merrill Ave,

Rochester Ave.   Etiwanda Ave.   Kaiser Steel Fontana Plant   Cherry Ave.   Randall Ave.   Oleander Ave.   Cypress Ave.   Juniper Ave.

23

Fontana Kaiser Hospital   9

4 Th. St.   San Bernardino Ave.

Hemlock Ave.   Marygold Ave.

Valley Blvd.   27

110/ 496   San Bernardino Freeway I - 10   110

Palm Ct.

Slover Ave.   21   23

Laurel Ave.   Linden Ave.

Santa Ana Ave.

Citrus Ave.   Oleander Ave.   Cypress Ave.   Juniper Ave.

Jurupa Ave.

Cypress Ave.

Mary Vagel Science & Nature Center   Jurupa Hills Regional Park

Mulberry Ave.

Phildelphia Ave.

Country Village Rd.   21

Country Club Dr.   496

Rialto Station

Station Connecting Transit Information

The Rialto Metrolink Station is located at 261 S. Palm Avenue. The station can be reached by taking the Riverside Avenue exit from the San Bernardino Freeway I - 10. From the I-10 go north on Riverside Avenue to Rialto Avenue and turn left. Go one block on Rialto Avenue to Orange Street and turn left. Orange Street terminates at the Metrolink 168-car parking lot. The train boarding platform is well lighted and has a fair amount of shelter. The parking lot is well lighted and maintained. Metrolink personnel man the station during the morning and evening rush hours. The station is not manned midday when the flex trains arrive.

The station is served by the Omnitrans 9, 22 and 26 bus lines. The bus stops are located on Riverside Avenue just north of the tracks. The station vicinity map provides the routes for bus transit options from the Rialto Metrolink Station. The following tables provide the schedules for bus

Rialto Metrolink Station

connections at the Rialto Metrolink Station. For schedule and route updates call Omnitrans on (800) 966-6428.

Points of Interest

Rialto was first settled in 1853 at the same time as San Bernardino by George Lord. He took up residence on

RIALTO STATION WEEKDAY BUS CONNECTIONS

WESTBOUND TRAINS FROM SAN BERNARDINO TO LOS ANGELES

TRAIN NUMBER	DAYS OF OPERATION	TRAIN ARRIVAL	OMNITRANS 9 WESTBOUND HOURLY	OMNITRANS 9 EASTBOUND HOURLY	OMNITRANS 22 NORTHBOUND 30 MINUTES	OMNITRANS 22 SOUTHBOUND 30 MINUTES	OMNITRANS 26 WESTBOUND HOURLY	OMNITRANS 26 EASTBOUND HOURLY
BUS FREQUENCY								
METROLINK 301	M - F	4:30A			4:26/5:13A	5:13A		
METROLINK 303	M - F	5:19A	5:30A	5:47A	5:13/5:45A	5:13/5:46A	5:29A	5:53A
METROLINK 305	M - F	5:55A	5:30/6:33A	5:47/6:55A	5:45/6:19A	5:46/6:18A	5:29/6:18A	5:53/6:58A
METROLINK 307	M - F	6:25A	5:30/6:33A	5:47/6:55A	6:19/6:56A	6:18/6:54A	6:18/7:50A	5:53/6:58A
METROLINK 309	M - F	7:03A	6:33/7:33A	6:55/7:46A	6:56/7:36A	6:54/7:39A	6:18/7:50A	6:58/8:23A
METROLINK 313	M - F	10:38A	10:33/11:33A	9:46/10:46A	10:36/11:06A	10:13/10:43A	9:50/10:50A	10:23/11:23A
METROLINK 315	M - F	1:29P	12:33/1:33P	12:46/1:46P	1:06/1:49P	1:09/1:47P	12:50/1:50P	1:23/2:30P
METROLINK 317	M - F	2:43P	2:33/3:22P	1:46/2:46P	2:42/3:06P	2:39/3:13P	1:50/3:10P	2:30/3:23P
METROLINK 323	M - F	L6:35P	5:33/6:46P	5:55/7:05P	6:17/6:48P	6:16/6:50P	5:51/7:20P	6:23P

EASTBOUND TRAINS FROM LOS ANGELES TO SAN BERNARDINO

METROLINK 302	M - F	L10:12A	9:33/10:33A	9:46/10:46A	9:36/10:10:15A	9:39/10:13A	9:50/10:50A	9:23/10:23A
METROLINK 304	M - F	L12:32P	11:33/12:33P	11:46A/12:46P	12:06/12:36P	12:09/12:39P	12:50/1:50P	12:23/1:23P
METROLINK 306	M - F	L2:17P	1:33/2:33P	1:46/2:46P	2:09/2:42P	1:47/2:39P	1:50/3:10P	1:23/2:30P
METROLINK 312	M - F	L6:12P	5:33/6:46P	5:55/7:05P	5:36/6:17P	5:53/6:16P	5:51/7:20P	5:23/6:23P
METROLINK 314	M - F	L6:44P	5:33/6:46P	5:55/7:05P	6:17/6:48P	6:16/6:50P	5:51/7:20P	6:23P
METROLINK 316	M - F	L7:12P	6:46/7:42P	7:05/8:15P	6:48/7:17P	6:50/7:18P	5:51/7:20P	
METROLINK 318	M - F	L8:01P	7:42/8:31P	7:05/8:15P	7:40/8:17P	7:50/8:13P	7:20/8:05P	
METROLINK 320	M - F	L8:41P	8:31/9:46P	8:15/9:00P	8:17/8:49P	8:13/8:50P	8:05P	
METROLINK 322	M - F	L10:02P	9:46P	9:00P	9:24/10:06P	9:22/10:06P		

L: Regular stop to discharge or pick up passengers except train may leave ahead of schedule

RIALTO STATION SATURDAY BUS CONNECTIONS

WESTBOUND TRAINS FROM SAN BERNARDINO TO LOS ANGELES

TRAIN NUMBER	DAYS OF OPERATION	TRAIN ARRIVAL	OMNITRANS 9	OMNITRANS 9	OMNITRANS 22	OMNITRANS 22	OMNITRANS 26	OMNITRANS 26
			WESTBOUND	EASTBOUND	NORTHBOUND	SOUTHBOUND	WESTBOUND	EASTBOUND
BUS FREQUENCY			HOURLY	HOURLY	HOURLY	HOURLY	HOURLY	HOURLY
METROLINK 391	SATURDAY	7:30A	8:33A	9:57A	8:36A	8:09A	7:55A	7:22/8:22A
METROLINK 393	SATURDAY	10:57A	10:33/11:33A	10:57/11:57A	10:36/11:36A	10:09.11:09A	10:50/11:50A	10:22/11:22A
METROLINK 395	SATURDAY	2:52P	2:33/3:33P	1:57/2:57P	2:36/3:36P	2:09/3:09P	2:50/3:50P	2:22/3:22P
METROLINK 397	SATURDAY	6:12P	5:33P	5:51P	5:36/6:36P	6:09P	5:50P	5:23P

EASTBOUND TRAINS FROM LOS ANGELES TO SAN BERNARDINO

METROLINK 390	SATURDAY	L10:29A	9:33/10:33A	9:57/10:57A	9:36/10:36A	10:09/11:09A	9:50/10:50A	9:22/10:22A
METROLINK 392	SATURDAY	L1:47P	1:33/2:33P	12:57/1:57P	1:36/2:36P	1:09/2:09P	12:50/1:53P	1:22/2:22P
METROLINK 394	SATURDAY	L5:44P	5:33	4:57/5:51P	5:36/6:36P	5:09/6:09P	4:50/5:50P	5:23P
METROLINK 396	SATURDAY	L9:04P						

L: Regular stop to discharge or pick up passengers except train may leave ahead of schedule

the west bank of Lytle Creek when the Mormons in San Bernardino would not sell him land. In 1887 the Semi-Tropic Land & Water Company purchased 28,500 acres of land west of Lytle Creek which eventually became the township of Rialto. The town was laid out along the line of the new Santa Fe Railway line. The town continued to grow and was incorporated as a city in 1911.

Today Rialto is a city of 75,000 residents where housing tracts have replaced the orange groves and vineyards of yesterday. The old downtown district lies north of the Metrolink tracks along Riverside Avenue. The business district is comprised of a number of buildings that date back to the 1920's.

Rialto Historical Society Museum

The Rialto Historical Society operates a museum in the old First Christian Church located at 201 N. Riverside Avenue. The church was first dedicated in 1907 and its architecture is in the Victorian style popular in the early 1900's. The museum has several rooms with antique furniture from the early days of Rialto. The most interesting exhibit in the museum is the Orange Packing Crate Label collection. These labels are works of art with full color lithographs. The museum has on display labels from virtually every citrus packing house in the Rialto area. The museum is only a couple of blocks north of the Metrolink station. The Museum is open 2:00 P.M. to 4:00 P.M. Wednesday and 10:00 A.M. to 2:00 P.M. Saturday.

Rialto Historical Society Museum

Places to Stay

Best Western Empire Inn

The Best Western Empire Inn is located at 475 W. Valley Boulevard. The hotel has a van which will pick you up at the Rialto Metrolink Station. Call the hotel before your arrival and tell them when your train will arrive and they will pick you up. The hotel phone number is (909) 877-0690. For reservations call (800) 528-1234.

Rialto Travelodge

The Rialto Travelodge is located at 425 West Foothill Boulevard. The hotel phone number is (909) 820-0705. For reservations call (800) 578-7878.

134

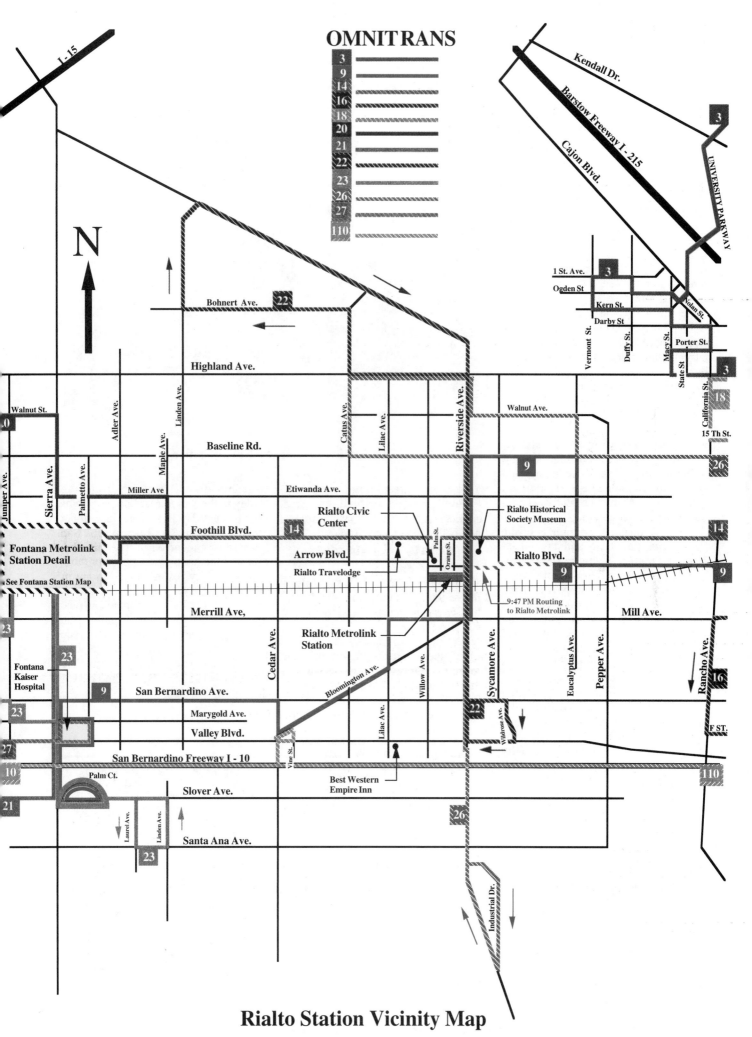

OMNITRANS

| 3 |
| 9 |
| 14 |
| 16 |
| 18 |
| 20 |
| 21 |
| 22 |
| 23 |
| 26 |
| 27 |
| 110 |

N

I - 15

Kendall Dr.

Barstow Freeway I - 215

Cajon Blvd.

UNIVERSITY PARKWAY

3

1 St. Ave.
Ogden St
3
Kern St.
Nolan St.
Darby St
Duffy St.
Macy St.
Porter St.
Vermont St.
State St
California St.
3
18
15 Th St.

Bohnert Ave.
22

Highland Ave.

Walnut St.
Adler Ave.
Linden Ave.
Maple Ave.
Cattus Ave.
Lilac Ave.
Riverside Ave.
Walnut Ave.

Baseline Rd.
9
26

Juniper Ave.
Sierra Ave.
Palmetto Ave.
Miller Ave
Etiwanda Ave.

Foothill Blvd.
14
Rialto Civic Center
Rialto Historical Society Museum
14

Arrow Blvd.
Palm St.
Orange St.
Rialto Blvd.
9
9

Rialto Travelodge

Fontana Metrolink Station Detail
See Fontana Station Map

9:47 PM Routing to Rialto Metrolink
Mill Ave.

Merrill Ave,

23

Rialto Metrolink Station

Cedar Ave.
Bloomington Ave.
Willow Ave.
Sycamore Ave.
Eucalyptus Ave.
Pepper Ave.
Rancho Ave.

23

Fontana Kaiser Hospital

9
San Bernardino Ave.
22
16

23
Marygold Ave.
Wildrose Ave.
F ST.

27
Valley Blvd.
Lilac Ave.
Vine St.

San Bernardino Freeway I - 10
10
110

10
Palm Ct.

21
Slover Ave.
Best Western Empire Inn
Laurel Ave.
Linden Ave.
Santa Ana Ave.
23
26

Industrial Dr.

Rialto Station Vicinity Map

San Bernardino Station

Station Connecting Transit Information

The San Bernardino Metrolink Station is located at 1204 West Third Street. The station can be reached by taking the Second Street exit from the northbound I-215 Freeway. From the I-215 go west on Second Street to K Street Turn right on K Street and the station will be at the end of K at Third Street. From the southbound I-215 take the Third Street exit. Go west on Third Street and the station will be on your right. The train boarding platform is well lighted with limited shelter. The parking lot is not well maintained or lighted.

The San Bernardino Station building was completed in 1927 in the California Spanish Colonial Revival Architectural style. It is one of the more elaborate and interesting station buildings on the Metrolink system. The building has seen better days and is in much need of repair and maintenance. Amtrak presently operates out of the station building

The station is the terminus of the San Bernardino Line and the Inland Empire-Orange County Line. The Omnitrans 1, 9, and 26 bus lines serve the station. The bus stops for these lines are located directly in front of the station on Third Street. In addition the Omnitrans line 16 has a stop at Second Street and K Street about a block from the station. The station vicinity map provides the routes for bus transit options from the San Bernardino Metrolink Station. The following tables provide the schedule of bus connections with Metrolink.

Outside of the immediate vicinity of the San Bernardino Metrolink Station the 1 line provides service to Colton. The 9 line provides service to Rialto and Fontana. The 26 line provides service to Rialto and Colton.

In downtown San Bernardino Omnitrans has its major Transit Mall along Fourth Street. San Bernardino has a fairly extensive local bus system and virtually any place in the city can be reached by one of the busses that stop along Fourth Street. There is a blow up of the Fourth Street Transit Mall on the San Bernardino Station vicinity map. The station vicinity map provides the routes and stop locations

San Bernardino Metrolink Station

for the Fourth Street Transit Mall.

For updated schedules, and complete route maps for Omnitrans lines, call (800) 966-6428.

Points of Interest

San Bernardino is the administrative center of the Inland Empire with a population of 170,000. The city was founded by a contingent of 500 Mormons in 1851. Three years later the city was officially incorporated. In 1857 approximately 60 percent of the Mormons living in San Bernardino returned to Utah. In 1860 William F.

Holcomb found gold in Holcomb Valley in the San Bernardino mountains near present day Big Bear Lake, about 60 miles from San Bernardino. San Bernardino prospered during this time as it was the jumping off point for those who would try to find their fortune in Holcomb Valley.

In the 1880's the railroads arrived in San Bernardino transforming San Bernardino into an important trade center for the Inland Empire. Citrus became the farm crop in the surrounding area and in 1911 San Bernardino hosted the National Orange Show.

SAN BERNARDINO STATION SATURDAY BUS CONNECTIONS

WESTBOUND TRAINS FROM SAN BERNARDINO TO LOS ANGELES

TRAIN NUMBER	DAYS OF OPERATION	TRAIN DEPARTURE	OMNITRANS 9	OMNITRANS 9	OMNITRANS 26
			EASTBOUND	WESTBOUND	EASTBOUND
BUS FREQUENCY			HOURLY	HOURLY	HOURLY
METROLINK 391	SATURDAY	7:23A		7:04A	
METROLINK 393	SATURDAY	10:50A	10:21A	10:09A	
METROLINK 395	SATURDAY	2:45P	2:21P	2:09P	
METROLINK 397	SATURDAY	6:05P	5:21P	5:09P	6:00P

EASTBOUND TRAINS FROM LOS ANGELES TO SAN BERNARDINO

METROLINK 390	SATURDAY	10:38A	11:21A	11:09A	
METROLINK 392	SATURDAY	1:56P	2:21P	2:09P	
METROLINK 394	SATURDAY	5:53P	6:12P		6:00P
METROLINK 396	SATURDAY	9:13P			

L: Regular stop to discharge or pick up passengers except train may leave ahead of schedule

Downtown San Bernardino

Downtown San Bernardino is the administrative center of San Bernardino County. The local government center includes the San Bernardino City Hall, County Government Center, County Courthouse and State Government offices. There are several high rise office buildings and an interesting downtown shopping district which is anchored by the Carousel Mall. The California Theater for the Performing Arts is on Fourth Street.

California Theater

The California Theater of the Performing Arts is located at 562 W. Fourth Street in downtown San Bernardino. The theater is an excellent example of Spanish Colonial Revival architecture popular in the 1920's. The theater originally opened in 1928 as a movie theater and hosted vaudeville

California Theater

acts in the 1930's. Today the theater is home to the San Bernardino Civic Light Opera and the Inland Empire Philharmonic. For information about current bookings please call (909) 386-7353 or (800) 228-1155.

Carousel Mall

The Carousel Mall is located at Second and F streets in downtown San Bernardino. It features a train ride and carousel in the promenade.

San Bernardino Valley College

The San Bernardino Valley College is located at 701 South Mt. Vernon Avenue. The college can be reached by taking the Omnitrans 1 line from Metrolink or the Fourth Street Transit Mall. The college is a two-year institution and offers an Associate of Arts Degree in a wide range of majors. The campus has an outdoor Greek Theater at the center of the campus. There is also a planetarium which offers shows to the public during the school year. For information on the planetarium call (909) 888-6511 Extension 1635. There is a small

SAN BERNARDINO STATION WEEKDAY BUS CONNECTIONS
WESTBOUND TRAINS FROM SAN BERNARDINO TO LOS ANGELES

TRAIN NUMBER	DAYS OF OPERATION	TRAIN DEPARTURE	OMNITRANS 1	OMNITRANS 1	OMNITRANS 9	OMNITRANS 9	OMNITRANS 26	OMNITRANS 26
			SOUTHBOUND	NORTHBOUND	EASTBOUND	WESTBOUND	EASTBOUND	WESTBOUND
BUS FREQUENCY			HOURLY	HOURLY	HOURLY	HOURLY	HOURLY	HOURLY
METROLINK 301	M - F	4:22A						
METROLINK 303	M - F	5:11A	5:06A			5:08A		
METROLINK 305	M - F	5:47A	5:06A	5:42A		5:08A		5:40A
METROLINK 307	M - F	6:17A	6:12A	6:10A	6:10A	6:11A		
METROLINK 309	M - F	6:55A			6:10A	6:11A	6:27A	
METROLINK 313	M - F	10:30A			10:10A	10:09A		
METROLINK 315	M - F	1:21P			1:10P	1:09P		
METROLINK 317	M - F	2:35P			2:10P	2:09P		
METROLINK 323	M - F	L6:28P	6:25P		6:19P	6:26P		6:26P

WESTBOUND TRAINS FROM SAN BERNARDINO TO IRVINE

METROLINK 301	M - F	5:26A	5:06A			5:08A		
METROLINK 303	M - F	6:28A	6:12A	6:10A	6:10A	6:11A	6:27A	5:40A
METROLINK 305	M - F	3:03P			2:10P	2:53P		

EASTBOUND TRAINS FROM LOS ANGELES TO SAN BERNARDINO

METROLINK 302	M - F	10:21A			11:10A	11:09A		
METROLINK 304	M - F	12:41P			1:10P	1:09P		
METROLINK 306	M - F	2:26P			3:10P	2:53P		
METROLINK 312	M - F	6:22P	6:25P	6:30P	7:27P	6:26P		6:26P
METROLINK 314	M - F	6:54P		6:59P	7:27P	7:22P	7:00P	
METROLINK 316	M - F	7:22P	7:38P		7:27P	7:22P		7:26P
METROLINK 318	M - F	8:12P	8:57P	8:16P	8:37P	8:13P		
METROLINK 320	M - F	8:53P	8:57P		9:22P	9:30P		
METROLINK 322	M - F	10:12P						

EASTBOUND TRAINS FROM IRVINE TO SAN BERNARDINO

METROLINK 302	M - F	9:38A			10:10A	10:09A		
METROLINK 304	M - F	6:16P	6:25P	6:30P	6:19P	6:26P		6:26P
METROLINK 306	M - F	6:58P	7:38P	6:59P	7:27P	7:22P	7:00P	7:26P

L: Regular stop to discharge or pick up passengers except train may leave ahead of schedule

At the time of publication Metrolink has not developed the schedule for the extention of the Inland Empire-Orange County Line to San Bernardino. Call Metrolink at 808-LINK for the current schedule.

**Greek Theater at
San Bernardino Valley College**

observatory associated with the planetarium that is open to the public in conjunction with the planetarium shows. For general information call (909) 888-6511.

California State University
San Bernardino

California State University-San Bernardino is located at 5500 University Parkway. It can be reached by taking the Omnitrans 3 or 5 line from the Fourth Street Transit Mall. The University is a part of the 20-campus State University system. It is a full four-year institution which offers bachelors and masters degrees. The campus has a student art gallery and theater. For Information call (909) 880-5200.

Inland Center Mall

The Inland Center Mall is located at Inland Center Drive and "E" Street. The mall features Gottschalks, Sears and The Broadway, plus 100 stores and services. The mall also boasts a food court, Pacific Theaters and a full Customer Service Center with stroller rentals and courtesy wheelchairs. Monthly events and promotions occur throughout the year. The mall can be

reached by taking the Omnitrans 2 line from the Fourth Street Transit Mall.

National Orange Show

The National Orange Show is located at 689 E Street. The show grounds can be reached by taking the Omnitrans 17 line from the Fourth Street Transit Mall. The National Orange Show Citrus Fruit Fair and Music Festival is held in mid-May of each year . The Fair includes a large number of carnival rides, numerous exhibits of arts and crafts and vendors hawking all types of wares. In the evenings there is NASCAR racing at the Orange Show auto race track. The Music Festival features many name entertainers; the 1994 Festival included The Temptations, Eddie Money, Los Lobos, Gladys Knight, Merle Haggard, just to name a few. During the rest of the year the show grounds are used for a wide variety of events. For information about current events call (909) 888-6788.

Places to Stay
San Bernardino Hilton

San Bernardino Hilton is located at 285 East Hospitality Lane. The hotel has a van which will pick you up at the San Bernardino Metrolink Station. Call the hotel before your arrival and tell them when your train will arrive and they will pick you up. The hotel phone number is (909) 889-0133. For reservations call (800) HILTONS.

National Orange Show

Radisson

The Radisson is located at 295 North E Street. The hotel has a van which will pick you up at the San Bernardino Metrolink Station. Call the hotel before your arrival and tell them when your train will arrive and they will pick you up. The hotel phone number is (909) 381-6181. For reservations call (800) 333-3333.

San Bernardino Comfort Inn

San Bernardino Comfort Inn is located at 1909 S. Business Center Drive. The hotel can be reached by taking the Omnitrans 17 bus line to the stop just west of Waterman Avenue. The hotel phone number is (909) 889-0090. For Reservations call (800) 228-5150.

San Bernardino Travelodge

The San Bernardino Travelodge is located at 225 East Hospitality Lane. The hotel can be reached by taking the Omnitrans 17 bus line to the stop just west of Waterman Avenue. The hotel phone number is (909) 888-6777. For reservations call (800) 578-7878.

La Quinta Inn

The La Quinta Inn is located at 205 East Hospitality Lane. The hotel can be reached by taking the Omnitrans 17 bus line to the stop just west of Waterman Avenue. The hotel phone number is (909) 888-7571. For reservations call (800) 531-5900.

Super 8 Lodge

The Super 8 Lodge is located at 294 East Hospitality Lane. The hotel can be reached by taking the Omnitrans 17 bus line to the stop just west of Waterman Avenue. The hotel phone number is (909) 381-1681. For reservations call (800) 800-8000.

E-Z 8 Motel

The E-Z 8 Motel is located at 1750 South Waterman Avenue. The hotel can be reached by taking the Omnitrans 9 bus line to the Waterman Avenue and Vanderbilt Way stop. The hotel phone number is (909) 888-4827. For reservations call (800) 32 MOTEL.

California State University San Bernardino Campus

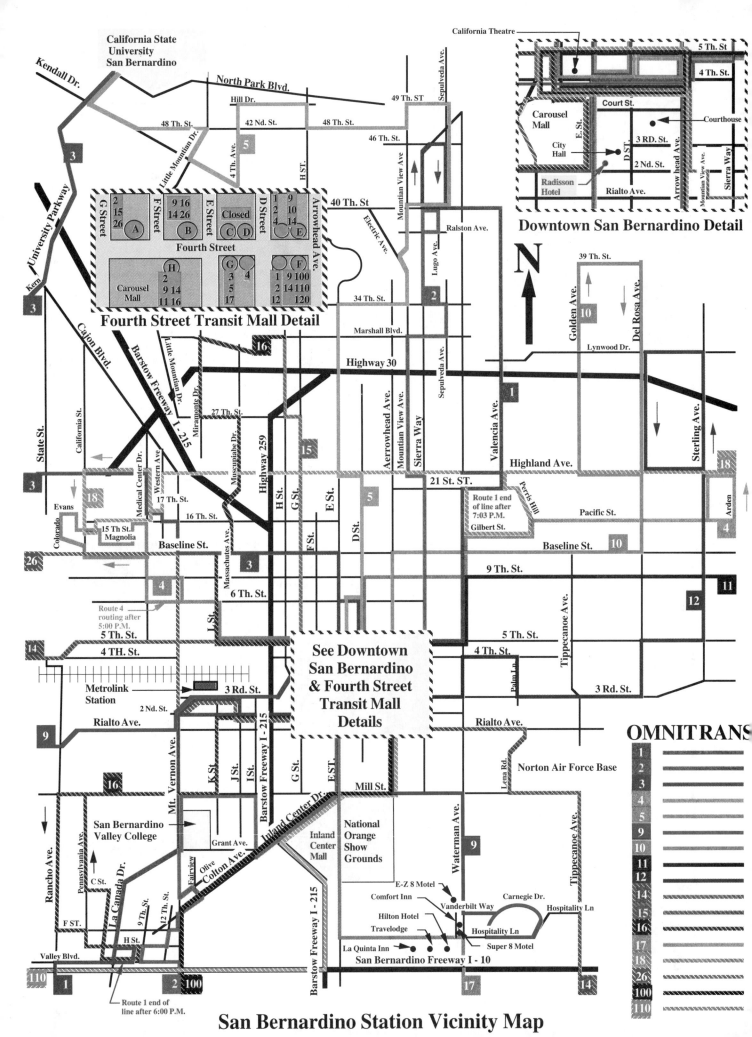

San Bernardino Station Vicinity Map

Riverside Line

The Riverside Line has five stations located at L.A. Union Station, Industry, East Ontario, The Pedley Station, and Riverside-Downtown. Metrolink operates six trains in each direction Monday thru Friday. The schedules below indicate the times and number of trains traveling in each direction on the Riverside Line at the time of publication. For updates to Metrolink schedules please call 808-LINK in the 213, 310, 714, 805, 818, and 909 area codes.

The Riverside Line was originally built by the San Pedro, Los Angeles & Salt Lake Railroad in the early 1900's. This line connected Southern California to the Union Pacific Railroad at Salt Lake City, Utah. Metrolink purchased operating rights on the portion of this line between Los Angeles and Riverside from the Union Pacific Railroad in July, 1992 for $17 million. After completion of $77.1 million of capital improvements for stations, track, and the purchase of Metrolink rolling stock, regular Metrolink service on this line began on June 14, 1995. The length of this line is 59 miles from Riverside to L.A. Union Station. Total transit time is one hour and eight minutes. The first stop along this line is the Industry Station which is located between the rural communities of Walnut and Diamond Bar.

After passing through downtown Ontario the line makes a slight turn to the south and heads for the southern boundary of the Ontario International Airport property. At the southeast corner of the Ontario Airport property is the East Ontario Station. The station is located in the middle of some of the last

Metrolink train leaving the East Ontario Station from the Vineyard

remaining vineyards that have not yet succumbed to the bulldozers to make way for residential or industrial development.

The countryside from the East Ontario Station to The Pedley Station is rural. After leaving the Ontario Station the vineyards give way to small horse ranches in the communities of Glen Avon and Pedley. The Jurupa hills will be visible to the north where the Jurupa Cultural Center is located.

From The Pedley Station the line continues to the Santa Ana River. The track follows the Santa Ana River for a short distance past upscale residential horse properties on the hills. The Jurupa Hills Country Club Golf Course is located at the turn just before the track crosses the Santa Ana River going into the city of Riverside and the Riverside-Downtown Station. The Riverside-Downtown Station is the end of the line.

RIVERSIDE LINE SCHEDULE
WESTBOUND FROM RIVERSIDE TO LOS ANGELES

	METROLINK	METROLINK	METROLINK	METROLINK	METROLINK	METROLINK
TRAIN NUMBER	401	403	405	407	409	411
DAYS OF OPERATION	M - F	M - F	M - F	M - F	M - F	M - F
RIVERSIDE-DOWNTOWN	5:00A	6:10A	6:40A	7:35A	2:47P	5:29P
THE PEDLEY STATION	5:10A	6:20A	6:50A	7:44A	2:57P	
EAST ONTARIO	5:19A	6:29A	6:59A	7:53A	3:05P	
INDUSTRY	5:36A	6:46A	7:16A	8:11A	L3:24P	
L.A. UNION STATION	6:08A	7:18A	7:48A	8:43A	4:02P	7:09P

EASTBOUND FROM LOS ANGELES TO RIVERSIDE

	METROLINK	METROLINK	METROLINK	METROLINK	METROLINK	METROLINK
TRAIN NUMBER	400	402	404	406	408	410
DAYS OF OPERATION	M - F	M - F	M - F	M - F	M - F	M - F
L.A. UNION STATION	5:55A	1:20P	4:14P	4:55P	5:30P	6:35P
INDUSTRY		1:54P	4:45P	5:26P	6:01P	7:06P
EAST ONTARIO		2:13P	5:02P	5:43P	6:18P	7:23P
THE PEDLEY STATION		L2:22P	L5:11P	L5:52P	L6:27P	L7:32P
RIVERSIDE-DOWNTOWN	7:27A	2:36P	5:23P	6:04P	6:39P	7:44P

L: Regular stop to discharge or pick up passengers except train may leave ahead of schedule

Santa Ana River Bridge

Industry Station

Station Connecting Transit Information

The Industry Metrolink Station is located at 600 S. Brea Canyon Road. The station can be reached by taking the Brea Canyon Road offramp from the 60 Freeway. From the freeway go north on Brea Canyon Road. The station is about one-half mile north on the right. The station has a 500-car parking lot. The train boarding platform is well lighted with a fair amount of shelter. The parking lot is well lighted and maintained. This station is not manned.

Adjacent to the boarding platform, Foothill Transit has established a Bus Transit Center where the Foothill Transit 179, 482, 701/702 and the MTA 484 lines stop. The station vicinity map provides the routes for bus transit options from the Industry Metrolink Station. The following table provides the schedule for bus connections to Metrolink. For schedule and route updates call Foothill Transit at (800) RIDE-INFO or MTA at (818) 443-1307 or (909) 620-1871.

Outside of the immediate vicinity of the Industry Metrolink Station, the Foothill Transit 179 line provides service to Mt. San Antonio College and Cal Poly Pomona to the east and West Covina and El Monte to the west with the line terminating at the El Monte Bus Station. Lines 701/702,

Industry Metrolink Station

called FasTrax, provides shuttle service to the industrial and business sites west of the station. Look for the distinctively decorated busses. Service is free for Metrolink passengers, 85 cents for those not carrying Metrocard or other Foothill Transit bus passes. The Foothill Transit 482 line provides service to Cal Poly Pomona and downtown Pomona to the east and, to the west, Hacienda Heights, El Monte and express service to Los Angeles from the El Monte bus

station via the El Monte Busway.

The MTA 484 line provides service to Pomona, Montclair, and the Ontario Airport to the east and, to the west, La Puente, Bassett, El Monte and express service to Los Angeles from the El Monte bus station via the El Monte Busway.

Points of Interest

The City of Industry has unusual boundaries. It extends about 12 miles east to west and is between one and two

INDUSTRY STATION BUS CONNECTION SCHEDULE
WESTBOUND TRAINS FROM RIVERSIDE TO LOS ANGELES

TRAIN NUMBER	DAYS OF	TRAIN	FOOTHILL 179	FOOTHILL 179	FOOTHILL 482	FOOTHILL 482	FOOTHILL 701/702*	MTA 484	MTA 484
	OPERATION	ARRIVAL	WESTBOUND	EASTBOUND	WESTBOUND	EASTBOUND		WESTBOUND	EASTBOUND
BUS FREQUENCY			HOURLY	HOURLY	30 MINUTES	30 MINUTES	COMMUTER	15-30 MIN.	15-30 MIN.
METROLINK 401	M - F	5:36A			6:30A		5:41A	5:22/5:42A	5:16/5:36A
METROLINK 403	M - F	6:46A	6:51A	7:05A	6:30/7:00A	6:59A	6:18/6:51A	6:39/6:52A	6:32/6:54A
METROLINK 405	M - F	7:16A	6:51/7:51A	7:05/8:05A	7:00A	6:59/7:51A	6:18/7:21A	7:07/7:24A	7:10/7:27A
METROLINK 407	M - F	8:11A	7:51/8:51A	8:05/9:05A		7:51A	7:58/8:16A	8:05/8:23A	8:01/8:15A
METROLINK 409	M - F	L3:24P	2:51/3:51P	3:05/4:05A			4:03P	3:12/3:41P	3:14/3:34P

EASTBOUND TRAINS FROM LOS ANGELES TO RIVERSIDE

METROLINK 402	M - F	1:54P	1:51/2:51P	1:05/2:05P				1:32/1:58P	1:47/2:08P
METROLINK 404	M - F	4:45P	3:51/4:51P	4:05/5:05P			4:40/5:19P	4:39/4:56P	4:34/4:52P
METROLINK 406	M - F	5:26P	5:21/6:51P	5:05/6:05P	5:37P	5:30P	5:21/6:24P	5:21/5:43P	5:10/5:27P
METROLINK 408	M - F	6:01P	5:21/6:51P	5:05/6:05P	5:37/6:39P	5:30/6:22P	5:56/6:24P	5:43/6:11P	5:56/6:09P
METROLINK 410	M - F	7:06P	6:51P	7:05P	6:39P	6:22P	7:01P	6:41/7:18P	6:56/7:16P

L: Regular stop to discharge or pick up passengers except train may leave ahead of schedule

* Foothill Transit 701/702 busses are designed to meet Metrolink trains and schedules may vary due to unforeseen Metrolink delays.

miles wide. It is bordered by El Monte on the west and Diamond Bar on the east. The station is located in the eastern part of the city and serves the surrounding communities of Diamond Bar and Walnut. These are upscale bedroom communities in the southeastern part of the San Gabriel Valley.

Diamond Bar, as with much of the San Gabriel Valley, began with a Spanish land grant. In 1840 Jose de la Luz Linares was deeded 4,340 acres which included Brea Canyon and the eastern Walnut Valley, which became Rancho Los Nogales. The next owner of the Grant was Ricardo Vejar who bought the rancho from Linares widow after her husband's death in 1847. Vejar already owned Rancho Los Nogales to the east which brought his holdings to over 10,000 acres. The land changed hands a number of times. In 1918, Frederick E. Lewis bought up most of the original Rancho Nogales and registered the Diamond Bar brand with the California Department of Agriculture. The ranch was next sold to the Bartholme family in 1943. In 1956, Transamerica Corporation purchased 8,000 acres of the Diamond Bar ranch

for $10 million. They began to develop the planned community of Diamond Bar.

Walnut has much the same history as Diamond Bar and was incorporated in 1959. Since that time it has grown to become a community of 31,000 residents. The city is home to Mt. San Antonio College and borders Cal Poly Pomona to the east.

Mount San Antonio College

Mount San Antonio College is located at 1100 N. Grand Avenue, Walnut. The college is a two-year institution which offers an Associate of Arts Degree in a wide range of majors and an Associate in Science degree for vocational majors. The college has set aside ten acres as a wildlife sanctuary which includes a natural stream, artificial ponds and a marsh. The sanctuary provides a habitat for native plants and animals. Paths through the sanctuary provide access for visitors. Guided tours are provided by the College's Technical Services Office. For information call (909) 594-5611 Ext. 4794.

The college also has a planetarium which offers a wide variety of programs

Cal Poly Pomona Campus

to the general public. For information on planetarium shows call the 24-hour hotline (909) 594-5611 Ext. 3810. The college can be reached by taking the Foothill Transit 179 line or the MTA 484 line.

California State Polytechnic University Pomona

Cal Poly Pomona began on the site of the Voorhis School for Boys, a 157-acre campus located in the San Jose Hills. In 1938 the Voorhis family donated the property to the State of California and the campus became the Southern California branch of California State Polytechnic School in San Luis Obispo. In 1949 W. K. Kellogg, the cereal magnate, donated his 813-acre Arabian Horse Ranch to the State of California. A 970-acre campus was thus established seven years later with 550

METROLINK

143

Old Kellogg Ranch Stables

students and 30 faculty members moving onto the Kellogg campus. The college became a part of the California State College System when it was established in 1961. Cal Poly Pomona was granted University status in 1972 and today is one of the 20 campuses of the California State University System.

The University has six academic colleges: Agriculture, Arts, Business Administration, Engineering, Environmental Design and Science. In addition, there is a School of Education and a School of Hotel and Restaurant Management. Cal Poly today has a student body of over 17,000 students and is well known for its pioneering efforts in solar-powered and electric vehicles, endangered species and resource management. For general information about the university call (909) 869-POLY.

The University is also home to the W. K. Kellogg Arabian Horse Center. The Arabian Horse Center is the fulfillment of Kellogg's boyhood dream to own an Arabian Horse ranch. Kellogg established his ranch in 1925, which soon became one of the world's foremost Arabian Horse Breeding farms. Sunday exhibitions of these beautiful horses were started in 1926. When Kellogg donated his ranch to Cal Poly he stipulated that the university retain the Arabian Horse breeding and training program and continue the Sunday performances.

Cal Poly continues to offer Sunday performances the first Sunday of each month during the school year (October thru June) in a specially designed arena with covered stands. In addition, two shows a month are staged on a weekday for elementary school children.

Admission is $2.00 for adults, $1.50 for senior citizens, and $1.00 for weekdays for elementary school children K-12th grade. For information call the center on (909) 869-2224.

From the Industry Metrolink Station take the Foothill Transit 179 line or the MTA 484 line.

Places to Stay

Radisson Diamond Bar

The Radisson Diamond Bar is located at 21725 East Gateway Drive, Diamond Bar. The hotel has a shuttle van and will pick you up at the Metrolink station with advance notice. The hotel phone number is (909) 860-5440. For reservations call (800) 333-3333

Best Western Executive Inn

The Executive Inn is located at 18880 E. Gale Avenue, Rowland Heights. The hotel has a shuttle van and will pick you up at the Metrolink station with advance notice. The hotel phone number is (818) 810-1818. For reservations call (800) 528-1234.

Best Western Hotel Diamond Bar

The Best Western Hotel Diamond Bar is located at 259 Gentle Springs Lane, Diamond Bar. The hotel has a shuttle van and will pick you up at the Metrolink station with advance notice. The hotel phone number is (909) 860-3700. For reservations call (800) 528-1234.

Shilo Inn

The Shilo Inn is located at 3200 Temple Street, Pomona. The hotel has a shuttle van and will pick you up at the Metrolink station with advance notice. The hotel phone number is (909) 598-0073. For reservations call (800) 222-2244.

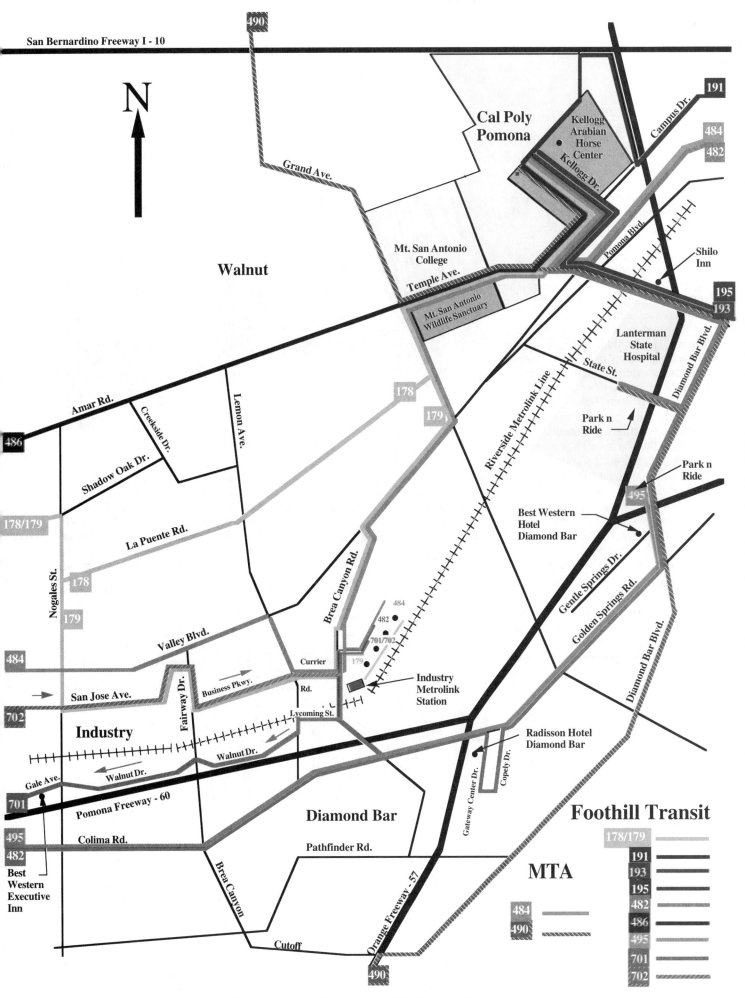

Industry Station Vicinity Map

East Ontario Station

Station Connecting Transit Information

The East Ontario Metrolink Station is located at 3330 East Francis Street. The station can be reached by taking the Haven Avenue exit from the San Bernardino Freeway (I-10). Go south on Haven to Francis Street and turn right. Turn right on Metro Way and the station will be on your right. The train boarding platform is well lighted and has a good shelter. The 300-car parking lot is well maintained and has excellent lighting.

The station is served by the Omni Transit 71 bus line. The bus stop is located directly in front of the station. The station vicinity map provides the routes for bus transit options from the East Ontario Metrolink Station. The following table provides the schedule for bus connections to Metrolink.

The Omni Transit 71 line connects with the 61, 62, 64, 65 and 70 lines at the Plum Avenue and D Street stop at the Ontario Civic Center.

For updated schedules, and complete route maps for Omni Transit lines call (909) 983-2671 from East Ontario.

Points of Interest

Ontario is a city in transition. It has a population of 138,000 spread out over 36.8-square miles. The landscape is a mixture of farmland, industry and housing developments. The city was founded in 1882 by George Chaffey who was responsible for planting trees along Euclid Avenue to make Ontario more like his native Ontario, Canada. In 1904 the city of Ontario was recognized as a model of progressiveness at the St. Louis World's Fair.

Old Downtown Ontario

The old downtown district extends from Mission Boulevard to Fourth Street along Euclid Avenue. Euclid Avenue is a wide tree-lined street with a wide grassy center divider. The store fronts along this thoroughfare date back to the 1920's. The Museum of History & Art and the Graber Olive House are both located in downtown Ontario. Someday Metrolink plans to add a station in downtown Ontario. Presently downtown Ontario can be reached by taking the Omni Transit 71 bus line from the East Ontario Metrolink Station

East Ontario Metrolink Station

on the Riverside Line or by taking the Omni Transit 62 bus line from the Upland Metrolink Station on the San Bernardino Line.

Ontario Museum of History and Art

The museum is located at 225 S. Euclid Avenue. The museum can be reached from East Ontario Metrolink Station by taking the Omni Transit 71 line to the Lemon Avenue and B Street stop. From there the museum is a short-two-block walk. From the Upland

EAST ONTARIO STATION BUS CONNECTION SCHEDULE
WESTBOUND TRAINS FROM RIVERSIDE TO LOS ANGELES

TRAIN NUMBER	DAYS OF	TRAIN	OMNITRANS
	OPERATION	ARRIVAL	71
			WESTBOUND
BUS FREQUENCY			HOURLY
METROLINK 401	M - F	5:19A	
METROLINK 403	M - F	6:29A	6:24/6:34A
METROLINK 405	M - F	6:59A	6:24/7:58A
METROLINK 407	M - F	7:53A	7:48/7:58A
METROLINK 409	M - F	3:05P	

EASTBOUND TRAINS FROM LOS ANGELES TO RIVERSIDE

TRAIN NUMBER	DAYS OF	TRAIN	OMNITRANS
	OPERATION	ARRIVAL	71
			EASTBOUND
BUS FREQUENCY			HOURLY
METROLINK 402	M - F	2:13P	
METROLINK 404	M - F	5:02P	4:57/5:07P
METROLINK 406	M - F	5:43P	4:57/6:23P
METROLINK 408	M - F	6:18P	6:13/6:23P
METROLINK 410	M - F	7:23P	7:18/7:28P

L: Regular stop to discharge or pick up passengers except train may leave ahead of schedule

Graber Olive House

P.M. Sunday. Closed holidays. For information call (909) 983-1761.

Guasti, and the
Joseph Filippi Winery

The old town of Guasti and the old Brookside Winery lies along Old Guasti Road between Archibald Avenue and Turner Avenue. The town is mostly abandoned today with the small homes that were used for housing the farm-workers that tended the vineyards in the Ontario area. San Secondo d'Asti Catholic Church, dedicated in 1927, is an excellent example of Spanish Colonial Revival style architecture. Masses are still said on Saturday and Sunday.

The Joseph Filippi Winery presently occupies the wine cellars in Guasti and they operate a wine tasting room at the facility. The wine tasting room is open seven days a week 9:00 A.M. to 6:00 P.M.

Ontario International Airport

Ontario International Airport is one of the major satellite airports in the Greater Los Angeles Region. The Omni Transit 71 line provides bus service between the East Ontario Metrolink Station and the Ontario International Airport. If you are planning to spend any time in the Inland Empire (San Bernardino and Riverside counties and vicinity) Ontario International Airport would be preferable to LAX as your

Metrolink Station take the Omni Transit 62 bus line to the Euclid Avenue and Holt Boulevard stop. The museum's history wing provides visitors a view of Ontario's heritage and the art wing features ever changing exhibitions by local and regional artists which is coordinated by the Chaffey Community Art Association. The museum is open Noon to 4:00 P.M. Wednesday thru Sunday. Closed holidays. Admission is free. For information call (909) 983-3198.

Graber Olive House

The Graber Olive House is located at 315 E. 4th. Street. The house can be reached from the East Ontario Metrolink Station by taking the Omni Transit 62 bus line from the Plum Avenue and D Street Transit Center in downtown Ontario, to the Euclid Avenue and

Fourth Street stop. From the Upland Metrolink Station take the Omni Transit 62 bus line to the same stop. The Olive House is located about one and one-half blocks east of Euclid Avenue. This is a family-run business founded by C.C. Graber in 1894. The grounds include a gift shop, museum, and picnic area. Tours of the Olive processing facility are available. It is open 9:00 A.M. to 5:30 P.M. Monday thru Saturday and 9:30 A.M. to 6:00

San Secondo d'Asti Catholic Church in old Guasti

147

Horse Drawn Trolley on Display in Center Median of Euclid Boulevard in Downtown Ontario

destination airport. It is over an hour and one-half driving time from LAX to Ontario International Airport. There are several major hotel chains that have hotels near the Ontario International Airport (See Places to Stay below). Most of them will provide free shuttle service to/from the Ontario International Airport. In addition many hotels in destination cities such as Baldwin Park, Diamond Bar, Claremont, Pomona, Riverside, San Bernardino, just to name a few, provide free shuttle service to the Ontario International Airport. Most of these hotels will also provide free shuttle service to the local Metrolink station.

The Airport is served by Aeromexico, Alaska Airlines, American Airlines, America West, Continental, Delta, Mexicana, Northwest, Reno Air, Southwest Airlines, and United Airlines.

Plaza Continental Factory Stores

This Factory Outlet Mall is located at 3700 E. Inland Empire Boulevard. The mall can be reached by taking the Omni Transit 61 line to the Inland Empire Boulevard and Haven Avenue stop. The Mall is two blocks east of Haven on Inland Empire Boulevard, just past the Hilton. The mall stores offer name brand merchandise at 20 to 75 percent savings over regular retail prices.

Places to Stay
Holiday Inn

Holiday Inn is located at 3400 Shelby Street (Haven Avenue and Inland Empire Boulevard). The hotel has a van which will pick you up at the East Ontario Metrolink Station. Call the hotel before your arrival and tell them when your train will arrive and they will pick you up. The hotel phone number is (909) 466-9600. For reservations call (800) 642-2617 or (800) HOLIDAY.

Goodnight Inn

The Goodnight Inn is located at 1801 East G Street. The hotel has a van which will pick you up at the East Ontario Metrolink Station. Call the hotel before your arrival and tell them when your train will arrive and they will pick you up. The hotel phone number is (909) 983-3604.

Ontario International Airport Hilton

The Hilton is located at 700 N. Haven Avenue. The hotel has a van which will pick you up at the East Ontario Metrolink Station. Call the hotel before your arrival and tell them when your train will arrive and the will pick you up. The hotel phone number is (909) 980-0400. For Reservations call (800) HILTONS.

Country Side Suites

The Country Side Suites is located at 204 N. Vineyard Avenue. The hotel has a van which will pick you up at the East Ontario Metrolink Station. Call the hotel before your arrival and tell them when your train will arrive and they will pick you up. The hotel phone number is (909) 986-8550.

Country Suites

The Country Suites is located at 231 N. Vineyard Avenue. The hotel has a van which will pick you up at the East Ontario Metrolink Station. Call the hotel before your arrival and tell them when your train will arrive and they will pick you up. The hotel phone number is (909) 983-8484. For reservations call (800) 456-4000.

Ontario International Airport Marriott

The Marriott is located at 2200 East Holt Boulevard. The hotel has a van which will pick you up at the East Ontario Metrolink Station. Call the hotel before your arrival and tell them when your train will arrive and they will pick you up. The hotel phone number is (909) 986-8811. For reservations call (800) 228-9290.

Red Lion Hotel

The Red Lion Hotel is located at 222 N. Vineyard Avenue. The hotel has a van which will pick you up at the East Ontario Metrolink Station. Call the hotel before your arrival and tell them when your train will arrive and they will pick you up. The hotel phone number is (909) 983-0909. For reservations call (800) 547-8010.

DoubleTree Club Hotel

The DoubleTree Club Hotel is located at 429 N. Vineyard Avenue. The hotel has a van which will pick you up at the East Ontario Metrolink Station. Call the hotel before your arrival and tell them when your train will arrive and they will pick you up. The hotel phone number is (909) 391-6411. For reservations call (800) 222-TREE.

Red Roof Inn

The Red Roof Inn is located at 1818 East Holt Boulevard. The hotel has a van which will pick you up at the East Ontario Metrolink Station. Call the hotel before your arrival and tell them when your train will arrive and they will pick you up. The hotel phone number is (909) 988-8466. For reservations call (800) THE-ROOF.

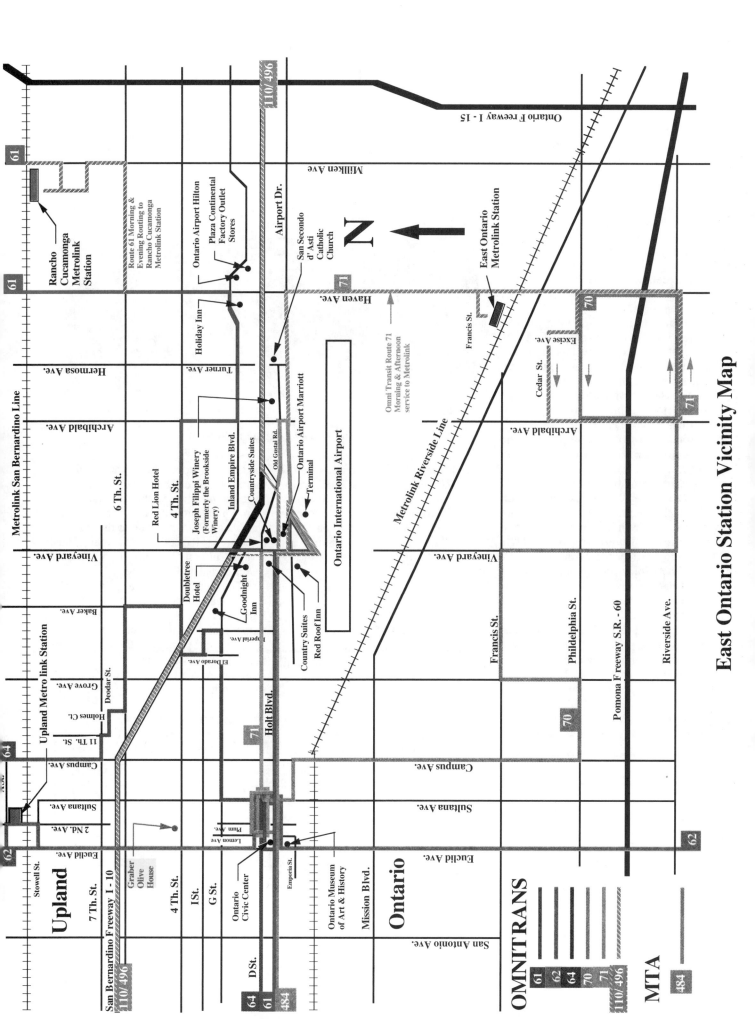

East Ontario Station Vicinity Map

The Pedley Station

Station Connecting Transit Information

The Pedley Metrolink Station is located at 6001 Pedley Road. The station can be reached by taking the Pedley Road exit from the Pomona Freeway (Route 60). Go south on Pedley Road about four miles and the station will be on your left just before you reach Limonite Avenue. The train boarding platform is well lighted and has excellent shelter. The 300-car parking lot is well maintained and has excellent lighting.

The station is served by the Riverside Transit Agency (RTA) 21 and 29 bus lines. The bus stops for these lines are located in the new bus transit center directly in front of the station. The station vicinity map provides the routes for the bus transit options from The Pedley Metrolink Station. The table below provides the schedule for bus connections with Metrolink.

Outside of the immediate vicinity of The Pedley Metrolink Station, the RTA 21 line provides service to Mira Loma. The 29 line provides service to downtown Riverside and RTA's Downtown Riverside Terminal.

The Pedley Station is located in a rural part of Riverside County. In the vicinity of the station there is a shopping district along Limonite Avenue. The RTA 21 line provides access to the RTA Transfer Terminal at the Galleria at Tyler where connections can be made with the 1, 2, 10, 12, 13, 14, 15, 21, 27, Orange County commuter busses and Inland Empire Connection 149.

In addition, all of the points of

The Pedley Metrolink Station

interest listed in this chapter can also be accessed using RTA lines originating from the RTA's Downtown Riverside Terminal described in the Chapter on the Riverside-Downtown Station.

For updates on the routes and schedules for RTA bus lines call (909) 682-1234.

Points of Interest
Jurupa Mountains Cultural Center

The Jurupa Mountains Cultural Center is located at 7621 Granite Hill Drive. The center can be reached by taking the RTA 21 line to the Mission

and Pedley stop. There you need to transfer to the eastbound RTA 496 line. Take the 496 line to the Camino Real stop. You could also catch the westbound RTA 496 line at the RTA's Downtown Riverside Terminal. The Jurupa Cultural Center is 200 yards up Camino Real under the freeway.

The Jurupa Mountains Cultural Center was founded 30 years ago by Sam and Ruth Kirkby, with the purpose of acquainting children of all ages with our planet and the wonders it holds for everyone. The center has a museum of sorts where old books, rocks, minerals and fossil collections

THE PEDLEY STATION BUS CONNECTION SCHEDULE
WESTBOUND TRAINS FROM RIVERSIDE TO LOS ANGELES

TRAIN NUMBER	DAYS OF OPERATION	TRAIN ARRIVAL	RTA 21 NORTHBOUND	RTA 21 SOUTHBOUND	RTA 29 WESTBOUND	RTA 29 EASTBOUND
BUS FREQUENCY			2 HOURS	2 HOURS	2 HOURS	2 HOURS
METROLINK 401	M - F	5:10A	5:05A**			5:40A#
METROLINK 403	M - F	6:20A	6:05A*&6:15A**			
METROLINK 405	M - F	6:50A	6:20A#/8:10A#	7:25A	7:19A	
METROLINK 407	M - F	7:44A	6:20A#/8:10A#	7:25A	7:19A	
METROLINK 409	M - F	2:57P	2:10P/4:19P#	1:15P#/3:17P#	2:36P#	2:48P

EASTBOUND TRAINS FROM LOS ANGELES TO RIVERSIDE

METROLINK 402	M - F	L2:22P	2:10P/4:19P#	1:15P#/3:17P#	12:53P#	2:48P
METROLINK 404	M - F	L5:11P	4:19P#	5:16P**&5:25P*	4:19P#	
METROLINK 406	M - F	L5:52P				
METROLINK 408	M - F	L6:27P	6:28P	6:31P**		6:39P
METROLINK 410	M - F	L7:32P	8:33P#	7:34P		6:39P/8:37P#

L: Regular stop to discharge or pick up passengers except train may leave ahead of schedule
* Metrolink Express service from the Riverside-La Sierra Station on the RTA Route 21.
** Metrolink Express Service from the RTA Bus Transfer Terminal located at the Galleria at Tyler.
# Bus stops at intersection of Van Buren Boulevard and Limonite Avenue.

Dinosaurs at Jurupa Mountains Cultural Center

acquired the property from one of Cornelius and Mercedes Alavarado Jensen's decedents in 1981. The parks district has completed a significant amount of restoration of the ranch house and winery building. The ranch house was damaged during the January 17, 1994 Northridge Earthquake. The winery building has been converted into a museum where several items from the mid 1800's are on display. The park is operated as a living history experience. Docents dress up in costumes from the late 1800's and provide the visitors a taste of what life was like a century ago. The park is open on Saturdays only 10:00 A.M. to 3:00 P.M. Admission is $3.00 for adults and $1.50 for children. For Information call (909) 369-6055 or 275-4310.

Louis Rubidoux Nature Center

The Louis Rubidoux Nature Center is located at 5370 Riverview Drive in Rubidoux. There is no public transit access to the center. The nearest bus stop is at Peralta and Limonite on the RTA 29 line about one and one-half miles from the center. The center has exhibits of the area wildlife, a picnic area, and hiking and equestrian trails. The center is open 10:00 A.M. to 4:00 P.M. Saturdays.

Places To Stay

There are no hotels near The Pedley Station. See the chapter on the Downtown-Riverside or the Riverside-La Sierra stations.

are intermixed with samples of the same for sale. The center also provides earth science kits for elementary school students. The center offers a variety of classes in a nature school for young children 6 to 12 years of age in the summer. On Saturdays, at 9:00 A.M., there is a Dinosaurs Walk where a guide will take a group of parents and children out on a trail to where the center has several life size dinosaurs made by local school children (6 to 12 years old) over the years. In the area at the top of the bluff the center has spread a mixture of different minerals over the ground. Each participant is issued an egg carton in order to start the adventure of collecting an assortment of minerals.

At 10:30 A.M. on Saturdays, there is a Kids' Fossil Shack where kids of all ages can learn how to collect fossils, learn their names and how to determine their age. The fee for these activities is $3.00 each.

The center is open Tuesday thru Saturday, 9:00 A.M. to 5:00 P.M. Admission to the center and museum is free. Activities and classes require a nominal charge. For information call (909) 685-5818.

Jensen Alvarado Ranch Historic Park

The Jensen Alvarado Ranch Historic Park is located off Briggs Street in Rubidoux. The ranch can be reached by taking the RTA 29 line to the Tilton and Briggs stop. You can also catch the RTA 29 line at the RTA's Downtown Riverside Terminal.

From there you need to walk two blocks through a residential district to the park entrance. The park consists of 30 acres of the original Jensen Alvarado Ranch which included the Ranch House and Winery. Cornelius Jensen was a Danish sea Captain who had the misfortune to arrive in San Francisco in 1849. The crew of his ship abandoned him to seek their fortunes in the gold fields in the Sierra Nevada mining camps. Cornelius disposed of the ship and its contents and moved to Southern California where he married Mercedes Alavarado. In 1868-70 they established a ranch in the Riverside area.

The Riverside County Parks

Women Making Tortillas Over Wood Burning Stove at Jensen Ranch

151

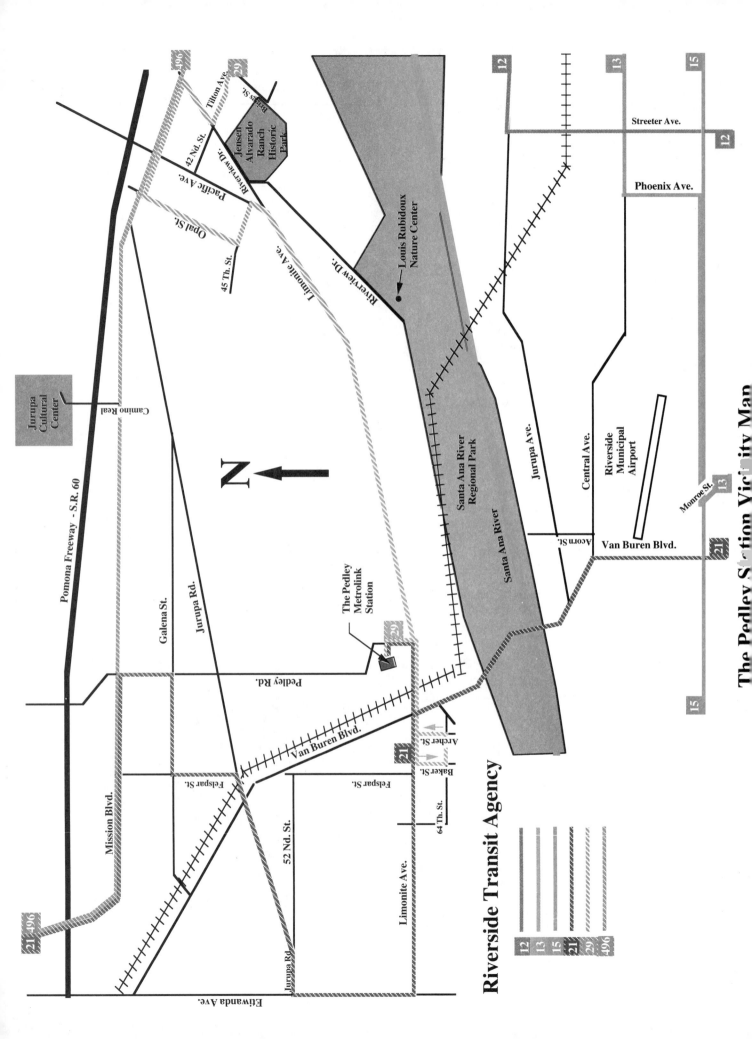

Riverside Transit Agency

The Pedley Station Vicinity Map

Legend routes: 12, 13, 15, 21, 29, 496

Streeter Ave.

Phoenix Ave.

Jensen Alvarado Ranch Historic Park

Louis Rubidoux Nature Center

Santa Ana River Regional Park

Santa Ana River

Jurupa Cultural Center

Pomona Freeway - S.R. 60

Camino Real

Mission Blvd.

Tilton Ave.

Briggs St.

42 Nd. St.

Pacific Ave.

Riverview Dr.

Opal St.

45 Th. St.

Limonite Ave.

Riverview Dr.

Jurupa Ave.

Central Ave.

Acorn St.

Riverside Municipal Airport

Monroe St.

Van Buren Blvd.

Galena St.

Jurupa Rd.

The Pedley Metrolink Station

Pedley Rd.

Van Buren Blvd.

Archer St.

Baker St.

Felspar St.

Felspar St.

64 Th. St.

52 Nd. St.

Limonite Ave.

Jurupa Rd.

Eltiwanda Ave.

N

Riverside-Downtown Station

Station Connecting Transit Information

The Riverside-Downtown Metrolink Station is located at 4066 Vine Street. The station can be reached by taking the University Avenue exit from the Riverside Freeway (Route 91). From the westbound Riverside Freeway turn right on Seventh Street which is at the end of the off-ramp. Go to Vine and turn right. The Metrolink station will be about a block away on the left. From the eastbound Riverside freeway turn right on Tenth Street which is at the end of the off-ramp. Go to Vine and turn left. The station will be on your right. The train boarding platform is well lighted and has a good shelter. The 300-car parking lot is well maintained and has excellent lighting.

The Riverside-Downtown Metrolink Station is the eastern terminus of the Riverside Line and is on the Inland Empire-Orange County Line.

The station is served by the Riverside Transit Agency (RTA) 2 and 16 bus lines. In addition the Orange Blossom Express Trolley serve the station. The bus stops for these lines are located directly in front of the station. The station vicinity map provides the route map for bus transit options in the vicinity of the Riverside-Downtown Metrolink Station. The following table provides the schedule for bus connections with Metrolink.

In downtown Riverside RTA has its downtown terminal located between Seventh Street and University Avenue. There is a blow-up of the RTA's Downtown Riverside Terminal on the Riverside-Downtown Station vicinity map. All of the points of interest listed

Riverside Metrolink Station

in the chapter on The Pedley Station and Riverside-La Sierra Station can be easily reached using RTA lines that originate from the Downtown Riverside Bus Terminal.

For updated schedules, and complete route maps for RTA lines call (909) 682-1234 from Riverside.

METROLINK

RIVERSIDE-DOWNTOWN STATION BUS CONNECTION SCHEDULE
WESTBOUND TRAINS FROM RIVERSIDE TO LOS ANGELES

TRAIN NUMBER	DAYS OF OPERATION	TRAIN DEPARTURE	RTA 2	RTA 16	ORANGE BLOSSOM ROUTE B
BUS FREQUENCY			30 -45 MIN.	30 MIN.	5 - 10 MIN.
METROLINK 401	M - F	5:36A		*5:30A	
METROLINK 403	M - F	6:46A		*6:35A	
METROLINK 405	M - F	7:16A	7:16A	7:03A	
METROLINK 407	M - F	8:11A		*7:30A	
METROLINK 409	M - F	L3:24P	2:25P	2:24P	3:20P

WESTBOUND TRAINS FROM RIVERSIDE TO IRVINE

METROLINK 801	M - F	5:46A		*5:30A	
METROLINK 803	M - F	6:48A		*6:35A	
METROLINK 805	M - F	3:25P	2:25P	2:24P	3:20P

EASTBOUND TRAINS FROM LOS ANGELES TO RIVERSIDE

METROLINK 402	M - F	1:54P	2:36P		2:00P
METROLINK 404	M - F	4:45P			
METROLINK 406	M - F	5:26P		*5:28P	
METROLINK 408	M - F	6:01P		*6:04P	
METROLINK 410	M - F	7:06P	7:19P	7:41P	

EASTBOUND TRAINS FROM IRVINE TO RIVERSIDE

METROLINK 801	M - F	L9:12A			11:00A
METROLINK 803	M - F	L5:51P		*6:04P	
METROLINK 805	M - F	L6:34P	7:19P	*6:43P	

L: Regular stop to discharge or pick up passengers except train may leave ahead of schedule

* Indicates RTA Route 16 Metrolink Express service.

Points of Interest

Riverside is one of the few remaining communities in Southern California that still has an abundance of space. The city is the administrative center of Riverside County and home to 200,000 residents. The city was founded by Judge John Wesley North's Southern California Colony Association. These eastern immigrants came to California to develop the citrus industry in the Riverside area. They initiated many of the innovative methods in irrigation, cooperative marketing, packing-house techniques and machinery. Riverside was home to the University of California's Citrus Experiment Station and Graduate School of Tropical Agriculture.

With the success of the citrus industry the citizens of Riverside became the wealthiest city per capita in 1895. The first golf course and polo field in Southern California were built in Riverside. Today, downtown Riverside still retains a gentile elegance that reflects the heyday of the Citriculture era that reached its peak in the 1920's.

Downtown Riverside

Walking around downtown Riverside is like taking a time trip to an earlier era in Southern California's history, where citrus agriculture was the primary industry for much of the region. Downtown Riverside is populated with an abundance of elegant buildings built with the profits from the groves. Main Street has been converted into a pedestrian mall between Sixth and Ninth streets. It is lined with several sidewalk cafes, boutiques and museums.

Mission Inn

The Mission Inn, the architectural

Chinese Pagoda in Downtown Riverside

center of downtown Riverside, was built in several phases between 1902 and 1932 by owner Frank A. Miller. The hotel is a kaleidoscopic example of Spanish Colonial architecture run amok with a final result that works. It is a wild assemblage of flying buttresses, spiral staircases, catacombs, carillon towers, balconies, turrets, gardens and domes. The inn is classified as a National Historic Landmark and offers tours to the general public at 10:00 and 10:30 A.M. and 1:30 and 2:00 P.M Monday thru Friday. On Saturdays and Sundays tours start every half hour 10:00 A.M. to 3:00 P.M. Cost is $6.00 per person. For information and reservations call (909) 781-8421 weekdays and (909) 784-0300 ext. 5035.

Mission Inn Museum

The Mission Inn Museum is

located at the corner of Seventh Street and the Main Street Pedestrian Mall. Several pieces of furniture, tableware, and art from the Mission Inn are included in the permanent collection. The museum also has frequent temporary exhibits. The Museum is open daily 11:00 A.M. to 4:00 P.M., donation $1.00. For information call (909) 788-9556 or (909) 781-8241.

Riverside Municipal Museum

The Riverside Municipal Museum is located at 3720 Orange Street. The museum has exhibits that focus upon the local history of Riverside and its industry. There is an extensive exhibit focusing on Joseph Hunter and Hunter-Douglas Corporation, a local metal fabrication business. There are exhibits on the citrus industry, local indian cultures and the early settlers in the local area. The Natural Science section

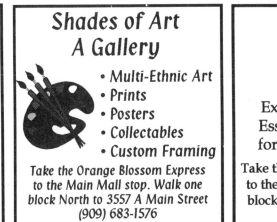

features exhibits that demonstrate how plate tectonics cause earthquakes, shows important minerals and fossils from the local landscape as well as exhibits of native desert plants and animals. The museum is open 9:00 A.M. to 5:00 P.M. Tuesday thru Friday, 1:00 P.M. to 5:00 P.M. Saturday and Sunday. It is closed Mondays and major holidays. Admission is free. For information call (909) 782-5273.

Riverside Art Museum

The Riverside Art Museum is located at 3425 Seventh Street. The museum building was built in 1929 in the Spanish Colonial revival style by architect Julia Morgan, who also designed William Randolph Hearst's San Simeon Estate. The YWCA occupied the building until 1966 when the Riverside Art Museum acquired the property. The museum features an ever-changing traveling exhibits. The museum is open Monday thru Saturday 10:00 A.M. to 4:00 P.M. The museum is closed Sunday. Donation $1.00. For information call (909) 684-7111.

California Museum of Photography

The California Museum of Photography is located at 3824 Main Street. It is operated by the University of California-Riverside. It is one of the largest museums of photography in the west. There is a large display of photographs from the 19th and early 20th centuries. The museum has exhibits that explore the various ways photography is used as an art form. The museum offers a number of workshops throughout the year. These workshops range from one day to a few days in duration. The museum is open 11:00 A.M. to 5:00 P.M. Monday and Wednesday to Saturday, 12:00 Noon to 5:00 P.M. Sunday and is closed on Tuesday. Admission is $2.00 for adults, $1.00 for seniors, and free on Wednesdays. For information call (909) 784-FOTO.

Heritage House

Heritage House is located at 8193 Magnolia Avenue. The house can be reached by taking the RTA 2 line from the Metrolink or the RTA 1 & 2 lines from RTA's Downtown Riverside Terminal. The house was completed in 1892 and was built by Mrs. James Bettner a recent widow of a civil engineer and orange grower who moved to Riverside in 1877. The house was

Heritage House

designed by Los Angeles architect John Walls in the Queen Anne style. The house is furnished with some of the original furnishings that were custom made for the house when built. The house gives a fairly accurate rendition of the lifestyle of the wealthy citrus growers from the late 19th and the early 20th-century Riverside. The house is open to the public Tuesdays, Thursdays 12:00 noon to 2:30 P.M. and Sundays 12:00 noon to 3:30 P.M. The house is closed July thru Labor Day. For information call (909) 782-5273.

Riverside Plaza

The Riverside Plaza is the older and smaller mall in Riverside. The mall is located at Central and Riverside avenues and can be reached by taking the RTA 2 bus line from Metrolink or RTA's Downtown Riverside Terminal.

The anchor department stores are Harris' and Montgomery Ward.

University of California Riverside

The University of California Riverside is one of the nine campuses and the smallest of the University of California system with a student population of 10,000. The university got its start with the establishment of the University of California Citrus Experiment Station on the present day campus site in 1907. In February 1954 UCR enrolled its first undergraduate class with 127 students in its innovative College of Letters and Science. It is the only liberal arts college in the U.C. system. In 1959 the UCR was made a general campus of the U.C. system. For general information

The Mall at U.C. Riverside

about campus activities call (909) 787-4571.

The university has an extensivebotanic garden which is open 8:00 A.M. to 5:00 P.M. Admission is free. For information call (909) 787-4650.

There is a student Art Gallery which features a number of different exhibits throughout the year. For information call (909) 787-3918.

The University Theater presents a number of stage productions and cultural events throughout the year. For information call (909) 787-4629.

The University can be reached by taking the RTA 16 from Metrolink or the RTA 1 line from the RTA's Downtown Riverside Terminal.

Riverside Community College

The Riverside Community College, Riverside City Campus is located at Magnolia Avenue and Ramona Drive. The college can be reached by taking the RTA 2 line from Metrolink or RTA's Downtown Riverside Terminal. The college is a two-year institution and offers an Associate of Arts Degree in a wide range of majors. The campus Art Gallery offers exhibitions by student artists and established artists throughout the year. The gallery is open 10:00 A.M. to 3:00 P.M. Monday thru Friday, and 5:00 P.M. to 7:00 P.M. Wednesday evenings during exhibitions. For Information about exhibitions at the Art Gallery call (909)

684-3240 Ext. 5480. There is a performing Arts Center on campus which offers professional stage productions throughout the school year. For general information about activities on campus call (909) 888-6511.

Places to Stay
Dynasty Suites

The Dynasty Suites is located at 3735 Iowa Avenue. The hotel can be reached by taking the RTA 16 bus line. The hotel phone number is (909) 369-8200.

Mission Inn

Mission Inn is located at 3649 Seventh Street. The hotel has a van

Botanical Garden U.C. Riverside

which will pick you up at the Metrolink Station. The hotel phone number is (909) 784-0300. For reservations call (800) 843-7755.

Holiday Inn

The Holiday Inn is located at 3400 Market Street. The hotel can be reached by taking the RTA 2 line from RTA's Downtown Riverside Terminal. The hotel phone number is (909) 784-8000. For reservations call (800) HOLIDAY.

Hampton Inn

Riverside Hampton Inn is located at 1590 University Avenue. The hotel can be reached by taking the RTA 16 bus line. The hotel phone number is (909) 683-6000. For reservations call (800) HAMPTON.

Courtyard by Marriott

The Courtyard by Marriott is located at 1510 University Avenue. The hotel can be reached by taking the RTA 16 bus line. The hotel phone number is (909) 276-1200. For reservations call (800) 943-9149.

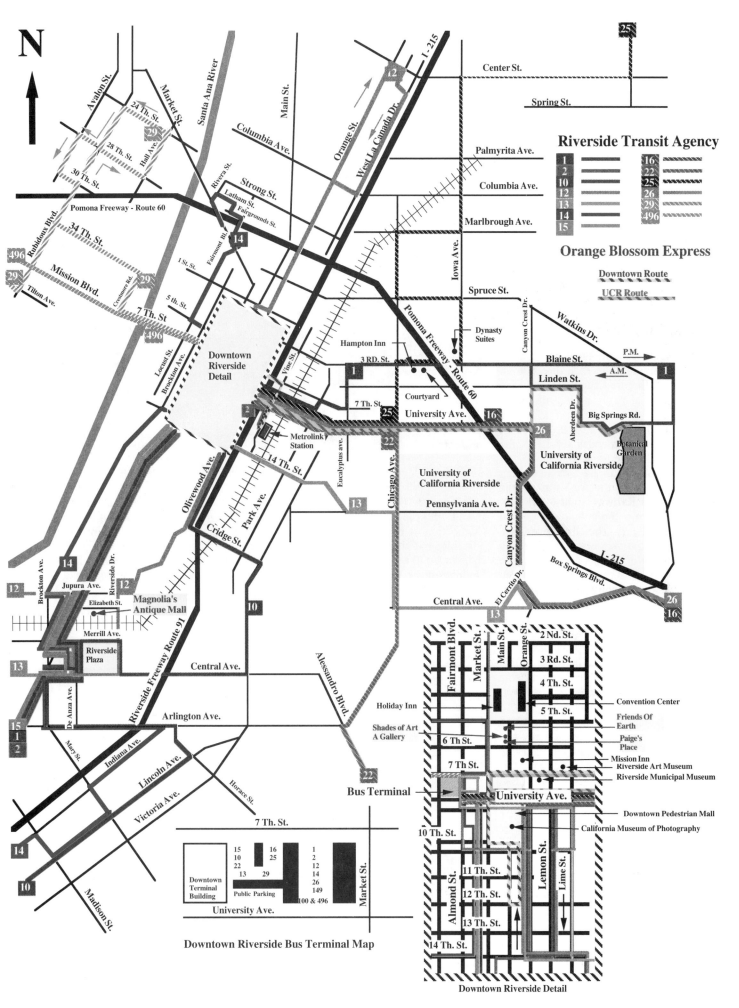

Riverside Station Vicinity Map

Inland Empire - Orange County Line

The Inland Empire-Orange County Line has seven stations located at San Bernardino, Riverside-Downtown, Riverside-La Sierra, West Corona, Orange, Santa Ana and Irvine. This is the sixth line to be opened by Metrolink. Regular service began on October 2, 1995 which saw the opening of the two new stations on this line located at Riverside-La Sierra and West Corona. Initial service consisted of three trains in each direction, Monday thru Friday, from Riverside to Irvine. Service to San Bernardino was initiated on March 4, 1996. The following schedule indicate the times and number of trains traveling in each direction on the Inland Empire-Orange County Line at the time of publication. Due to the rapid expansion of Metrolink service please call from 213, 310, 714, 805, 818, and 909 area codes 808-LINK for current updates to the schedule.

The Inland Empire-Orange County Line operates on the Atchison Topeka & Santa Fe Railway right-of-way. In traveling from the Inland Empire to Orange County the line uses the alignment that was originally built by the Atchison, Topeka & Santa Fe Railroad. The railroad was incorporated as a subsidiary known as the Riverside, Santa Ana & Los Angeles Railway in 1885. The line was completed and passenger service between San Bernardino and Santa Ana began on September 15, 1887. The route of this line passes through scenic Santa Ana Canyon parallel to the Santa Ana River. After leaving Santa Ana Canyon the line joins the Orange County Line and operates on the same right-of-way and shares the Orange, Santa Ana, Irvine and San Juan Capistrano stations with that line. Connections with Amtrak San Diegans and Metrolink's Orange County Line trains can be made at the Santa Ana and Irvine stations. Metrolink Orange County Line connections are possible from the Orange Station, but Amtrak does not stop there. The station chapters for the stations shared with the Orange County Line will be found in the Orange County Line section of this book.

The Riverside-Downtown Station

Passengers Waiting Board to Metrolink Train at Riverside-La Sierra Station

and the San Bernardino Station is shared with the San Bernardino Line. Connection with Metrolink trains is possible on these two lines. The chapter on the Riverside-Downtown Station will be found in the Riverside Line section of this book. The chapter on the San Bernardino Station will be found in the San Bernardino Line section of this book.

The total length of the line from San Bernardino to Irvine is 59 miles.

INLAND EMPIRE-ORANGE COUNTY LINE SCHEDULE
WESTBOUND FROM SAN BERNARDINO TO IRVINE

	METROLINK	METROLINK	METROLINK
TRAIN NUMBER	**801**	**803**	**805**
DAYS OF OPERATION	**M - F**	**M - F**	**M - F**
SAN BERNARDINO	5:26A	6:28A	3:03P
RIVERSIDE-DOWNTOWN	5:46A	6:48A	3:25P
RIVERSIDE-LA SIERRA	5:57A	6:59A	3:37P
WEST CORONA	6:08A	7:10A	3:48P
ORANGE	L6:33A	L7:35A	L4:13P
SANTA ANA	L6:37A	L7:39A	L4:17P
IRVINE	6:50A	7:52A	4:32P

EASTBOUND FROM IRVINE TO SAN BERNARDINO

	METROLINK	METROLINK	METROLINK
TRAIN NUMBER	**800**	**802**	**804**
DAYS OF OPERATION	**M - F**	**M - F**	**M - F**
SAN JUAN CAPISTRANO			5:18P
IRVINE	8:10A	4:47P	5:30P
SANTA ANA	8:20A	4:57P	5:40P
ORANGE	8:24A	5:02P	5:45P
WEST CORONA	8:49A	5:27P	6:10P
RIVERSIDE-LA SIERRA	L8:59A	L5:38P	L6:21P
RIVERSIDE-DOWNTOWN	L9:12A	L5:51P	L6:34P
SAN BERNARDINO	9:38A	6:16P	6:59P

L: Regular stop to discharge or pick up passengers except train may leave ahead of schedule

158

Riverside - La Sierra Station

Station Connecting Transit Information

The Riverside-La Sierra Metrolink Station is located at 10901 Indiana Avenue. The station can be reached by taking the La Sierra Avenue exit from the Riverside Freeway (Route 91). Go south on La Sierra Avenue to Indiana Avenue and turn left. The station is on the left, one-half block from the intersection of La Sierra and Indiana avenues. The train boarding platform is well lighted and has excellent shelter. The 350-car parking lot is well maintained and has excellent lighting.

The station is served by the Riverside Transit Authority (RTA) 2, 15 and 21 bus lines. The bus stops for these lines are located in the new bus transit center directly in front of the station. The station vicinity map provides the routes for the bus transit options from the Riverside-La Sierra Metrolink Station. The following table provides the schedule for bus connections with Metrolink.

Outside of the immediate vicinity of the Riverside-La Sierra Metrolink Station the RTA 21 line provides service to Mira Loma.

The RTA lines serving the station provide access to the RTA Transfer Terminal at the Galleria at Tyler where connections can be made with the 1, 10, 12, 13, 14, 21, 27, Orange County commuter busses and Inland Empire Connection 149. From that point you can access all of the points of interest

Riverside-La Sierra Metrolink Station

listed in this chapter.

In addition, all of the points of interest listed in this chapter can also be accessed using RTA lines originating from the RTA's Downtown Riverside Terminal described in the Chapter on the Riverside Station.

For updates on the routes and schedules for RTA bus lines call (909) 682-1234.

Points of Interest
La Sierra University

La Sierra University is located at

4700 Pierce Street. It can be reached by taking the RTA 1 line from the Transit Terminal at the Galleria at Tyler. This line originates from the RTA's Downtown Riverside Terminal. It is a private four-year institution which offers Bachelors and Masters degrees. The campus has a student Art Gallery, Theater and World Museum of Natural History. The Museum is open 2:00 P.M. to 5:00 P.M. on Saturdays. The museum has two main displays. The first deals with specimens of reptiles, birds and mammals preserved by

RIVERSIDE-LA SIERRA STATION BUS CONNECTION SCHEDULE
WESTBOUND TRAINS FROM SAN BERNARDINO TO IRVINE

TRAIN NUMBER	DAYS OF OPERATION	TRAIN ARRIVAL	RTA 2 WESTBOUND 20 - 40 MIN.	RTA 2 EASTBOUND 20 - 40 MIN.	RTA 15 WESTBOUND 30 MIN.	RTA 15 EASTBOUND 30 MIN.	RTA 21 METROLINK EXPRESS**	RTA 21 2 HOURS
METROLINK 801	M - F	5:57A	5:48/6:55A		5:46A			
METROLINK 803	M - F	6:59A	6:55A		6:56A			
METROLINK 805	M - F	3:37P						* 1:40/3:53P

EASTBOUND TRAINS FROM IRVINE TO SAN BERNARDINO

METROLINK 800	M - F	L8:59A						*9:41A
METROLINK 802	M - F	L5:38P		5:45P		5:45P		*3:47/6:03P
METROLINK 804	M - F	L6:21P		6:15P		6:15P	5:47P	*8:07P

L: Regular stop to discharge or pick up passengers except train may leave ahead of schedule

* Stop is at Indiana and La Sierra avenues.

** Metrolink Express provides service between the Riverside-La Sierra Metrolink Station and The Pedley Station only.

La Sierra University Campus

taxidermy. The displays are well done and arranged to show the relationships between similar species. The second display deals with mineral spheres and mineral samples, fluorescent minerals, meteorites and petrified wood. The sphere collection is one of the largest and finest collection of spheres made out of various minerals. For information about the museum call (909) 785-2209. For general information about the University call (909) 785-2000.

California State Citrus Historic Park

The park is located at 1879 Jackson Street (Van Buren Boulevard and Dufferin Avenue). It can be reached by taking the RTA 27 line from the Transfer Terminal at the Galleria at Tyler. The park is dedicated to preserving a small part of Riverside's history, as urban sprawl has eliminated most of the remaining citrus groves in the area. It is situated on land considered to be the finest naval orange growing region in the world. The park has several California Bungalow-style buildings popular in the early 20th century. These buildings and the Sunkist center provide visitors a glimpse of life in the groves when citrus was the primary industry in this region of Southern California. For information call (909) 780-6222.

Galleria at Tyler

The Galleria is located off the 91 Freeway at Tyler Street. The mall can be reached by taking any RTA line from the Riverside-La Sierra Metrolink Station. This facility is the primary shopping mall in Riverside with Nordstrom's, The Broadway, J. C. Penney and Robinson's-May as the anchor department stores.

Castle Amusement Park

The park is located at 3500 Polk Street. The park is within walking distance from the Riverside-La Sierra Metrolink Station. It can also be reached by taking the RTA 2 line from the station. Exit at the Magnolia Avenue and Park Sierra Drive stop. The park is one-block down Park Sierra Drive behind the Kaiser Hospital. The park features a miniature golf course, 26 rides and an arcade. The golf course and arcade are open daily 10:00 A.M. to 10:00 P.M. and until midnight Friday and Saturday. The ride park is open at 6:00 P.M. Tuesdays thru Fridays in the summer. Winter hours for the ride park are 6:00 P.M. to 11:00 P.M. Friday, Noon to 11:00 P.M. Saturday and Noon to 8:00 P.M. Sunday. For information call (909) 785-4140.

Places to Stay
Riverside Travelodge

The Riverside Travelodge is located at 11043 Magnolia Avenue. The hotel phone number is (909) 688-5000. For reservations call (800) 225-3050.

Entrance to Citrus State Park

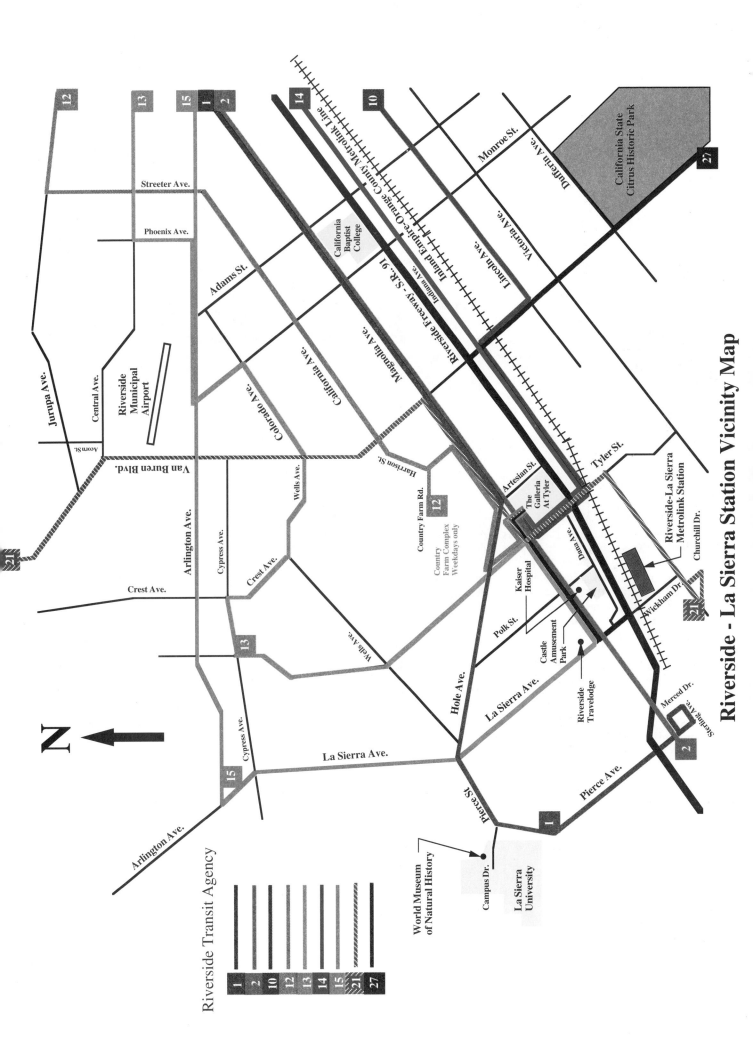

Riverside - La Sierra Station Vicinity Map

Riverside Transit Agency

| 1 | 2 | 10 | 12 | 13 | 14 | 15 | 21 | 27 |

West Corona Station

Station Connecting Transit Information

The West Corona Metrolink Station is located at 155 South Auto Center Drive. The station can be reached by taking the Auto Center Drive exit from the Riverside Freeway (Route 91). Go north on Auto Center Drive to the station. The train boarding platform is well lighted and has excellent shelter. The 500-car parking lot is well maintained and has excellent lighting.

The station is served by the Riverside Transit Authority (RTA) 2, bus line. The bus stop for this line is located in the new bus transit center directly in front of the station. The station vicinity map provides the routes for the bus transit options from the West Corona Station. The following table provides the schedule for bus connections with Metrolink.

For updates on the routes and schedules for RTA bus lines call (909) 682-1234.

Points of Interest

Corona was founded by Robert Taylor and the South Riverside Land & Water Company in 1886. Mr. Taylor and his engineer, H. Clay Kellogg, decided to build the city within a circular street, one mile in diameter. Thus Corona is also known as *The Circle City*. From the early days until as recently as 1954, citrus culture dominated the local economy. The biggest employer in town, in that year was the Exchange Lemon Products Company, with a staff of 700.

Today Corona is a mid-sized community with a population that exceeds 92,500.

West Corona Metrolink Station

Corona Public Library

The Corona Public Library is located at 650 S. Main Street. The library is a 62,300 square-foot facility which is well stocked with books of all sorts. In addition, the library hosts the Heritage Room which displays articles from Corona's past and traces the community's history.

Riverside Community College
Norco Campus

The Riverside Community College Norco Campus is located at 2001 Third Street in Norco. The college can be reached by taking the RTA route 2 bus to the Sixth and Main streets stop. Transfer to the northbound RTA route 3 bus. Take the route 3 bus to the college.

The college, which opened in 1991 is a two-year institution that offers an Associate of Arts degree in a variety of majors. For general campus information call (909) 372-7000.

Places to Stay
Best Motel

The Best Motel is located at 1248 West Sixth Street. The hotel phone number is (909) 272-4900.

Howard Johnson Lodge

The Howard Johnson Lodge is located at 1695 Hamner Avenue in Norco. The hotel phone number is (909) 278-8886. For reservations call (800) 770-HOJO.

TRAIN NUMBER	DAYS OF OPERATION	TRAIN DEPARTURE	RTA 2
BUS FREQUENCY			20 - 40 MIN.
METROLINK 801	M - F	6:08A	5:58A
METROLINK 803	M - F	7:10A	7:10A
METROLINK 805	M - F	3:48P	
EASTBOUND TRAINS FROM IRVINE TO SAN BERNARDINO			
METROLINK 800	M - F	8:49A	
METROLINK 802	M - F	5:27P	5:24/5:34P
METROLINK 804	M - F	6:10P	6:05P

WEST CORONA STATION BUS CONNECTION SCHEDULE
WESTBOUND TRAINS FROM SAN BERNARDINO TO IRVINE

L: Regular stop to discharge or pick up passengers except train may leave ahead of schedule

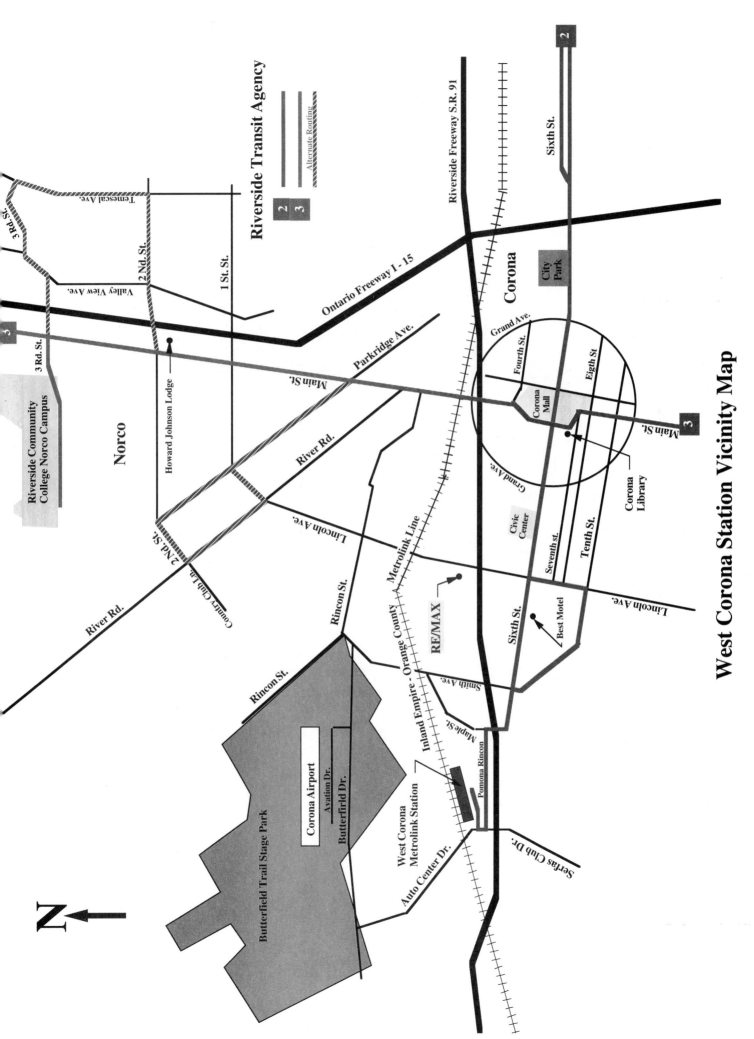

West Corona Station Vicinity Map

Riverside Transit Agency

2 3

Alternate Routing

N

Riverside Community College Norco Campus

Norco

Howard Johnson Lodge

Temescal Ave.

2 Nd. St.

Valley View Ave.

1 St. St.

3 Rd. St.

3 Rd. St.

Ontario Freeway I - 15

Parkridge Ave.

Main St.

River Rd.

River Rd.

Country Club Ln.

2 Nd. St.

Lincoln Ave.

Rincon St.

Rincon St.

Metrolink Line

Inland Empire - Orange County

Smith Ave.

Maple St.

Pomona Rincon

Serfas Club Dr.

Auto Center Dr.

West Corona Metrolink Station

Butterfield Trail Stage Park

Corona Airport

Avation Dr.

Butterfild Dr.

RE/MAX

Sixth St.

Best Motel

Lincoln Ave.

Tenth St.

Seventh st.

Civic Center

Grand Ave.

Corona Mall

Corona Library

Main St.

Eigth St

Fourth St.

Grand Ave.

City Park

Corona

Riverside Freeway S.R. 91

Sixth St.

2

3

Orange County Line

The Orange County Line has 12 stations located at L.A. Union Station, Commerce, Norwalk/Santa Fe Springs, Fullerton, Anaheim, Orange, Santa Ana, Irvine, San Juan Capistrano, San Clemente, and Oceanside. In addition, Amtrak has a station in San Clemente next to the municipal pier. Primary service along this line is provided by Amtrak which operates eight trains daily in each direction. Metrolink operates four trains Monday thru Friday in each direction. The schedules below indicate the times and number of trains traveling in each direction on the Orange County Line at the time of publication. For updates to Metrolink schedules please call 808-LINK in the 213, 310, 714, 805, 818, and 909 area codes. For updates to Amtrak schedules please call (800) USA-RAIL.

Amtrak and Metrolink tickets are not interchangeable. You must purchase an Amtrak ticket for travel on Amtrak and a Metrolink ticket for travel on Metrolink. Presently the only exception to this policy is the Step-Up Program where Metrolink monthly pass holders can purchase coupons for passage on

Amtrak Train Passing by the Norwalk/Santa Fe Springs Metrolink Station

Amtrak Train Nos. 576, 578 and 786 on Monday thru Friday only. The coupons are sold at Amtrak ticket counters at the Orange County Amtrak stations and L.A. Union Station. These coupons are sold in books of ten for $18.00. When riding one of these Amtrak trains you must show the

ORANGE COUNTY LINE SCHEDULE
NORTHBOUND FROM OCEANSIDE TO LOS ANGELES

TRAIN NUMBER	METROLINK 601	METROLINK 603	METROLINK 681	METROLINK 605	AMTRAK 769	AMTRAK 771	AMTRAK 573	AMTRAK 775	AMTRAK 577	AMTRAK 779	AMTRAK 781	AMTRAK 791	AMTRAK 583	AMTRAK 585	AMTRAK 587
DAYS OF OPERATION	M - F	M - F	M - F	M - F	SA.SU.H	M - F	M - F	DAILY	DAILY	DAILY	M - F	SA.SU.H	DAILY	DAILY	FRIDAY
OCEANSIDE	4:51A	5:30A		6:52A	6:58A	7:17A	8:28A	9:22A	11:20A	1:17P	3:24P	3:39P	5:22P	7:52P	9:49P
SAN CLEMENTE AMTRAK											3:43P	3:58P			
SAN CLEMENTE METROLINK	5:11A	5:51A		7:13A											
SAN JUAN CAPISTRANO	5:20A	6:00A		7:22A	7:31A		9:00A	9:52A	11:50A	1:47P	4:02P	4:09P	6:00P	8:30P	10:09P
IRVINE	5:32A	6:13A	7:10A	7:35A	7:46A		9:14A	10:06A	12:04P	2:00P	4:15P	4:22P	6:14P	8:44P	10:23P
SANTA ANA	5:42A	6:23A	7:21A	7:45A	7:58A	8:05A	9:26A	10:18A	12:16P	2:11P	4:27P	4:34P	6:30P	8:56P	10:35P
ORANGE	5:47A	6:28A	7:26A	7:50A											
ANAHEIM	5:51A	6:32A	7:30A	7:54A	8:08A		9:35A	10:26A	12:26P	2:20P	4:38P	4:44P	6:40P	9:06P	10:45P
FULLERTON	5:59A	6:40A	7:39A	8:02A	8:17A	8:22A	9:44A	10:38A	12:36P	2:31P	4:48P	4:54P	6:50P	9:16P	10:55P
NORWALK/SANTA FE SPRINGS	6:08A	6:49A	7:48A	8:11A											
COMMERCE		L6:57A					10:02A		12:54P				7:05P		
L.A. UNION STATION	6:36A	7:20A	8:15A	8:39A	8:58A	8:58A	10:25A	11:20A	1:20P	3:12P	5:30P	5:35P	7:25P	9:50P	11:35P

SOUTHBOUND FROM LOS ANGELES TO OCEANSIDE

TRAIN NUMBER	AMTRAK 570	AMTRAK 772	AMTRAK 572	AMTRAK 574	AMTRAK 774	AMTRAK 776	AMTRAK 578	METROLINK 684	METROLINK 604	AMTRAK 780	AMTRAK 782	METROLINK 606	AMTRAK 584	METROLINK 608	AMTRAK 786
DAYS OF OPERATION	DAILY	M - F	SA.SU.H	DAILY	SA.SU.H	DAILY	DAILY	M - F	M - F	M - F	SA.SU.H	M - F	SU. - F	M - F	DAILY
L.A. UNION STATION	6:40A	8:35A	8:35A	10:30A	10:30A	12:30P	2:30P	3:39P	4:35P	5:15P	5:15P	5:37P	6:10P	6:29P	9:00P
COMMERCE				10:46A	10:46A				L4:51P			L5:53P	6:26P		
NORWALK/SANTA FE SPRINGS								4:02P	5:01P			6:03P		6:52P	
FULLERTON	7:14A	9:14A	9:14A	11:04A	11:04A	1:03P	3:04P	4:11P	5:10P	5:47P		6:12P	6:46P	7:01P	9:33P
ANAHEIM	7:23A	9:24A	9:24A	11:14A	11:14A	1:13P	3:14P	4:19P	5:18P		5:56P	6:20P	6:55P	7:10P	9:42P
ORANGE								4:23P	5:22P			6:24P		7:14P	
SANTA ANA	7:32A	9:34A	9:34A	11:24A	11:24A	1:23P	3:24P	4:28P	5:26P	6:02P	6:06P	6:28P	7:03P	7:18P	9:51P
IRVINE	7:44A	9:46A	9:46A	11:36A	11:36A	1:35P	3:36P	L4:39P	5:37P		6:18P	6:39P	7:14P	7:29P	10:02P
SAN JUAN CAPISTRANO	7:58A	10:03A	10:03A	11:51A	11:51A	1:57P	3:50P	4:54P	L5:49P		6:29P	L6:52P	7:27P	L7:41P	10:13P
SAN CLEMENTE METROLINK									L6:01P			L7:04P		L7:53P	
SAN CLEMENTE AMTRAK		10:15A	10:15A												
OCEANSIDE	8:29A	10:35A	10:35A	12:20P	12:20P	2:28P	4:21P		6:26P	6:49P	6:59P	7:29P	8:01P	8:18P	10:43P

L: Regular stop to discharge or pick up passengers except train may leave ahead of schedule

Metrolink Train Traveling Along Coast Near Dana Point

conductor your monthly pass and present him with one of the coupons. Coupons are not sold on Amtrak trains. Step-Up Coupons sold for use on the Orange County Line are not valid for travel on the Ventura County Line nor are the Step-Up Coupons sold for use on the Ventura County Line valid on the Orange County Line.

The Orange County Line was originally built by the Atchison, Topeka & Santa Fe Railway in the latter part of the 1880's. Presently the line is owned by three different public agencies. The Los Angeles County Metropolitan Transit Authority owns the segment between L.A. Union Station and Redondo Junction; the Orange County Transit Authority owns the segment from Fullerton to the San Diego County line; and the North County Transit District owns the segment down to Oceanside through Camp Pendleton. The cost of Metrolink service along this line was $218.3 million which included track upgrades, stations and Metrolink rolling stock.

The length of the line is 87.3 miles from Oceanside to L.A. Union Station. The alignment roughly follows the I-5 Santa Ana Freeway along the entire route. The total trip time takes approximately one hour-50 minutes. The average speed along the entire route is 45 mph with top speeds of 79 mph. This speed should improve when Metrolink completes its program to improve the roadbed and install a second track along much of this line through southern Orange County.

The southern half of the Orange County Line is one of the most scenic routes on the Metrolink system.

The more picturesque portion of the line starts at the Irvine Ranch, some of the last remaining agriculture land in Orange County.

From San Juan Capistrano the tracks follows San Juan Creek to the City of Dana Point. At Dana Point Harbor the tracks run along the beach to San Clemente.

From San Clemente, the tracks enter San Diego County and traverse Camp Pendleton along the top of the bluffs that line the coastline all the way to Oceanside. The first landmark after entering San Diego County, will be the famous Trestles surfing beach named for the wooden railroad trestle that passes over San Onofre Creek. After passing over San Onofre Creek the track passes by the San Onofre Nuclear Power Generating Station.

The Oceanside Station is the end of the Metrolink Orange County Line. Rail travel further south to San Diego is available on all Amtrak trains or on the Coaster. For more information on these services see the chapter in this book on the Oceanside Station.

165

Commerce Station

Station Connecting Transit Information

The Commerce Amtrak/Metrolink Station is located at 6344 26th Street off Garfield Avenue between I-5 Freeway and Bandini Boulevard. The station has a 150-car parking lot. The train boarding platform is well lighted but with limited shelter. The parking lot is well lighted and maintained. The station is unmanned.

The station is served by the City of Commerce Orange Bus Line. The bus stop is located just off the boarding platform. The MTA 262 Line runs along Garfield and has stops at Bandini and Garfield, about one-third mile from the station. The MTA 462 Line runs along Telegraph Road and has stops at Garfield and Telegraph, about one-half mile from the station. The City of Commerce Orange line will take you to these stops when it stops at the Metrolink station.The station vicinity map provides the routes for the bus transit options from the Commerce Amtrak/Metrolink Station. The following tables below provide the schedule for bus connections to Amtrak and Metrolink. For a City of Commerce Bus schedule and route updates call (213) 887-4419. For MTA updates call (213) 626-4455.

Commerce Amtrak/Metrolink Station

Points of Interest

The City of Commerce was once part of the Indian lands that became part of San Gabriel Mission when it was founded in 1771. In 1810 the area was included in the boundaries of Rancho San Antonio which was granted to Don Antonio Maria Lugo. He held the property for the next 60 years. Eventually Lugo divided up his holdings and distributed them to his children. When one of his daughters died, he sold her acreage to Able Sterns. He eventually amassed 6,000 acres which became Rancho Laguna. The bulk of the property remained with the Sterns family and his heirs until the

COMMERCE STATION WEEKDAY BUS CONNECTIONS
NORTHBOUND TRAINS FROM OCEANSIDE TO LOS ANGELES

TRAIN NUMBER	DAYS OF OPERATION	TRAIN ARRIVAL	CITY OF COMMERCE ORANGE HOURLY	MTA 262 NORTHBOUND 45 - 60 MIN.	MTA 262 SOUTHBOUND 45 - 60 MIN.	MTA 462 WESTBOUND 20 - 60 MIN.	MTA 462 EASTBOUND 20 - 60 MIN.
BUS FREQUENCY							
METROLINK 603	M - F	L6:57A	6:05/7:10A	6:41/7:21A	6:51/7:31A	6:39/7:18A	6:51/7:13A
AMTRAK 573	M - F	10:02A	10:02/10:10A	9:36/10:21A	9:43/10:28A	9:29/10:59A	9:32/10:34A
AMTRAK 577	DAILY	12:54P	12:37/1:45P	12:31/1:16P	12:43/1:28P	11:59A/1:01P	12:35/1:35P
AMTRAK 583	DAILY	7:05P		6:24/7:53P	6:38/7:28P	6:59/7:49P	6:25/7:44P

SOUTHBOUND TRAINS FROM LOS ANGELES TO OCEANSIDE

AMTRAK 574	M - F	10:46A	10:02/11:45A	10:21/11:06A	10:28/11:13A	9:59/10:59A	10:34/11:35P
METROLINK 604	M - F	L4:51P	4:37/5:45P	4:16/4:56P	4:23/5:08P	4:32/5:06P	4:29/5:14P
METROLINK 606	M - F	L5:53P	5:37P	5:40/6:24P	5:08/6:38P	5:46/6:20P	5:33/6:25P
AMTRAK 584	SU. - F	6:26P		5:40/7:08P	5:51/6:38P	6:20/6:57P	5:55/7:05P

L: Regular stop to discharge or pick up passengers except train may leave ahead of schedule
Stop for MTA 262 line is at corner of Garfield Avenue and Bandini Boulevard.
Stop for MTA 462 line is at corner of Garfield Avenue and Telegraph Road

COMMERCE STATION WEEKEND BUS CONNECTIONS

NORTHBOUND TRAINS FROM OCEANSIDE TO LOS ANGELES

TRAIN NUMBER	DAYS OF OPERATION	TRAIN ARRIVAL	MTA 262	MTA 262	MTA 262	MTA 262	MTA 462	MTA 462
			NORTHBOUND	NORTHBOUND	SOUTHBOUND	SOUTHBOUND	WESTBOUND	EASTBOUND
DAYS OF OPERATION			SATURDAY	SUNDAY - H.	SATURDAY	SUNDAY - H.	SA.SU.H.	SA.SU.H.
BUS FREQUENCY			HOURLY	HOURLY	HOURLY	HOURLY	HOURLY	HOURLY
AMTRAK 577	DAILY	12:54P	12:45/1:25P	12:13/1:32P	12:15/1:35P	12:02/1:01P	11:53A/1:53P	12:34/1:34P
AMTRAK 583	DAILY	7:05P	6:54/7:54P	6:54/7:53P	6:26/7:24P	6:24/7:24P	6:42/7:37P	6:31/7:31P

SOUTHBOUND TRAINS FROM LOS ANGELES TO OCEANSIDE

AMTRAK 774	SA.SU.H.	10:46A	10:29/11:25A	10:33/11:33A	10:02/10:55A	10:02/11:02A	9:53/10:53A	10:34/11:34A
AMTRAK 584	SU. - F	6:26P		5:54/6:54P		5:24/7:24P	5:52/6:42	6:31/7:31P

Stop for MTA 262 line is at corner of Garfield Avenue and Bandini Boulevard.

Stop for MTA 462 line is at corner of Garfield Avenue and Telegraph Road

1920's. Since that time industrial giants such as B. F. Goodrich, Uniroyal Rubber, Chrysler, and Lever Brothers have built plants in Commerce. The city was incorporated in 1960. Today the City of Commerce is in the middle of Los Angeles' heavy industry area. The city has a small residential area sandwiched between Washington Boulevard and the I-5 Freeway. There is a small commercial shopping district along Washington Boulevard between the I-5 and I-710 freeways. Points of interest in the city would be the Citadel Outlet Mall and the Commerce Casino.

Citadel Outlet Mall

The Citadel was built on the site of the Samson Tire & Rubber Company facility, which operated an automobile tire manufacturing plant. The building was a copy of an Assyrian palace. The original plant was built in 1929. Eventually Uniroyal acquired the castle and continued to produce tires there until 1978. From that time, until 1990, the castle lay abandoned. The Citadel has reopened as a Factory Outlet Mall. The mall has stores representing many name-brand manufacturing labels, such as Eddie Bauer, Corning, Benetton, Paul Jardin to name a few. The Citadel has an office complex and a hotel, The Wyndham Garden, behind the Wall. The Citadel is located at 5675 East Telegraph Road. From the Metrolink station take the City of Commerce Orange line or MTA 462 Line.

The Commerce Casino

In California, card casinos are legal providing the local community has not outlawed them. Commerce is one of the communities that has welcomed this type of establishment. While not on the same scale as a Las Vegas or Atlantic City gambling establishment, the Commerce Casino is reminiscent of the establishments that grace those cities. The games include Poker, Pan, Pai Gow, Asian Poker, Asian Stud Poker, Omaha, Hold'Em, 7-Card Stud, Super Pan Nine and California Aces, California's answer to Blackjack. The casino features a lounge with live entertainment and three restaurants. The casino is open 7 days a week 24, hours a day.

The Commerce Casino is located at 6131 East Telegraph Road. From Metrolink take the City of Commerce Orange Line or the MTA 462 line.

The Citadel

167

Commerce Casino

Metrolink station with advance notice. The hotel phone number is (800) 547-4777. For reservations call (800) 2-RAMADA.

Travelodge Suites

The Travelodge Suites is located at 7701 Slauson Avenue. The hotel has a shuttle van and will pick you up at the Metrolink station with advance notice. The hotel phone number is (213) 728-5165. For reservations call (800) 578-7878.

Super 8 Motel

The Super 8 Motel is located at 7810 East Telegraph Road. The hotel has a shuttle van and will pick you up at the Metrolink station with advance notice. The hotel phone number is (310) 806-3791. For reservations call (800) 800-8000.

Wyndham Garden Hotel

The Wyndham Garden Hotel is located at 5757 East Telegraph Road. The hotel has a shuttle van and will pick you up at the Metrolink station with advance notice. The hotel phone number is (213) 887-8100. For reservations call (800) 822-4200.

Places to Stay

Commerce Holiday Inn

The Commerce Holiday Inn is located at 6300 East Telegraph Road. The hotel has a shuttle van and will pick you up at the Metrolink station with advance notice. The hotel phone number is (213) 888-8878. For reservations call (800) HOLIDAY.

Howard Johnson

The Howard Johnson Hotel is located at 7709 Telegraph Road in Montebello. The hotel phone number is

(213) 724-1400. For reservations call (800) 300-5110.

Ramada Inn

The Ramada Inn is located at 7272 Gage Avenue. The hotel has a shuttle van and will pick you up at the

City of Commerce

TAKE A FREE RIDE

City of Commerce Municipal Bus Lines Provides

Free Transportation within the City.

For Information call (213) 887-4419

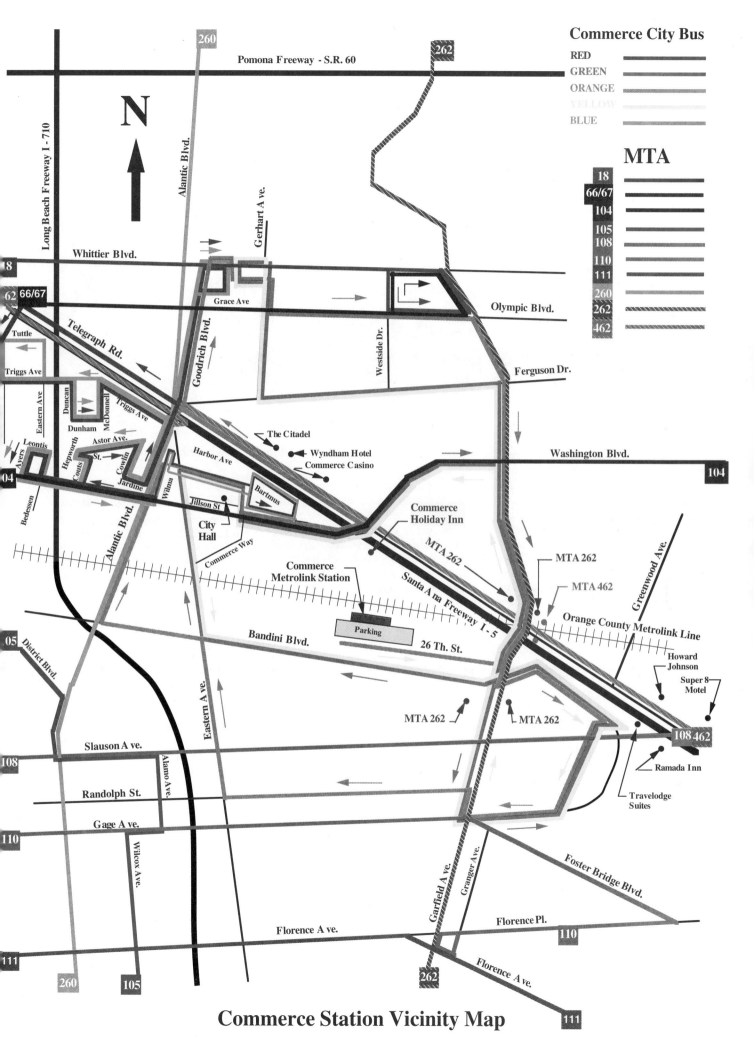

Commerce Station Vicinity Map

Norwalk/Santa Fe Springs Station

Station Connecting Transit Information

The Norwalk/Santa Fe Springs Transportation Center is located at 12700 Imperial Highway. The transportation center has a 268-car parking lot which is well lighted. There are boarding platforms are on each side of the tracks with a pedestrian bridge over the tracks. The boarding platforms are well lighted and have excellent shelter. A Metrolink Ambassador mans the transportation center during the morning and evening rush hours. The transportation center can be reached by taking the Imperial Highway offramp from the Santa Ana Freeway I-5. Go east on Imperial Highway to the transportation center which will be on your right. The entrance to the parking lot will be just before the railroad underpass on Imperial Highway.

The transportation center is served by the Norwalk Transit Route 3 and Route 4 (*Green Line Shuttle Bus*), the City of Santa Fe Springs MetroExpress, and the MTA 120 line. The station vicinity map provides the routes for the fixed route bus transit options from the Norwalk/Santa Fe Springs Transportation center.

The Santa Fe Springs MetroExpress provides door-to-door connecting transfer from Metrolink

Norwalk/Santa Fe Springs Transportation Center

trains stopping at the transportation center to places of employment within the City of Santa Fe Springs. To make your reservation call (310) 868-0511.

The following table provides the schedule for fixed route bus connections with Metrolink. For updates to schedules and routes for Norwalk Transit System bus service please call (310) 929-5550. For MTA schedule and route updates call (310) 868-0511.

MTA Green Line Connection

The eastern terminus of the MTA Green Line light rail line from Norwalk to LAX and Manhattan Beach is only 2.2 miles from the Norwalk/Santa Fe Springs Transportation Center. The Green line has 14 stations located at Norwalk I-605 and I-105, Lakewood Boulevard, Long Beach Boulevard,

NORWALK/SANTA FE SPRINGS STATION BUS CONNECTIONS

NORTHBOUND TRAINS FROM OCEANSIDE TO LOS ANGELES

TRAIN NUMBER	DAYS OF OPERATION	TRAIN ARRIVAL	NORWALK ROUTE 3 CLOCKWISE HOURLY	NORWALK ROUTE 3 C. CLOCKWISE HOURLY	NORWALK ROUTE 4 EASTBOUND 20 - 30 MIN.	NORWALK ROUTE 4 WESTBOUND 20 - 30 MIN.	MTA 121 15 - 20 MIN.
BUS FREQUENCY							
METROLINK 601	M - F	6:08A	6:10A	6:16A	6:00/6:20A	6:00/6:20A	6:01/6:20A
METROLINK 603	M - F	6:49A	6:10/7:10A	6:16/7:05A	6:40/7:00A	6:40/7:00A	6:42/7:00A
METROLINK 681	M - F	7:48A	7:10/8:10A	7:05/8:10A	7:40/8:00A	7:20/7:50A	7:41/8:00A
METROLINK 605	M - F	8:11A	8:10/9:10A	8:10/9:05A	8:00/8:20A	7:50/8:20A	8:01/8:20A

SOUTHBOUND TRAINS FROM LOS ANGELES TO OCEANSIDE

METROLINK 684	M - F	4:02P	3:10/4:10P	3:55/4:55P	4:00/4:20P	4:00/4:20P	3:58/4:10P
METROLINK 604	M - F	5:01P	4:10/5:10P	4:55/5:55P	5:00/5:20P	5:00/5:20P	4:57/5:10P
METROLINK 606	M - F	6:03P	5:10/6:10P	5:55/7:05P	6:00/6:20P	6:00/6:20P	5:56/6:10P
METROLINK 608	M - F	6:52P	6:10P	5:55/7:05P	6:40/7:00P	6:40/7:00P	6:50/7:20P

L: Regular stop to discharge or pick up passengers except train may leave ahead of schedule

Norwalk Green Line Station

Imperial Highway/Wilmington Avenue, Avalon Boulevard, Harbor Freeway I-110 and I-105, Vermont Boulevard, Crenshaw Boulevard, Hawthorne Boulevard, Aviation Boulevard, Mariposa Avenue, El Segundo Boulevard and Nash Street, Douglas Street and Rosecrans Avenue, and Marine and Redondo Beach avenues.

Connections between Metrolink and the Green Line are provided by Norwalk Transit System Route 4 and the MTA 121 line.

The Green Line provides connections to the MTA Blue Line at the Imperial Highway/Wilmington Avenue Station and access to Los Angeles International Airport at the Aviation Boulevard Station. For more information on the MTA Green Line call (213) 620-7245.

Points of Interest

The cities of Norwalk and Santa Fe Springs were originally part of Spanish land grant ranchos. Norwalk was a part of the Rancho Los Coyotes and Santa Fe Springs was a part of the Santa Gertrudes Rancho. Cattle and sheep were grazed on the land during the days of the rancho's. Mexico built a fort near present day Norwalk and Pioneer boulevards.

In the mid 1870's Dr. J. W. Fulton built a resort on the stagecoach route between Los Angeles and San Diego. Passengers en-route between these two cities would stop for a few days to enjoy the mineral springs at the resort.

The Los Angeles & Anaheim Railroad, now the Southern Pacific Company, built the first railroad through this area in 1888. The name on the railroad station serving this area was Fulton Wells. In 1889 the California Southern Railroad, now the Santa Fe Railway, completed its line through these communities. Metrolink operates on the Santa Fe tracks.

From the mid 1800's to 1921, when oil was discovered, the area was a farming community with many large dairies and some of the largest sugar beet farms in Southern California. With the discovery of oil, the community of Santa Fe Springs was transformed overnight into a boom town. Living conditions near the oil fields were abysmal, explosions rattled windows, mud ran through streets and fires burned for weeks. Many of the original residents fled.

After World War II the oil boom had receded and developers were building residential housing tracks in Norwalk. Norwalk and Santa Fe Springs both incorporated in 1957. Santa Fe Springs today is primarily an industrial community with a population of only 15,000 in its 8.67 square miles. In contrast, Norwalk is home to 91,000 residents in its 11 square miles.

Norwalk Civic Center

The Norwalk Civic Center is about two blocks west of the transportation center. In addition to the Norwalk City Hall on the corner of Imperial Highway and Norwalk Boulevard, the civic center complex includes the Norwalk Branch of the Los Angeles County Library, Los Angeles County Hall of Records Branch, Sheriff's Station, Superior Court House and a newly completed parking structure with a pedestrian overhead crossing to the AMC Theater Complex.

Norwalk Arts and Sports Complex

The Norwalk Arts and Sports Complex is located at 13000 Clarkdale Avenue. The complex has 42,000 square feet devoted to the fitness of the citizens of Norwalk. The sports center has a fully equipped gym, a basketball court, boxing rings, four indoor racquetball/handball courts. There is a daily fee of $5.00 for nonresidents. For more information call (310) 406-2221.

Take the westbound Norwalk Transit Route 3 line to the San Antonio Drive and Olive Street stop. Walk one block southeast on Olive.

Norwalk Arts and Sports Complex

Santa Fe Springs Town Center

The Santa Fe Springs Town Center is comprised of the City Hall, Fire Station, Santa Fe Springs Library, Town Center Hall, Post Office, Aquatic Center and Clarke Estate. At the intersection of Pioneer Boulevard and Telegraph Road, in front of the post office, there is a spectacular fountain which is titled *Soaring Dreams* by artist Dennis Smith.

Take the westbound MTA 121 line or the Norwalk Transit Route 3 or 4 lines to the Imperial Highway and Norwalk Boulevard stop. Transfer to the northbound MTA 462 line and take it to the Telegraph Road and Pioneer Boulevard stop.

The Clarke Estate

The Clarke Estate is located at 10211 Pioneer Boulevard in Santa Fe Springs, directly behind the library. The estate was built by Architect Irving Gill in 1919 for Chauncey and Marie Rankin Clarke and is listed on the National Register of Historic Places.

Clarke Estate

Soaring Dreams **Fountain**

Gill's architectural design philosophy was to design buildings without the ornamentation of the Victorian era. As a result of this philosophy, he became one of the most influential architects of this century. The Clarke Estate was completed in 1921. It is built around a central courtyard and has an exterior pergola (covered walkway). The home is of unadorned concrete construction. This home is one of the few remaining buildings designed by Gill. The Clarke Estate features some of Gill's innovations which include closets in the bedrooms and skylights in halls and bathrooms. Other innovations designed to reduce the collection of dust on the building surfaces include rounded interior corners, flat panel doors, and the elimination of moldings.

The estate is open to the public for tours Tuesday and Friday and on the first Sunday of the month from 11:00 A.M. to 2:00 P.M. The Clarke Estate is available for weddings, receptions and meetings for both the business and residential communities. Along with the basic accommodations, a concierge service is also available for a service fee in which all arrangements are handled by the staff. For information call (310) 863-4896 or 868-3876.

The Clarke Estate can be reached by taking westbound MTA 121 line or the Norwalk Transit Route 3 or 4 lines to the Imperial Highway and Norwalk Boulevard stop. Transfer to the northbound MTA 462 line and take it to the Telegraph Road and Pioneer

Boulevard stop. Walk one block south on Pioneer to the driveway which leads to the estate.

Cerritos College

Cerritos College is located at 11110 Alondra Boulevard in Norwalk.

The college was founded in 1956 and is a two year community college. The college offers Associate of Arts degrees and certificates in 87 different areas of study. The student body is over 22,000. For general campus information call (310) 860-2451.

From The transportation center take the MTA 121 line to the Metro Green Line Station and transfer to the MTA 270 line. Take this line to the Studebaker Road and Alondra Boulevard stop. You can also take the Norwalk Transit Route 3 or 4 lines to the Imperial Highway and Norwalk

Antique Tractors at the Hathaway Ranch Museum

Boulevard Stop. Transfer to the Southbound Norwalk Transit Route 1 or 2 lines and take them to the Cerritos College stop.

The college has an art gallery with professional and student shows throughout the school year. For current information call (310) 860-2451 ext. 395.

The Burnight Theater on campus offers a variety of student productions during the school year. The Theater Department at the college offers the internationally recognized Lee Korf Playwriting Award each year. The school receives over 1,000 scripts each year in this competition many, from recognized playwrights. The winning scripts are produced by the Theater Department with student participation. These productions are the highlight of the theater calendar. For information on current productions call (310) 924-2100.

Hathaway Ranch Museum

The Hathaway Ranch Museum is located at 11901 East Florence Avenue in Santa Fe Springs. The museum is located on what remains today of the Hathaway ranch. Jesse Hathaway and his new bride Lola moved to Santa Fe Springs shortly after their marriage in 1902. They purchased a 40-acre ranch and began farming their property. They had three sons on the ranch, Elwood, Richard and Julian. When oil was discovered in Santa Fe Springs in 1921

the fortunes of the Hathaways increased dramatically. By 1929 the Hathaways had started an independent oil company and in 1933 they built a new house on their ranch. Richard Hathaway remained in Santa Fe Springs and married Nadine Appplegate in 1935. They raised six children in the house that today is the museum. The Hathaways never threw anything away. They would keep on repairing any equipment that they

acquired for either farming or operation of their oil business. In order to preserve this rich heritage Nadine Hathaway founded the Hathaway Ranch Museum in 1986. The museum displays items used by the Hathaways over almost a century of living on the property. Antique farming and oil equipment, most of which are still in working condition, are on display in addition to the domestic items and furniture in the Hathaway house.

The museum is open Monday, Tuesday, Thursday, Friday 11:00 A.M. to 4:00 P.M. and on the first Sunday of each month from 2:00 to 4:00 P.M. Admission is free but donations are accepted. For information call (310) 944-6563.

From the transportation center take Norwalk Transit Route 3 or 4 lines to the Imperial Highway and Norwalk Boulevard stop. Transfer to the northbound Norwalk Transit Route 1 and take it to the Florence Avenue and Pioneer Boulevard stop. Walk one-quarter block back on Florence. The museum is on the north side of Florence.

Heritage Park

Heritage Park is located at 12100 Mora Drive in Santa Fe Springs. The park is a nationally-recognized historic site. It is a reconstruction of the ranch estate of a wealthy farmer named Hawkins. In the 1880's, Hawkins

Windmill at Heritage Park

174

A.T. & S.F. 870 at Heritage Park

purchased 100 acres of land from Dr. J. E. Fulton, the Santa Fe Springs mineral spring health resort owner. Hawkins built his estate in the Victorian architectural style known as Carpenter Gothic. While most farmers in the area built barns for a few hundred dollars Hawkins, spent $5,000.00 on his carriage barn.

The estate began to deteriorate in the 1920's with the onset of the oil boom in the Santa Fe Springs area. The Hawkins house was destroyed in the 1940's. The buildings and gardens in Heritage Park are recreations of those located on the original Hawkins estate.

The Carriage Barn houses a number of turn-of-the-century exhibits and an 1880's vintage carriage. The park site has been the site of numerous archeological diggings representing several era, starting with the Ontiveros family. Patricio Ontiveros first came to the area in the late 1700's. In 1815 Ontiveros built a large adobe home on the park site adjacent to the present site of the Carriage Barn. Ontiveros was not the owner of the property but was appointed mayordomo of the vast cattle rancho operated by the Mission San Juan Capistrano. The carriage barn is open Sunday, Tuesday, Friday and Saturday 12:00 Noon to 4:00 P.M., Wednesday and Thursday 9:00 A.M. to 4:00 P.M. and is closed on Monday.

There is a replica of the Santa Fe Springs Railroad Depot on the park site along with a restored steam locomotive, the A.T.&S.F. 870, a boxcar and caboose.

The park is open from 7:00 A.M. to 10:00 P.M. every day of the year. This beautiful park with its secluded gardens and fountains is an ideal location for outdoor summer weddings, receptions and photo opportunities. For further information call (310) 946-6476.

To reach the park from the transportation center take the westbound MTA 121 line or Norwalk Transit Route 3 or 4 lines to the Imperial Highway and Norwalk Boulevard stop. Transfer to the northbound MTA 462 line and take it to the Telegraph Road and Heritage Park Drive stop. Walk one block south on Heritage Park Drive. Alternately, at Imperial Highway and Norwalk Boulevard you can transfer to the northbound Norwalk Transit Route 1 line and take it to the Florence Avenue and Hathaway Drive Stop. Transfer to the Santa Fe Springs Tram and it will take you to the park.

Places to Stay

Best Western Norwalk Inn

The Best Western Norwalk Inn is located at 10902 Firestone Boulevard. The hotel phone number is (310) 929-8831. For reservations call 528-1234.

Comfort Inn

The Comfort Inn is located at 12512 S. Pioneer Boulevard. The hotel phone number is (310) 868-3453. For reservations call (800) 221-2222.

Sheraton Norwalk Hotel

The Sheraton Norwalk Hotel is located at 13111 Sycamore Drive. The hotel has a shuttle van which will pick you up at the transportation center with advance notice. The hotel phone number is (310) 863-6666. For reservations call (800) 325-3535.

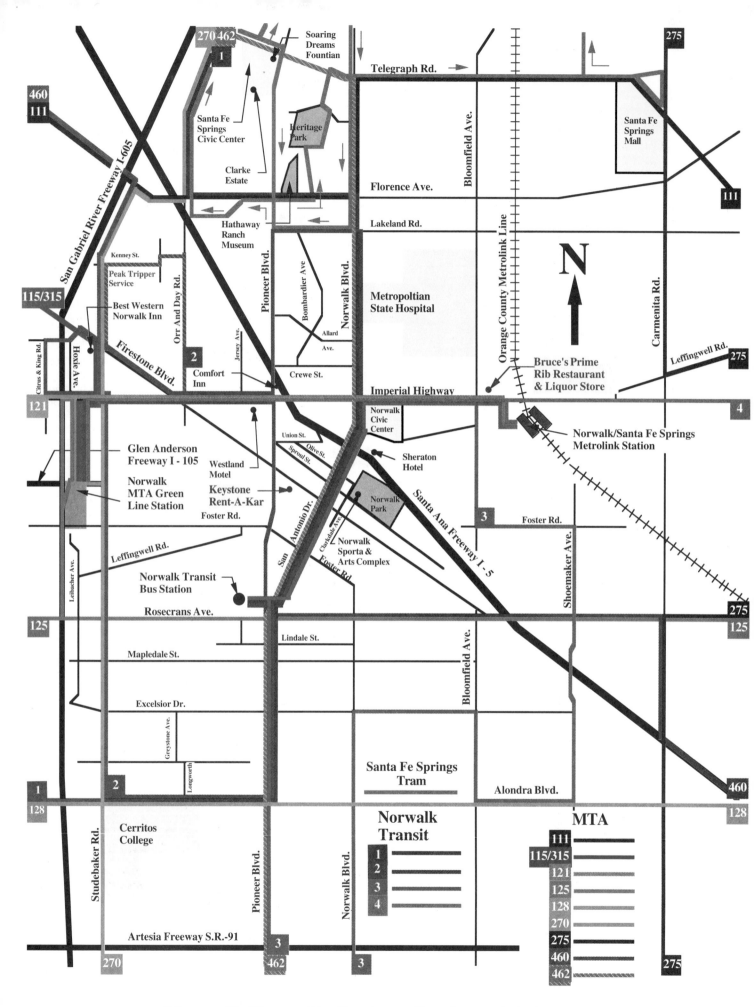

Norwalk/Santa Fe Springs Station Vicinity Map

Fullerton Station

Station Connecting Transit Information

The Fullerton Amtrak/Metrolink Station is located at 120 E. Santa Fe Avenue off Harbor Boulevard. The station has several parking lots on both sides of the tracks and a parking structure. Parking is free, but has a variety of time restrictions to accommodate adjacent restaurants and shops.

There are two historic railroad station buildings located at the Fullerton Amtrak/Metrolink Station. The newly restored station building used by Metrolink and Amtrak is the old Fullerton Santa Fe Station. The Fullerton Union Pacific Station is home to the Old Spaghetti Factory restaurant. The Fullerton Union Pacific Station, is in the Southern California variant of the Colonial Spanish Revival Style architecture, while the Santa Fe station has a distinct New Mexican theme.

The train boarding platform is well lighted but with limited shelter. The station is manned by Amtrak personnel.

Fullerton Amtrak/Metrolink Station

The station can be reached by taking the Harbor Boulevard offramp from the 91 Freeway. From the 91 Freeway go north on Harbor Boulevard to Santa Fe Avenue and turn right. The station and its parking lot will be on your right just past the Old Spaghetti Factory.

FULLERTON STATION WEEKDAY BUS CONNECTIONS
NORTHBOUND TRAINS FROM OCEANSIDE TO LOS ANGELES

TRAIN NUMBER	DAYS OF OPERATION	TRAIN ARRIVAL	OCTA 26 WESTBOUND 30-60 MIN.	OCTA 26 EASTBOUND 30-60 MIN.	OCTA 41 WESTBOUND 45 MIN.	OCTA 41 EASTBOUND 45 MIN.	OCTA 43 15 MIN.	OCTA 47 30 MIN.
METROLINK 601	M - F	5:59A	6:24A	6:11A	5:30/6:15A	5:55/6:35A	5:55/6:00A	6:24A
METROLINK 603	M - F	6:40A	6:24/6:54A	6:39/7:11A	6:15/6:50A	6:35/7:25A	6:30/6:44A	6:36/6:54A
METROLINK 681	M - F	7:39A	7:24/7:54A	7:11/7:39A	7:25/8:15A	7:25/8:05A	7:37/7:42A	7:11/7:54A
METROLINK 605	M - F	8:02A	7:54/8:24A	7:39/8:11A	7:25/8:15A	7:25/8:05A	7:57/8:02A	7:41/8:24A
AMTRAK 771	M - F	8:22A	7:54/8:24A	8:11/8:39A	8:15/8:55A	8:05/8:45A	8:15/8:27A	8:11/8:24A
AMTRAK 573	M - F	9:44A	9:25/9:55A	9:41/10:41A	9:35/10:15A	9:25/10:10A	9:35/9:54A	9:41/9:54A
AMTRAK 775	DAILY	10:38A	9:55/10:55A	9:41/10:41A	10:15/11:00A	10:10/10:55A	10:25/10:39A	10:36/10:50A
AMTRAK 577	DAILY	12:36P	11:55A/12:55A	12:34/1:34P	12:30/1:17P	12:25/1:10P	12:30/12:39P	12:06/12:50P
AMTRAK 779	DAILY	2:31P	1:55/2:55P	1:34/2:34P	2:00/2:45P	1:50/2:37P	2:30/2:37P	2:09/2:50P
AMTRAK 781	M - F	4:48P	4:25/4:55P	4:37/5:09P	4:11/4:50P	4:40/5:20P	4:42/4:53P	4:41/4:49P
AMTRAK 583	DAILY	6:50P	5:54/6:54P	6:41/7:41P	6:48/7:43P	6:44/7:25P	6:32/6:56P	6:48/6:58P
AMTRAK 585	DAILY	9:16P	7:54P	7:41P	8:45/10:04P	8:36/10:00P	9:15/9:53P	9:07P
METROLINK 587	FRIDAY	10:55P			10:04P	10:00P	10:36	

TRAIN NUMBER	DAYS OF OPERATION	TRAIN ARRIVAL	OCTA 333 NORTHBOUND COMMUTER	OCTA 333 SOUTHBOUND COMMUTER	OCTA 373 NORTHBOUND COMMUTER	OCTA 373 SOUTHBOUND COMMUTER	OCTA 424 WESTBOUND COMMUTER	OCTA 424 EASTBOUND COMMUTER
METROLINK 601	M - F	5:59A		6:37A		5:40/6:10A		
METROLINK 603	M - F	6:40A	6:44/7:15A	6:37A		6:10/6:40A	6:44A	
METROLINK 681	M - F	7:39A	7:15A	7:53A			7:40A	
METROLINK 605	M - F	8:02A		7:53A			8:15A	
AMTRAK 771	M - F	8:22A						
AMTRAK 573	M - F	9:44A						
AMTRAK 775	DAILY	10:38A						
AMTRAK 577	DAILY	12:36P						
AMTRAK 779	DAILY	2:31P						
AMTRAK 781	M - F	4:48P		4:19/4:50P	5:19P			
AMTRAK 583	DAILY	6:50P	6:00P	6:03P	6:19P			
AMTRAK 585	DAILY	9:16P						
METROLINK 587	FRIDAY	10:55P						

SOUTHBOUND TRAINS FROM LOS ANGELES TO OCEANSIDE

TRAIN NUMBER	DAYS OF OPERATION	TRAIN ARRIVAL	OCTA 26 WESTBOUND 30-60 MIN.	OCTA 26 EASTBOUND 30-60 MIN.	OCTA 41 WESTBOUND 45 MIN.	OCTA 41 EASTBOUND 45 MIN.	OCTA 43 15 MIN.	OCTA 47 30 MIN.
AMTRAK 570	DAILY	7:14A	6:54/7:24A	7:11/7:39A	6:50/7:25A	6:35/7:25A	7:11/7:22A	7:11/7:24A
AMTRAK 772	M - F	9:14A	8:54/9:25A	8:39/9:41A	8:55/9:35P	8:45/9:25A	9:05/9:27A	9:11/9:24A
AMTRAK 574	M - F	11:04A	10:55/11:55A	10:41/11:34A	11:00/11:45A	10:55/11:42A	10:55/11:09A	10:36/11:20A
AMTRAK 776	DAILY	1:03P	12:55/1:55P	12:34/1:34P	12:30/1:17P	12:25/1:10P	1:00/1:09P	12:36/1:20P
AMTRAK 578	DAILY	3:04P	2:55/3:25P	2:34/3:09P	2:45/3:20P	2:37/3:10P	3:00/3:07P	2:39/3:17P
METROLINK 684	M - F	4:11P	3:55/4:25P	3:37/4:09P	3:20/4:50P	4:00/4:40P	4:08/4:13P	4:09/4:17P
METROLINK 604	M - F	5:10P	4:55/5:24P	5:09/5:37P	4:50/5:30P	4:40/5:20P	5:02/5:23P	4:41/5:19P
AMTRAK 780	M - F	5:47P	5:24/5:54P	5:37/6:41P	5:30/6:11P	5:20/6:05P	5:42/6:05P	5:41/5:49P
METROLINK 606	M - F	6:12P	5:54/6:54P	5:37/6:41P	6:11/6:48P	6:05/6:44P	6:02/6:25P	5:41/6:28P
AMTRAK 584	SU. - F	6:46P	5:54/6:54P	6:41/7:41P	6:11/6:48P	6:44/7:25P	6:32/6:56P	6:18/6:58P
METROLINK 608	M - F	7:01P	6:54/7:54P	6:41/7:41P	6:48/7:43P	6:44/7:25P	6:52/7:16P	6:48/7:28P
AMTRAK 786	DAILY	9:33P	7:54P	7:41P	8:45/10:04P	8:36/10:00P	9:15/9:53P	9:07P

TRAIN NUMBER	DAYS OF OPERATION	TRAIN ARRIVAL	OCTA 333 NORTHBOUND COMMUTER	OCTA 333 SOUTHBOUND COMMUTER	OCTA 373 NORTHBOUND COMMUTER	OCTA 373 EASTBOUND COMMUTER	OCTA 424 WESTBOUND COMMUTER	OCTA 424 EASTBOUND COMMUTER
AMTRAK 570	DAILY	7:14A	7:15A	6:37/7:53A		6:40A	7:40A	
AMTRAK 772	M - F	9:14A						
AMTRAK 574	M - F	11:04A						
AMTRAK 776	DAILY	1:03P						
AMTRAK 578	DAILY	3:04P						
METROLINK 684	M - F	4:11P		4:19P				
METROLINK 604	M - F	5:10P		4:50P	5:19P			5:00P
AMTRAK 780	M - F	5:47P	6:00P	6:03P	5:19/5:49P			
METROLINK 606	M - F	6:12P	6:00P	6:03P	5:49/6:19P			6:02P
AMTRAK 584	SU. - F	6:46P			6:19P			
METROLINK 608	M - F	7:01P						
AMTRAK 786	DAILY	9:33P						

L: Regular stop to discharge or pick up passengers except train may leave ahead of schedule

FULLERTON STATION WEEKEND BUS CONNECTIONS
NORTHBOUND TRAINS FROM OCEANSIDE TO LOS ANGELES

TRAIN NUMBER	DAYS OF OPERATION	TRAIN ARRIVAL	OCTA 26 WESTBOUND SATURDAY HOURLY	OCTA 26 EASTBOUND SATURDAY HOURLY	OCTA 41 WESTBOUND SATURDAY 75 MIN.	OCTA 41 EASTBOUND SATURDAY 75 MIN.	OCTA 41 WESTBOUND SUNDAY/HO. 75 MIN.	OCTA 41 EASTBOUND SUNDAY/HO. HOURLY	OCTA 43 SATURDAY 20 MIN.	OCTA 43 SUNDAY/HO. 20 MIN.	OCTA 47 SATURDAY 45-60 MIN.	OCTA 47 SUNDAY/HO. 45-60 MIN.
AMTRAK 769	SA.SU.H.	8:17A	9:24A	9:11A	7:13/8:31A	7:21/8:36A	7:33/8:36A	7:18/8:33A	8:16/8:24A	8:12/8:35A	7:19/8:24A	7:28/8:51A
AMTRAK 775	DAILY	10:38A	10:24/11:24A	10:11/11:11A	9:46/11:01A	9:50/11:05A	9:51/11:06A	9:45/11:00A	10:18/10:44A	10:29/10:47A	10:26/11:23A	10:06/11:06A
AMTRAK 577	DAILY	12:36P	12:24/1:24P	12:11/1:11P	12:16/1:31P	12:20/1:35P	12:21/1:36P	12:15/1:30P	12:25/12:37P	12:33/12:47P	11:58A/12:55P	11:50A/12:45P
AMTRAK 779	DAILY	2:31P	2:24/3:24P	2:11/3:11P	1:31/2:46P	1:35/2:50P	1:36/2:51P	1:30/2:45P	2:25/3:37P	2:13/2:47P	2:16/3:27P	2:08/3:23P
AMTRAK 791	SA.SU.H.	4:54P	4:24/5:24P	4:11/5:11P	4:01/5:16P	4:05/5:20P	4:06/5:21P	4:00/5:15P	4:49/4:58P	4:53/5:07P	4:34/5:35P	4:26/5:15P
AMTRAK 583	DAILY	6:50P			6:31/7:43P	6:35/7:53P	6:41/7:49P	6:30/7:50P	6:45/7:17P	6:33/7:05P	6:29P	6:05P
AMTRAK 585	DAILY	9:16P			7:43P	7:53P	7:49P	7:50P	8:48/9:17P	9:07P	7:29P	

SOUTHBOUND TRAINS FROM LOS ANGELES TO OCEANSIDE

TRAIN NUMBER	DAYS OF OPERATION	TRAIN ARRIVAL	OCTA 26	OCTA 26	OCTA 41	OCTA 41	OCTA 41	OCTA 41	OCTA 43	OCTA 43	OCTA 47	OCTA 47
AMTRAK 570	DAILY	7:14A			7:13/8:31A	6:13/7:21A	7:33A	7:18A	7:09/7:29A	7:12/7:21A	7:24A	7:35A
AMTRAK 572	SA.SU.H.	9:14A	9:24A	9:11/10:11A	8:31/9:46A	8:36/9:50A	8:36/9:51A	8:33/9:45A	8:57/9:24A	8:49/9:15A	8:19/9:51A	8:24/9:40A
AMTRAK 774	SA.SU.H.	11:04A	10:24/11:24A	10:11/11:11A	11:01A/12:16P	9:50/11:05A	9:51/11:06A	11:00A/12:15P	10:58/11:17A	10:49/11:07A	10:26/11:23A	11:01/11:06A
AMTRAL 776	DAILY	1:03P	12:24/1:24P	12:11/1:11P	12:16/1:31P	12:20/1:35P	12:21/1:36P	12:15/1:30P	12:45/1:17P	12:53/1:07P	12:44/1:41P	12:36/1:31P
AMTRAK 578	DAILY	3:04P	2:24/3:24P	2:11/3:11P	2:46/4:01P	2:50/4:05P	2:51/4:06P	2:45/4:00P	2:45/3:17P	2:53/3:07P	3:02/3:27P	2:54/3:23P
AMTRAK 782	SA.SU.H.	5:47P	5:24P	5:11P	5:16/6:31P	5:20/6:35P	5:21/6:41P	5:15/6:30P	5:45/5:58P	5:33/6:03P	5:29/6:35P	5:09/6:11P
AMTRAK 584	SU.-F	6:46P					6:41/7:49P	6:30/7:50P	6:45/7:17P	6:33/7:05P	6:29P	6:05P
AMTRAL 786	DAILY	9:33P			7:43P	7:53P	7:49P	7:50P	9:18P	9:07P	7:29P	

Everything in downtown Fullerton is within easy walking distance of the station. The station is served by the Orange County Transit Authority (OCTA) 26, 41, 43, 47, 333, 373, and 424 bus lines. The stops for these lines are located at the Fullerton Bus Transit Center located across the parking lot from the station building. The station vicinity map provides the bus transit options from the Fullerton Amtrak/Metrolink Station. The preceding tables provide the schedule for bus connections with Amtrak and Metrolink. For updates to schedules call OCTA at (714) 636-RIDE.

Points of Interest

In 1887 the township of Fullerton was laid out on 430 acres of land where downtown district exists today. The community leaders that accomplished this were Edwin and George Amerige and the Wilshire brothers. The new town was named after George H. Fullerton who was responsible for bringing the Los Angeles-to-San Diego branch of the Santa Fe Railway to the town. Today Fullerton is a city occupying 23-square miles with a population over 121,000. The city's downtown district is home to the Fullerton Museum Center, art galleries, antique shops, book stores, restaurants, boutiques, office buildings and Fullerton Community College. On Thursdays, April through mid-November, from 4:00 P.M. to 9:00 P.M. Wilshire Avenue between Harbor Boulevard and Pomona Avenue becomes the Fullerton Marketplace. The Marketplace features a Farmers Market with fresh produce, Arts and Crafts displays, food, fun and

Fullerton Bus Transit Center

Fullerton Community College Campus

Downtown Fullerton

Fullerton Antique District

The Fullerton Antique District is located primarily along Harbor Boulevard in downtown Fullerton. However there are several antique shops located on many of the side streets that intersect with Harbor Boulevard. In fact, right across the parking lot from the station is a couple of antique shops. In addition there are several boutiques and restaurants throughout the surrounding downtown district of Fullerton.

Fullerton Museum Center

The Fullerton Museum Center is located at 301 N. Pomona Avenue. Pomona Avenue dead ends at Santa Fe Avenue just to the right of the station building. The museum is a short three-block walk up Pomona Avenue from the station. The museum offers the visitor a unique mix of exhibits and cultural events in science, history and art. The museum is open Wednesday thru Sunday 12:00 P.M. to 4:00 P.M. and Thursdays till 8:00 P.M. Closed Mondays and Major Holidays. Admission is $2.50 for adults, $2.00 for senior citizens, $1.50 for students and children under 12 are free. For information call (714) 738-6545.

Muckenthaler Cultural Center

The Muckenthaler Cultural Center is located at 1201 W. Malvern Avenue. The Center can be reached from

entertainment.

Metrolink by walking five blocks to Chapman and Lemon Street and catching the westbound OCTA 25 line to the Malvern Avenue and Euclid Street stop. The center will be one block west on the north side of Malvern Avenue. The center offers ever-changing fine art exhibitions, a variety of workshops, classes, and an outdoor summer theater. The center was built in 1924 and served as the home of the Muckenthaler family. The center is open noon to 4:00 P.M. Tuesday thru Sunday. For information call (714) 738-6595. For information on Theater-on-the-Green summer productions in June, July and August call (714) 992-7432.

Plummer Auditorium

Plummer Auditorium is the performing arts center for Fullerton. It is located at the corner of Chapman Avenue and Lemon Street. The Fullerton Civic Light Opera offers several productions throughout the year at the auditorium. For information on Civic Light Opera Productions call (714) 526-3832. The North Orange County Community College district sponsors a number of professional productions throughout the year. For information call (714) 525-5836 or (714) 525-8617.

Fullerton Community College

The Fullerton Community College is located at 321 E. Chapman Avenue. The college is a short five-block-walk from the Metrolink Station at the corner of Lemon Street and Chapman Avenue.

The college was established as a department of Fullerton Union High School in 1913 and is the oldest continuously-operating community college in the state of California. It was reorganized as a district Junior College in 1922. In 1964 the North Orange County Community College District was formed and Fullerton college became the first college in the new district. The college is a two-year institution offering an Associate of Arts degree in a wide variety of majors. For information call (714) 992-7000.

Heritage House at the Fullerton Arboretum

Chase Suites Hotel

The Chase Suites Hotel is located at 2932 E. Nutwood Avenue. The hotel has a shuttle van and will pick you up at the Metrolink station with advance notice. The hotel phone number is (714) 579-7400. For reservations call (800) 237-8811.

Fullerton Holiday Inn

The Fullerton Holiday Inn is located at 222 West Houston Avenue. The hotel has a shuttle van and will pick you up at the Metrolink station with advance notice. The hotel phone number is (714) 992-1700 or (800) 553-3441. For reservations call (800) HOLIDAY.

Red Roof Inn

The Red Roof Inn is located at 1251 North Harbor Boulevard. The hotel phone number is (714) 635-6461. For reservations call (800) THE-ROOF.

California State University Fullerton

California State University Fullerton is located at 800 N. State College Boulevard. It can be reached by taking the OCTA 26 or 328 lines from the Fullerton Transit Mall. The University is a part of the 20-campus State University system. It is a full four-year institution which offers Bachelors and Masters degrees.

The University was originally named Orange County State College and was established in 1957 by an act of the State Legislature. The following year the present site in northeast Fullerton was designated and purchased by the state in 1959. The college opened in September 1959 with 452 full and part-time students. In 1964 the name was changed to California State College-Fullerton. In 1972 the school qualified for University status and the name was changed again to California State University, Fullerton. Today the university enrollment has climbed to over 25,000 students and is a major institution of higher learning in the State of California.

The campus has a student Art Gallery and Theater. The Fullerton Arboretum is located on the Cal State Fullerton campus. For Information call (714) 773-2011.

The Fullerton Arboretum

The Fullerton Arboretum is located on the northeast corner of the Cal State-Fullerton campus. The Arboretum can be reached by taking the OCTA 26 or 328 line from Metrolink to the Cal State-Fullerton stop at the corner of Nutwood Avenue and State College Boulevard. There you need to transfer to the northbound OCTA 49 line to the Yorba Linda Boulevard and Associated Road stop. The arboretum features plantings from all over the world. A restored victorian cottage, the home of Fullerton's first doctor, is on the grounds. Tours are available by appointment. The arboretum is open 8:00 A.M. to 4:45 P.M. For information call (714) 773-3579.

Places to Stay
Fullerton Marriott Hotel

The Fullerton Marriott Hotel is located at 2701 E. Nutwood Avenue. The hotel can be reached by taking the OCTA 26 or 328 line to the Nutwood Avenue and Langsdorf Drive stop. The hotel phone number is (714) 738-7800. For reservations call (800) 228-9290.

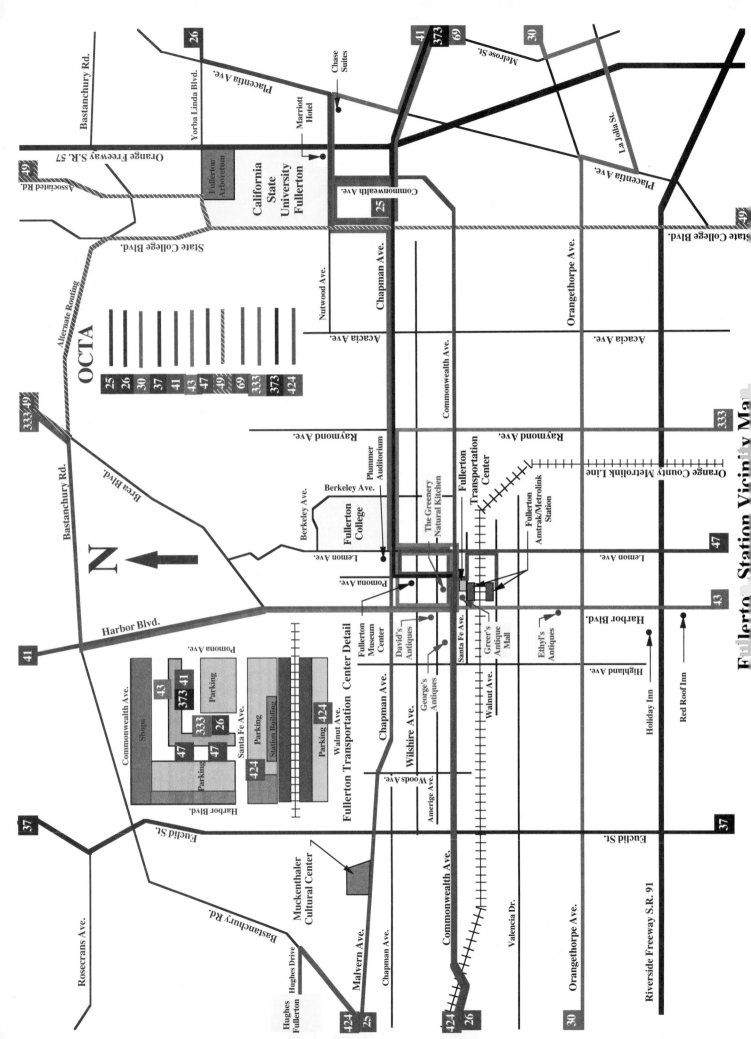

Fullerton Station Vicinity Map

Buena Park

The Buena Park Station is scheduled to be built some time in the future. Until the station is completed, Buena Park can be reached by taking the westbound OCTA 25 Line from the Chapman Avenue and Lemon Street stop which is a short four-block walk from the Fullerton Amtrak/Metrolink Station. Transfer to the southbound OCTA 29 or 29A line at the Beach Boulevard and Commonwealth Avenue stop. The OCTA 29 or 29A line will take you to the Buena Park Entertainment District and Knott's Berry Farm. An alternative to this would be to book a hotel in Buena Park which provides shuttle service to/from the Fullerton Amtrak/Metrolink Station. The Buena Park vicinity map provides the route map for these lines in the vicinity of the Buena Park Entertainment District. For schedules call OCTA on (714) 636-RIDE.

Points of Interest

Buena Park is home to Knott's Berry Farm one of Southern California's major theme parks. The city has prospered from the association with the Knott family. An entertainment corridor along Beach Boulevard between the 91 Freeway and Knott's Berry Farm includes such attractions as Wild Bill's Wild West Dinner Extravaganza, Movieland Wax Museum, Medieval Times Dinner & Tournament and Ripley's "Believe It or Not" Museum. A number of hotels and restaurants are dispersed in this same area.

Cypress College

Cypress college is located at 9200 Valley View Street in Cypress, California. The college is a member of the North Orange County Community

Buena Park's Entertainment District on Beach Boulevard

College District. Cypress college opened on September 12, 1966. Since that time the college has built twelve major instructional buildings on the 110-acre site and the student population has grown from 1,200 to over 15,000. The school offers a two-year Associate of Arts Degree in a wide range of majors. For information call (714) 826-2220. On campus there is a theater which offers a number of student stage and dance productions throughout the school year. For information call (714) 821-6320 days or (714) 821-4221 evenings.

Buena Park Mall

The Buena Park Mall is located at Stanton and La Palma avenues one block east of Knott's Berry Farm. The

mall anchor department stores include Sears, Fedco and J. C. Penney. The mall provides a shopper shuttle which stops at the major tourist hotels in the Anaheim area. For information about the shopper shuttle call (714) 826-4266.

International Printing Museum

The International Printing Museum is located at 8469 Kass Drive. To reach the museum by bus take the OCTA 30 bus line to the Orangethorpe Avenue and Thomas Street stop. Kass Drive intersects Thomas Drive a short block south of Orangethorpe Avenue. The Museum is one block east at the end of Kass Avenue The museum has a large collection of antique printing presses. The museum offers a series of educational tours. The Pages of Invention tour combines a general tour of the museum's galleries, which highlights inventions which have changed history, with a character performance by either Ben Franklin or Mark Twain. The Pages of Freedom tour is a reenactment of the Constitutional Convention along with a guided tour of exhibits of watershed documents of freedom throughout history. The Pages of Adventure Tour explores the history of books for over 3,000 years. Demonstrations of papermaking and bookbinding are presented. The museum is open Tuesday thru Saturday 10:00 A.M. to 5:00 P.M. Closed Sundays, Mondays and major holidays. Admission is $6.50 for adults, $4.00 for students and seniors. For information call (714) 523-2080.

Knott's Berry Farm

Knott's Berry Farm is located at 8039 Beach Boulevard. The park is America's first theme amusement park dating back to 1940 when Walter Knott opened the Ghost Town and offered visitors a real wild west adventure. The Ghost Town is still one of the major attractions at the park. The Ghost Town offers visitors a ride on a real steam train from the latter part of the 19th century, stage coach rides, saloon shows, gunfights and a myriad of activities. The Mystery Lodge is a special effects family attraction based upon native american folklore continues to astound audiences daily.

The Roaring Twenties area features roller coaster rides, a parachute ride, the Kingdom of the Dinosaurs, the Goodtime Theater, just to name a few. Plus, don't miss Knott's blockbuster new attraction Jaguar, the streaking big cat of roller coasters.

For small children there is Camp Snoopy where you just might run into Charlie Brown, Lucy, and of course Charles Shultz's lovable beagle, Snoopy. A trip to Southern California without a visit to Knott's Berry Farm would be incomplete. The park is open every day except Christmas. For information on current admission prices and operating hours call (714) 523-2070.

Medieval Times Dinner & Tournament

Medieval Times is located at 7662 Beach Boulevard. This attraction offers visitors a trip back to medieval England in the year of 1093, for a traditional feast where you get your fill of roasted chicken and spare ribs while being entertained by a jousting tournament with real horses. For show times and reservations call (714) 521-4740.

Movieland Wax Museum

The museum is located at 7711 Beach Boulevard. The museum opened in 1962 and has continually expanded its collection of lifesize wax figures of motion picture stars from yesteryear and today. There are 300 wax figures representing over 74 years of film and television personalities. For information call (714) 52-1154.

Ripley's "Believe It or Not" Museum

The museum is located at 7850 Beach Boulevard. The museum is a commercial entertainment venture where many of the oddities collected by Robert L. Ripley are on display. Ripley was born in 1893 in Santa Rosa, California. At age sixteen he began his newspaper career as a sports cartoonist. He originated the "Believe It or Not" series that delighted readers the world over for over 70 years. The museum is a monument to his achievements as a reporter who traveled the world in search of the odd and unusual. For information call (714) 522-1152.

Wild Bill's Wild West Dinner Extravaganza

Wild Bill's is located at 7600 Beach Boulevard. This attraction offers the visitor a rip roar'n wild west musical extravaganza. The meal includes roast chicken, barbecue ribs, corn on the cob, potatoes and dessert, beer, wine and Coca-Cola to drink. For show times and reservations call (714) 522-6414.

Places to Stay
Buena Park Hotel

The Buena Park Hotel is located at 7675 Crescent Avenue. The hotel has a shuttle van and will pick you up at the Fullerton Amtrak/Metrolink Station with advance notice. The hotel phone number is (714) 995-1111. For

Cypress College Campus

reservations call (800) 422-4444 in California or (800) 854-8792 outside California.

Embassy Suites Hotel

The Embassy Suites Hotel is located at 7762 Beach Boulevard. The hotel has a shuttle van and will pick you up at the Fullerton Amtrak/Metrolink Station with advance notice. The hotel phone number is (714) 739-5600. For reservations call (800) EMBASSY.

Buena Park Holiday Inn

The Buena Park Holiday Inn is located at 7000 Beach Boulevard. The hotel has a shuttle van and will pick you up at the Fullerton Amtrak/Metrolink Station with advance

notice. The hotel phone number is (714) 522-7000 or (800) 522-7006. For reservations call (800) HOLIDAY.

Courtyard by Marriott

The Courtyard by Marriott is located at 7621 Beach Boulevard. The hotel phone number is (714) 670-6600. For reservations call (800) 321-2211.

The Inn at Buena Park

The Inn at Buena Park is located at 7828 Orangethorpe. The hotel has a shuttle van and will pick you up at the Fullerton Amtrak/Metrolink Station

with advance notice. The hotel phone number is (714) 670-7200.

Fairfield Inn by Marriott

The Fairfield Inn by Marriott is located at 7032 Orangethorpe Avenue. The hotel phone number is (714) 523-1488. For reservations call (800) 228-2800.

Ramada Inn

The Ramada Inn is located at 7555 Beach Boulevard. The hotel phone number is (714) 522-7360 or (800) 862-8987. For reservations call (800) 2RAMADA.

Travelers Inn

The Travelers Inn is located at 7121 Beach Boulevard. The hotel phone number is (714) 670-9000. For reservations call (800) 633-8300.

Best Western Buena Park Inn

The Best Western Buena Park Inn is located at 8580 Stanton Avenue. The hotel phone number is (714) 828-5211. For reservations call (800) 528-1234.

Travelodge

The Travelodge is located at 7039 Orangethorpe Avenue. The hotel phone number is (714)521-9220. For reservations call (800) 854-8299.

Super 8 Motel

The Super 8 Motel is located at 7930 Beach Boulevard. The hotel phone number is (714) 994-6480. For reservations call (800) 800-8000.

Knott's Berry Farm Main Gate

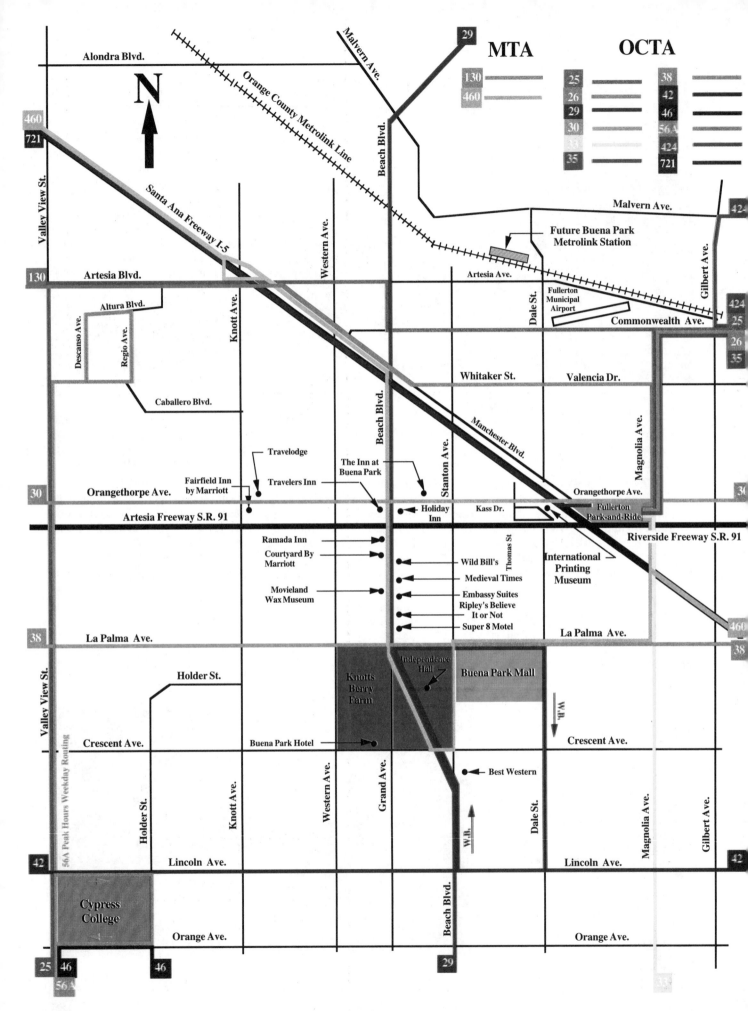

Buena Park Vicinity Map

Anaheim Station

Station Connecting Transit Information

The Anaheim Amtrak/Metrolink Station is located at 2150 E. Santa Fe Avenue on the grounds of Anaheim Stadium. The station parking lot is a part of the parking lot for the stadium which has been separated from the latter and space for 400 cars is available. The train boarding platform is well lighted, but there is no shelter. The station building is manned daily by Amtrak personnel.

The station is accessible from the Santa Ana I-5 and Orange 57 freeways. From the Santa Ana Freeway take the Katella Avenue offramp and then go east. Enter the Anaheim Stadium parking lot via the entrance just past State College Boulevard. Follow the signs to the Amtrak/Metrolink station parking lot. From the Orange Freeway take the Katella offramp and go west. The entrance to the stadium parking lot will be on your left just before State College Boulevard

The station is served by the Orange County Transit Authority (OCTA) 49, 50, and 439 bus lines and the Anaheim Transportation Network (ATN) Commuter Route. The stops for the OCTA 439 line and ATN Commuter Route are located in front of the Anaheim Station building. The stops for the 49 line are locate on Katella Avenue a good one-quarter mile walk from the station building. The 50

Anaheim Amtrak/Metrolink Station

line stops are located at the corner of State College Boulevard and Katella Avenue. The station vicinity map provides the routes of bus transit options from the Anaheim Amtrak/Metrolink Station. The following tables provide the schedules for bus connections with Metrolink and Amtrak. For updates to schedules and routes call OCTA at (714) 636-RIDE and ATN at (714) 563-5287.

Outside the immediate vicinity of the Anaheim Metrolink Station the

OCTA 49 line provides service to Brea, Fullerton to the north, and Orange and Santa Ana to the south. The OCTA 50 line provides service to Orange to the east and Garden Grove, Los Alamitos and Long Beach to the west.

Points of Interest

Anaheim's original residents were a group of German emigrants who came to America as a result of the German Revolution of 1848. Two German emigrants had experience in the wine-making business. When they settled in

ANAHEIM STATION WEEKEND BUS CONNECTIONS
NORTHBOUND TRAINS FROM OCEANSIDE TO LOS ANGELES

TRAIN NUMBER	DAYS OF OPERATION	TRAIN ARRIVAL	OCTA 49 NORTHBOUND SATURDAY 20 - 60 MIN.	OCTA 49 SOUTHBOUND SATURDAY 20 - 60 MIN.	OCTA 49 NORTHBOUND SUNDAY - H. 20 - 60 MIN.	OCTA 49 SOUTHBOUND SUNDAY - H. 20 - 60 MIN.	OCTA 50 EASTBOUND SATURDAY 30 - 60 MIN.	OCTA 50 WESTBOUND SATURDAY 30 - 60 MIN.	OCTA 50 EASTBOUND SUNDAY - H. HOURLY	OCTA 50 WESTBOUND SUNDAY - H. HOURLY
AMTRAK 769	SA.SU.H.	8:08A	7:19/8:26A	7:22/8:22A	8:30A	9:10A	7:21/8:21A	7:06/9:06A	7:34/8:34A	7:19/8:19A
AMTRAK 775	DAILY	10:26A	10:06/10:48A	10:19/10:59A	9:40/10:39A	10:00/10:50A	9:21/11:05A	10:06/10:41A	9:31/11:31A	9:19/11:23A
AMTRAK 577	DAILY	12:26P	12:08/12:38P	12:19/12:55P	12:04/12:29P	11:40A/12:41P	12:16/12:51P	11:51A/1:04P	11:31A/1:29P	11:23A/1:20P
AMTRAK 779	DAILY	2:20P	2:08/2:48P	1:51/2:47P	1:44/2:32P	2:11/2:33P	2:01/2:36P	1:39/2:49P	1:29/3:29P	1:20/3:23P
AMTRAK 791	SA.SU.H	4:44P	4:06/5:26P	4:21/5:21P	4:12/5:02P	4:23/5:28P	4:22/5:22P	4:34/5:09P	4:28/5:31P	4:23/5:23P
AMTRAK 583	DAILY	6:40P	6:26/7:26P	6:21/7:21P	5:52/6:42P	6:18P	6:17/7:22P	6:09/7:01P	6:31/7:31P	6:21/7:21P
AMTRAK 585	DAILY	9:06P	8:26P	7:51P			8:22/9:34P	8:06P	8:34P	8:21/9:21P

SOUTHBOUND TRAINS FROM LOS ANGELES TO OCEANSIDE

AMTRAK 570	DAILY	7:23A	6:19/8:26A	6:23/8:22A	8:30A		6:18/8:21A	7:06/8:06A	7:34A	5:56/8:19A
AMTRAK 572	SA.SU.H.	9:24A	8:26/9:46A	9:02/9:42A	8:30/10:20A	9:10/10:00A	8:21/10:29A	9:06/10:06A	8:34/9:31P	8:19/10:23A
AMTRAK 774	SA.SU.H.	11:14A	10:58/11:28A	10:59/11:39A	10:39/11:34P	10:50/11:40P	11:05/11:40A	10:41/11:51A	10:31/11:31A	10:23/11:23A
AMTRAK 776	DAILY	1:13P	12:48/1:28P	12:59/1:39P	12:54/1:44P	12:41/1:21P	12:51/1:26P	1:04/1:39P	12:29/1:29P	12:23/2:19P
AMTRAK 578	DAILY	3:14P	2:48/3:28P	3:01/3:41P	2:32/3:22P	3:01/3:28P	2:36/3:46P	2:49/3:24P	2:29/3:29P	2:19/3:23P
AMTRAK 782	SA.SU.H.	5:56P	5:26/6:26P	5:21/6:21P	5:02/6:42P	5:28/6:18P	5:22/6:17P	5:09/6:09P	5:31/6:31P	5:23/6:21P
AMTRAK 584	SU. - F	6:55P			6:42P	6:18P			6:31/7:31P	6:21/7:21P
AMTRAK 786	DAILY	9:42P	8:26P	7:51P			9:34P	9:06P	8:34P	9:21P

ANAHEIM STATION WEEKDAY BUS CONNECTIONS
NORTHBOUND TRAINS FROM OCEANSIDE TO LOS ANGELES

TRAIN NUMBER	DAYS OF OPERATION	TRAIN ARRIVAL	OCTA 49/49A NORTHBOUND 30 MIN.	OCTA 49/49A SOUTHBOUND 30 MIN.	OCTA 50 EASTBOUND 30 - 60 MIN.	OCTA 50 WESTBOUND 30 - 60 MIN.	OCTA 439 COMMUTER	ATN COMMUTER ROUTE
BUS FREQUENCY								
METROLINK 601	M - F	5:51A	5:37/6:07A	5:30/6:05A	5:39/6:09A	5:25/6:25A		
METROLINK 603	M - F	6:32A	6:07/7:15A	6:05/7:05A	6:09/7:09A	6:25/6:55A	6:35A	6:35A
METROLINK 681	M - F	7:30A	7:15/7:40A	7:05/7:38A	7:09/7:39A	6:55/7:59A	7:55A	7:55A
METROLINK 605	M - F	7:54A	7:40/8:15A	7:38/8:09A	7:39/8:09A	7:25/8:29A	7:55A	7:55A
AMTRAK 573	M - F	9:35A	9:16/9:51A	9:19/9:56A	9:09/9:39A	9:29/9:59A		
AMTRAK 775	DAILY	10:26A	9:51/11:01A	9:56/11:06A	10:09/10:39A	9:59/10:59P		
AMTRAK 577	DAILY	12:26P	12:15P/12:51P	12:10/12:45P	12:09/12:39P	11:59A/12:59P		
AMTRAK 779	DAILY	2:20P	2:01/2:36P	1:55/2:30P	2:09/2:39P	1:59/2:29P		
AMTRAK 781	M - F	4:38P	4:21/4:51P	4:28/4:57P	4:05/5:05P	4:30/5:00P		
AMTRAK 583	DAILY	6:40P	6:13/7:13P	6:31/7:04P	5:41/7:43P	6:30/7:28P	5:48P	6:10P
AMTRAK 585	DAILY	9:06P	8:39/9:37P	8:41/9:23P	8:43/9:43P	8:28/9:26P		
AMTRAK 587	FRIDAY	10:45P	9:37P	9:23P	9:43P	10:26P		

SOUTHBOUND TRAINS FROM LOS ANGELES TO OCEANSIDE

TRAIN NUMBER	DAYS OF OPERATION	TRAIN ARRIVAL	OCTA 49/49A NORTHBOUND	OCTA 49/49A SOUTHBOUND	OCTA 50 EASTBOUND	OCTA 50 WESTBOUND	OCTA 439 COMMUTER	ATN COMMUTER ROUTE
AMTRAK 570	DAILY	7:23A	7:15/7:40A	7:05/7:38A	7:09/7:39A	6:55/7:59A	7:55A	7:55A
AMTRAK 772	M - F	9:24A	9:16/9:51A	8:44/9:56A	9:09/9:39A	8:59/9:59A		
AMTRAK 574	M - F	11:14A	11:01/11:36A	11:06/11:35A	10:39/11:39A	10:59/11:29A		
AMTRAK 776	DAILY	1:13P	12:51P/1:26P	12:45/1:20P	12:39/1:39P	12:59/1:29P		
AMTRAK 578	DAILY	3:14P	2:36/3:46P	3:00/3:30P	3:05/3:35P	2:59/3:29P		
METROLINK 684	M - F	4:19P	3:46/4:51P	3:58/4:28P	4:05/4:35P	4:00/4:30P	4:38P	
METROLINK 604	M - F	5:18P	4:51/5:43P	4:57/5:28P	5:05/5:41P	5:00/5:30P	5:48P	5:07P
METROLINK 606	M - F	6:20P	6:13/6:43P	5:54/6:31P	5:41/6:41P	5:30/6:30P		6:10P
AMTRAK 584	SU. - F	6:55P	6:43/7:13P	6:31/7:04P	6:41/7:43P	6:30/7:28P		
METROLINK 608	M - F	7:10P	6:43/7:39P	6:31/7:41P	6:41/7:41P	6:30/7:28P		
AMTRAK 786	DAILY	9:42P	8:39P	9:23P	8:43/10:43P	9:30/10:26P		

L: Regular stop to discharge or pick up passengers except train may leave ahead of schedule

Anaheim they quickly formed and headed the Los Angeles Vineyard Society. The city's name "Anaheim" means "home by the river" which reflects the fact that the Santa Ana River traverses the city. The city was officially founded in 1857, and incorporated in 1870, thus making it the oldest city in Orange County. In the 1880's disaster struck the vineyards. A grapevine disease destroyed the wine making business in Anaheim. The local farmers eventually turned to citrus as the primary farm crop for the region. Orange Groves remained the predominant fixture in the region until the 1950's. It was then that industry and Walt Disney came to town. Disneyland opened in 1955. This event changed Orange County forever. Today Anaheim is Southern California's number one tourist attraction and Orange County's second largest city with a population of 280,000.

Downtown Anaheim

The Anaheim Civic Center can be reached by taking the ATN Commuter Route from the Anaheim Amtrak/Metrolink Station. Downtown Anaheim is populated by a number of high-rise office buildings with some shops at street level. The Anaheim Museum is located in downtown Anaheim across the street from City Hall.

The Anaheim Museum

The Anaheim Museum is located at 241 S. Anaheim Boulevard. The museum can be reached by taking the ATN Commuter Route to the Anaheim Civic Center stop. The museum is housed in the restored Carnegie Library, built in 1908 with funds donated by the steel magnate Andrew Carnegie. It is one of 1,678 libraries built by Carnegie during the early part of the 20th century. It features exhibits which trace the history of Anaheim from its founding by German immigrants in 1857 with artifacts from the vineyards and citrus groves which replaced the vineyards in the 1880's. The majority of the exhibits focus upon Walt Disney and Disneyland. Memorabilia from the early days of Disneyland are on display. Everything from mouse ears to ticket books with the "E" tickets unused is on display. The museum is open 10:00 A.M. to 4:00 P.M. Wednesday thru Friday and 12:00 P.M. to 4:00 P.M. on Saturday. Donations are appreciated.

Disneyland

Disneyland, Walt Disney's dream, which at once reinvented and defined what amusement parks should be when it opened in 1955. It is more than a amusement park, it is a place where dreams are born; a place where anything can happen and usually does. The streets are clean, crime is not a problem, and mass public transportation is a reality and works. As you enter the park you travel through a tunnel under the Main Street Station serving Main Street, USA. From here vintage 19th century steam trains take you on a grand central tour of the Magic Kingdom. Main Street, USA, which is

Anaheim Museum

lined with stores and shops that resemble an idealized downtown district of a midwestern farming community, is just like the one that Walt Disney grew up in, Marceline, Missouri. In walking down Main Street you are gently transported to a simpler time, where the stresses and complexities of modern life were not yet invented. Walt Disney's placing Main Street, USA, between the entrance of the park and the various attractions in the lands of Disneyland was no accident. It allows the visitors time to transition from the reality of modern urban existence to a place where one can let his imagination go and experience what is to come. By the time you reach the Hub at the end of Main Street, USA, you are ready to escape to any one of the various lands of Disneyland. Walt Disney knew there was a child in every one of us. This child should be allowed to escape and experience some magic and adventure. Thus, Disneyland was actually designed for adults and children. The layout of the park, and the placement of everything in the park, was done to take the adults of Disney's generation back to their childhood. Adults were then allowed to escape to any number of fantasy worlds, of their childhood. While most of us today grew up in large cities of America, the effect is much the same. By the time we reach the Hub we are ready to believe anything that the rest of the park presents as reality if only for a day.

From the Anaheim Amtrak/

Metrolink Station take either the OCTA 50 line or ATN Commuter Route to the Disneyland Hotel stop. From there you can enter the park by taking the parking lot tram to the Disneyland Main Gate or by taking the Disneyland Monorail from the Disneyland Hotel Monorail Station.

The park is open daily. For information about operating hours and passport prices call (714) 999-4565.

Anaheim Stadium

Anaheim Stadium is just across the parking lot from the Metrolink station. The stadium was built by the city in 1964 and today is the home of the *California Angles* American League baseball team. For information about games and events at the stadium call (714) 254-3000.

Arrowhead Pond of Anaheim

Arrowhead Pond is located at 2695 E. Katella Avenue. The facility is about a one-half mile walk from the station. The OCTA 452 bus will take you to the Pond when in operation. The Pond opened in 1993 and seats 19,200 spectators. It is the home of the *Mighty Ducks,* the Disney owned NHL franchise. For information about games and other events at the Pond call (714) 704-2400.

Anaheim Convention Center

The Anaheim Convention Center is located at 800 W. Katella Avenue just about one-half mile from Disneyland. The center hosts a wide variety of consumer and trade shows

throughout the year. For information about current activities and shows call (714) 999-8900.

Places to Stay

There is an abundance of hotels in Anaheim around the vicinity of Disneyland. All of the major hotels provide free shuttle service to/from Disneyland during park-operating hours. Check with the hotel prior to making reservations to verify the availability of a shuttle to Disneyland. At the same time most of these hotels <u>do not</u> provide any service to/from the Anaheim Amtrak/Metrolink Station. The OCTA dial-a-ride, OCTA bus lines or local taxis are the only transportation available to most of the hotels listed below. Those that do provide shuttle service to/from the Anaheim Station are listed first and so noted.

Hotels and Motels with shuttle service to/from the Anaheim Station

Anaheim Center Holiday Inn

The Anaheim Center Holiday Inn is located at 1221 S. Harbor Boulevard. The hotel phone number is (714) 758-0900. For reservations call (800) HOLIDAY.

Anaheim Hilton Hotel

The Anaheim Hilton Hotel is located at 777 W. Convention Way. The hotel phone number is (714) 750-4321 or (800) 222-9923. For reservations call (800) HILTONS.

Anaheim Pan Pacific Hotel

The Anaheim Pan Pacific Hotel is located at 1717 S. West Street. The hotel phone number is (714) 999-0990. For reservations call (800) 327-8585 US or (800) 321-8976 CA.

Anaheim Ramada Inn

The Anaheim Ramada Inn is located at 1331 E. Katella Avenue. The hotel phone number is (714) 978-8088. For reservations call (800) 2-RAMADA.

Castle Inn & Suites

The Castle Inn & Suites is located at 1734 S. Harbor Boulevard. The hotel phone number is (714)774-8111. For reservations call (800)521-5653.

Hampton Inn Anaheim

The Hampton Inn Anaheim is located at 300 E. Katella Way. The hotel will pay for taxi fare from the Metrolink station. The hotel phone

View of the Arrowhead Pond

number is (714) 772-8713. For reservations call (800) HAMPTON.

Howard Johnson Hotel

The Howard Johnson Hotel is located at 1380 S. Harbor Boulevard. The hotel phone number is (714) 776-6120. For reservations call (800) 446-4656.

Hotels <u>without</u> shuttle service to/from the Anaheim Station

Anaheim Days Inn Maingate

The Anaheim Days Inn Maingate is located at 1604 S. Harbor Boulevard. The hotel phone number is (714) 635-3630 or (800) 864-8005. For reservations call (800) 329-7466.

Anaheim Days Inn & Suites

The Anaheim Days Inn & Suites is located at 1111 S. Harbor Boulevard. The hotel phone number is (714) 533-8830. For reservations call (800) 329-7466.

Anaheim Desert Inn & Suites

The Anaheim Desert Inn & Suites is located at 1600 Harbor Boulevard. The hotel phone number is (714) 772-

5050. For reservations call (800) 433-5270.

Anaheim Desert Palm Inn & Suites

The Anaheim Desert Palm Inn & Suites is located at 631 W. Katella Avenue. The hotel phone number is (714) 535-1133. For reservations call (800) 635-5423.

Anaheim Holiday Inn Express

The Anaheim Holiday Inn Express is located at 435 W. Katella Avenue. The hotel phone number is (714) 772-7755 or (800) 833-7888. For reservations call (800) HOLIDAY.

Anaheim Marriott Hotel

The Anaheim Marriott Hotel is located at 700 W. Convention Way. The hotel phone number is (714) 750-8000. For reservations call (800) 228-9290.

Anaheim/Orange Hilton Suites

The Anaheim/Orange Hilton Suites is located at 400 N. State College Boulevard. The hotel phone number is (714) 938-1111. For reservations call (800) HILTONS.

Anaheim Ramada LTD

The Anaheim Ramada LTD is located at 921 S. Harbor Boulevard. The hotel phone number is (714) 999-0684. For reservations call (800) 2-RAMADA.

Anaheim Stadium Travelodge

The Anaheim Stadium Travelodge is located at 1700 E. Katella Avenue. The hotel phone number is (714) 634-1920. For reservations call (800) 578-7878.

Convention Center Inn

The Convention Center Inn is located at 2017 S. Harbor Boulevard The hotel phone number is (714) 740-2500. For reservations call (800) 521-5628.

Crystal Suites

The Crystal Suites is located at 1752 Clementine Street. The hotel phone number is (714) 535-7773. For reservations call (800) 992-0810.

Disneyland Hotel

The Disneyland Hotel is located at 1150 W. Cerritos Avenue. The hotel phone number is (714) 956-6400.

Econo Lodge

The Econo Lodge is located at 1570 S. Harbor Boulevard. The hotel phone number is (714) 772-5721. For reservations call (800) 854-0199 Ext. 437.

Hyatt Regency Allicante

The Hyatt Regency Allicante is located at Harbor Boulevard and Chapman Avenue. The hotel phone number is (714) 750-1234 or (800) 972-2929. For reservations call (800) 233-1234.

Peacock Suites

The Peacock Suites is located at 1745 Haster Street. The hotel phone number is (714) 535-8255. For reservations call (800) 522-6407.

Sheraton Anaheim Hotel

The Sheraton Anaheim Hotel is located at 1015 W. Ball Road. The hotel phone number is (714) 778-1700 or (800) 331-7251. For reservations call (800) 325-3535.

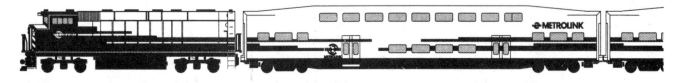

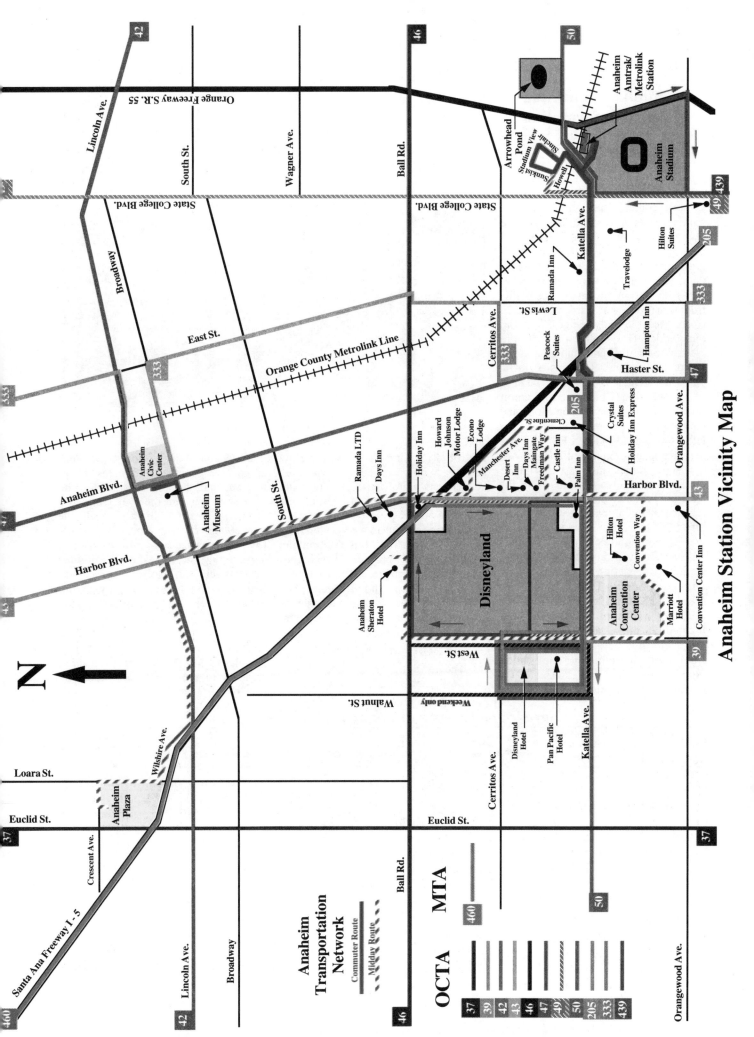

Anaheim Station Vicinity Map

Orange Station

Station Connecting Transit Information

The Orange Metrolink Station is located at Atchison Street and Chapman Avenue. The station has a medium-sized parking lot located one block east of the station at Maple Avenue and Cypress Street. The entrance for the parking lot is on Lemon Street and the exit is on Cypress Street. The train boarding platform is well lighted with good shelter. The station is manned for the morning and evening rush hours.

The station is easily accessible from three freeways, Garden Grove 22 , Costa Mesa 55 and Orange 57 . From the Garden Grove Freeway take the Glassell Street offramp and go north to Chapman Avenue. There is a traffic circle at Chapman Avenue and you need to go west on Chapman to Lemon Street. Turn right on Lemon Street and the parking lot entrance will be on your left. From the Costa Mesa Freeway take the Chapman Avenue exit and go west to Lemon Street, just past the traffic circle in downtown Orange. From the Orange Freeway take the Chapman Avenue offramp and go east to Lemon Street and turn left.

Everything in downtown Orange is within easy walking distance of the station. The station is served by the Orange County Transit Authority (OCTA) 53, 54, 59, 69, 453 and 454 bus lines. The stops for these lines are located at the Orange Bus Transit Center located across the parking lot from the station building. The station vicinity map provides the routes for the bus transit options from the Orange

Orange Metrolink Station

Metrolink Station. The table below provides the schedule for bus connections with Metrolink. For route and schedule updates call OCTA on (714) 636-RIDE.

Outside of the immediate vicinity of the Orange Metrolink Station the OCTA 53 line provides service to Santa Ana, Irvine, Costa Mesa, Newport Beach and Balboa. The OCTA 69 line provides service to Santa Ana to the south and Anaheim, Placentia and Fullerton to the North.

Points of Interest

The town of Orange got its start in 1869 when two lawyers, Alfred

Beck Chapman and Andrew Glassell, accepted as legal fees 1,385 acres of land that was until that date a part of Rancho Santiago. With the help of Glassell's brother, Captain William Glassell, the new owners laid out a one-square-mile township. The remaining property surrounding the townsite was divided into 10-acre farm lots. The city was incorporated in 1887 to prevent the establishment of a saloon in the townsite. Today the city of Orange is, for the most part, just another suburban city that makes up the greater Los Angeles region. The downtown district, adjacent to the Metrolink station and centered around the Central Plaza, still

ORANGE STATION BUS CONNECTIONS
NORTHBOUND TRAINS FROM OCEANSIDE TO LOS ANGELES

TRAIN NUMBER	DAYS OF OPERATION	TRAIN ARRIVAL	OCTA 53/53A NORTHBOUND 45 MIN.	OCTA 53/53A SOUTHBOUND 45 MIN.	OCTA 54 EASTBOUND 30 MIN	OCTA 54 WESTBOUND 30 MIN	OCTA 59 NORTHBOUND PEAK	OCTA 59 SOUTHBOUND PEAK	OCTA 69 NORTHBOUND 30 MIN	OCTA 69 SOUTHBOUND 30 MIN	OCTA 453 PEAK	OCTA 454 PEAK
BUS FREQUENCY												
METROLINK 601	M - F	5:47A	6:16A	5:10/5:55A	5:30/6:00A	5:18/5:48A	5:52A	5:19/5:49A	5:35/6:05A	5:34/6:04A		
METROLINK 603	M - F	6:28A	6:16/6:56A	5:55/6:33A	6:00/6:35A	6:18/6:48A	6:22/6:52A	6:23/6:55A	6:05/6:30A	6:04/6:38A	6:32A	6:37A
METROLINK 681	M - F	7:26A	6:56/7:36A	7:11/7:56A	7:05/7:35A	7:14/7:44A	7:25/7:55A	7:25/7:55A	7:00/7:30A	7:08/7:38A	7:52A	7:45A
METROLINK 605	M - F	7:50A	7:36/8:58A	7:11/7:56A	7:35/8:05A	7:44/8:14A	7:25/7:55P	7:25/7:55A	7:30/8:00A	7:38/8:08A	7:52A	

WESTBOUND FROM RIVERSIDE TO IRVINE

METROLINK 801	M - F	L6:33A	6:16/6:56A	5:55/6:33A	6:00/6:35A	6:18/6:48A	6:22/6:52A	6:23/6:55A	6:30/7:00A	6:04/6:38A	6:37A	6:37A
METROLINK 803	M - F	L7:35A	6:56/7:36A	7:11/7:56A	7:05/8:05A	7:14/7:44A	7:25/7:55A	7:25/7:55A	7:30/8:00A	7:08/7:38A	7:52A	7:45A
METROLINK 805	M - F	L4:13P	3:40/4:22P	3:49/4:29P	4:07/4:37P	4:11/4:41P	3:55/4:25P	3:57/4:28P	3:58/4:28P	4:08/4:38P		

SOUTHBOUND TRAINS FROM LOS ANGELES TO OCEANSIDE

METROLINK 684	M - F	4:23P	4:22/5:02P	3:49/4:29P	4:07/4:37P	4:11/4:41P	3:55/4:25P	3:57/4:28P.	3:58/4:28P	4:08/4:38P		
METROLINK 604	M - F	5:22P	5:02/5:42P	5:09/6:04P	5:07/5:37P	5:11/5:41P	4:55/5:26P	4:58/5:28P	4:58/5:28P	5:08/5:38P	5:11P	4:52P
METROLINK 606	M - F	6:24P	6:22/7:02P	6:04/6:44P	6:07/6:33P	6:15/6:45P	6:02P	5:58P	5:58/6:28P	6:08/6:38P	6:14P	
METROLINK 608	M - F	7:14P	7:02/7:37P	6:44/7:24P	7:03/7:33P	6:45/7:15P			6:58/7:35P	7:06/7:36P		

EASTBOUND FROM IRVINE TO RIVERSIDE

METROLINK 800	M - F	8:24A	8:18/8:58A	7:56/8:32A	8:05/8:35A	8:14/8:44P	7:55/8:27A	8:21/8:51A	8:00/8:30A	8:08/8:38A		7:45A
METROLINK 802	M - F	5:02P	5:02/5:42P	4:29/5:09P	4:37/5:07P	4:41/5:11P	4:55/5:26P	4:58/5:28P	4:58/5:28P	4:38/5:08P	4:52P	4:52P
METROLINK 804	M - F	5:45P	5:42/6:22P	5:09/6:04P	5:37/6:07P	5:11/5:45P	5:26/6:02P	5:28/5:58P	5:28/5:58P	5:38/6:08P	5:25P	5:25P

L: Regular stop to discharge or pick up passengers except train may leave ahead of schedule

Plaza in Downtown Orange

Chapman University Campus

has the small town feel of the earlier part of the 20th century.

Downtown Orange

The centerpiece of downtown Orange is the Plaza, located in the center of the traffic circle, at the intersection of Chapman Avenue and Glassell Street. The Plaza is a short four-block walk east from Metrolink along Chapman Avenue. There is an attractive Spanish style fountain in the center of the Plaza. The downtown district extends a couple of blocks in each direction from the Plaza along Chapman Avenue and Glassell Street. There are several restaurants, sidewalk cafes, antique shops and boutiques.

Chapman University

Chapman University is located at Glassell and Palm streets. The university is within easy walking distance from the Orange Metrolink Station. Walk up Maple to Glassell Street and turn left. The university is one block north. The university traces its roots to Hesperian College, opened the very hour of Abraham Lincoln's inauguration as the 16th President of the United States. After merging with several other institutions in Los Angeles, the college was renamed after its most generous benefactor, and one of the founders of the city of Orange, C.C. Chapman. The college moved to the city of Orange in 1954, and in 1991, became Chapman University. The University is an independent private institution. For information call (714) 997-6711.

Main-Place Santa Ana

Main-Place Santa Ana is located at 2800 N. Main Street, Santa Ana. This

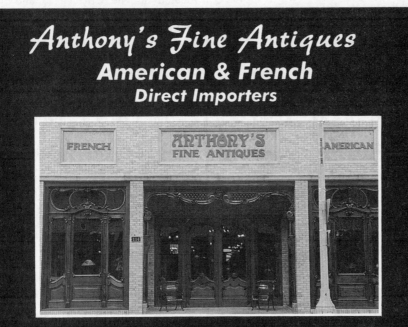

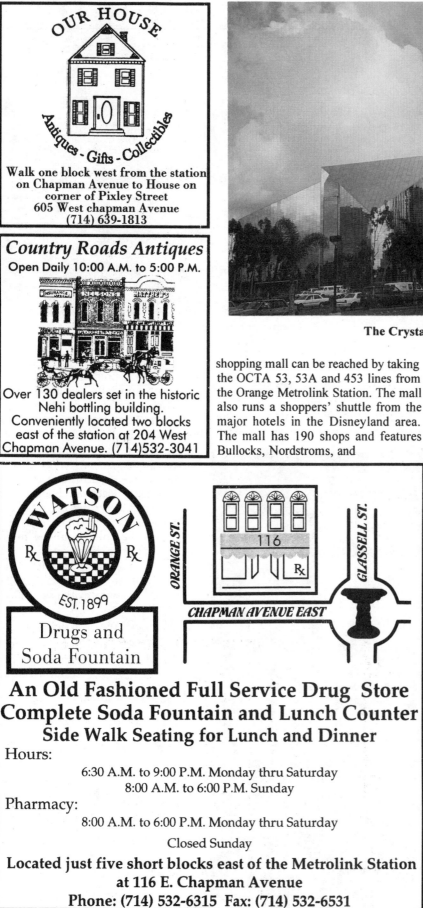

The Crystal Cathedral

shopping mall can be reached by taking the OCTA 53, 53A and 453 lines from the Orange Metrolink Station. The mall also runs a shoppers' shuttle from the major hotels in the Disneyland area. The mall has 190 shops and features Bullocks, Nordstroms, and Robinson's-May as anchor department stores. There is also an AMC-6 theater at the mall.

The City Shopping Center

The City Shopping Center is located at The City Drive and the Garden Grove Freeway 22. From Metrolink it can be reached by taking the OCTA 454 line. The mall provides free shuttle bus service from all the major hotels in the vicinity of Disneyland. For information about this service call (714) 535-2211.

The Crystal Cathedral

The Crystal Cathedral is the located at 12141 Lewis Street in Garden Grove. The Cathedral is famous for its two major holiday productions, *The Glory of Christmas* and *The Glory of Easter.* For information call (714) 971-4000. The Cathedral can be reached by taking the OCTA 454 line.

Places to Stay

Doubletree Hotel- Orange County

The Doubletree Hotel-Orange County is located at 100 The City Drive. The hotel phone number is (714) 634-4500. For reservations call (800) 222-TREE.

Orange Travelodge

The Orange Travelodge is located at 1302 West Chapman Avenue. The hotel phone number is (714) 633-7720. For reservations call (800) 578-7878.

194

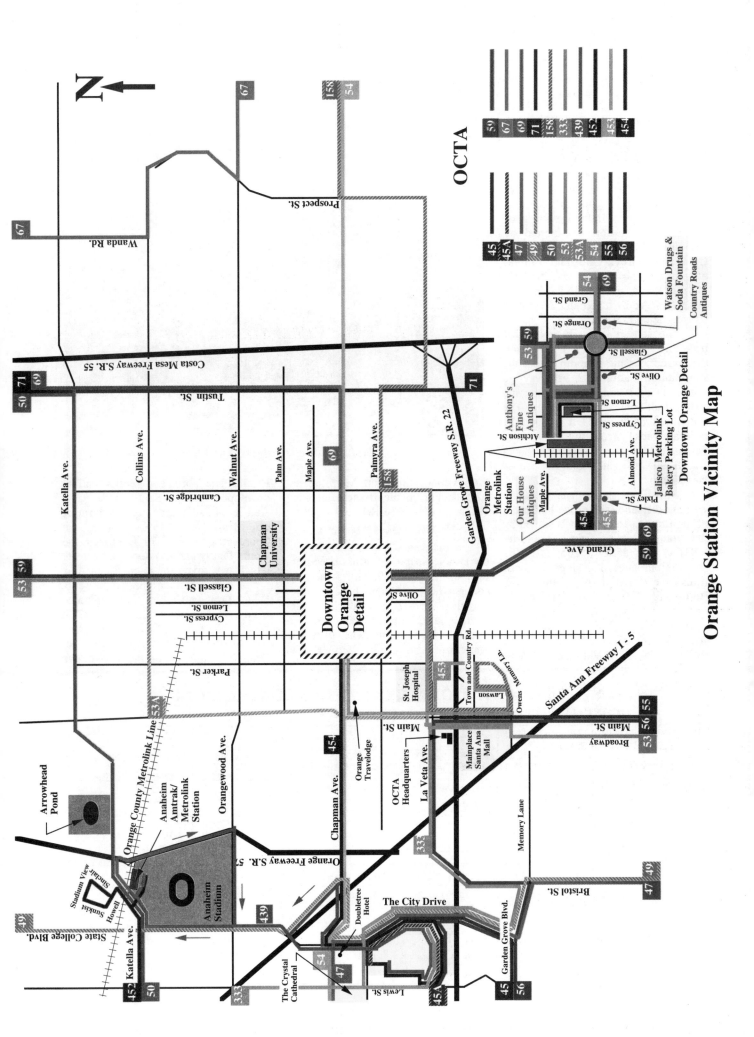

Orange Station Vicinity Map

Santa Ana Station

Station Connecting Transit Information

The Santa Ana Amtrak/Metrolink Station is located at 1000 E. Santa Ana Boulevard. The station has parking for over 400 vehicles. The train boarding platform is well lighted with good shelter. The station is manned by Amtrak, and connecting long-haul Bus Company (Greyhound and others) personnel. The station was built in 1985 in the Spanish Colonial Revival Style to serve as the center for public transportation in Santa Ana.

The station is easily accessible from Santa Ana Freeway I-5 by taking the Grand Avenue offramp. From the southbound Santa Ana Freeway go south on Grand under the Freeway and turn left on Santa Ana Boulevard. The station will be on your left just past the railroad tracks. From the northbound Santa Ana Freeway turn left on Santa Ana Boulevard which is at the end of the offramp.

Downtown Santa Ana is within walking distance (about one-half mile) of the station. The station is served by the Orange County Transit Authority (OCTA) 69, 85/85A, 205, 461, 462 and 463 bus lines. The stops for these lines are located on Santa Ana Boulevard. The station vicinity map provides the routes of the bus transit options from the Santa Ana Amtrak/Metrolink Station. The following tables provide the schedules

Santa Ana Amtrak/Metrolink Station

for bus connections with Metrolink and Amtrak. For updates to schedules call OCTA on (714) 636-RIDE.

Points of Interest

Santa Ana's history dates back to the Don Gaspar De Portola expedition to California in 1769. This same party continued north to found the city of Los Angeles. Portola named the valley Santa Ana in honor of Saint Anne. A Spanish land grant was given to Antonio Yorba and his nephew Juan

Peralta. The Yorba and Peralta families developed Rancho Santiago de Santa Ana as a cattle grazing and farming operation. In 1869 William H. Spurgeon purchased 70 acres from the Yorba family and developed a townsite which was given the name Santa Ana. Santa Ana was incorporated in 1886. When Orange County was separated from Los Angeles County in 1889, it became the County Seat. Today Santa Ana is the administrative center of Orange County with the Downtown

SANTA ANA STATION WEEKEND BUS CONNECTIONS
NORTHBOUND TRAINS FROM OCEANSIDE TO LOS ANGELES

TRAIN NUMBER	DAYS OF OPERATION	TRAIN ARRIVAL	OCTA 69 NORTHBOUND SATURDAY 30 - 60 MIN.	OCTA 69 SOUTHBOUND SATURDAY 30 - 60 MIN.	OCTA 69 NORTHBOUND SUNDAY, H. 45 - 60 MIN.	OCTA 69 SOUTHBOUND SUNDAY, H. 45 - 60 MIN.	OCTA 205 NORTHBOUND SATURDAY 30 MIN.	OCTA 205 SOUTHBOUND SATURDAY 30 MIN.	OCTA 205 NORTHBOUND SUNDAY HOURLY	OCTA 205 SOUTHBOUND SUNDAY HOURLY
DAYS OF OPERATION / BUS FREQUENCY										
AMTRAK 769	SA.SU.H.	7:58A	7:57/9:12A	7:25/8:40A	8:59A	9:15A	7:31/8:01A	7:49/8:19A	8:01A	7:49/8:19A
AMTRAK 775	DAILY	10:18A	10:17/10:52A	9:45/10:48A	9:46/10:33A	10:02/10:49A	10:01/10:31A	9:49/10:19A	9:31/10:31A	9:19/10:19A
AMTRAK 577	DAILY	12:16P	11:57A/12:27P	11:53A/12:28P	12:07/12:54P	11:36A/12:23P	12:01/12:31P	11:49A/12:19P	11:31A/12:31P	11:19A/12:19P
AMTRAK 779	DAILY	2:11P	2:07/2:32P	2:03/2:43P	1:41/2:28P	1:58/2:45P	2:01/2:31P	1:49/2:19P	1:31/2:31P	1:49/2:19P
AMTRAK 791	SA.SU.H	4:34P	4:12/4:52P	4:15/4:50P	4:02/4:49P	4:19/5:06P	4:31/5:01P	4:19/4:49P	4:31/5:01P	4:19/5:19P
AMTRAK 583	DAILY	6:30P	5:47/6:39P	6:10/6:40P	6:23P	5:53/6:40P	6:01/6:31P	6:19/6:49P	5:31/6:31P	6:19/6:49P
AMTRAK 585	DAILY	8:56P		7:42P			9:24P	8:49P	9:24P	8:49P

SOUTHBOUND TRAINS FROM LOS ANGELES TO OCEANSIDE

AMTRAK 570	DAILY	7:32A	6:55/7:57A	7:25/8:40A			7:31/8:01A	7:19/7:49A	8:01A	7:19/8:19A
AMTRAK 572	SA.SU.H.	9:34A	9:12/9:42A	8:40/9:45A	8:59/9:46A	9:15/10:02A	9:31/10:01A	9:19/9:49A	9:31/10:01A	9:19/10:19A
AMTRAK 774	SA.SU.H.	11:24A	11:22/11:57A	11:23A/11:53A	11:20A/12:07P	10:49/11:36A	11:01/11:31A	11:19/11:49A	10:31/11:31A	11:19A/12:19P
AMTRAK 776	DAILY	1:23P	1:02/1:32P	12:58/1:33P	12:54/1:41P	1:11/1:58P	1:01/1:31P	1:19/1:49P	12:31/1:31P	1:19/2:19P
AMTRAK 578	DAILY	3:24P	3:17/3:47P	3:13/3:38P	3:15/4:02P	2:45/3:32P	3:01/3:31P	3:19/3:49P	2:31/3:31P	3:19/4:19P
AMTRAK 782	SA.SU.H.	6:06P	5:47/6:39P	5:15/6:10P	5:36/6:23P	5:53/6:40P	6:01/6:31P	5:49/6:19P	5:31/6:31P	5:49/6:19P
AMTRAK 584	SU. - F	7:03P	6:39/7:14P	6:40/7:42P	6:23P	6:40P	7:01/7:31P	6:49/7:19P	6:31/7:31P	6:49P
AMTRAK 786	DAILY	9:51P					10:24P	9:19P	10:24P	9:19P

SANTA ANA STATION WEEKDAY BUS CONNECTIONS
NORTHBOUND TRAINS FROM OCEANSIDE TO LOS ANGELES

TRAIN NUMBER	DAYS OF OPERATION	TRAIN ARRIVAL	OCTA 69 NORTHBOUND 30 MIN.	OCTA 69 SOUTHBOUND 30 MIN.	OCTA 85/85A NORTHBOUND COMMUTER	OCTA 85/85A SOUTHBOUND COMMUTER	OCTA 205 NORTHBOUND 30 - 60 MIN.	OCTA 205 SOUTHBOUND 30 - 60 MIN.	OCTA 461 & 463 COMMUTER	OCTA 462 COMMUTER
METROLINK 601	M - F	5:42A	5:27/5:57A	5:43A	6:17A	5:38/6:00A	5:30/6:02A	5:20/5:50A		
METROLINK 603	M - F	6:23A	6:19/6:49A	6:13/6:50A	6:17/6:47A	6:08/6:30A	6:02/6:32A	6:20/6:50A	6:40A	6:25A
METROLINK 681	M - F	7:21A	7:19/7:49A	6:50/7:50A	7:17/7:47A	7:08/7:28A	7:02/7:32A	7:18/7:48A	7:49A	7:00/7:23A
METROLINK 605	M - F	7:45A	7:19/7:49A	7:20/7:50A	7:17/7:47A	7:38/7:58A	7:32/8:02A	7:18/7:48A	7:49A	7:43/7:46A
AMTRAK 771	M - F	8:05A	7:49/8:19A	7:50/8:20A	7:47/8:22A	7:58/8:08A	8:02/8:32A	7:48/8:18A		
AMTRAK 573	M - F	9:26A	9:19/9:49A	9:20/9:50A	9:22A	8:58A	9:02/9:32A	9:18/10:18A		
AMTRAK 775	DAILY	10:18A	9:49/10:19A	9:50/10:20A			10:02/10:32A	9:18/11:18A		
AMTRAK 577	DAILY	12:16P	11:49A/12:19P	11:50A/12:20P			11:32A/12:32P	11:18A/12:18P		
AMTRAK 779	DAILY	2:11P	1:49/2:16P	1:50/2:20P			1:32/2:32P	1:18/2:18P		2:50P
AMTRAK 781	M - F	4:27P	4:16/4:46P	4:20/4:53P	4:22/4:53P	3:58/4:28P	4:32/5:02P	4:18/4:48P		4:10/4:56P
AMTRAK 583	DAILY	6:30P	6:16/6:46P	6:23/6:53P	6:27P	5:28P	6:02/6:32P	6:18/6:48P		6:20P
AMTRAK 585	DAILY	8:56P	8:30/9:10P	8:16/9:16P			7:32P	7:18P		
AMTRAK 587	FRIDAY	10:35P	10:10P	10:16P						

EASTBOUND FROM IRVINE TO SAN BERNARDINO

METROLINK 800	M - F	8:20A	8:19/8:49A	8:20/8:50A	7:47/8:22A	8:08/8:28A	8:02/8:32A	8:18/8:48A		7:43A
METROLINK 802	M - F	4:57P	4:46/5:16P	4:53/5:23P	4:52/5:22P	4:28/4:58P	4:32/5:02P	4:48/5:18P	4:42P	4:47/5:25P
METROLINK 804	M - F	5:40P	5:16/5:46P	5:23/5:53P	5:22/5:42P	5:28P	5:32/6:02P	5:18/5:48P	5:15P	5:16/6:00P

SOUTHBOUND TRAINS FROM LOS ANGELES TO OCEANSIDE

AMTRAK 570	DAILY	7:32A	6:49/7:19A	7:20/7:50A	7:17/7:47A	7:28/7:38A	7:02/8:02A	7:18/7:48A	7:49A	7:00/7:46A
AMTRAK 772	M - F	9:34A	9:19/9:49A	9:20/9:50A	9:22A	8:58A	9:32/10:02A	9:18/10:18A		
AMTRAK 574	M - F	11:24A	11:19/11:49A	11:20/11:50A			10:32/11:32A	11:18A/12:18P		
AMTRAK 776	DAILY	1:23P	1:19/1:49A	1:20/1:50P			12:32/1:32P	1:18/2:18P		
AMTRAK 578	DAILY	3:24P	3:16/3:46P	3:20/3:50P	3:42P	2:58/3:28P	3:02/3:32P	3:18/3:48P		3:10/3:50P
METROLINK 684	M - F	4:28P	4:16/4:46P	4:20/4:53P	4:22/4:53P	3:58/4:58P	4:02/4:32P	4:18/4:48P		4:10/4:56P
METROLINK 604	M - F	5:26P	5:16/5:46P	5:23/5:53P	5:22/5:42P	4:58/5:28P	5:02/5:32P	5:18/5:48P	5:15P	5:16/6:00P
AMTRAK 780	M - F	6:02P	5:46/6:16P	5:53/6:23P	5:52/6:12P	5:28P	5:32/6:32P	5:48/6:18P		5:45P
METROLINK 606	M - F	6:28P	6:16/6:46P	6:23/6:53P	6:27P		6:02/6:32P	6:18/6:48P		6:20P
AMTRAK 584	SU. - F	7:03P	6:46/7:16P	6:53/7:16P			7:02/7:32P	6:48/7:18P		
METROLINK 608	M - F	7:18P	6:46/7:25P	7:16/7:46P			7:02/7:32P	7:18P		
AMTRAK 786	DAILY	9:51P	9:10/10:10P	9:16/10:16P						

WESTBOUND FROM SAN BERNARDINO TO IRVINE

METROLINK 801	M - F	L6:37A	6:19/6:49A	6:13/6:50A	6:17/6:47A	6:30/6:40A	6:32/7:02A	6:20/6:50A	6:40A	6:40A
METROLINK 803	M - F	L7:39A	7:19/7:49A	7:20/7:50A	7:17/7:47A	7:38/7:58A	7:32/8:02A	7:18/7:48A	7:49A	7:00/7:46A
METROLINK 805	M - F	L4:17P	4:16/4:46P	3:50/4:21P	3:52/4:23P	3:58/4:28P	4:02/4:32P	3:48/4:18P		4:10/4:27P

L: Regular stop to discharge or pick up passengers except train may leave ahead of schedule

Government Center. The city has a population of 300,000 residents which makes it Orange County's largest city.

Downtown Santa Ana

Downtown Santa Ana is about one-half mile from the Amtrak/Metrolink station and transportation center. Any of the OCTA bus lines provide transportation from the station to the Civic Center and the Santa Ana Transit Terminal. It is populated with numerous government buildings necessary for the administration of Federal, State, County and City governments in Orange County.

Fiesta Marketplace

The Fiesta Marketplace is centered at Fourth and Main streets in downtown Santa Ana. The marketplace is less than one-half mile from the Amtrak/Metrolink station. For bus transportation take any OCTA bus to downtown and exit at the Santa Ana Boulevard and Main Street stop. Walk two blocks south on Main to Fourth Street. The old downtown shopping district that runs along Fourth Street

Fiesta Marketplace

has been restored and revitalized with shops catering to the large Hispanic population residing in Santa Ana. There are over 40 shops featuring Mexican products and gifts. There are several good Mexican restaurants and a Spanish language movie theater. Mariachis serenade passersby on street corners on the weekends and there is a carousel located at Spurgeon and Fourth streets.

The Bowers Museum of Cultural Art

The Bowers Museum of Cultural Art is Orange County's premier museum. It is located at 2002 N. Main Street. From Amtrak/Metrolink station take the northbound OCTA 205 line to the Main and 20th streets stop.

This museum has an extensive collection of Native American Art, Pre-Columbian archaeological finds from

The Bowers Museum

Mexico and Central America, indigenous art from the Pacific rim, Africa and the Americas. The museum also has an extensive collection of dolls which has been a central part of the museums permanent exhibit since 1942. The museum is open Tuesday through Sunday 10:00 A.M. to 5:00 P.M. Admission is $4.50 for adults, $1.50 for children under 12, $3.00 for seniors over 65 and students with identification. For information call (714) 567-3600.

Old Courthouse Museum

The Old Courthouse Museum is located at 211 W. Santa Ana Boulevard. The museum can be reached by taking the OCTA 362 Commuter line or the OCTA 69 bus line to the Santa Ana Boulevard and Sycamore Street stop. The museum focuses on the history of Orange County and the history of law and government. The museum also features everchanging traveling exhibits. The museum is open 9:00 A.M. to 5:00 P.M. Monday thru Friday. Admission is free. For information call (714) 834-3703.

Old Courthouse Museum

Kellogg House at The Discovery Museum

Discovery Museum of Orange County

The Discovery Museum of Orange County is located at 3101 W. Harvard Street. To reach the museum from the Santa Ana Amtrak/Metrolink Station take any OCTA bus to the Santa Ana Transit Terminal and transfer to the OCTA 55 line. Take the 55 line to the Fairview Street and Warner Avenue stop. There you need to transfer to the northbound OCTA 45 line. Take the OCTA 45 line to the Fairview Boulevard and Harvard Street stop. The museum is about one-half block west on Harvard Street. The museum is situated on a site which recreated a small portion of the Citrus Groves which once covered most of Orange County. The H. Clay Kellogg House has been restored to its Victorian splendor. The house is in the Queen Anne Style and is furnished with antiques from the 19th century. The museum is open to the public Wednesday thru Friday 1:00 P.M. to 5:00 P.M. and Sundays 11:00 A.M. to 3:00 P.M. Suggested donations $2.50 adults, $2.00 students and seniors, and $1.50 for children. For information call (714) 540-0404.

Rancho Santiago College

The college is located at 1530 W. 17th. Street. To reach the college from the Amtrak/Metrolink station take any one of the OCTA bus lines to the Santa

Ana Transit Terminal in the Civic Center and transfer to the OCTA 60 line. Take the 60 line to the 17th and Bristol streets stop. The college is a part of the Rancho Santiago Community College District. The Santa Ana campus was first opened in 1915 as an upward extension of Santa Ana High School. It is the fourth oldest community college in California. In 1947 it was moved from downtown Santa Ana to its present 58-acre site. It offers a two-year curriculum in a wide range of majors. The college grants an Associate of Arts degree to two-year graduates. For information call (714) 564-6000. The college has a Fine Arts Gallery, Planetarium and Theater. The Fine Arts Gallery is open Monday thru Thursday 10:00 A.M. to 2:00 P.M. and Tuesday and Wednesday 6:30 P.M. to

Rancho Santiago College Campus

8:30 P.M. Admission is free. For information about exhibits and events call (714) 564-5615. The Rancho Santiago College Theater offers a number of student stage, dance and musical productions throughout the school year. For information call (714) 564-5661. The Tessmann Planetarium offers a number of programs in association with the Orange County Astronomers. For information about current shows call (714) 641-3860.

Santa Ana Zoo

The Santa Ana Zoo is located at Elm Lane and Chestnut Avenue. The zoo is about three-quarters of a mile from the Santa Ana Amtrak/Metrolink Station. To reach the zoo by bus take any bus to the OCTA bus transit terminal in Santa Ana and connect with the OCTA 61 line. Take the 61 bus to the Chestnut Avenue and Lyon Street stop. This is a rather small zoo with approximately 250 animals. The zoo is primarily known for its collection of monkeys and other primates. The zoo features an elephant ride on weekends which is a favorite for the children. The zoo is open 10:00 A.M. to 5:00 P.M. June thru August and 10:00 A.M. to 4:00 P.M. September thru May. It is closed Christmas and New Years Day. Admission is $3.00 for adults and $1.00 for children 3 thru 12 and seniors 60 and over. For information call (714) 835-7484.

Places to Stay

Comfort Suites

The Comfort Suites is located at 2620 Hotel Terrace Drive. The hotel has a shuttle van and will pick you up

Amazon's Edge Primate Exhibit at the Santa Ana Zoo

at the Metrolink station with advance notice. The hotel phone number is (714) 966-5200. For reservations call (800) 221-2222.

Howard Johnson's Lodge - Hotel Terrace

The Howard Johnson's Lodge - Hotel Terrace is located at 2700 Hotel Terrace Drive. The hotel phone number is (714) 432-8888. For reservations call (800) 446-4656.

Howard Johnson's Lodge - Santa Ana

The Howard Johnson's Lodge-Santa Ana is located at 939 E. 17th. Street. The hotel has a shuttle van and will pick you up at the Amtrak/Metrolink station with advance notice. The hotel phone number is (714) 558-3700. For reservations call (800) 446-4656.

Crown Sterling Suites

The Crown Sterling Suites is located at 1325 E. Dyer Road. The hotel phone number is (714) 241-3800. For reservations call (800) 433-4600.

Quality Suites

The Quality Suites is located at 2701 Hotel Terrace Drive. The hotel has a shuttle van and will pick you up at the Amtrak/Metrolink station with advance notice. The hotel phone number is (714) 957-9200. For reservations call (800) 221-2222.

Radisson Suites

The Radisson Suites is located at

2720 Hotel Terrace Drive. The hotel phone number is (714) 556-3838. For reservations call (800) 333-3333.

Ramada Grand Avenue

The Ramada Grand Avenue is located at 2726 S. Grand Avenue. The hotel has a shuttle van and will pick you up at the Amtrak/Metrolink station with advance notice. The hotel phone number is (714) 966-1955. For reservations call (800) 2RAMADA.

Tustin Suites

The Tustin Suites is located at 2151 E. First Street. The hotel phone number is (714) 558-2772. For reservations call (800) 558-2772.

Woolley's Petite Suites

The Woolley's Petit Suites is located at 2721 Hotel Terrace Drive. The hotel phone number is (714) 540-1111. For reservations call (800) 762-2597.

Saddleback Inn

The Saddleback Inn is located at 1660 E. First Street. The hotel phone number is (714) 835-3311.

Best Western Santa Ana Inn

The Best Western Santa Ana Inn is located at 2600 N. Main Street. The hotel phone number is (714) 836-5141. For reservations call (800) 528-1234.

California Lodge Suites

The California Lodge Suites is located at 2909 S. Bristol Street. The hotel phone number is (714) 540-2300. For reservations call (800) 628-9755.

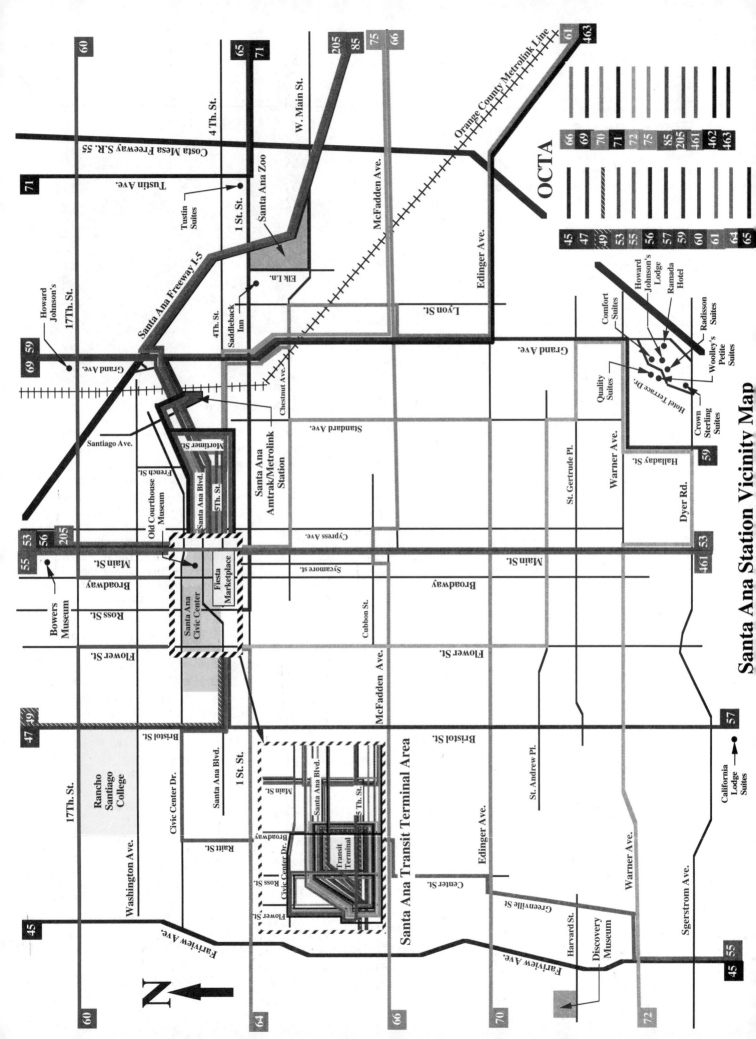

Santa Ana Station Vicinity Map

Santa Ana Transit Terminal Area

OCTA

Irvine Station

Station Connecting Transit Information

The Irvine Transportation Center is located at 15215 Barranca Parkway. The transportation center has parking for 525 vehicles. The train boarding platform is well lighted with good shelter. The station is manned by Amtrak and other staff personnel.

The transportation center is easily accessible from I-5 Freeway by taking the Alton Parkway offramp. Go east on Alton Parkway to Ada Drive. Turn left on Ada Drive and the transportation center will be at the end of Ada Drive. From the San Diego Freeway I-405 take the Irvine Center Drive offramp and go north to Alton Parkway and turn right. Turn left on Ada Drive and the transportation center will be at the end of Ada Drive.

The Irvine Transportation Center is served by the Orange County Transit Authority (OCTA) 211, 309, 382, 388 and 488 bus lines. The stops for these lines, except the OCTA 211 line, are located at the OCTA bus transit center. The station vicinity maps provides the routes for bus transit options from the Irvine Transportation Center. The following tables provide the schedule

Irvine Transportation Center

IRVINE STATION WEEKEND TRAIN SCHEDULE NORTHBOUND TRAINS FROM OCEANSIDE TO LOS ANGELES

TRAIN NUMBER	DAYS OF OPERATION	TRAIN ARRIVAL
AMTRAK 769	SA.SU.H.	7:46A
AMTRAK 775	DAILY	10:06A
AMTRAK 577	DAILY	12:04P
AMTRAK 779	DAILY	2:00P
AMTRAK 791	SA.SU.H	4:22P
AMTRAK 583	DAILY	6:14P
AMTRAK 585	DAILY	8:44P

SOUTHBOUND TRAINS FROM LOS ANGELES TO OCEANSIDE

AMTRAK 570	DAILY	7:44A
AMTRAK 572	SA.SU.H.	9:46A
AMTRAK 774	SA.SU.H.	11:36A
AMTRAK 776	DAILY	1:35P
AMTRAK 578	DAILY	3:36P
AMTRAK 782	SA.SU.H.	6:18P
AMTRAK 584	SU. - F	7:14P
AMTRAK 786	DAILY	10:02P

for bus connections with Amtrak and Metrolink. For updates to schedules call OCTA at (714) 636-RIDE.

In addition the transportation center has a Greyhound bus station. For information on Greyhound bus service call (800) 231-2222.

Points of Interest

In 1876, James Irvine put together a 186,000-acre parcel of land and dubbed it The Irvine Ranch. This land was passed on to his son James Irvine, Jr., when Irvine Sr. passed on in 1886. The ranch was operated as a vast agricultural kingdom until Irvine Jr.'s death in 1947. The James Irvine Foundation was deeded 53.7 percent of the stock in The Irvine Company (TIC), a holding company, into which James Irvine Jr. had incorporated his land holdings. The remainder of the estate went to members of Irvine's family. In 1959 architect William Pereira was retained to develop a master planned community around the 1,000 acre plot of land deeded to the State of California. This land was to be used for a campus of the University of California.

As the City of Irvine grew beyond the small community around the university site, TIC staff with a myriad of consultants completed planning for the entire Irvine Ranch property. The city was incorporated after approval by the voters in a December 21, 1971, election. Today Irvine is an upscale suburban community of 121,000 residents, and has an employment base of 165,000 jobs.

University of California-Irvine

The currently 1,500-acre University of California-Irvine campus is bounded by University Drive and Campus Drive. The university can be reached by taking the OCTA 382 line from the Irvine Transportation Center to the UCI Marketplace stop. The University of California-Irvine opened in 1965 with 116 faculty and 1,589 students. In the succeeding years the university has grown to become a major campus of the University of California with 17,000 students. The student body is comprised of 13,800 undergraduate students, 2,100 graduate students and 1,100 medical students and residents at the UCI Medical Center. The university is the major attraction in Irvine which provides a wide variety of cultural, athletic, recreational and entertainment events throughout the academic year. For general campus information call (714) 856-5011.

Bren Events Center

The Bren Events Center is home to the UCI Anteaters Basketball team

Bren Events Center UCI Campus

and is used throughout the year for a wide variety of sporting events, concerts, and symposiums. For event information call (714) 856-5000.

Irvine Barclay Theater

The Irvine Barclay Theater is home to the UCI Symphony Orchestra and the UCI Concert Choir. In addition the theater presents stage productions by student and professional production companies. For information call (714) 854-4646.

UCI Fine Arts Gallery

The UCI Fine Arts Gallery provides a variety of student and traveling exhibits throughout the academic year. The gallery is open to the general public 12:00 Noon to 5:00 P.M., Tuesday through Saturday. Admission is free. For Information call (714) 856-6610.

UCI Arboretum

The UCI Arboretum is located just south of Jamboree Road on Campus Drive. Take the OCTA 382 line to the Campus Drive and Jamboree Road stop. The arboretum contains plants which adapted to climates similar to Southern California. The arboretum maintains a gene bank devoted to the conservation are of African monocot flora and contains several important collections of rare plants. The arboretum is open 9:00 A.M. to 3:00 P.M. Monday thru Saturday. Admission is free. For Information please call (714) 856-5833.

Irvine Valley College

Irvine Valley College is located at 5500 Irvine Center Drive. The college can be reached by taking the OCTA 382 bus to the Lake Forrest Drive and Rockfield Boulevard stop. There you need to transfer to the OCTA 75/75A bus which will take you to Irvine Valley College.

Irvine Valley College is one of the newest of California's 107 community colleges. The college opened in 1979 as

IRVINE STATION WEEKDAY BUS CONNECTIONS

NORTHBOUND TRAINS FROM OCEANSIDE TO LOS ANGELES

TRAIN NUMBER	DAYS OF OPERATION	TRAIN ARRIVAL	OCTA 211 EASTBOUND COMMUTER	OCTA 211 WESTBOUND COMMUTER	OCTA 309 EASTBOUND COMMUTER	OCTA 309 WESTBOUND COMMUTER	OCTA 382 COMMUTER	OCTA 388 CLOCKWISE COMMUTER	OCTA 388 COUNTER C.W. COMMUTER	OCTA 488 COMMUTER
METROLINK 601	M - F	5:32A					6:04A	6:18A	5:51A		
METROLINK 603	M - F	6:13A	6:41A				6:04/7:23A	6:05/6:18A	5:51/6:36A	6:23A	6:54A
METROLINK 681	M - F	7:10A	6:41/7:11A				6:04/7:23A	6:59/7:35A	6:36/7:21A	6:23/7:14A	
METROLINK 605	M - F	7:35A	7:11/7:41A				7:23A	6:59/7:35A	7:21/8:12A	7:14/7:59A	8:02A
AMTRAK 573	M - F	9:14A						8:39A	8:57A	8:44A	
AMTRAK 775	DAILY	10:06A									
AMTRAK 577	DAILY	12:04P									
AMTRAK 779	DAILY	2:00P									
AMTRAK 781	M - F	4:15P		3:49/4:19P				4:45P	3:35/4:21P	4:08/4:59P	
AMTRAK 583	DAILY	6:14P			5:42/6:49P			6:05/6:15P	5:57P	5:44/6:29P	5:10P
AMTRAK 585	DAILY	8:44P									
AMTRAK 587	FRIDAY	10:23P									

EASTBOUND FROM IRVINE TO SAN BERNARDINO

METROLINK 800	M - F	8:10A	7:41A				7:23A	8:01A	7:21A	7:59A	
METROLINK 802	M - F	4:47P		4:45P				4:29P	4:21P	4:08P	4:37P
METROLINK 804	M - F	5:30P			5:13/5:42P			5:10P	5:06/5:57P	4:59/5:44P	5:10P

SOUTHBOUND TRAINS FROM LOS ANGELES TO OCEANSIDE

AMTRAK 570	DAILY	7:44A	7:41A				7:23A	6:59/8:02A	7:21/8:12A	7:14/7:59A	8:02A
AMTRAK 772	M - F	9:46A							8:57A	8:44A	
AMTRAK 574	M - F	11:36A									
AMTRAK 776	DAILY	1:35P									
AMTRAK 578	DAILY	3:36P		3:49P					3:35/4:21P	3:23/4:08P	
METROLINK 684	M - F	L4:39P		4:19/4:45P				4:29/4:45P	4:21/5:06P	4:08/4:59P	4:37P
METROLINK 604	M - F	5:37P		4:45P	5:13/5:42P			5:20/5:40P	5:06/5:57P	4:59/5:44P	5:10P
METROLINK 606	M - F	6:39P				5:42/6:49P		6:29/6:40P	5:57P	6:29P	
AMTRAK 584	SU. - F	7:14P				6:49P		7:05P			
METROLINK 608	M - F	7:29P									
AMTRAK 786	DAILY	10:02P									

WESTBOUND FROM SAN BERNARDINO TO IRVINE

METROLINK 801	M - F	6:50A	7:11A				7:23A	6:55A	7:21A	7:14A	6:54A
METROLINK 803	M - F	7:52A						8:02A	8:12A	7:59A	8:02A
METROLINK 805	M - F	4:32P		4:45P	5:13P			4:45P	5:06P	4:59P	

L: Regular stop to discharge or pick up passengers except train may leave ahead of schedule

Irvine Valley College Campus

a satellite campus of Saddleback College North with a student body of 1,500 students. In July 1985 the college received its current name and became an independent institution. Present enrollment is over 10,000 students. The college offers an Associate of Arts degreein a full complement of programs. For general campus information call (714) 559-9300. The college has a theater and Fine Arts Gallery on campus. The Forum theater offers a full schedule of dramatic and musical productions which feature student and community actors. For information on current productions please call (714) 559-3303. The college's fine arts gallery is located in building A300. The gallery offers exhibits of professional artists, students and facility. For information about current exhibits call (714) 559-3488.

Irvine Fine Arts Center in Heritage Park

The Irvine Museum

The museum is housed on the 12th floor of a high rise building located at 18881 Von Karman Avenue. It can be reached by taking the OCTA 382 line from Irvine Transportation Center to the Von Karman Avenue and Martin Street stop. The Irvine Museum was founded by Joan Irvine Smith in 1992 and opened to the public on January 15, 1993. The museum is dedicated to the preservation of California art from 1890 to 1930. The backbone of the museum collection are works depicting scenes of California donated by the founder. The museum is open Tuesday thru Saturday, 11:00 A.M. to 5:00 P.M. Admission is free. For Information call (714) 476-2565.

Irvine Spectrum Entertainment Center

The Irvine Spectrum Entertainment Center is located at 31 Fortune Drive. This is Orange County's latest and hottest locale for night life. The center has a Edwards 21 Theaters and Edwards IMAX-3D Theater as centerpieces. There are several trendy restaurants such as Bertolini's Authentic Trattoria, Blueberry Hill Hamburgers, P.F. Chang's China Bistro and Wolfgang Puck Cafe. An assortment of coffee bars, retail shops, outdoor specialty vendors, and Sega City complement the theaters and restaurants. From the Irvine Transportation Center take the OCTA 309 line to the Fortune Loop and Spectrum stop.

Irvine Fine Arts Center

The Irvine Fine Arts Center is located at 14321 Yale Avenue in Heritage Park. The Irvine Fine Arts Center provides a wide range of cultural opportunities for the residents of Irvine. The center offers classes, workshops, art exhibits, open studio activities and many special events. Exhibits by local Orange County artists are the mainstay of this facility. The center is open

Irvine Spectrum Entertainment Center

203

Serrano Adobe in Heritage Hill Historical Park

12:00 Noon to 9:00 P.M. Monday, 9:00 A.M. to 9:00 P.M. Tuesday thru Thursday, 9:00 A.M. to 4:00 P.M. Friday, 9:00 A.M. to 3:00 P.M. Saturday, and 1:00 P.M. to 5:00 P.M. Sunday. Admission is free. For information call (714) 552-1078.

Irvine Meadows Amphitheater

The Irvine Meadows Amphitheater is located at 8808 Irvine Center Drive. The Amphitheater is host to a full schedule of rock & Roll concerts during the summer. For information call (714) 855-4515. From the Irvine Transportation Center take the OCTA 388 line to the Wild Rivers stop.

Heritage Hill Historical Park

The park is located at 25151 Serrano Road in Lake Forest. The park can be reached by taking the OCTA 309 line to the Trabuco Road and Lake Forest Drive stop. From there walk one block south on Lake Forest Drive to Serrano Road. The park will be just up Serrano to your right behind the shopping center on the corner of Lake Forrest and Serrano. The park features four early California structures complete with period furnishings and landscaping spanning the time from the great Mexican ranchos to the beginning of the citrus industry in Orange County. The buildings include the Serrano Adobe, Street George's Episcopal Mission, the Bennett Ranch House, and the El Toro Grammar School. Tours of the buildings are offered at 2:00 P.M. Wednesday thru Friday, and at 11:00 A.M. and 2:00 P.M. Saturdays and Sundays. The park is open 9:00 A.M. to 5:00 P.M. Wednesday thru Sunday. Admission is free. For Information call (714) 855-2028.

Laguna Hills Mall

The Laguna Hills Mall is located just off I-5 and El Toro Road in Laguna Hills. The mall can be reached by taking the OCTA 388 line to the mall stop. The mall has J. C. Penney, the Broadway, and Sears as anchor department stores.

Orange County
John Wayne Airport

The John Wayne Airport is served by most of the major airlines. There is a modern terminal building and gate facility. This airport provides convenience for visitors and residents of Orange County without the commute to Los Angeles International Airport. Most of the hotels listed under the Irvine and Santa Ana stations provide shuttle service to/from the airport. Those that also provide shuttle service to these stations would be a good choice for the visitor who wishes to base his visit at one of the airport hotels.

Wild Rivers

Wild Rivers is orange county's water park. It is located on the site of the now defunct Lion Country Safari theme park. As such it has an African theme to its ride venues. There is a Lake Victoria for adults, Safari River Expedition for a one-quarter mile tube float, the African Queen Picnic area, the Cobras water slides, Sweitzer Falls with a speedy slide with a three-foot drop into the pool and much more. The park is open May through September. Please call (714) 768-WILD for operating hours. From the Irvine Transportation Center take the OCTA 388 line to the Wild Rivers stop.

Places to Stay
Airporter Garden Hotel

The Airporter Garden Hotel is located at 18700 MacArthur Boulevard. The hotel phone number is (714) 833-2770. For reservations call (800) 854-3012.

Courtyard by Marriott

The Courtyard by Marriott is located at 2701 Main Street. The hotel phone number is (714) 757-1200. For reservations call (800) 321-2211.

Embassy Suites

The Embassy Suites is located at 2120 Main Street. The hotel has a shuttle van and will pick you up at the Metrolink Transportation Center with advance notice. The hotel phone number is (714) 553-8332. For reservations call (800) 362-2779.

Holiday Inn
Laguna Hills/Irvine Spectrum

The Holiday Inn Laguna Hills/Irvine Spectrum is located at 25205 La Paz Road in Laguna Hills. The hotel phone number is (714) 586-5000. For reservations call (800) HOLIDAY.

Holiday Inn Irvine at
Orange County Airport

The Holiday Inn Irvine at Orange County Airport is located at 17941 Von Karman Avenue. The hotel phone number is (714) 863-1999. For reservations call (800) HOLIDAY.

Hyatt Regency Irvine

The Hyatt Regency Irvine is located at 17900 Jamboree Road. The hotel phone number is (714) 975-1234. For reservations call (800) 233-1234.

Irvine Marriott Hotel

The Irvine Marriott Hotel is located at 18000 Von Karman Avenue. The hotel phone number is (714) 553-0100. For reservations call (800) 228-9290.

La Quinta Inn

The La Quinta Inn is located at 14972 Sand Canyon Avenue. The hotel shares the Old Town Irvine site and is housed in the Granary Building, a 1947 addition to the original sack house built in 1895. These buildings were used by the Irvine Ranch as the loading facility for railroad transportation of the ranch's prodigious output. The hotel has a shuttle van and will pick you up at the Irvine Transportation Center with advance notice. The hotel phone number is (714) 551-0909. For reservations call (800) 531-5900

Radisson Plaza Hotel

The Radisson Plaza Hotel is located at 18800 Mac Arthur Boulevard. The hotel phone number is (714) 833-9999. For reservations call (800) 333-3333.

Residence Inn by Marriott

The Residence Inn is located at 10 Morgan Street. The hotel has a shuttle van and will pick you up at the Irvine Transportation Center. The hotel phone number is (714) 380-3000. For reservations call (800) 331-3131.

Travelodge Laguna Hills

The Travelodge Laguna Hills is located at 23150 Lake Center Drive, El Toro. The hotel phone number is (714) 855-1000. For reservations call (800) 830-4447.

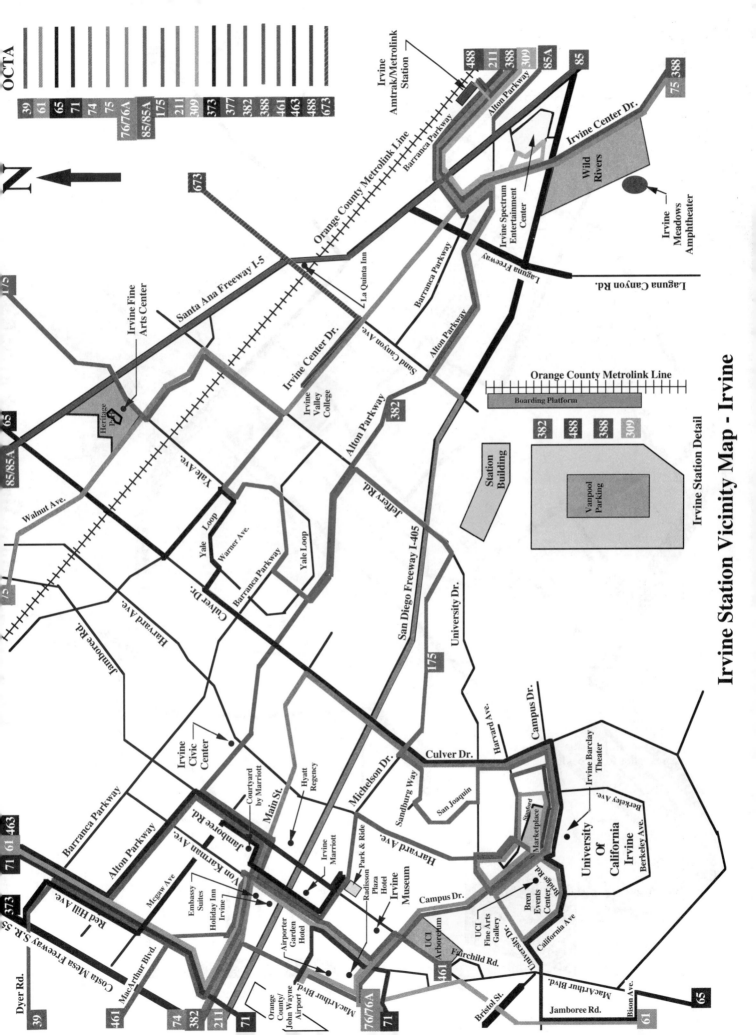

Irvine Station Vicinity Map - Irvine

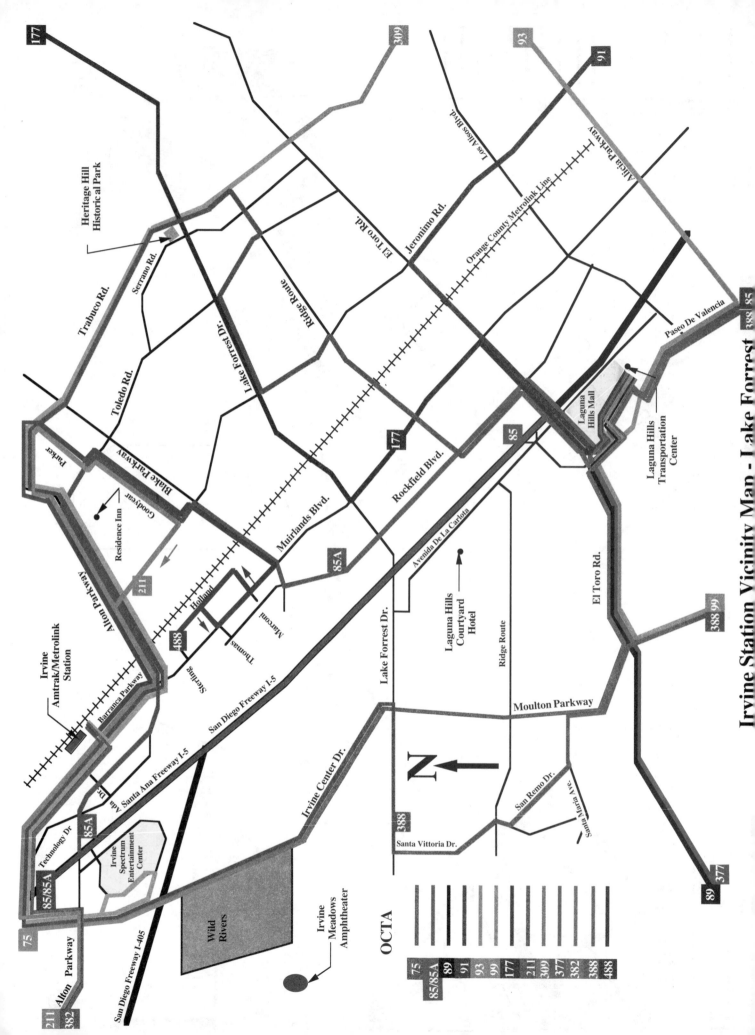

Irvine Station Vicinity Map - Lake Forrest

San Juan Capistrano Station

Station Connecting Transit Information

The San Juan Capistrano Amtrak/Metrolink Station is located at the end of Verdugo Street in the middle of Old San Juan Capistrano. There is limited public parking at the station. Be careful if you park at the station that you do not park in one of the four-hour limit spaces. The station is well maintained and is an integral part of historic Old San Juan Capistrano. Across from the old station is a new parking structure for the Edwards movie theater and associated shops. The station can be reached by taking the Ortega Highway offramp from Interstate 5 and heading west to Camino Capistrano. Turn left on Camino Capistrano and go one short block to Verdugo Street where you turn right. Verdugo terminates at the tracks with the parking structure on the left and open parking on the right.

The station is served by the OCTA 91 and 394 lines which travel north and south on Camino Capistrano. The nearest bus stop is at the corner of Ortega Highway and Camino Capistrano, two short blocks from the station. The station vicinity map provides the routes for the bus transit options from the San Juan Capistrano Station. The following tables provide the schedule for bus connections with

San Juan Capistrano Station

Amtrak and Metrolink. For updates to schedules and routes call OCTA on (800) 636-7433.

Points of Interest
Los Rios Historic District

The Los Rios Historic District begins with Capistrano Depot which was built by the Atchison, Topeka & Santa Fe Railway in 1894. It is the oldest Spanish Colonial station in Southern California.

From the end of Verdugo Street you can walk across the tracks into the 1880's. Here the San Juan Capistrano Historical Society has preserved a bit of the Old West. The first structure you will encounter is the Combs house built in 1878 in Foster City near San Onofre. It was moved to San Juan in 1882. From there you can stroll north or south on Los Rios Street where many of the historic buildings from San Juan's past are now located. The San Juan Historic Society provides walking tours on Sundays at 1:00 P.M. The tours start in front of El Peon Plaza on Ortega Highway. The cost is $1.00 for adults and $.50 for children.

O'Neill Museum

The O'Neill Museum is located

SAN JUAN CAPISTRANO STATION WEEKDAY BUS CONNECTIONS
NORTHBOUND TRAINS FROM OCEANSIDE TO LOS ANGELES

TRAIN NUMBER	DAYS OF OPERATION	TRAIN ARRIVAL	OCTA 91 NORTHBOUND 30 - 60 MIN.	OCTA 91 SOUTHBOUND 30 - 60 MIN.	OCTA 394 NORTHBOUND HOURLY	OCTA 394 SOUTHBOUND HOURLY
BUS FREQUENCY						
METROLINK 601	M - F	5:20A	5:33A		5:49A	
METROLINK 603	M - F	6:00A	5:56/6:26A	6:20A	5:49/7:05A	6:53A
METROLINK 605	M - F	7:22A	6:56/7:26A	7:20/7:55A	7:05/8:05A	6:53/7:53A
AMTRAK 573	M - F	9:00A	8:56/9:26A	8:55/9:25A	8:45/9:49A	8:53/9:41A
AMTRAK 775	DAILY	9:52A	9:26/9:56A	9:25/9:55A	9:49/10:49A	9:41/10:41A
AMTRAK 577	DAILY	11:50A	11:26/11:56A	11:25/11:55A	11:49A/12:49P	11:41A/12:41P
AMTRAK 779	DAILY	1:47P	1:26/1:56P	1:25/1:57P	12:49/1:49P	1:41/2:41P
AMTRAK 781	M - F	4:02P	3:46/4:16P	3:57/4:27P	3:49/4:49P	3:41/4:41P
AMTRAK 583	DAILY	6:00P	5:58/6:28P	5:57/6:27P	5:49P	5:53/6:58P
AMTRAK 585	DAILY	8:30P	6:58P	7:20P		6:58P
AMTRAK 587	FRIDAY	10:09P				

SOUTHBOUND TRAINS FROM LOS ANGELES TO OCEANSIDE

TRAIN NUMBER	DAYS OF OPERATION	TRAIN ARRIVAL	OCTA 91 NORTHBOUND	OCTA 91 SOUTHBOUND	OCTA 394 NORTHBOUND	OCTA 394 SOUTHBOUND
AMTRAK 570	DAILY	7:58A	7:56/8:26A	7:55/8:25A	7:05/8:05A	7:53/8:53A
AMTRAK 772	M - F	10:03A	9:56/10:26A	9:55/10:25A	9:49/10:49A	9:41/10:41A
AMTRAK 574	M - F	11:51A	11:26/11:56A	11:25/11:55A	11:49A/12:49P	11:41/12:41P
AMTRAK 776	DAILY	1:57P	1:56/2:26P	1:25/2:27P	1:49/2:49P	1:41/2:41P
AMTRAK 578	DAILY	3:50P	3:46/4:16P	3:27/3:57P	3:49/4:49P	3:41/4:41P
METROLINK 684	M - F	4:54P	4:46/5:16P	4:27/4:57P	4:49/5:49P	4:41/5:53P
METROLINK 604	M - F	L5:49P	5:16/5:58P	5:27/6:27P	4:49/5:49P	4:41/5:53P
METROLINK 606	M - F	L6:52P	6:28/6:58P	6:50/7:20P	5:49P	5:53/6:58P
AMTRAK 584	SU. - F	7:27P	6:58P	7:20P		6:58P
METROLINK 608	M - F	L7:41P				
AMTRAK 786	DAILY	10:13P				

L: Regular stop to discharge or pick up passengers except train may leave ahead of schedule

SAN JUAN CAPISTRANO STATION WEEKEND BUS CONNECTIONS
NORTHBOUND TRAINS FROM OCEANSIDE TO LOS ANGELES

TRAIN NUMBER	DAYS OF OPERATION	TRAIN ARRIVAL	OCTA 91 NORTHBOUND HOURLY	OCTA 91 SOUTHBOUND HOURLY
BUS FREQUENCY				
AMTRAK 769	SA.SU.H.	7:31A	S7:02/S8:00A	S7:40A
AMTRAK 775	DAILY	9:52A	9:00/9:57A	9:40/10:47A
AMTRAK 577	DAILY	11:50A	10:57/11:57A	11:47A/12:47P
AMTRAK 779	DAILY	1:47P	12:57/1:57P	12:47/2:47P
AMTRAK 791	SA.SU.H	4:09P	3:57/5:02P	3:47/4:47P
AMTRAK 583	DAILY	6:00P	5:02/6:10P	5:47/6:47P
AMTRAK 585	DAILY	8:30P	7:10P	S7:47P

SOUTHBOUND TRAINS FROM LOS ANGELES TO OCEANSIDE

AMTRAK 570	DAILY	7:58A	S7:02/S8:00A	S7:40/8:40A
AMTRAK 572	SA.SU.H.	10:03A	9:57/10:57A	9:40/10:47A
AMTRAK 774	SA.SU.H.	11:51A	10:57/11:57P	11:47A/12:47P
AMTRAK 776	DAILY	1:57P	12:57/2:57P	1:47/2:47P
AMTRAK 578	DAILY	3:50P	2:57/3:57P	3:47/4:47P
AMTRAK 782	SA.SU.H.	6:29P	6:10/7:10P	5:47/6:47P
AMTRAK 584	SU. - F	7:27P	7:10P	6:47/S7:47P
AMTRAK 786	DAILY	10:13P		

NOTE: S INDICATES SATURDAY BUS ONLY

Combs House in Los Rios Historic District

just south of Verdugo Street on Los Rios in the Los Rios Historic District. The museum is the restored Albert Pryor residence and provides a glimpse into the home life of residents of San Juan in the 1880's. The Museum is operated by the San Juan Historical Society and the docents provide an interesting history of the house, its furnishings and former residents. The museum is open 10:00 A.M. till 5:00 P.M. daily except Monday. Admission is $1.00 for adults and $.50 for children. Information can be obtained by calling (714) 493-8444.

Mission San Juan Capistrano

The Mission San Juan Capistrano was founded by Father Junipero Serra on November 1, 1776. It is the seventh in a chain of 21 missions founded by Franciscan Padres. The mission grounds today are much as they were during the Spanish Colonial and Mexican periods of California history. The mission museum features rooms which trace the history of San Juan from the time of the Native Americans known as Acagchemem to the time of Mexican rule before California was ceded to the United States, after the Mexican American War, and became a state in 1850.

The gardens are meticulously maintained with colorful flowers and central fountains which are a part of all of the California missions. The gardens offer one a chance to stop, rest and enjoy the serenity that the surroundings evoke.

The Serra Chapel was built in 1777 and is the oldest standing church in California. The chapel is the last remaining church where Father Serra actually said Mass. The altar is made of cherrywood with gold-leaf overlay and is estimated to be over 300 years old.

The mission has a good collection of native American artifacts dating back to the time of the founding of the mission. There is a replica of a shelter used by the early native Americans who lived in the San Juan Capistrano area

Central Courtyard and Gardens Mission San Juan Capistrano

prior to the coming of the Spanish. The shelter was built by descendants of the original inhabitants of the San Juan area and is furnished with tools that were used by the early Californians.

The Mission is also famous for the annual return of the swallows from their winter stay in Argentina for nesting in the spring. Traditionally the Swallows return on March 19, Saint Joseph's Day. Today March 19 is celebrated in San Juan as Swallows Day with a parade and fiesta with native American performances and living history characters who mingle with visitors to the celebrations.

The mission is open daily from 8:30 A.M. to 5:00 P.M. except Thanksgiving, Christmas and the afternoon on Good Friday. Admission is $4.00 for adults and $3.00 for children under 12 and seniors 62 and over. For further information call (714) 248-2049.

South Orange County Community Theater

The South Orange County Community Theater is located at 31776 El Camino Real near the intersection of Ortega Highway and El Camino Real.

Replica of a Shelter used by Native Americans inhabiting San Juan Area

The theater features live stage productions usually on Friday and Saturday evenings. For information as to current offerings call (714) 489-8082.

Dana Point Harbor

Dana Point harbor can be reached by taking the southbound OCTA 91 bus line to the Pacific Coast Highway and Del Obispo Street stop. From there one can either walk to the harbor, which extends about a mile, or transfer to the OCTA 85 bus line to the Dana Point Harbor Drive and Golden Lantern Drive stop, approximately one-third mile from the harbor entrance. The harbor is a manmade haven for small craft and fishing boats in south Orange County. It is named after Richard Henry Dana who explored the California coast in the 1830's. The harbor features sportfishing in local waters, a New England style shopping village, several parks,

windsurfing and is home to the Orange County Marine Institute.

Orange County Marine Institute

The Orange County Marine Institute is located at the end of Dana Point Harbor Drive. The Institute features a small gift shop, some small aquariums with local Pacific Ocean sea creatures and two large classrooms where local school children have the opportunity for a hands-on learning experience in marine science. The Institute also trains teachers nationwide in effective teaching techniques for marine and environmental science. At the dock across from the Institute is a replica of Richard Henry Dana's Sailing Ship the *Pilgrim*. Admission is free. The Institute is open daily 10:00 A.M. till 3:30 P.M., except on major

Replica of Pilgrim

Holidays. The *Pilgrim* is open for tours on Sundays 11:00 A.M. till 2:30 P.M. For further information call (714) 496-2274.

Doheny State Park

Doheny State Park is located at the entrance to Dana Point Harbor. Doheny State Park can be reached by taking the southbound OCTA 91 bus line to the Pacific Coast Highway and Del Obispo Street stop. The park features picnic areas and camping facilities. It has an excellent surf break and the local surfers can be seen riding the waves anytime the surf is breaking. The park has a large sandy beach for beachgoers. The park is open for day use between 6:00 A.M. and 8:00 P.M. There is a day-use fee of $6.00 per car. If you walk into the park there is no fee. Campsites are available and cost $19.00 for beach front sites and $14.00 for inland sites. The Park information phone number is (714) 496-6171. For campsite reservations call (800) 444-7275.

Places to Stay
Mission Inn Motel

The Mission Inn Motel is located about 3 blocks from the Metrolink Station at 26891 Ortega Highway, San Juan Capistrano. The motel phone number is (714) 493-1151.

Capistrano Inn Best Western Motel

The Capistrano Inn is located at 27174 Ortega Highway. The hotel phone number is (714) 493-5661. For

reservations call (800) 528-1234.

Dana Point Marriott

The Dana Point Marriott is located at 25135 Park Lantern, Dana Point. The hotel provides free van pick-up at the Metrolink station. For pick-up call

(714) 661-5000. For reservations call (800) 228-9290.

Dana Point Hilton

The Dana Point Hilton is located at 34402 Pacific Coast Highway. The hotel phone number is (714) 661-1100. For reservations call (800) HILTONS.

The Ritz-Carlton Laguna Niguel

The Ritz-Carlton is located at 33533 Ritz-Carlton Drive. The hotel phone number is (714) 240-2000. For reservations call (800) 241-3333.

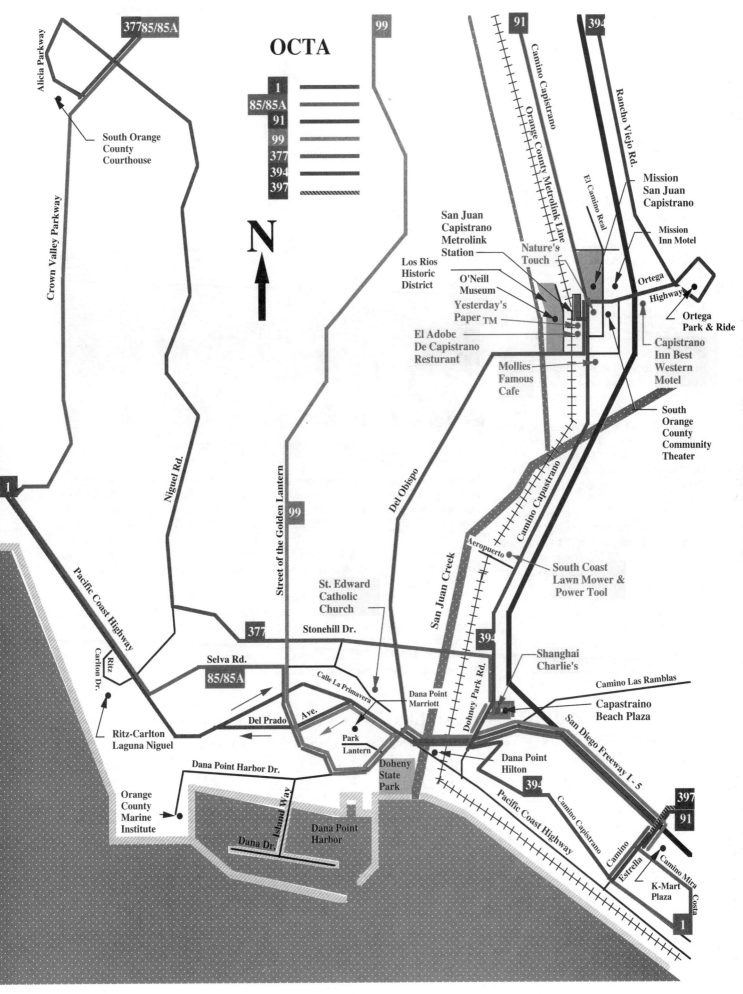

San Juan Capistrano Station Vicinity Map

San Clemente Stations

San Clemente presently has separate stations for Metrolink and Amtrak. The San Clemente Amtrak Station is located on Avenida Victoria at the San Clemente Pier. There is no parking associated with the station. The lack of parking and difficulty of access from the San Diego Freeway were the reasons that the City of San Clemente located the Metrolink station near the intersection of Avenida Pico and El Camino Real.

San Clemente Metrolink Station Connecting Transit Information

The San Clemente Metrolink Station is located at the intersection of El Camino Real and Avenida Estation. The station shares the parking lot with the Ole Hanson Beach Club and Calafia Beach. There are 145 parking spaces, numbered 1 thru 145, available for commuters at the station. Due to the fact that the parking lot is a City Beach Parking Lot, <u>parking is not free</u>. Parking costs $1.00 per day providing you purchase your daily parking permit from the centralized parking revenue collection device in front of the station before 9:00 A.M. Commuters enter their parking space number and keep the receipt. They do not have to display anything in their car. Alternately, commuters may purchase an annual commuter rail parking pass. The cost of a pass for a San Clemente resident is $30.00 and non-residents pay $45.00. Permits may be purchased at San

San Clemente Metrolink Station

Clemente City Hall or at a number of other city facilities. For information about parking permits call the City Planning Division at (714) 498-2533 Ext. 3311.

The station is well lighted and has excellent shelter. The station is manned in the morning and afternoon. The station is accessible from San Diego Freeway I-5. Take the Avenida Pico offramp and go west on Avenida Pico to El Camino Real and turn right. Go one more block and turn left on Avenida Estation which leads into the parking lot. The station is served by the Orange County Transit Authority (OCTA) 91 and 397 bus lines. The stops for these lines are located on El Camino Real and Avenida Pico adjacent to the station. The station vicinity map provides the route map for bus transit options in the vicinity of the San Clemente Metrolink and Amtrak stations. The following tables provide the schedule for bus connections with Metrolink and Amtrak. For updates to schedules call OCTA on (714) 636-RIDE.

SAN CELEMENTE METROLINK STATION BUS CONNECTIONS
NORTHBOUND TRAINS FROM OCEANSIDE TO LOS ANGELES

TRAIN NUMBER	DAYS OF OPERATION	TRAIN ARRIVAL	OCTA 91 SOUTHBOUND 30 MIN.	OCTA 91 NORTHBOUND 30 MIN.	OCTA 397 SOUTHBOUND HOURLY	OCTA 397 NORTHBOUND HOURLY
BUS FREQUENCY						
METROLINK 601	M - F	5:11A		5:09/5:22A		5:42A
METROLINK 603	M - F	5:51A	6:46A	5:22/5:52A	7:04A	5:42/6:22A
METROLINK 605	M - F	7:13A	6:46/7:16P	6:52/7:22A	7:04/7:34A	6:22/7:24A

SOUTHBOUND TRAINS FROM LOS ANGELES TO OCEANSIDE

METROLINK 604	M - F	L6:01P	5:59/6:29P	5:57/6:27P	5:26/6:34P	5:09/6:09P
METROLINK 606	M - F	L7:04P	6:59/7:17P	6:27P	6:34P	6:09/7:14P
METROLINK 608	M - F	L7:53P	7:47P			7:14P

L: Regular stop to discharge or pick up passengers train may leave ahead of schedule

San Clemente Amtrak Station

The Spanish Village from the San Clemente Pier

San Clemente Amtrak Station Connecting Transit Information

The San Clemente Amtrak Station is located on Avenida Victoria at the San Clemente Pier. The train boarding platform is extremely primitive and unmanned. There is only one Amtrak train in each direction between Los Angeles and San Diego that stops per day. The location of this station is outstanding from the standpoint of easy access to one of Southern California's premier beaches.

The station is accessible from the San Diego Freeway I-5. From the Southbound I-5 take the Avenida Pico offramp. Go west on Avenida Pico to El Camino Real and turn left. Go to Avenida Del Mar and turn right. Go to the end of Avenida Del Mar and the station will be at the San Clemente Pier. From the northbound I-5 Freeway take the El Camino Real offramp and go north to Avenida Del Mar and turn left.

The station is served by the OCTA 91 bus line. The stops for these lines are located on Avenida Victoria adjacent to the station.

Outside of the immediate vicinity of the San Clemente Amtrak and Metrolink stations the OCTA 91 line provides service to San Juan Capistrano, Mission Viejo and Lake Forest.

Points of Interest

The town of San Clemente is the dream of its founder Ole Hanson who, in partnership with Hamilton Cotton, planned a Spanish style village and named it San Clemente. The city was officially founded on December 6, 1925 when a crowd of 600 people listened to Hanson speak of his plans for San Clemente. Hanson dedicated 3,000 feet of beach along with a fishing pier to the residents. The original development included 8 miles of paved streets complete with street lights, bridle paths, community clubhouse, schoolhouse, beach club, park and swimming pool.

SAN CLEMENTE AMTRAK STATION BUS CONNECTIONS
NORTHBOUND TRAINS FROM OCEANSIDE TO LOS ANGELES

TRAIN NUMBER	DAYS OF OPERATION	TRAIN ARRIVAL	OCTA 91 SOUTHBOUND	OCTA 91 NORTHBOUND	OCTA 91 SOUTHBOUND	OCTA 91 NORTHBOUND
DAYS OF OPERATION			M - F	M - F	SA.SU.H	SA.SU.H
BUS FREQUENCY			HOURLY	HOURLY	HOURLY	HOURLY
AMTRAK 781	M - F	3:43P	3:39/4:09P	3:32/4:02P		
AMTRAK 791	SA.SU.H	3:58P			3:25/4:25P	3:18/4:28P

SOUTHBOUND TRAINS FROM LOS ANGELES TO OCEANSIDE

AMTRAK 772	M - F	10:15A	10:02/10:32A	10:14/10:44A		
AMTRAK 572	SA.SU.H.	10:15A			9:15/11:25A	9:18/10:18A

View along Avenida del Mar

In 1969, San Clemente was thrust into the national spotlight by Richard Nixon who purchased the Cotton Estate and named it the "Western White House".

The San Clemente Pier

The San Clemente Pier features two restaurants/bars which have indoor and outdoor seating with spectacular views of the ocean and coastline. The pier is a favorite of anglers of all ages. The beach along this stretch of coast is wide and sandy with excellent opportunities for swimming, body surfing, board surfing and sunbathing. On weekends many residents from northern Orange County board the morning southbound train which arrives at 10:15 AM for a day at the beach. The daily northbound train stops at 4:04 PM to take these same beachgoers back to their homes after a full day at the beach.

The Spanish Village

The area surrounding the Amtrak station and the Pier have several restaurants and hotels which cater to the beach crowd. Further up Avenida Del Mar is the commercial and administrative center of San Clemente.

Calafia Beach

This street has several upscale boutiques, antique shops, and restaurants in addition to the city hall, library, and community center.

Ole Hanson Beach Club

The Ole Hanson Beach Club features an olympic-sized swimming pool which is open to the public. For information call (714) 361-8207.

Calafia Beach

The access to Calafia beach is just south of the Metrolink station boarding platform. There is a small beach concession located with the beach restrooms.

Places to Stay

Best Western Casablanca Inn

The Best Western Casablanca Inn is located at 1601 N. El Camino Real. The hotel phone number is (714) 361-1644. For reservations call (800) 528-1234.

Casa Clemente Resort

The Casa Clemente Resort is located at 35 Calle de Industrias. The hotel phone number is (714) 498-8800.

Oceanview Inn & Suites

The Oceanview Inn & Suites is located at 1301 N. El Camino Real. The hotel phone number is (714) 361-0636. For reservations call (800) 346-6441.

Beachcomber Motel

The Beachcomber Motel is located at 533 Avenida Victoria just across from the Amtrak station. The hotel phone number is (714) 492-5457.

Holiday Inn

The Holiday Inn is located at 111 South Avenida De Estrella. The hotel phone number is (714) (714) 361-3000. For reservations call (800) HOLIDAY.

214

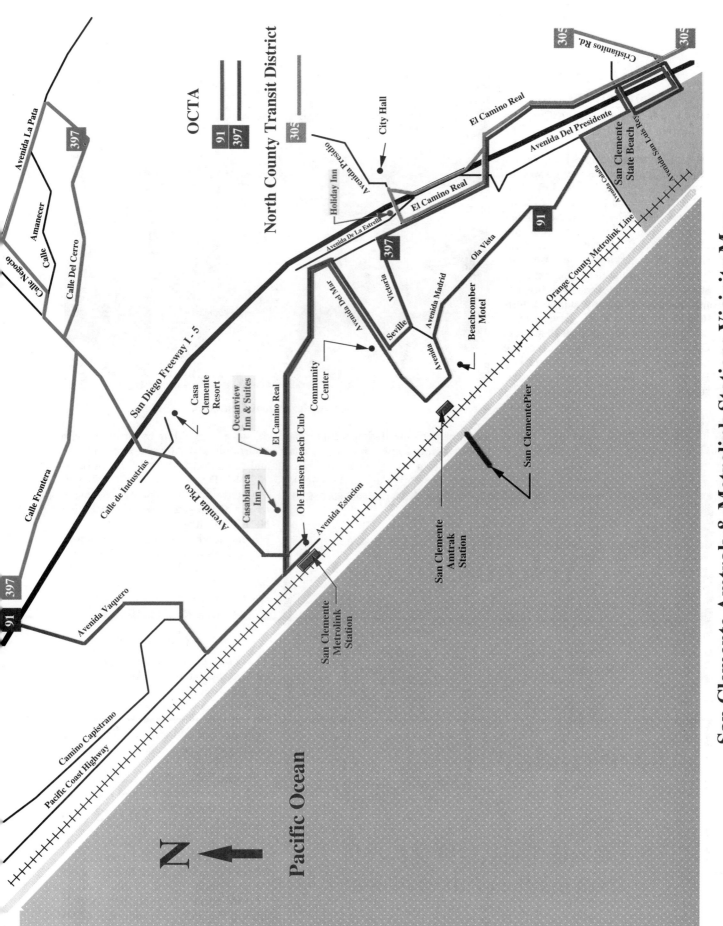

San Clemente Amtrak & Metrolink Stations Vicinity Map

Oceanside Station

Station Connecting Transit Information

The Oceanside Transit Center is located at 235 S. Tremont Street. The station can be reached by taking the Mission Avenue offramp from the I-5 Freeway. From the freeway go west to Tremont Street and turn left. The station will be one block from Mission on your right. The station has a large parking lot. The train boarding platform is well lighted with excellent shelter. The parking lot is also well lighted and maintained. The station is supervised by Metrolink ambassadors during the morning and afternoon rush hour. Amtrak has a full service ticket booth that is open seven days a week. Greyhound busses also serve the Oceanside Transit Center. There is a Burger King fast food restaurant and sundries shop located at the station.

The North County Transit District (NCTD) has a Bus Transit Center located to the north of the main Transit Center complex. NCTD 301, 302, 303, 305, 310, 312, 313, 314, 316, 317, 318, and 320 lines operate from the

Oceanside Transit Center

transit center. The station vicinity map provides the routes for bus transit options from the Oceanside Transit Center. The following tables provide

the schedule of bus connections with Metrolink and Amtrak. For schedule and route updates call NCTD at (619) 722-NCTD.

Outside of the immediate vicinity of the Oceanside Transit Center the NCTD 301 line and 310 Express line provide service to Carlsbad, Encinitas, Del Mar and University Town Center. The 302 line and 320 Express line provides service to San Marcos and Escondido. The 305 line provides service to Camp Pendleton and San Clemente.

Coaster

The Coaster commuter rail service, operated by NTCD, provides service from Oceanside to San Diego. Presently the Coaster operates 8 trains a day in each direction Monday thru Thursday and 10 trains on Fridays. The Coaster stops at Oceanside, Carlsbad, Poinsettia, Encinitas, Solana Beach, Sorrento Valley, Old Town and San Diego. For information and schedules for the Coaster call (800) COASTER.

Amtrak Service to San Diego

All Amtrak trains that stop at the Oceanside Transit Center continue on to San Diego with a stop in-route at the Solana Beach Amtrak/Coaster Station. For information regarding Amtrak service beyond Oceanside call (800) USA-RAIL.

Welcome to the

City
of
Oceanside

Please telephone (619) 966-4410 if we may be of assistance

216

OCEANSIDE STATION WEEKDAY BUS CONNECTIONS
NORTHBOUND TRAINS FROM OCEANSIDE TO LOS ANGELES

TRAIN NUMBER	DAYS OF OPERATION	TRAIN DEPARTURE	NCTD 301 NORTHBOUND	NTCD 302 WESTBOUND	NTCD 303 CLOCKWISE	NCTD 303 COUNTER CW	NCTD 305 SOUTHBOUND	NCTD 310 NORTHBOUND	NTCD 312 CLOCKWISE	NTCD 312 COUNTER CW
BUS FREQUENCY			30 MINUTES	15 - 30 MIN.	30 - 60 MIN.	30 - 60 MIN.	30 MIN. - 3 HRS.	45 - 60 MIN.	HOURLY	HOURLY
METROLINK 601	M - F	4:51A								
METROLINK 603	M - F	5:30A			5:19A					
METROLINK 605	M - F	6:52A	6:22A	6:46A	6:19A	6:49A	6:04A	6:10A	6:22A	
AMTRAK 771	M - F	7:17A	6:52A	7:06A	6:19A	6:49A		6:57A	6:22A	6:55A
AMTRAK 573	M - F	8:28A	8:24A	8:26A	8:19A	8:19A	8:25A	8:11A	8:22A	7:55A
AMTRAK 775	DAILY	9:22A	8:54A	9:06A	9:19A	9:19A		9:07A	9:22A	8:55A
AMTRAK 577	DAILY	11:20A	10:54A	11:06A	11:19A	11:19A	11:09A	11:09A	10:26A	10:55A
AMTRAK 779	DAILY	1:17P	12:54A	1:06P	12:49P	12:49P		1:16A	12:30P	1:05P
AMTRAK 781	M - F	3:24P	2:54P	3:10P	3:19P	3:19P	2:17P	2:53A	2:40P	3:15P
AMTRAK 583	DAILY	5:22P	4:52P	5:10P	4:49P	4:57P	5:22P	5:04P	4:50P	5:10P
AMTRAK 585	DAILY	7:52P	7:22P	7:46P	7:49P	7:49P	7:42P	7:08P	7:12P	7:35P
AMTRAK 587	FRIDAY	9:49P	9:22P	9:46P	9:19P	9:19P	9:42P	9:15P	8:52P	9:20P

TRAIN NUMBER	DAYS OF OPERATION	TRAIN DEPARTURE	NCTD 313 CLOCKWISE	NTCD 313 COUNTER CW	NTCD 314 LOOP 1	NCTD 314 LOOP 2	NCTD 316 CLOCKWISE	NCTD 316 COUNTER CW	NTCD 317	NTCD 318 WESTBOUND	NTCD 320 WESTBOUND
BUS FREQUENCY			45 MINUTES	45 MINUTES	HOURLY	HOURLY	HOURLY	HOURLY	30 - 60 MIN	30 MINUTES	30 MINUTES
METROLINK 601	M - F	4:51A									
METROLINK 603	M - F	5:30A									
METROLINK 605	M - F	6:52A	6:43A	6:10A	6:22A		6:45A			6:35A	6:47A
AMTRAK 771	M - F	7:17A	6:43A	7:05A	6:22A	7:00A	6:45A			7:05A	6:47A
AMTRAK573	M - F	8:28A	7:35A	7:55A	8:22A	8:00A	7:53A	7:34A		8:05A	8:17A
AMTRAK 775	DAILY	9:22A	9:09A	8:45A	8:22A	9:00A	8:51A	8:40A		8:35A	9:17A
AMTRAK 577	DAILY	11:20A	10:40A	11:00A	10:22A	11:00A	10:45A	10:32A		11:05A	11:17A
AMTRAK 779	DAILY	1:17P	12:50P	1:15P	12:22P	1:00P	12:51P	12:32P		1:05A	12:47P
AMTRAK 781	M - F	3:24P	3:20P	2:50P	3:22P	3:00P	3:10P	2:32P		2:35P	3:17P
AMTRAK 583	DAILY	5:22P	5:00P	5:20P	4:26P	5:18P	4:55P	4:38P	5:11P	5:09P	5:20P
AMTRAK 585	DAILY	7:52P	7:20P	7:40P	7:22P	7:00P	7:40P	7:28P	7:41P	6:59P	7:47P
AMTRAK 587	FRIDAY	9:49P	8:45P	9:05P	8:22P	9:00P	9:40P	9:28P	9:41P	9:09P	8:57P

SOUTHBOUND TRAINS FROM LOS ANGELES TO OCEANSIDE

TRAIN NUMBER	DAYS OF OPERATION	TRAIN ARRIVAL	NCTD 301 SOUTHBOUND	NCTD 302 EASTBOUND	NCTD 303 CLOCKWISE	NCTD 303 COUNTER CW	NTCD 305 NORTHBOUND	NCTD 310 SOUTHBOUND	NCTD 312 CLOCKWISE	NCTD 312 COUNTER CW
BUS FREQUENCY			30 MINUTES	15 - 30 MIN.	30 - 60 MIN.	30 - 60 MIN.	30 MIN. - 3 HRS.	45 - 60 MIN.	HOURLY	HOURLY
AMTRAK 570	DAILY	8:29A	8:30A	8:48A	9:00A	8:30A		9:13A	8:30A	9:00A
AMTRAK 772	M - F	10:35A	11:00A	10:48A	11:00A	11:00A	11:20A	11:14A	11:30A	11:00A
AMTRAK 574	M - F	12:20P	12:30P	12:28P	12:30P	12:30P		12:42P	12:35P	1:10P
AMTRAK 776	DAILY	2:28P	2:30P	2:48P	2:30P	2:30P		3:00P	2:45P	3:20P
AMTRAK 578	DAILY	4:21P	4:30P	4:28P	4:35P	4:35P	4:50P	4:30P	4:40P	5:00P
METROLINK 604	M - F	6:26P	6:30P	6:28P	6:30P	6:30P	6:50P	7:13P	7:00P	6:40P
AMTRAK 780	M - F	6:49P	7:00P	6:58P	7:00P	7:00P	6:50P	7:13P	7:00P	7:30P
METROLINK 606	M - F	7:29P	7:30P	7:58P	7:30P	7:30P	7:50P	8:13P	8:00P	7:30P
AMTRAK 584	SU. - F	8:01P	8:30P	8:28P	8:30P	8:30P	8:20P			8:30P
METROLINK 608	M - F	8:18P	8:30P	8:28P	8:30P	8:30P	8:20P			8:30P
AMTRAK 786	DAILY	10:43P			11:00P	11:30P	10:50P			

TRAIN NUMBER	DAYS OF OPERATION	TRAIN ARRIVAL	NCTD 313 CLOCKWISE	NCTD 313 COUNTER CW	NCTD 314 LOOP 1	NCTD 314 LOOP 2	NCTD 316 CLOCKWISE	NCTD 316 COUNTER CW	NCTD 317	NCTD 318 EASTBOUND	NCTD 320 EASTBOUND
BUS FREQUENCY			45 MINUTES	45 MINUTES	HOURLY	HOURLY	HOURLY	HOURLY	30 - 60 MIN	30 MINUTES	30 MINUTES
AMTRAK 570	DAILY	8:29A	8:50A	8:40A	9:00A	8:30A	8:45A	8:30A		8:45A	8:30A
AMTRAK 772	M - F	10:35A	11:05A	10:50A	11:00A	11:30A	10:45A	11:30A		11:15A	11:00A
AMTRAK 574	M - F	12:20P	12:35P	1:05P	1:00P	12:30P	12:45P	12:30P		12:45P	12:30P
AMTRAK 776	DAILY	2:28P	3:00P	2:40P	3:00P	2:30P	2:45P	2:30P		2:45P	2:30P
AMTRAK 578	DAILY	4:21P	4:40P	5:10P	5:00P	4:45P	4:30P	4:30P	4:45P	4:45P	4:30P
METROLINK 604	M - F	6:26P	7:05P	6:45P	7:00P	6:30P	6:45P	6:33P	6:45P	6:45P	6:30P
AMTRAK 780	M - F	6:49P	7:05P	7:30P	7:00P	7:30P	7:45P	7:33P	7:15P	7:03P	7:00P
METROLINK 606	M - F	7:29P	7:50P	7:30P	8:00P	7:30P	7:45P	7:33P	7:45P	8:08P	7:30P
AMTRAK 584	SU. - F	8:01P		8:15P			8:30P	8:45P	8:33P	8:15P	8:08P
METROLINK 608	M - F	8:18P					8:45P	8:33P	8:45P		
AMTRAK 786	DAILY	10:43P							10:45P		

OCEANSIDE STATION WEEKEND BUS CONNECTIONS
NORTHBOUND TRAINS FROM OCEANSIDE TO LOS ANGELES

TRAIN NUMBER	DAYS OF OPERATION	TRAIN DEPARTURE	NCTD 301 NORTHBOUND SA.SU.H 30 MINUTES	NTCD 302 WESTBOUND SA.SU.H 15-30 MIN.	NTCD 303 CLOCKWISE SA.SU.H 30-60 MIN.	NCTD 303 COUNTER CW SA.SU.H 30-60 MIN.	NCTD 305 SOUTHBOUND SA.SU.H 30 MIN.-3 HRS.	NCTD 310 NORTHBOUND SATURDAY 45-60 MIN.	NTCD 312 CLOCKWISE SATURDAY HOURLY	NTCD 312 COUNTER CW SATURDAY HOURLY	NCTD 313 CLOCKWISE SATURDAY 45 MINUTES	NTCD 313 COUNTER CW SATURDAY 45 MINUTES	NTCD 313 CLOCKWISE SUNDAY-H. 45 MINUTES	NTCD 313 COUNTER CW SUNDAY-H. 45 MINUTES
AMTRAK 769	SA.SU.H	6:58A	6:52A	6:54A	6:19A	6:49A	6:04A	6:08A				6:40A	6:10A	
AMTRAK 775	DAILY	9:22A	8:52A	8:54A	9:19A	8:49A	8:14A	8:07A			8:40A	9:10A		
AMTRAK 577	DAILY	11:20A	10:54A	10:54A	11:19A	11:19A	11:11A	11:08A	10:23A		10:50A	10:20A	10:40A	11:15A
AMTRAK 779	DAILY	1:17P	12:54P	12:54P	12:49P	12:49P	1:11P	1:16P	12:28P	1:03P	1:10P	12:40P	12:55P	12:25P
AMTRAK 791	SA.SU.H	3:39P	3:34P	3:24P	3:19P	3:19P	3:11P	2:53P	2:38P	3:13P	3:10P	3:30P	2:55P	3:15P
AMTRAK 583	DAILY	5:22P	4:52P	4:54P	4:49P	4:27P	5:11P	4:25P	4:48P	5:21P	4:50P	5:10P	4:35P	
AMTRAK 585	DAILY	7:52P	7:22P	7:24P SA. 7:17P SU.	7:49P	7:19P	7:42P	7:08P		7:26P	7:10P	7:40P		

TRAIN NUMBER	DAYS OF OPERATION	TRAIN DEPARTURE	NTCD 314 LOOP 1 SATURDAY HOURLY	NCTD 314 LOOP 2 SATURDAY HOURLY	NCTD 316 CLOCKWISE SATURDAY HOURLY	NCTD 316 COUNTER CW SATURDAY HOURLY	NCTD 316 CLOCKWISE SUNDAY-H. HOURLY	NCTD 316 COUNTER CW SUNDAY-H. HOURLY	NTCD 317 SA.SU.H 30-60 MIN	NTCD 318 WESTBOUND SATURDAY 30 MINUTES	NTCD 318 WESTBOUND SUNDAY-H. 30 MINUTES	NTCD 320 WESTBOUND SATURDAY 30 MINUTES	NTCD 320 WESTBOUND SUNDAY-H. 30 MINUTES
AMTRAK 769	SA.SU.H	6:58A	6:22A		6:40A							6:47A	
AMTRAK 775	DAILY	9:22A	9:22A	9:00A	8:45A	8:28A			9:11A SU	9:05A		9:17A	
AMTRAK 577	DAILY	11:20A	10:22A	11:00A	10:51A	10:32A	10:20A	10:56A	11:11A	10:35A	11:05A	11:17A	11:15A
AMTRAK 779	DAILY	1:17P	12:22P	1:00P	12:55P	12:38P	12:30P	12:40P	1:11P	12:50P	12:35P	1:17A	1:15A
AMTRAK 791	SA.SU.H	3:39P	3:22P	3:00P	2:55P	3:38P	3:03P	3:38P	3:30P	3:05P	3:35P	3:17A	3:15A
AMTRAK 583	DAILY	5:22P	4:26P	5:18P	4:55P	4:38P	4:08P	4:53P	5:15P	5:20P	5:50P	5:17P	5:15P
AMTRAK 585	DAILY	7:52P	7:22P	7:00P	6:51P	7:45P			7:50P	7:35P		7:47P	7:47P

SOUTHBOUND TRAINS FROM LOS ANGELES TO OCEANSIDE

TRAIN NUMBER	DAYS OF OPERATION	TRAIN ARRIVAL	NCTD 301 SOUTHBOUND SA.SU.H. 30 MINUTES	NCTD 302 EASTBOUND SA.SU.H. 15-30 MIN.	NCTD 303 CLOCKWISE SA.SU.H. 30-60 MIN.	NCTD 303 COUNTER CW SA.SU.H. 30-60 MIN.	NTCD 305 NORTHBOUND SA.SU.H. 30 MIN.-3 HRS.	NCTD 310 SOUTHBOUND SATURDAY 45-60 MIN.	NCTD 312 CLOCKWISE SATURDAY HOURLY	NCTD 312 COUNTER CW SATURDAY HOURLY	NCTD 313 CLOCKWISE SATURDAY 45 MINUTES	NCTD 313 COUNTER CW SATURDAY 45 MINUTES	NCTD 313 CLOCKWISE SUNDAY-H. 45 MINUTES	NCTD 313 COUNTER CW SUNDAY-H. 45 MINUTES
AMTRAK 570	DAILY	8:29A	8:30A	8:38A	8:30A	8:30A	8:50A	9:12A	8:30A			8:45A	9:15A	8:45A	9:15A
AMTRAK 572	SA.SU.H.	10:35A	11:00A	10:38A	11:00A	11:00A	10:50A	11:13A	11:30A	11:00A	10:55A	11:35A	10:45A	11:20A
AMTRAK 774	SA.SU.H.	12:20P	1:00P	12:38P	12:30P	12:30P	12:50P	12:42P	12:35A	1:10P	1:15P	12:45P	1:00P	12:30P
AMTRAK 776	DAILY	2:28P	2:30P	2:38P	2:30P	2:30P	2:50P	3:00P	2:45P	3:20P	2:55P	3:15P	2:40P	3:00P
AMTRAK 578	DAILY	4:21P	4:30P	4:38P	4:35P	4:30P	4:50P	4:30P	4:55P	4:25P	4:35P	4:55P		4:55P
AMTRAK 782	SA.SU.H.	6:59P	7:00P	7:08P	7:00P	7:00P	7:20P	7:13P		7:30P	7:15P	7:45P		7:45P
AMTRAK 584	SU.-F	8:01P	8:30P	9:08P	8:30P	8:30P	8:20P	8:13P			8:15P			
AMTRAK 786	DAILY	10:43P			11:00P	11:30P	10:50P							

TRAIN NUMBER	DAYS OF OPERATION	TRAIN ARRIVAL	NCTD 314 LOOP 1 SATURDAY HOURLY	NCTD 314 LOOP 2 SATURDAY HOURLY	NTCD 316 CLOCKWISE SATURDAY HOURLY	NCTD 316 COUNTER CW SATURDAY HOURLY	NTCD 316 CLOCKWISE SUNDAY-H. HOURLY	NCTD 316 COUNTER CW SUNDAY-H. HOURLY	NCTD 317 SA.SU.H. 30-60 MIN.	NCTD 318 EASTBOUND SATURDAY 30 MINUTES	NCTD 318 EASTBOUND SUNDAY-H. 30 MINUTES	NCTD 320 EASTBOUND SATURDAY 30 MINUTES	NCTD 320 EASTBOUND 30 MINUTES
AMTRAK 570	DAILY	8:29A	9:00A	8:30A	8:45A	9:30A			8:45A SU	9:15A	9:45P	8:30A	
AMTRAK 572	SA.SU.H.	10:35A	11:00A	11:30A	10:45A	11:30A	11:05A	11:35A	10:45A	10:45A	11:15A	10:50A	10:50A
AMTRAK 774	SA.SU.H.	12:20P	1:00P	12:30P	12:45P	12:30P	1:25P	12:40P	12:45P	1:00P	12:45P	12:30P	1:00P
AMTRAK 776	DAILY	2:28P	3:00P	2:30P	2:45P	2:30P	2:30P	3:10P	2:40P	2:30P	3:45P	2:30P	3:00P
AMTRAK 578	DAILY	4:21P	5:00P	4:45P	4:45P	4:30P	5:00P	5:30P	4:25P	4:45P	5:15P	4:30P	5:00P
AMTRAK 782	SA.SU.H.	6:59P	7:00P	7:30P	7:45P	7:33P			7:05P			7:00P	
AMTRAK 584	SU.-F	8:01P		8:30P		8:33P			8:15P				
AMTRAK 786	DAILY	10:43P							10:45P				

Points of Interest

The City of Oceanside is located at the southern boundary of the Camp Pendleton Marine Base, which separates San Diego County from the urban sprawl of Greater Los Angeles to the north. The city was officially founded in 1883 by early settlers who were mostly English gentry. Prior to this, the Mission San Luis Rey de Francia, four miles to the east of Oceanside was the center of Spanish and Mexican settlement in this region of the California coast. With the establishment of Camp Pendleton Marine Base in 1942, the character of the city changed forever as it was transformed from an agricultural distribution center to a place where the civilian and military personnel from the base would live and play.

Today the city is caught somewhere in time between the 1950's and the 1990's. The streets of downtown Oceanside are still crowded with many young men identified by their Marine haircuts as new recruits out on their first leave after boot camp on weekend evenings. However, the 1990's are rapidly remaking this city. There are plans for a Vietnam Memorial Sculpture Garden, an art museum in the old city hall at Pier View Way and Ditmar Streets, the Oceanside Sea Center at 221 North Coast Highway and the renovation of the former Towne Theater as a performing arts center for the community. For current information as to the status of these and other new venues in the Oceanside area call the visitors information center at (800) 350-7873. The visitors center is located at 928 North Coast Highway.

Within walking distance of the

218

Church at Mission San Luis Rey

Metrolink station is the downtown shopping district, the beaches, the Oceanside Pier, and the California Surfing Museum. The Oceanside small craft harbor is only a few miles to the north.

Oceanside Heritage Park

Oceanside Heritage park is located at 210 Peyri Road just around the corner from Mission San Luis Rey. The park has buildings from the "early days township" which consist of the old livery stable, newspaper building, general store, city jail, doctor's office, saloon and school house. For further information call (619) 433-8297. From Metrolink take the NCTD 303 bus to the Douglas Drive and El Camino Real stop. Walk two blocks east on El Camino Real to Peyri Drive. Walk one block North on Peyri Drive to the park.

Mission San Luis Rey
de Francia

Mission San Luis Rey de Francia is located at 4050 Mission Avenue, San Luis Rey. The mission was founded by Father Fermin Francisco de Lasuen in June 1798, the ninth and last mission founded by Father Fermin. Under the administration of Father Antonio Peyri the mission grew and prospered to become the largest of the California missions. Its farm and pasture lands extended in a radius of up to 15 miles. The quadrangle of the mission building was 500 feet by 500 feet occupying six acres. After Mexican independence the mission was secularized in 1834, and Father Bonaventura Fortuni turned over

the mission to Pio Pico and Pablo de la Portilla. Chaos ensued with the cattle being slaughtered for their hides, the lands were given to the Indians and then stolen from them. In 1843 Governor Michaeltorena returned the mission to Franciscan control. So little of the lands and stock was left that Father Zalvidea could not properly feed the remaining 400 Indians and the mission reverted back to secular control and was sold by Governor Pico in 1846 for $2,437. That same year Father Zalvidea died, the last successor of Father Peyri.

During the Mexican-American War, and for some time after, the U.S. Army stationed troops at the mission as attested to by the numerous signs on the mission grounds proclaiming the exploits of Captain Fremont and Kit Carson. In 1865 Abraham Lincoln returned the mission to the Franciscans. However, the mission remained

unoccupied until a group of Franciscans came up from Zacatecas, Mexico, to take up residence in 1892. Father Joseph Jeremiah O'Keefe arrived in 1893 with the intention of restoring the old mission and making it a Franciscan missionary college. Since that time the restoration efforts have been gradual at Mission San Luis Rey de Francia.

Today the mission serves as a parish and retreat center for the surrounding community and is still occupied by the Franciscans. The mission will be opening a conference center in the fall of 1996 which can accommodate up to 1,000 people. For further information call (619) 757-3651.

The mission museum is open 10:00 A.M. to 4:30 P.M. Monday thru Saturday and 12:00 P.M. to 4:30 P.M. on Sunday. Admission is $3.00 for adults, $1.00 for children 8 thru 14 and children and under are free.

The mission can be reached by taking the NCTD 313 Counter Clockwise bus to the Rancho Del Oro and Mission Avenue stop.

Oceanside Harbor

The Oceanside Harbor is located about two miles north of the Metrolink station. The harbor features a New England style village with numerous shops, restaurants and boutiques. The harbor has a significant sportfishing center with several boats offering daily full and half-day trips. Whale-watching trips are offered December 26 thru March 31 during the annual grey whale migrations between Baja and Alaska. For information on whale watching or sportfishing call (619) 722-2133.

The California
Surf Museum

The California Surf Museum is an internationally recognized surfing

Village at Oceanside Harbor

museum which annually draws growing numbers of tourists and surfing aficionados. The museum is located at 223 North Coast Highway. The Museum has on display a number of redwood and balsa wood surfboards from the early days of surfing in Southern California. The museum also has a large collection of early surfing publications, photos, surf art and surf paraphernalia from 50's and 60's. The people operating the museum are very knowledgeable about the Southern California surfing subculture. Admission is free. The museum is open Monday thru Friday noon to 4:00 P.M. and Saturday and Sunday 10:00 A.M. to 4:00 P.M. During the fall and winter the museum is closed Tuesday and Wednesday. For information call (619) 721-6876. The museum is a short three-block walk from the Metrolink station.

The Oceanside Pier

The Oceanside Pier is located at the end of Pier View Way. The pier is the longest over-water pier in Southern California with a length of 1,942 feet. There is a tram which will take you from the end of Pier View Way to the restaurant at the end of the pier for a quarter. You can rent a fishing pole from the bait shop and try your luck. No license is required for pier fishing. Below the Oceanside pier along the coast is one of the finest white sand beaches in Southern California.

Places to Stay
Best Western Oceanside Inn

The Best Western Oceanside Inn is located at 1680 Oceanside Boulevard. Take the NCTD 316 or 318 bus to the Oceanside Boulevard and Vine Street stop. The hotel phone number is (619) 722-1821. For reservations call (800) 443-9995.

Oceanside Marina Inn

The Oceanside Marina Inn is located at 2008 Harbor Drive North. This hotel is located at the north end of the harbor about a mile from the nearest bus stop on the NCTD 314 line. It is recommended that you either rent a car or take a taxi from Metrolink. The hotel phone number is (619) 722-1561. For reservations call (800) 252-2033.

Oceanside Travelodge

The Oceanside Travelodge is located at 1401 North Coast Highway. Take the NCTD 314 line to the Coast Highway and Monterey Drive stop. The hotel phone number is (619) 722-1244. For reservations call (800) 255-3050.

North Coast Village Condominium

The North Coast Village Condominium is located at 999 North Pacific Avenue. You can walk to the complex from the Metrolink station. For information call the Oceanside Visitors and Information center at (800) 350-7873.

Best Western Marty's Valley Inn

The Best Western-Marty's Valley Inn is located at 3240 Mission Avenue. Take the NCTD 303, 313 or 316 line to the Mission Boulevard and Airport Road stop. the hotel phone number is (619) 439-3311. For reservations call (800) 747-3529.

The Oceanside Pier

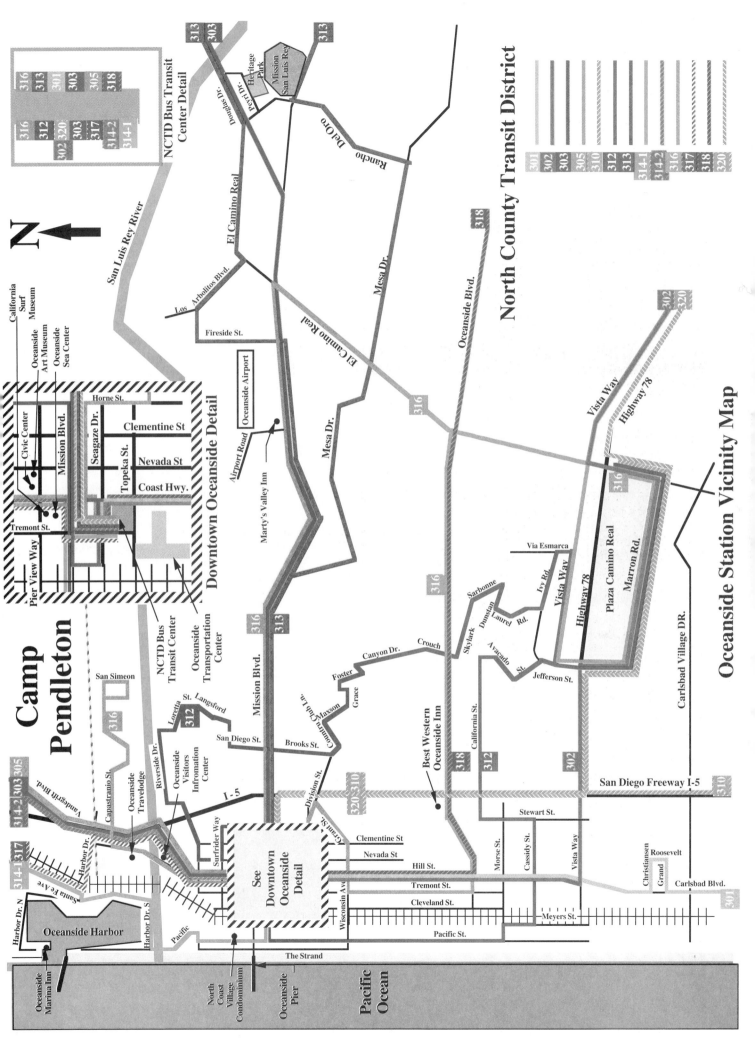

N

Camp Pendleton

North County Transit District

Oceanside Station Vicinity Map

Downtown Oceanside Detail

NCTD Bus Transit Center Detail

316	313	301	303	305	318
316	312	320	303	317	314-2	314-1
		302			

| 301 | 302 | 303 | 305 | 310 | 312 | 313 | 314-1 | 314-2 | 316 | 317 | 318 | 320 |

San Luis Rev River

Heritage Park
Mission San Luis Rey

313 303 313

Douglas Dr.
Peyri Dr.

El Camino Real

Rancho Del Oro

Los Arbolitos Blvd.

Fireside St.

Oceanside Airport
Airport Road

Mesa Dr.

El Camino Real

Oceanside Blvd.

318

316

Mesa Dr.

Marty's Valley Inn

316

Canyon Dr.   Crouch

Foster

Country Club Dr.

Maxson   Grace

Skylark   Sarbonne   Via Esmarca

Dunstan   Laurel Rd.   Ivy Rd.

Avacado St.

Jefferson St.

Vista Way

Highway 78

316

Plaza Camino Real

Marron Rd.

Vista Way   Highway 78   302   320

Best Western Oceanside Inn

318   California St.   312

316

Mission Blvd.
313

San Diego St.   Brooks St.

Loretta St. Langsford

312

Riverside Dr.

San Simeon

316

California Surf Museum
Oceanside Art Museum
Oceanside Sea Center

Civic Center
Mission Blvd.
Seagaze Dr.
Topeka St.
Tremont St.
Pier View Way

Horne St.
Clementine St
Nevada St
Coast Hwy.

Oceanside Visitors Infromation Center
Oceanside Travelodge

NCTD Bus Transit Center
Oceanside Transportation Center

Capastranio St.
Vandegrift Blvd.

314-2 303 305

314-1 317

Harbor Dr.
Harbor Dr. N
Santa Fe Ave

Oceanside Harbor

Oceanside Marina Inn

Harbor Dr. S

Pacific

Surfrider Way

Grant St.

See Downtown Oceanside Detail

North Coast Village Condominium
Oceanside Pier

The Strand

Division St.

I - 5

320 310

Clementine St
Nevada St
Hill St.
Tremont St.
Cleveland St.
Wisconsin Ave

Pacific St.

Stewart St.

Morse St.   Cassidy St.   Vista Way

San Diego Freeway I-5

302

310

Meyers St.

Christiansen   Roosevelt
Grand

Carlsbad Blvd.

301

Carlsbad Village DR.

Pacific Ocean

Index of Place Names